NIGHT SKY PHOTOGRAPHY

First published in the UK in 2021 by ILEX, an imprint of
Octopus Publishing Group Limited
Carmelite House
50 Victoria Embankment
London, EC4Y 0DZ
www.octopusbooks.co.uk
www.octopusbooksusa.com

Distributed in the US by Hachette Book Group
1290 Avenue of the Americas, 4th & 5th Floors
New York, NY 10104

Distributed in Canada by Canadian Manda Group
664 Annette St, Toronto, Ontario, Canada M6S2C8

Publisher: Alison Starling
Commissioner: Richard Collins
Managing Editor: Rachel Silverlight
Art Director: Ben Gardiner
Page Design: Tammy Kerr
Editorial Assistant: Ellen Sandford O'Neill
Senior Production Manager: Peter Hunt

ISBN 978-1-78157-750-9

A CIP catalogue record for this book is available from the British Library

Printed and bound in China

10 9 8 7 6 5

From First Principles to Professional Results

ADAM WOODWORTH

NIGHT SKY PHOTOGRAPHY

ilex

CONTENTS

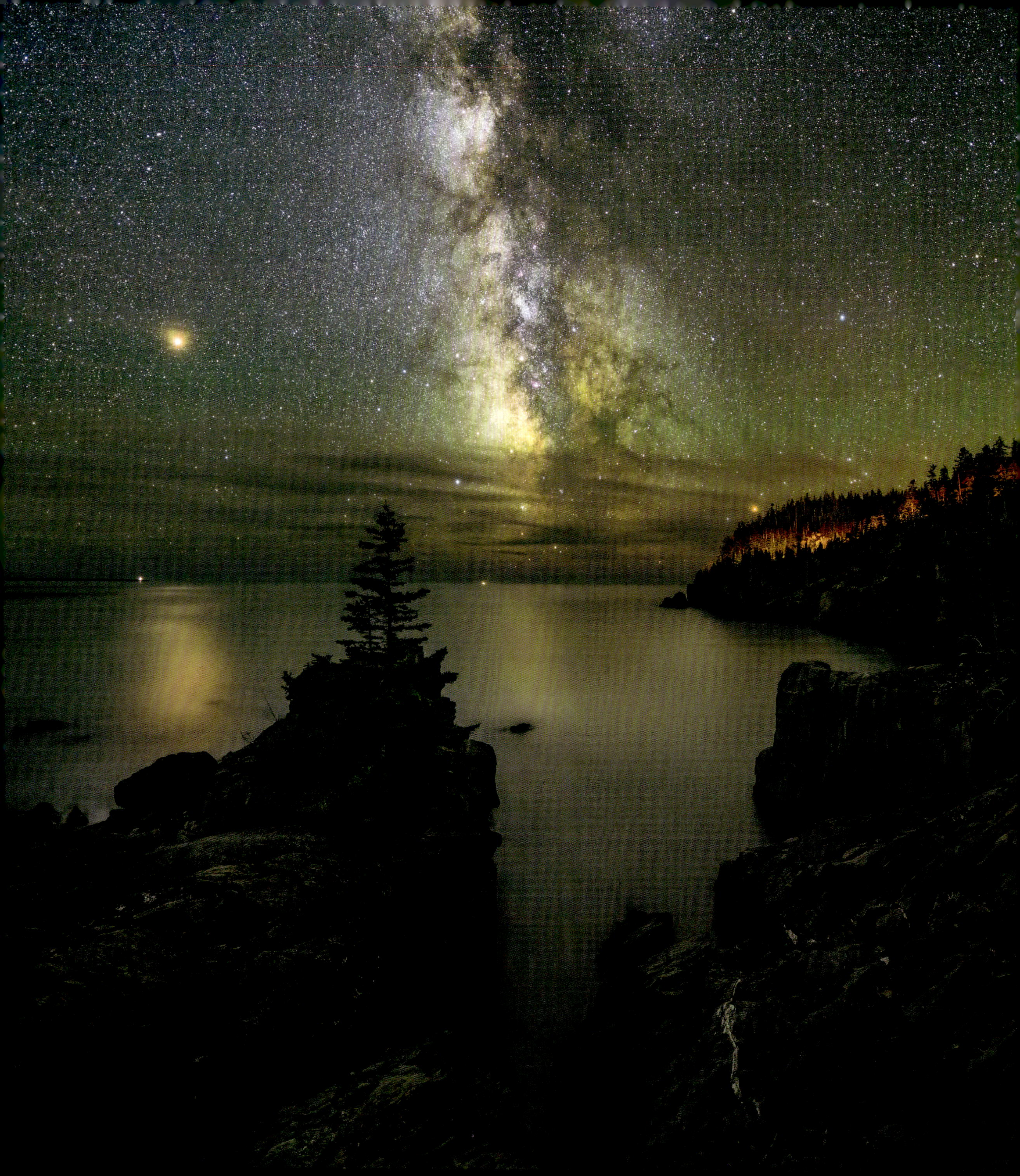

◀ The Milky Way and Mars (the bright orb on the left) reflect in the Atlantic Ocean on the rugged coast of Maine.

Nikon Z 7 with Mount Adapter FTZ and Nikon 14-24mm f/2.8 lens at 14mm and f/2.8. Like most of my landscape astrophotographs, this is a blend of multiple exposures for dynamic range and depth of field so that the image has detail, low noise, and is in focus from the foreground to the stars.

Sky: Ten shots each at ISO 6400 and 10 seconds that were star stacked for pinpoint stars and low noise.

Foreground: Focus and exposure stack of three shots, each at f/2.8 and ISO 1600, two exposures at 10 minutes and one exposure at 20 minutes.

Imagine standing on the edge of a cliff in a remote area, overlooking the ocean on a clear, moonless night. The Milky Way is so bright that it reflects in the ocean, and the way it shoots up into the sky lines up with the small cove in front of you. It's so dark you can barely see your camera in front of you when its LCD isn't lit up, and the crashing waves below are providing a great sonic backdrop to the experience.

I have been fascinated with the night sky ever since I was a kid, and I never get tired of scenes like this. Whether you're on the coast, in the desert, or in the mountains, viewing the night sky in a dark location is always incredible.

I remember seeing the Milky Way for the first time while lying down in a canoe on a lake in Maine, angling for catfish. In that moment, and ever since then, I was amazed by what it was possible to see in the night sky in the right location.

So it's fitting that I find myself, as an adult, regularly out in the middle of the night, in the middle of nowhere, taking pictures of the night sky over wilderness, lighthouses, or whatever looks promising. This type of photography is known as landscape astrophotography, and with modern digital cameras and lenses it is much easier to capture these images than ever before. Even an entry-level DSLR or a mirrorless interchangeable-lens camera with a kit lens will capture great images of the night sky.

It does take some practice, and standing around in the dark while your camera takes long-exposure images requires patience, but the results will make you glad you stayed up all night. Landscape astrophotography is one of the most rewarding types of photography that I've personally experienced. I still get excited when I see the Milky Way pop out on the image review on the LCD of my camera.

This book focuses on capturing "pinpoint stars" — where the stars appear as small, sharp points of light in the sky. The aim of this book is to show you how to achieve this while minimizing the level of noise (digital artifacts) in your images and simultaneously getting your entire scene well exposed and in focus. These are the main challenges to overcome in this type of landscape astrophotography and we'll look at different techniques for capturing dramatic, high-quality images of the night sky.

We won't touch on star trails or moon photography, although we will briefly cover photographing the aurora and how this differs from capturing just the stars. A much longer book would be needed to cover every aspect of landscape astrophotography.

At the end of this book you should be able to head out into the night with your camera gear and capture the exposures needed to create photographs that are in focus from the foreground to the stars, with little noise. You will also learn how to plan photos ahead of time and how to scout locations during the day in order to make it easier to find your composition in the dark.

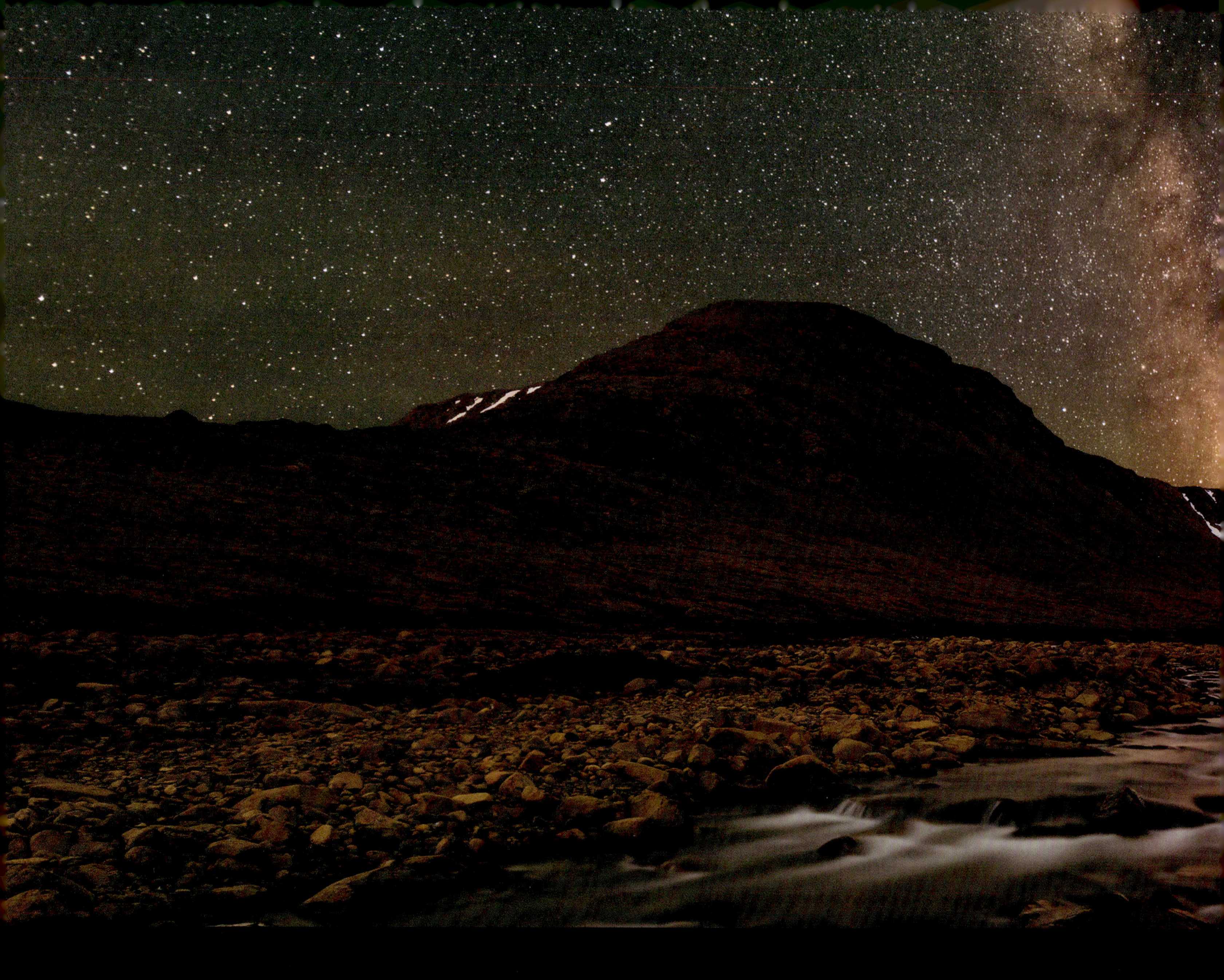

1 OVERVIEW OF TECHNIQUES

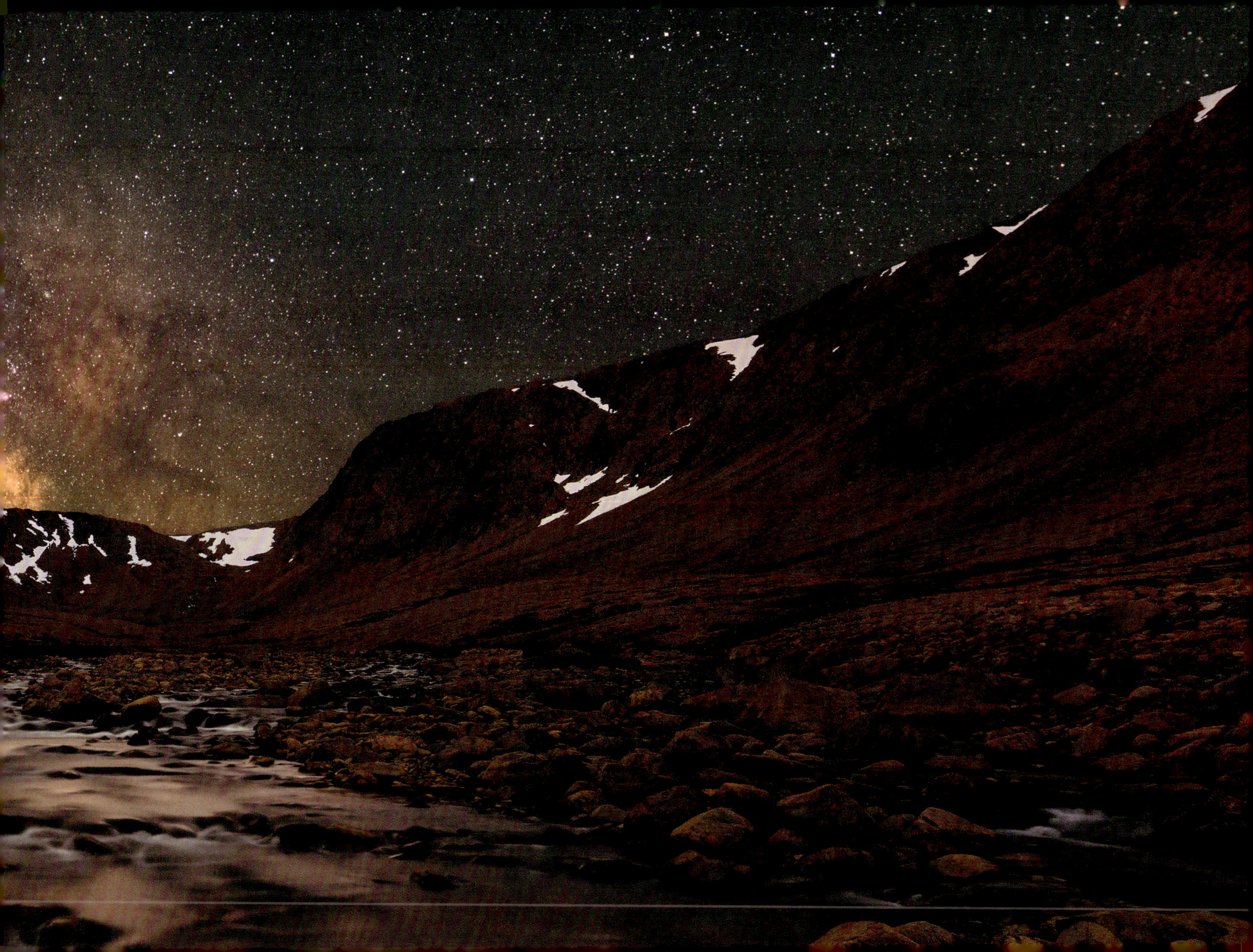

1.1 TECHNIQUES FOR LOW LIGHT

Using longer shutter speeds or widening your aperture are the obvious ways to let in more light. However, the longer the shutter is open, the more movement it will capture, and widening the aperture means that less of the scene will be in focus. Instead, we can use the following techniques to mitigate these issues.

Exposure blending is a method of combining multiple photographs taken at different settings together in software to create a perfectly exposed final image. Photographs captured with the settings needed for pinpoint stars often result in a very dark and out-of-focus foreground. Separate shots with settings appropriate for the foreground can be captured and then blended with the sky shots to make a final image that has plenty of detail in both the sky and foreground.

Sky exposures When I use this term I am referring to the photographs taken to capture the stars as pinpoints or with very small trails. The foreground is still in the frame, but it will often be very dark depending on the ambient light of your shooting location.

Foreground exposures This term refers to images taken with settings to capture a brighter foreground. These usually include a much longer shutter speed than would be possible for the stars.

Focus stacking combines multiple shots taken at different focus distances together in software to create an image with more depth of field (more in focus) than a single photograph. This is often necessary to get the entire foreground in focus, particularly when, at night, we are using apertures such as f/2.8 to let in a lot of light, but at the cost of less depth of field. (See **Aperture**, page 32 for more about the relationship between apertures and depth of field.)

Star stacking is a technique that involves capturing multiple photographs with settings appropriate for the sky to capture sharp stars and reasonably small star trails, and then blending them later using dedicated star-stacking software to give you an image with much less noise than would otherwise be present in a single shot.

We will cover all of these methods in detail throughout this book, but it is worth noting them now, as almost all of the images featured in this book are created using a combination of star stacking and exposure blending, and often focus stacking is used as well.

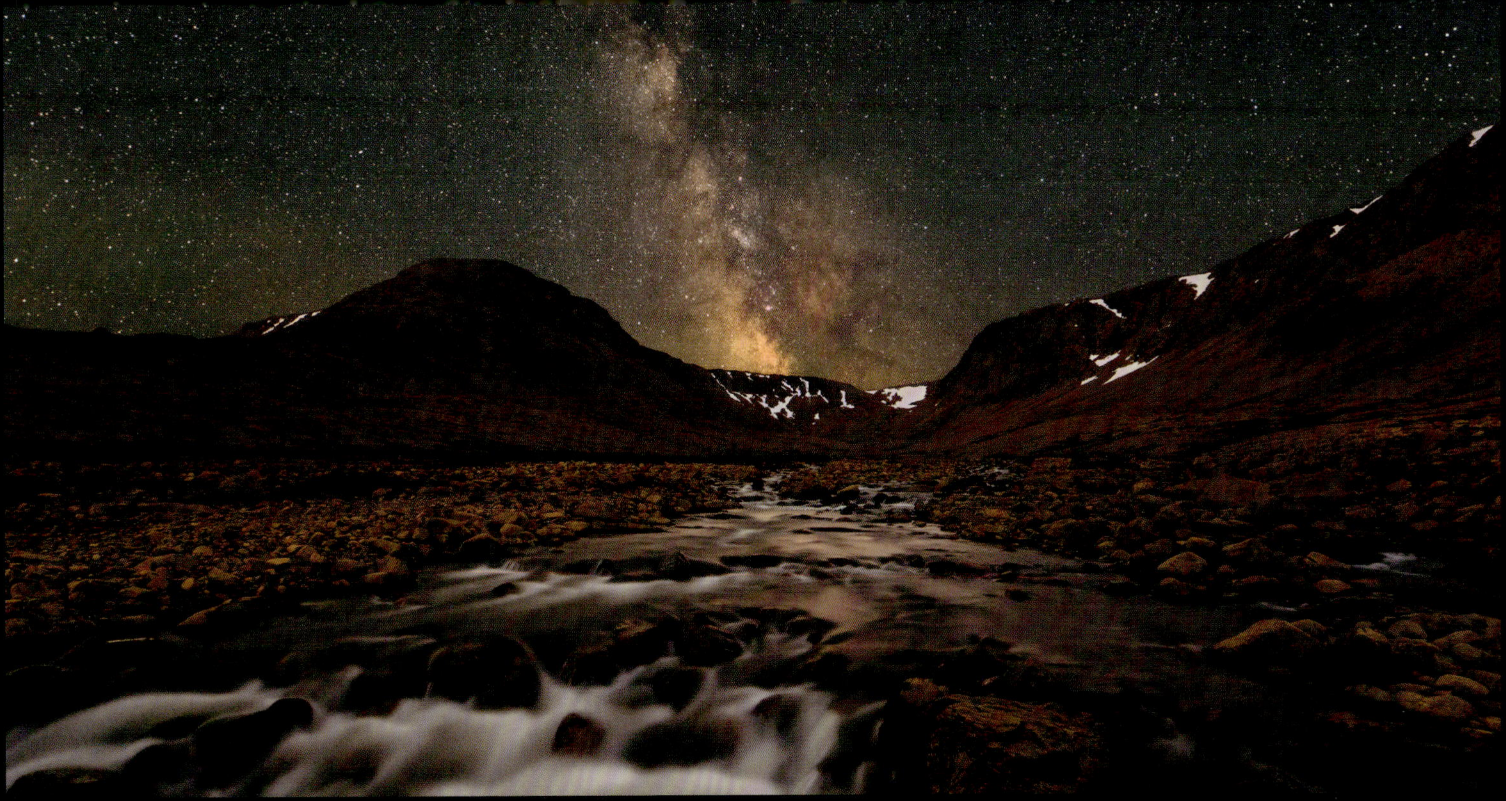

▲ Exposure blending: page 12

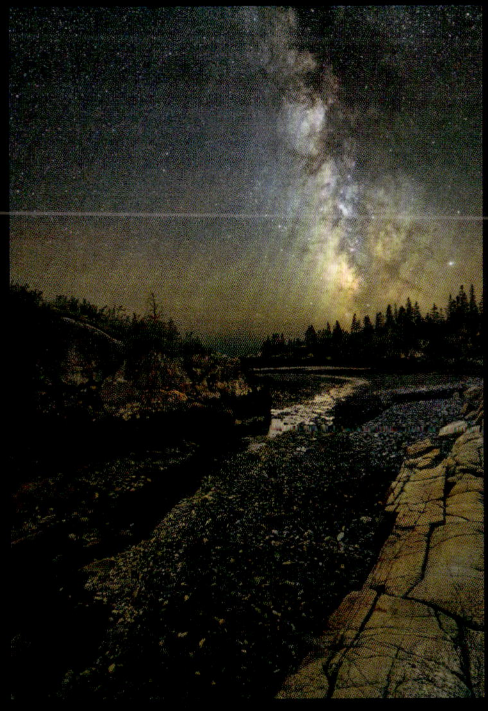

▲ Sky exposures, foreground exposures and focus stacking: page 56

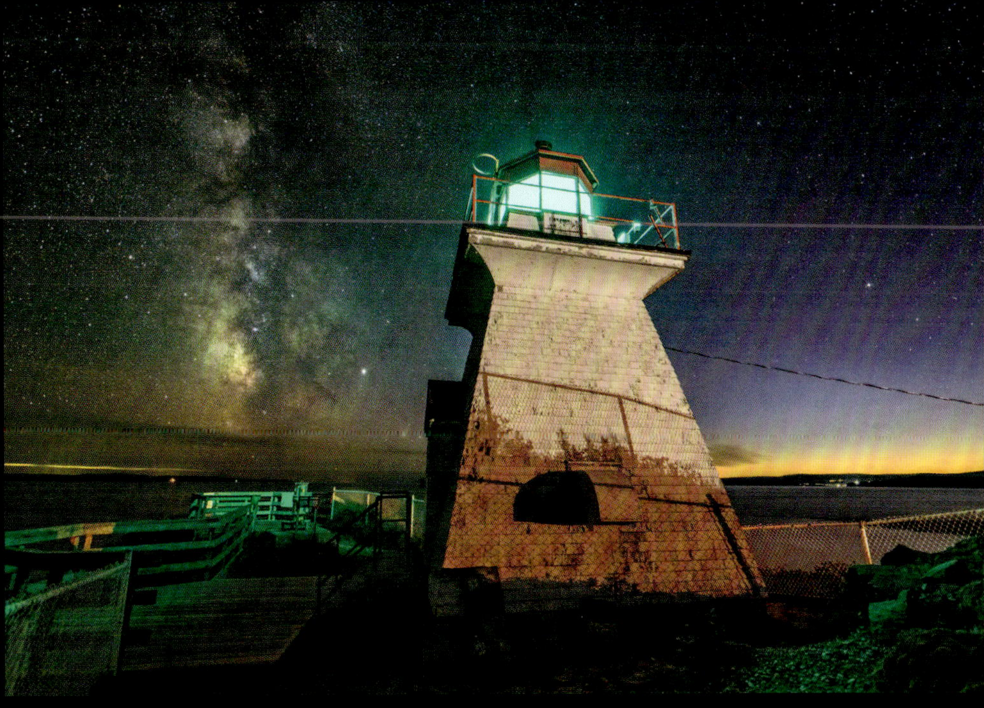

▲ Star stacking: page 76

1.2 EXPOSURE BLENDING

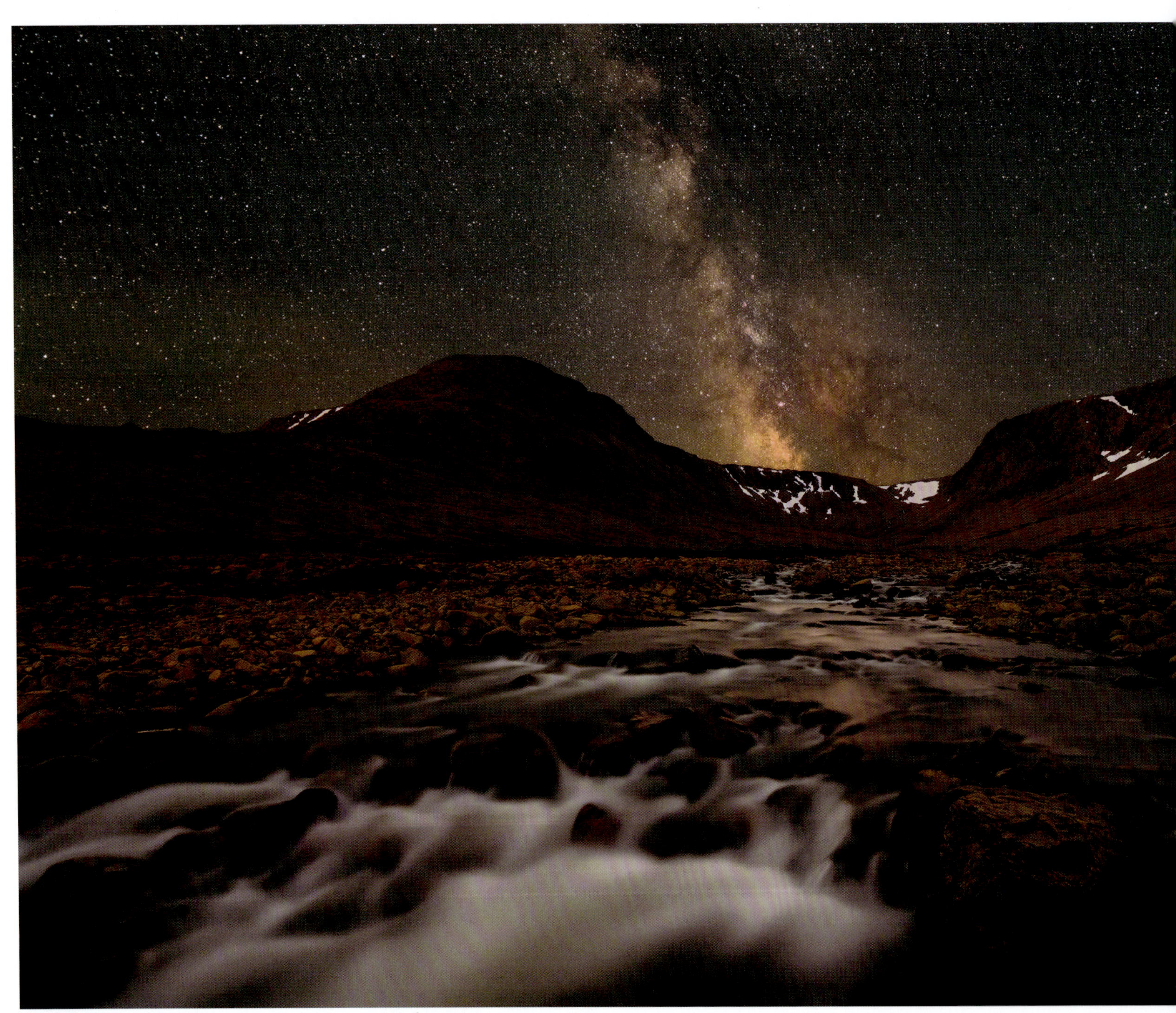

▲ Milky Way over the Tablelands in Newfoundland, Canada.
This photo actually consists of ten sky and two foreground images.
All exposures were taken with a Nikon D810A and Nikon 14-24mm f/2.8 lens.

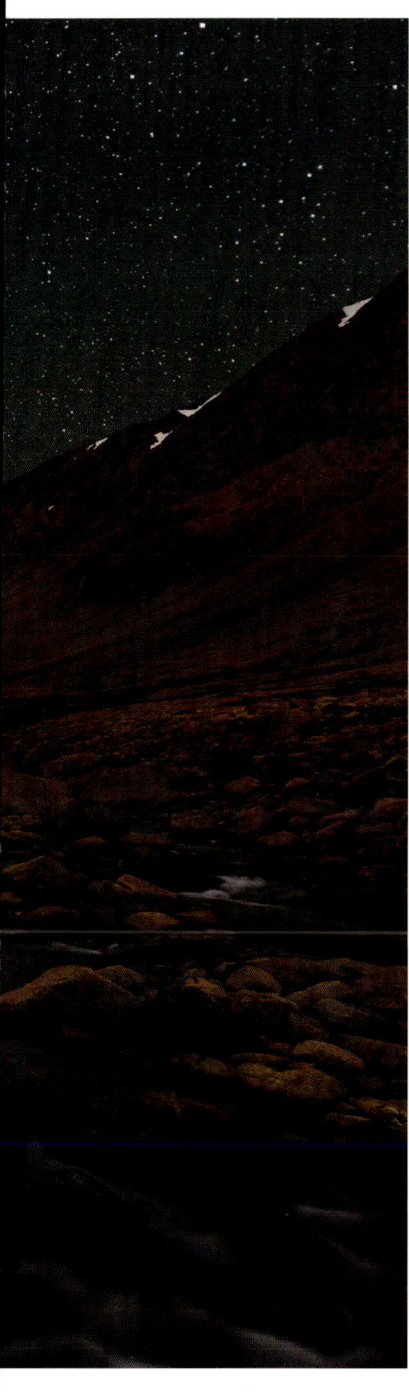

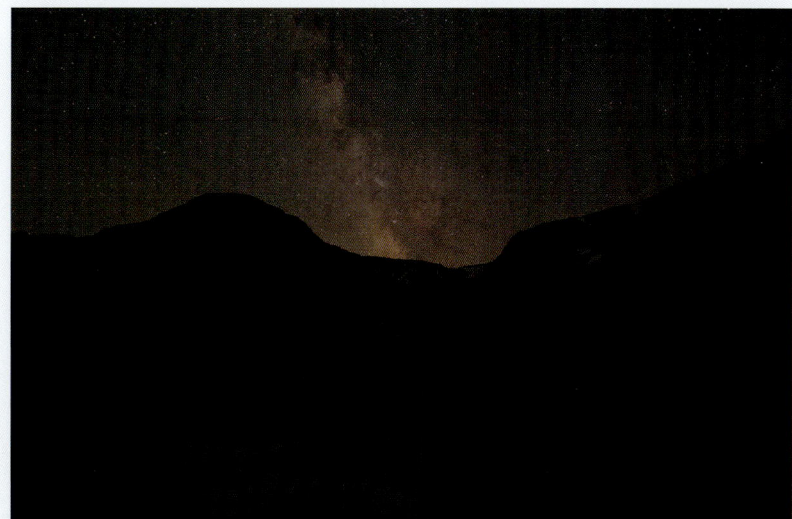

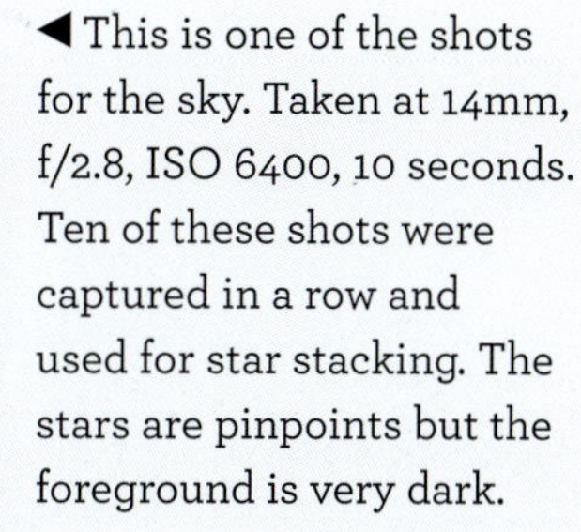

◀ This is one of the shots for the sky. Taken at 14mm, f/2.8, ISO 6400, 10 seconds. Ten of these shots were captured in a row and used for star stacking. The stars are pinpoints but the foreground is very dark.

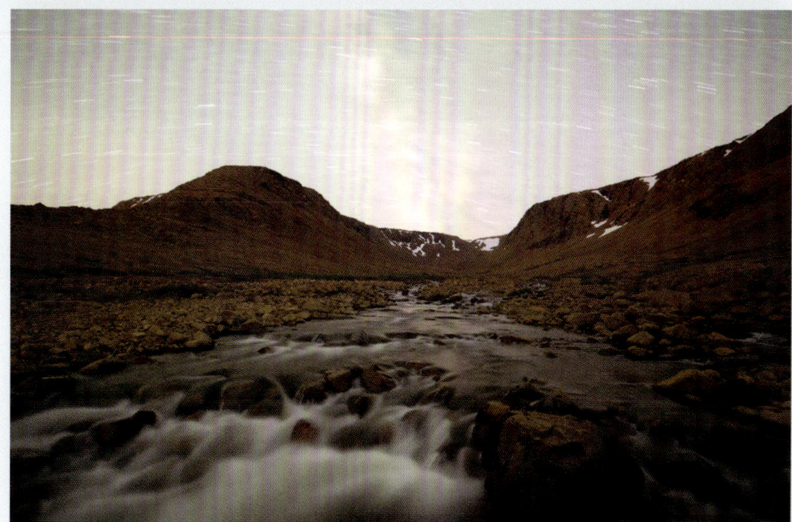

◀ This is one of the foreground shots, with the horizon and mid-ground in focus. Taken at 14mm, f/2.8, ISO 1600, 8 minutes. The foreground is bright and has lots of detail, but now the stars have trailed considerably.

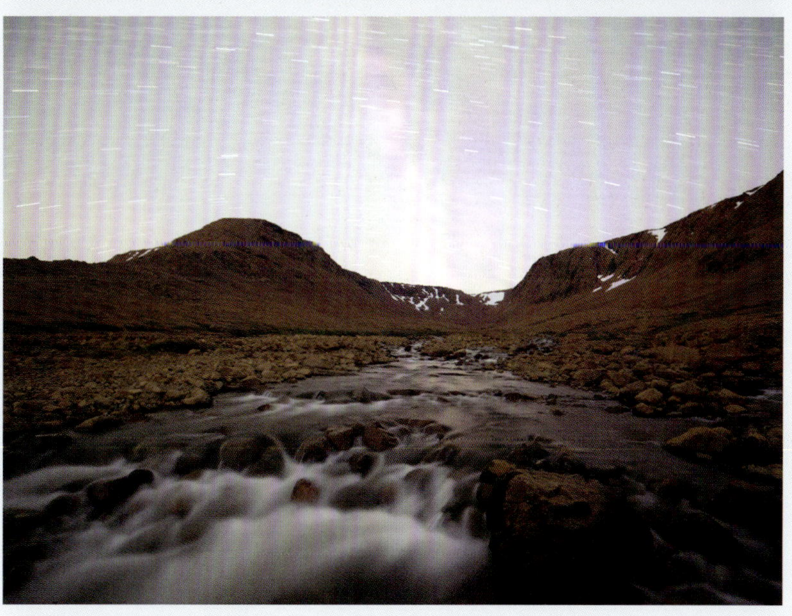

◀ The other foreground shot, with the close rocks in focus. Taken at 14mm, f/2.8, ISO 1600, 8 minutes.

The ten sky shots were combined to create a single image of the sky with low levels of noise. The foreground shots were then focus-stacked to achieve the greatest depth of field, and blended with the sky image to create the final image that is in focus from the foreground to the sky with low noise and pinpoint stars.

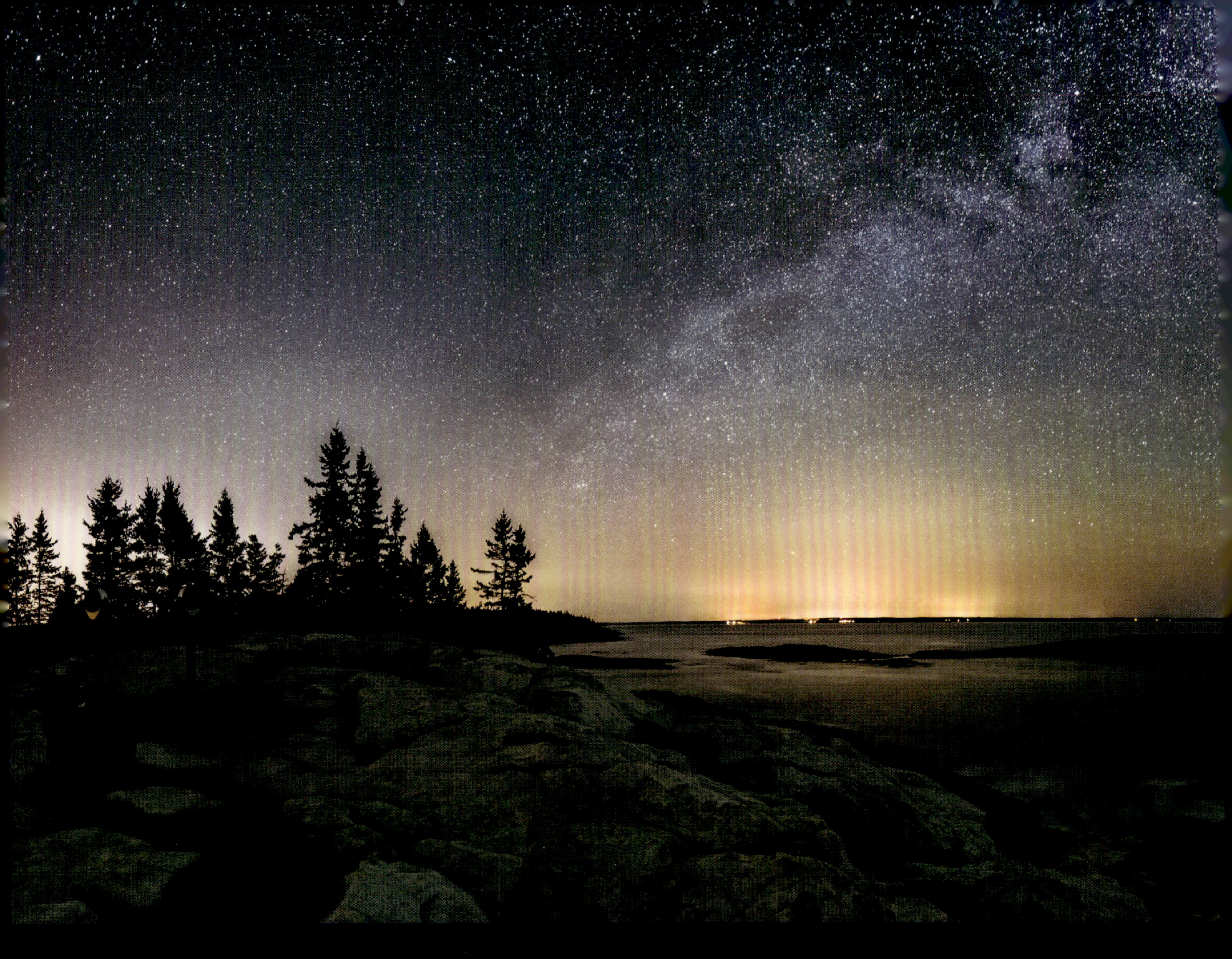

2 NIGHT SKY SUBJECTS

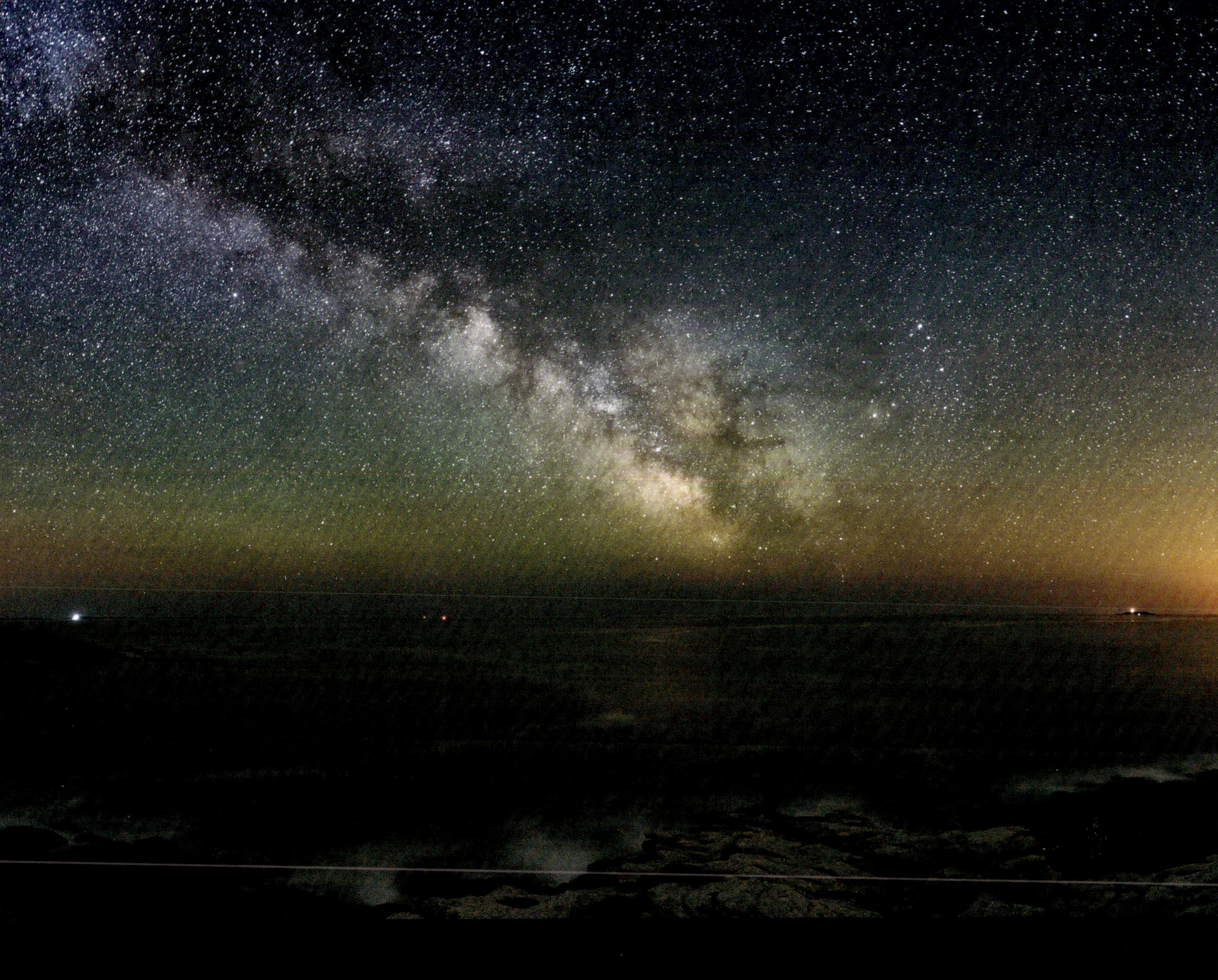

Welcome to the night sky. There's nothing quite like standing out under the stars, and there are a lot of different subjects you can photograph. In all cases, I like to use the sky as a backdrop to an interesting foreground. While the night sky is prominent in the photo, the foreground is often the star of the show, with the night sky playing a supporting role, just as a dramatic sunrise or sunset would do for a daytime landscape.

▲ A panorama of eight photographs. The Raw files were prepped in Lightroom, and stitched and further edited for contrast in Photoshop.

2.1 THE MILKY WAY

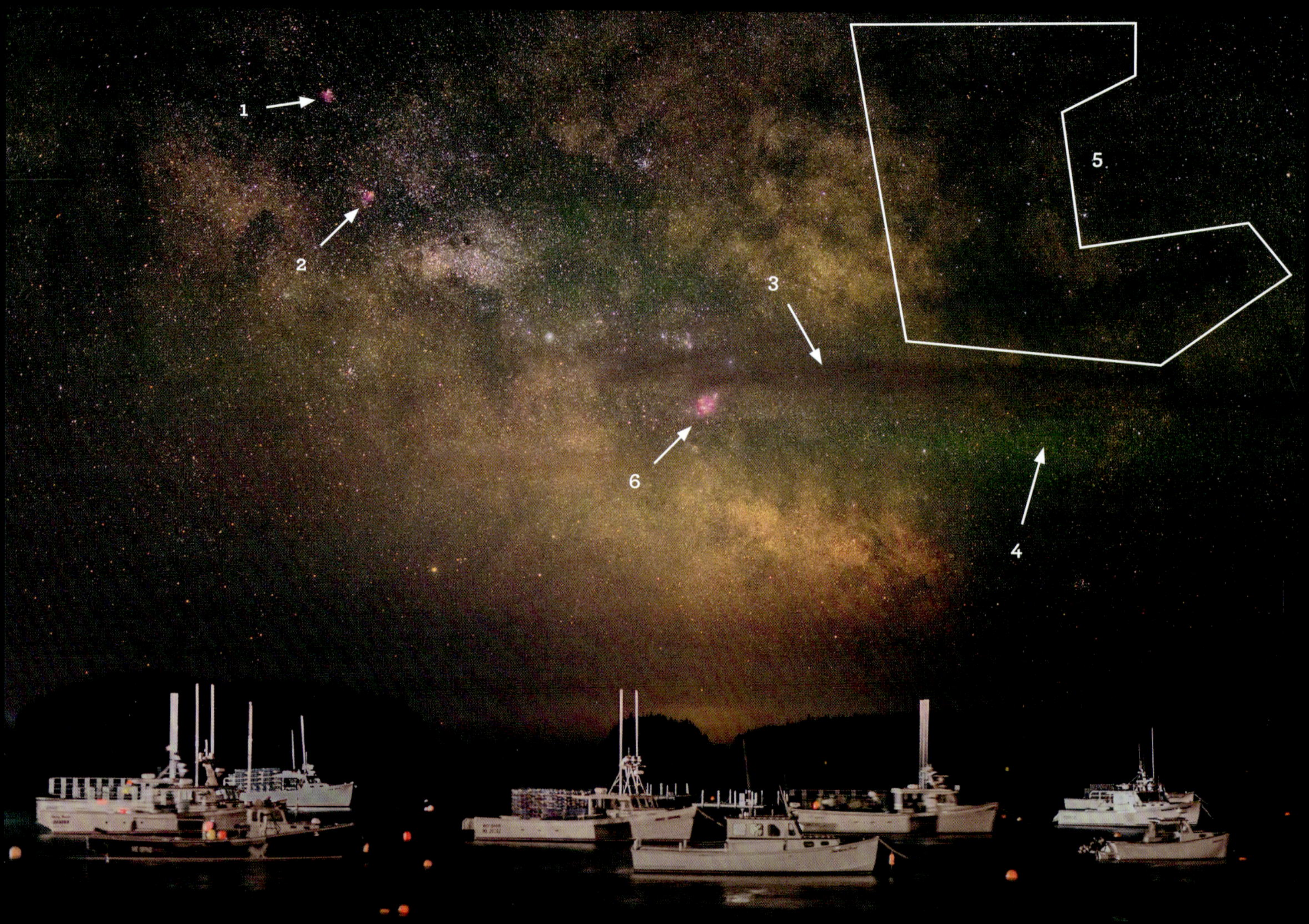

▲ The Milky Way over lobster boats on the coast of Maine. Shot at 58mm, making the Galactic Core appear huge above the boats.

1. **Eagle Nebula**
2. **Omega Nebula**
3. **Thin passing cloud**
4. **Faint band of green airglow**
5. **The Dark Horse**
6. **Lagoon Nebula**

The Milky Way is by far the most common night sky subject used in landscape astrophotography, and for good reason. The Galactic Core of the Milky Way is very big and bright. It will show up quite prominently even in ultra-wide-angle lenses. The rest of the Milky Way that arcs through the sky is also quite bright and makes a great subject for panoramas. There's quite a bit of color in the Milky Way from the stars and nebulae scattered throughout it, and the Galactic Core has an interesting texture caused by dust clouds that block light, creating dark areas, including the "Dark Horse," so named because if you look at it from the right angle it looks like the silhouette of a horse.

The Galactic Core of the Milky Way is the true center of our galaxy, around which the rest of the Milky Way rotates. It is home to the supermassive black hole Sagittarius A* (pronounced "A star"). Fun fact: A supermassive black hole is most likely at the center of every large galaxy in the universe.

The Galactic Core is sort of loosely used to mean the bright thick "bulge" around the center. It is this area that is featured in most Milky Way photos.

Even when the big bright Galactic Core is not visible, the part of the Milky Way that is visible can still be used as an interesting subject. It's fainter and has less dramatic punch, but it's still beautiful.

The Milky Way works well with most focal lengths, from ultra-wide fisheye lenses to the popular 14mm focal length, to 24mm, 50mm, and even beyond. A longer focal length will isolate more of the Milky Way against your foreground subject, making the Milky Way appear very large.

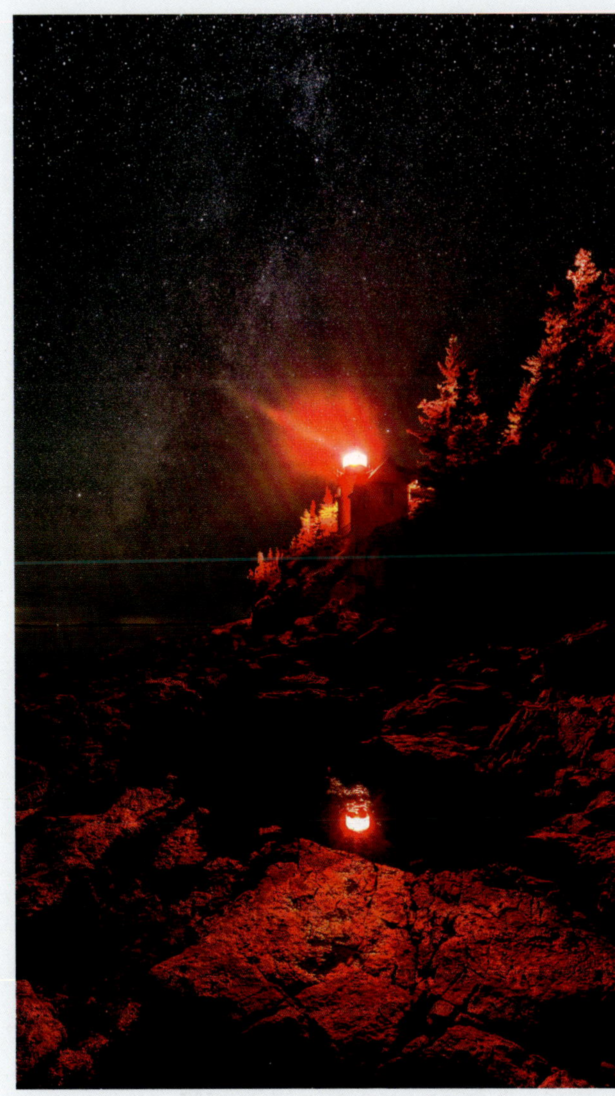

◀ The Milky Way next to Bass Harbor Lighthouse. Even after the Galactic Core has disappeared below the horizon late in the summer or in the fall in the Northern Hemisphere, the rest of the Milky Way can still be seen reaching up into the sky.

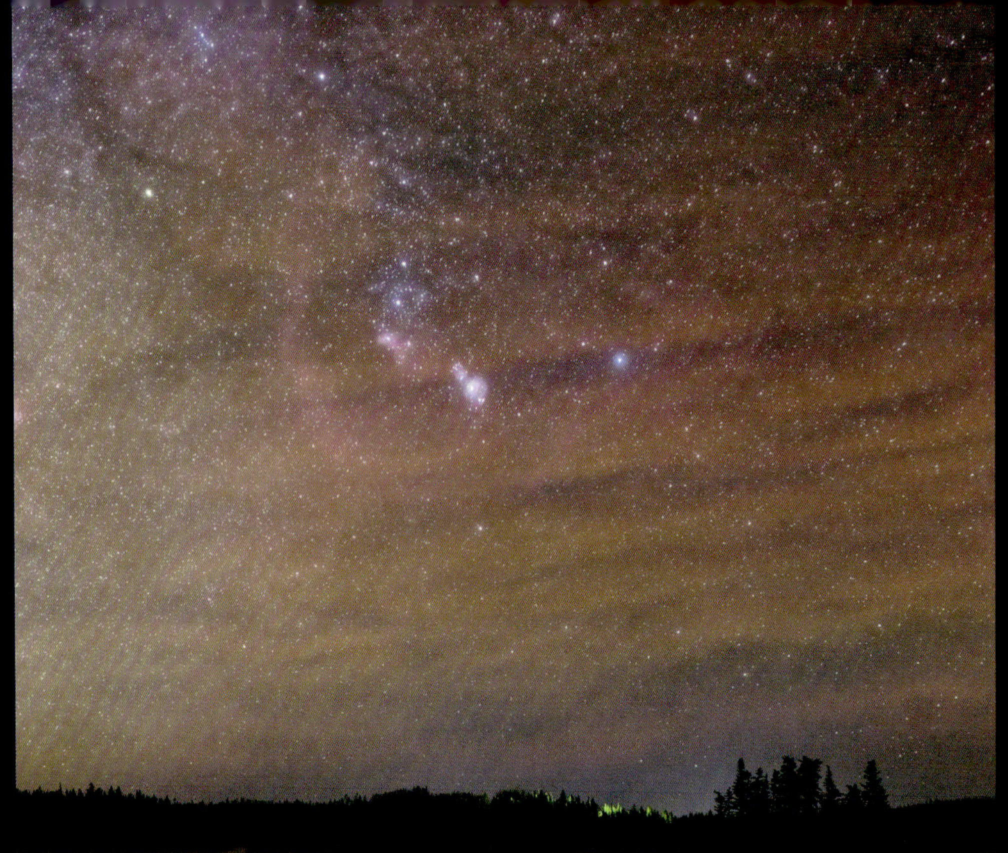

Orion is one of the most recognizable constellations in the night sky, being clearly visible even in twilight due to the bright stars that comprise it. The most prominent part of the constellation is an hourglass shape, with four bright stars at the corners and three bright stars that divide the hourglass in two—these three stars in the middle form the "belt" of Orion, and the full constellation creates Orion the Hunter.

◀ **The Orion Constellation and nebulae over the coast of Maine, shot with a 35mm lens.**

Orion also contains a number of colorful nebulae, with the Orion Nebula in the bottom half of the constellation being one of the brightest deep space objects in the sky. The Flame and Horsehead Nebulae are also visible around the left half of the belt stars, and there is a faint nebula called Barnard's Loop that forms a semi-circle around the lower half of the constellation. Altogether, these nebulae, plus others in the region, are known as the Orion Molecular Cloud Complex.

This all makes for a great subject. With the right edits you can really bring out the nebulae and make them pop, or you can focus on just the stars to bring more attention to the shape of the constellation.

If you wanted to capture just the sky rather than the landscape too, Orion makes for an easy wide-field astrophotography shot that you can take with just a 50mm lens on a full-frame camera (or a 35mm lens on APS-C, and a 25mm lens on Micro Four Thirds). Even without a star tracker, you can use star stacking to capture a lot of light, resulting in a lot of detail in the nebulae. (Star stacking and star trackers are covered in detail on pages 76–83.) The Orion Nebula itself is also a great subject for getting started with deep space astrophotography because it is so bright and easy to find. Using a star tracker with a zoom lens or telescope, it is one of the easiest deep space objects to locate and photograph.

WHEN AND WHERE TO SEE ORION

The Orion is considered a "winter constellation" because it is only visible during the winter and early spring in the Northern Hemisphere. This makes it a great alternative subject when the Milky Way's Galactic Core isn't visible during that same period.

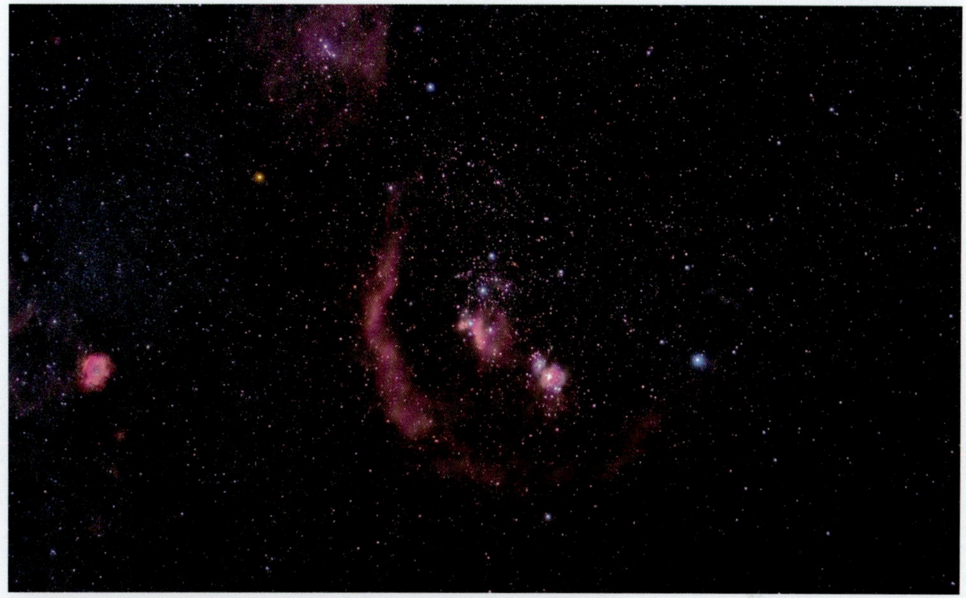

▲ The Orion Molecular Cloud Complex.

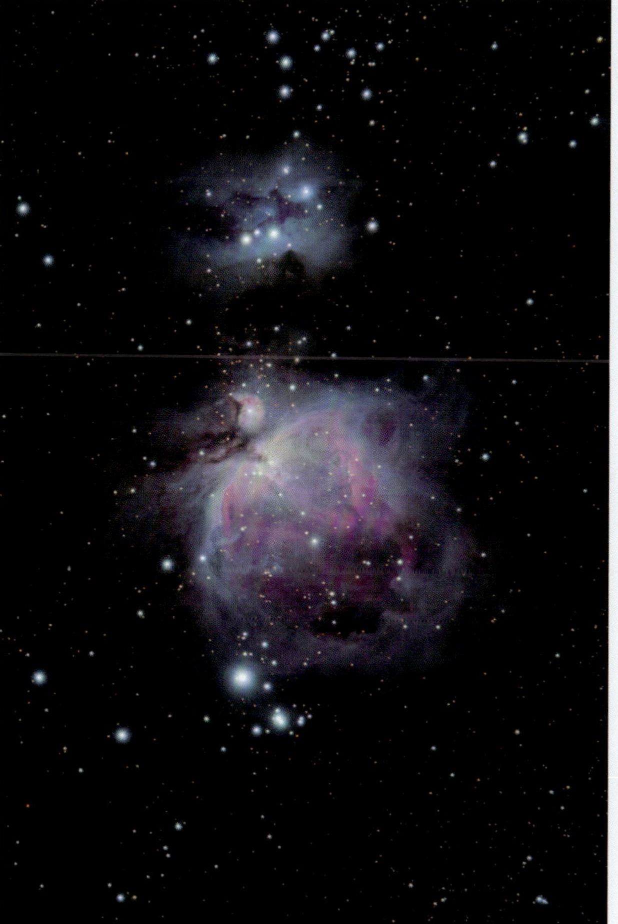

◀ The Orion Nebula with the Running Man Nebula above it. Photographed with a Nikon Z 6 attached to a William Optics Zenithstar 61 telescope. I used the iOptron SkyGuider Pro star tracker to allow me to take 30 and 60-second exposures without star trails. This final image is a stacked blend of almost 90 minutes' worth of exposures.

2.3 ZODIACAL LIGHT

Zodiacal light is the name given to what looks like a wide and tapered fuzzy beam of light shooting up from the horizon. It is caused by sunlight reflecting off dust particles in our solar system. In the first half of the year, it is most visible in the west during late winter or spring, and in the east before dawn during late summer and autumn. Those are Northern Hemisphere seasons, swap them for the Southern Hemisphere.

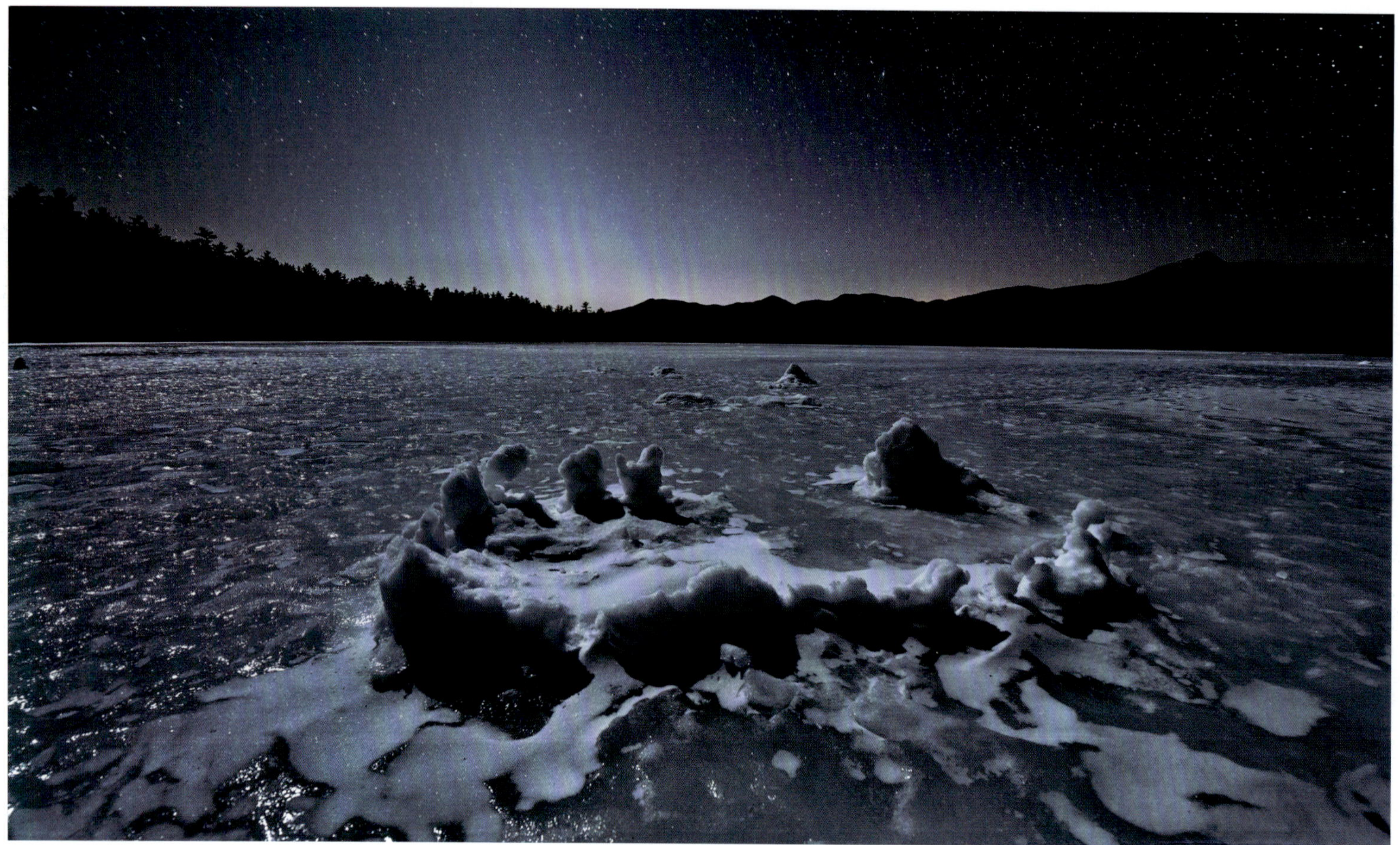

Zodiacal light can be incredibly beautiful, especially when used as a compositional element in a wider scene, taking care over its position in the frame. As with the Milky Way, for the best results you'll usually want to have the angle of the zodiacal light bending into the frame from the edge or centered in the frame. Try to avoid the light bending out of the frame when it is positioned near the edge.

▲ Zodiacal light over a frozen lake in New Hampshire.

2.4 THE BIG DIPPER

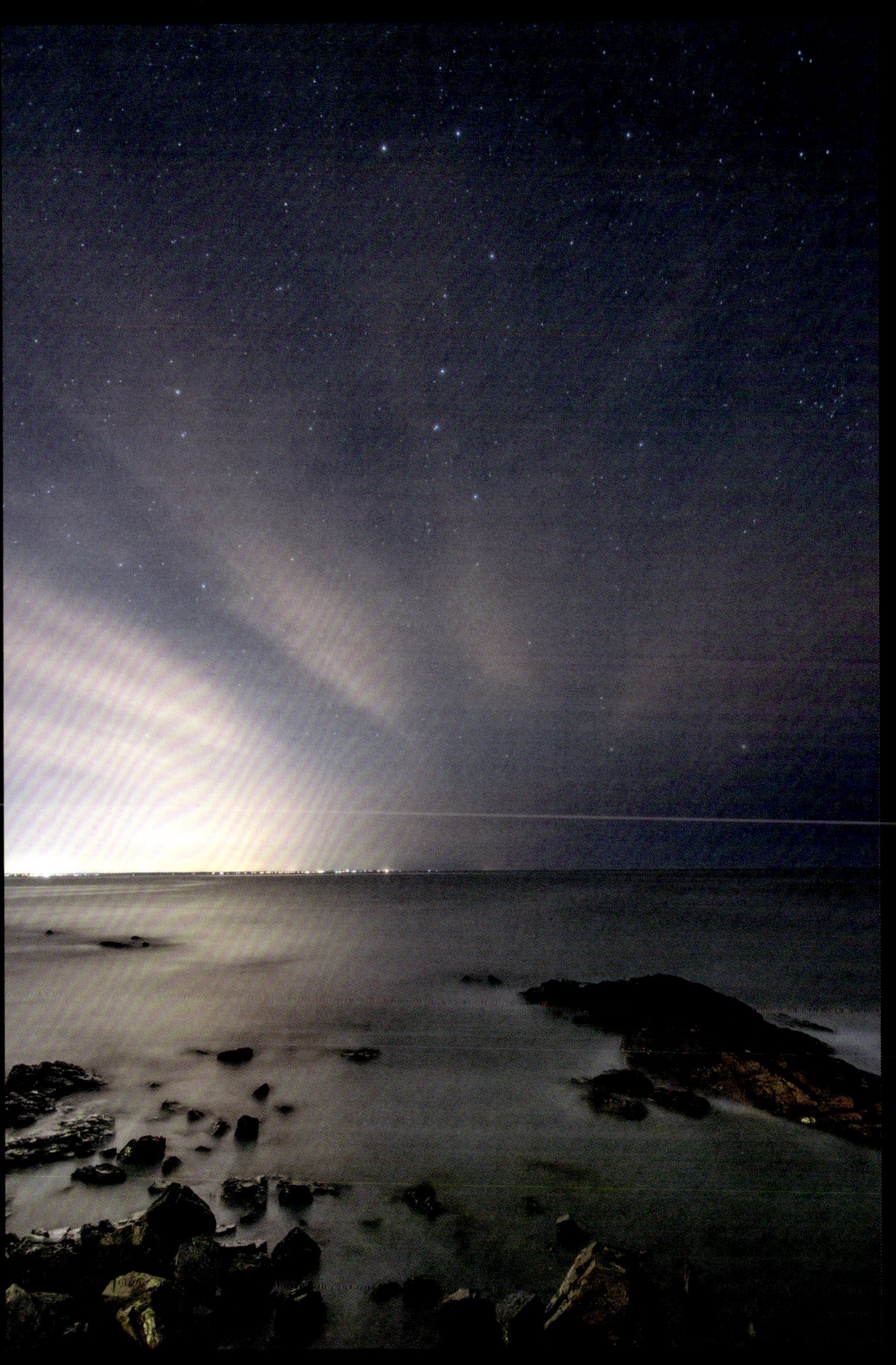

The Big Dipper is one of the easiest constellations to find in the Northern Hemisphere. Its bright stars are easy to spot early in the night and they will be clearly visible even during twilight or under light pollution.

At or above 41 degrees north latitude, the Big Dipper is visible all year long as it never sets below the horizon. Below 41 degrees though, you will want to check a star chart or an app such as Stellarium (see page 140) to determine when you can see the Big Dipper.

◀ The Big Dipper is visible in the top half of the frame.

2.5 LARGE MAGELLANIC CLOUD

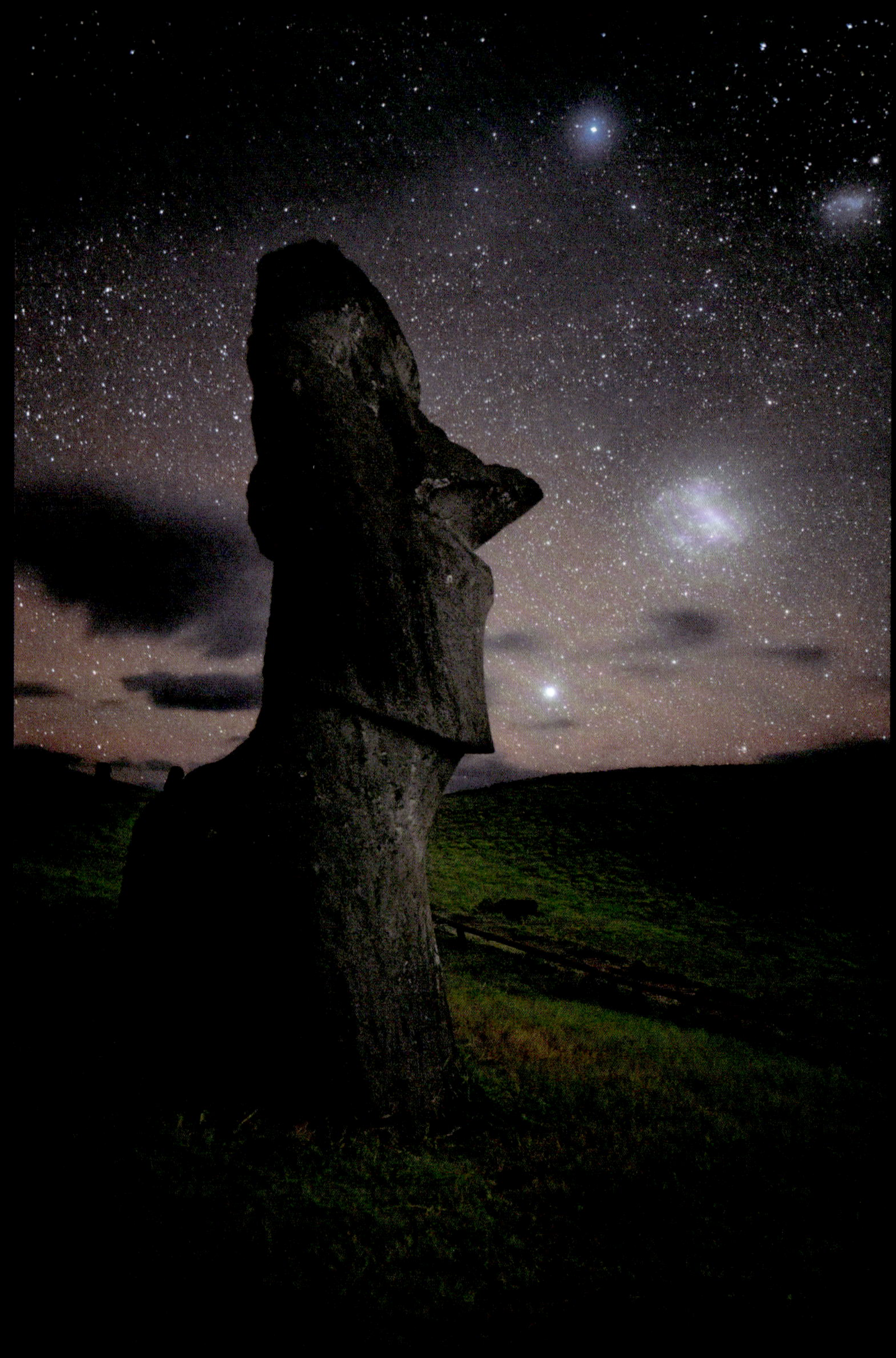

The Large Magellanic Cloud is a small galaxy that is near our own Milky Way galaxy. It is always visible in the night sky below 20 degrees south latitude. Between there and 20 degrees north latitude, it is only sometimes visible. Above 20 degrees north, it is never visible.

Just like the Milky Way, it is visible to the naked eye, but it really pops on camera.

◀ This photo by Yuri Beletsky shows the Large Magellanic Cloud next to a moai on Easter Island.

2.6 AIRGLOW

While not usually a night sky subject by itself, airglow is something you will likely run into when photographing in dark areas. Airglow is the result of various chemical reactions in the upper atmosphere that emit light, and on some nights it is much more active than others. It's very difficult to see airglow with the naked eye, but the camera has no problem capturing the dim light in a long exposure. Sometimes it colors the entire sky, and sometimes it appears just as ribbons passing through part of the frame. The color of airglow is most commonly green, red or yellow, and occasionally blue.

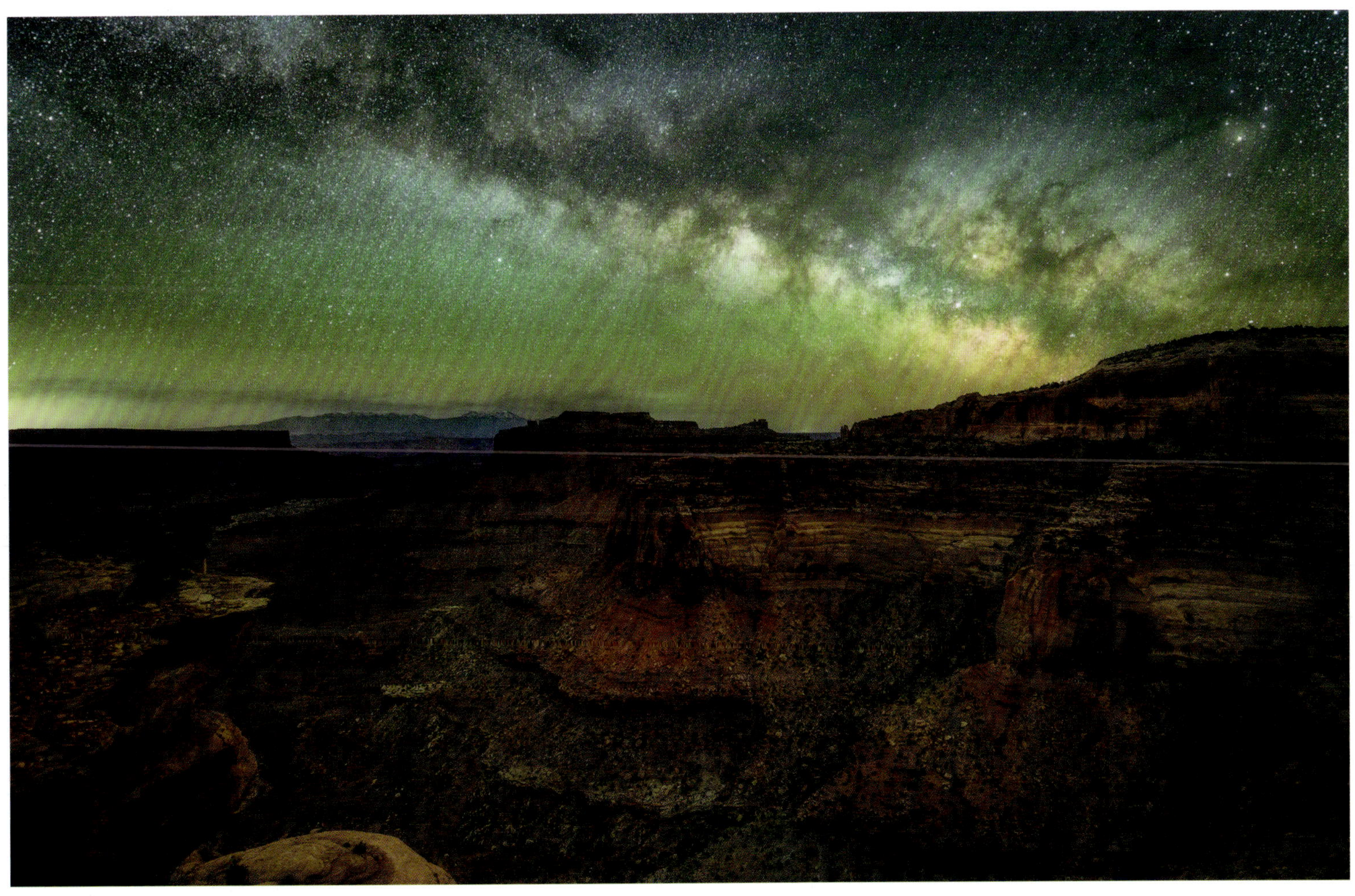

▲ Green airglow covering the sky above the desert of Utah, causing the entire sky and Milky Way to appear green.

GEAR

3

The gear required for landscape astrophotography isn't that different from the gear required for regular landscape photography, but there are some important things to consider. However, if you're just getting started, you might be able to shoot with whatever gear you have, depending on the focal length of your lens and the age of your camera.

Landscape astrophotography is one of those fields of photography where having better gear can really make a big difference, but that's not to say that you can't start out with entry-level gear. You can certainly get great shots with many modern digital cameras and lenses. The key features are how well a lens handles pinpoint sources of light, which will effect how the lens distorts the stars (if at all), and how much noise your camera creates in low light. However, technique plays just as much of a role in determining image quality, so don't worry if full-frame cameras and lenses are out of your budget. You can get amazing, high-resolution, print-worthy results with low noise by following the method laid out in this book.

But for now, let's dive into cameras.

▶ The Milky Way over Screw Auger Falls, Maine, in autumn.

Very little ambient light was hitting this gorge so I used a 20-minute exposure for the foreground. I could have used artificial lighting but I prefer natural ambient light, even if it's in a very dark gorge.

Nikon D800E and Nikon 14-24mm f/2.8 lens at 14mm and f/2.8 for all exposures.

Sky: 25 seconds at ISO 3200.

Foreground: 20 minutes at ISO 1600.

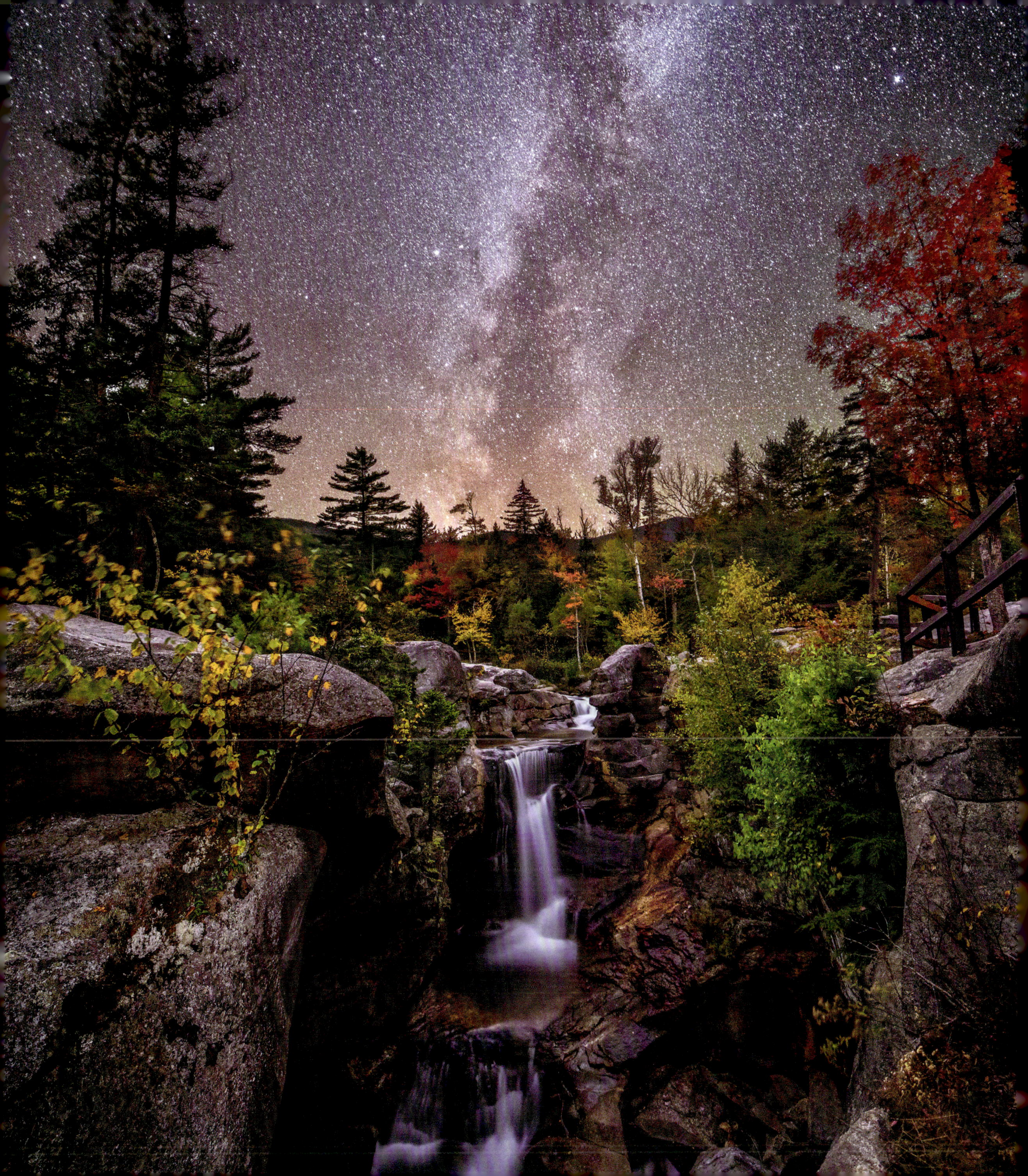

3.1 CAMERAS

By far, the question I most often get asked by landscape astrophotography newcom is, "I have a (insert brand and model name here) camera, will that work for this type of photography?"

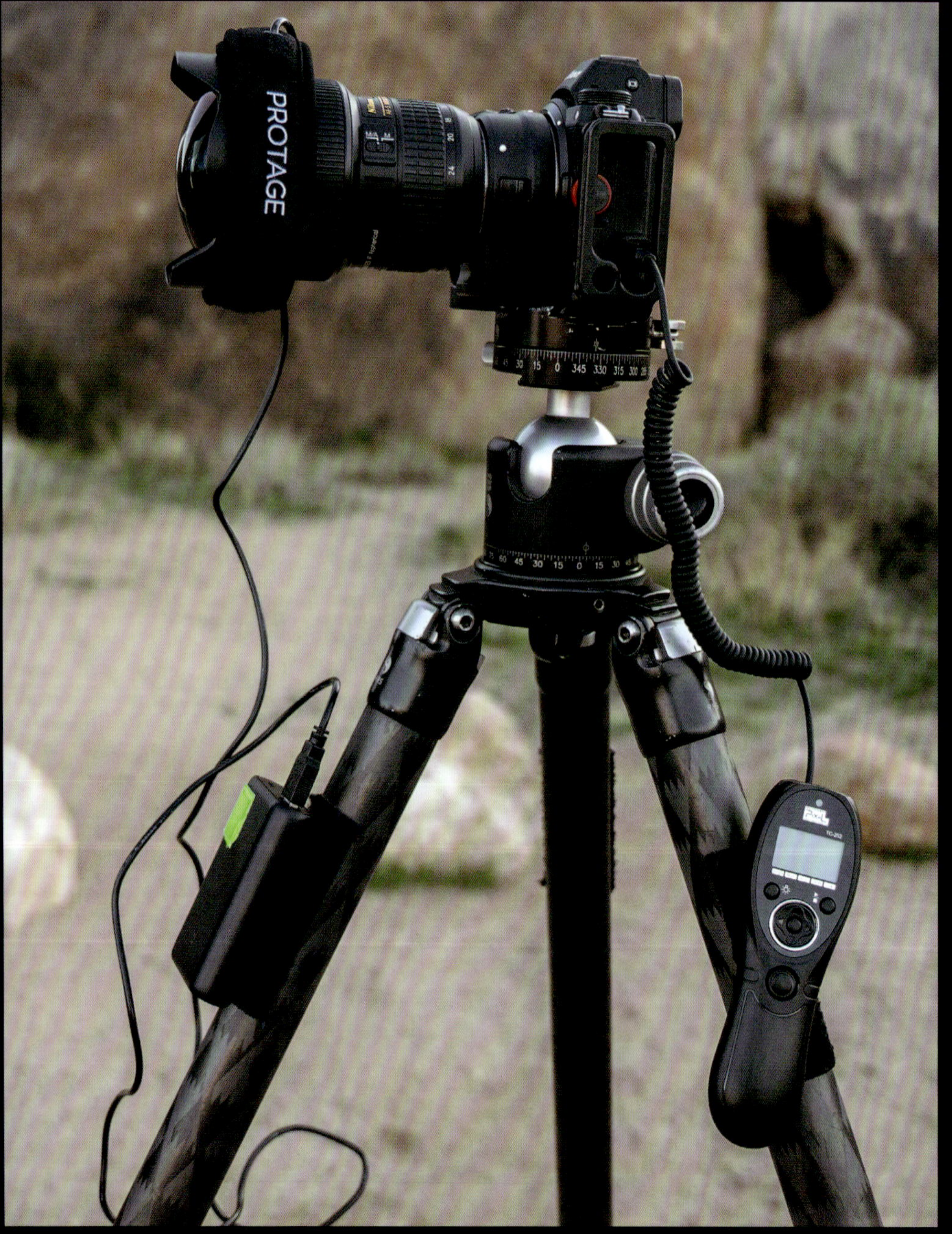

◀ My typical night photography setup, with lens heater (see page 46) and intervalometer (see page 44). I actually use an out-of-production Promote intervalometer, but the Pixel brand shown here is a much more affordable (and available) model. Note that I use hook-and-loop fasteners (such as Velcro) to attach the lens heater battery and intervalometer to the tripod.

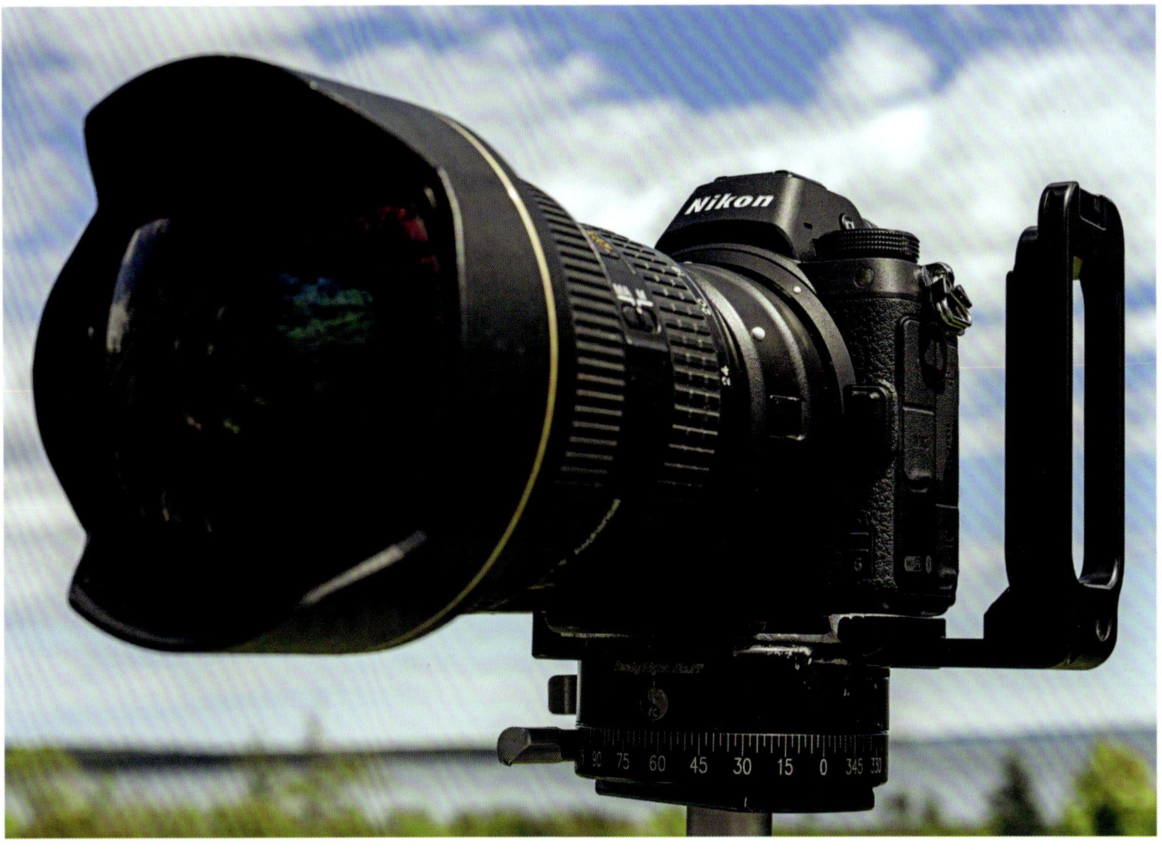

▶ Nikon Z 6 mirrorless full-frame camera with the Nikon AF-S Nikkor 14-24mm f/2.8 lens, attached using the Mount Adapter FTZ, which allows Nikon F-mount lenses to be attached to Nikon mirrorless cameras. The funny-looking thing sticking out from the right of the camera is an L-bracket (see page 42).

Almost always the answer is "Yes!" As long as you have a digital camera with interchangeable lenses, whether a DSLR or mirrorless camera, that was produced after, say, 2010, you should be capable of capturing great images. That's sort of an arbitrary date—it was around the time I started getting into landscape astrophotography, and digital cameras were rapidly improving their low-light capabilities at the time. Of course, more recent camera models will give you better low-light results, and older cameras will certainly have more trouble with noise, but if an upgrade is out of your budget, don't worry, just shoot!

SENSOR SIZE

There are quite a few digital cameras to choose from these days, with various sensor sizes and lens choices, but most serious landscape astrophotographers use a 35mm full-frame camera for higher quality results.

The term "full frame" means that the sensor size is the same as a single frame of 35mm film, which is 36mm x 24mm. A "crop" camera refers to any camera with a sensor that is smaller than a 35mm full-frame sensor. Then there are medium-format sensors that are larger than 35mm full-frame sensors, but by and large 35mm or smaller is the most common camera choice.

Full-frame cameras will deliver the best results. First, since a full-frame sensor is physically larger than a crop sensor, it will collect more light, and more light means less noise (we'll get into the details of this later in this book; see **Light & Noise**, page 62). Also, full-frame cameras typically contain better engineering and higher-end hardware, which will result in higher image quality and less noise. You'll also have more (and better) lens choices with full-frame cameras.

However, that's not to say that you can't shoot the night sky with a crop camera, or any other camera. I've had many students use crop cameras in my workshops, whether mirrorless or DSLR, and the results are always great.

With crop sensor cameras you have a magnifying effect since the smaller sensor

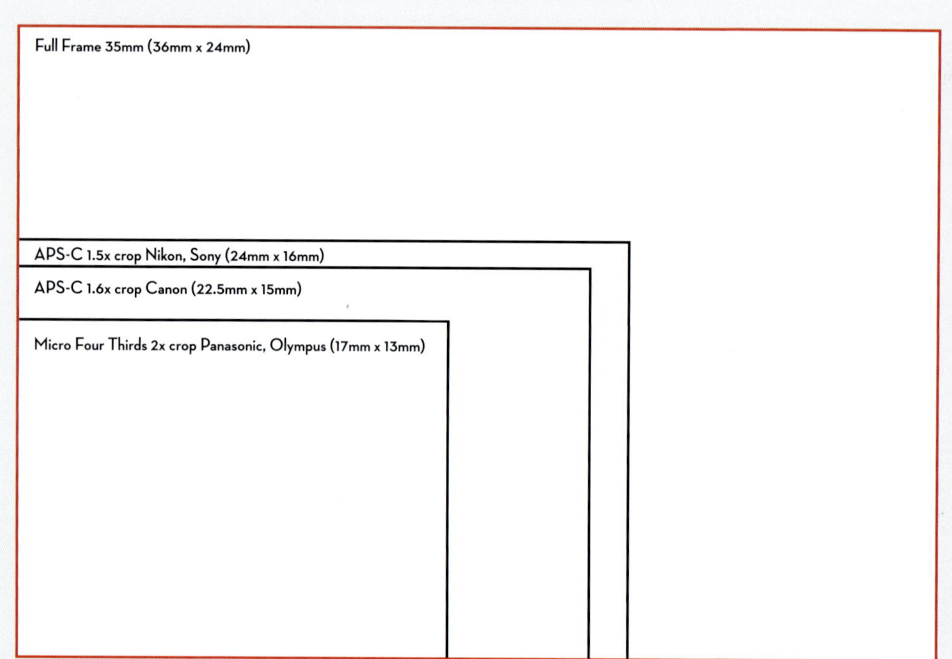

▲ A comparison of some standard sensor sizes. The red outer box is a full-frame 35mm sensor, with smaller sensor sizes drawn inside.

will only capture a portion of what a full-frame 35mm sensor can view. This means that if you use a full-frame lens on a crop camera, that crop camera will only capture the inner part of the image created by that lens, cropping the scene, hence the name "crop sensor."

There are a few different types of crop sensors. In DSLR or mirrorless cameras, APS-C sensors are the most common. Nikon and Sony APS-C cameras have a 1.5x magnification factor, and Canon APS-C cameras have a 1.6x magnification factor. This means that, for example, a 50mm lens used on an APS-C camera will actually have a field of view similar to a 75mm lens on a Nikon or Sony APS-C camera (50mm x 1.5 = 75mm), or 80mm on a Canon APS-C camera (50mm x 1.6 = 80mm).

Micro Four Thirds (abbreviated as Micro 4/3, M4/3 or MFT) cameras have a crop magnification factor of 2x, so a 50mm lens on an MFT camera actually has the field of view of a 100mm lens on a 35mm full-frame camera. Olympus and Panasonic are the most popular MFT camera brands.

MEGAPIXELS

Another factor to consider is megapixel count. A full-frame camera that has 20 megapixels (MP) has a lower resolution (lower pixel density) than a full-frame camera with 40 MP, but the size of a pixel on the sensor will be larger for the 20 MP camera because there is more room for each pixel, where as the 40 MP camera will have to use less space for each pixel in order to fit them all into the same physical dimensions. The result is that each pixel on the 20 MP sensor will collect more light (more photons, which are the particles of light), and thus each pixel will have a higher signal-to-noise ratio versus the 40 MP sensor. Given two cameras of the same brand and vintage, and thus similar hardware, this means that the 20 MP sensor will generate images with less noise, particularly in low-light situations where photons are scarce. This has long been why many night photographers look for a low-megapixel camera as their dedicated night photography camera, since it will generate less noise in photographs taken at night.

However, that's not the full story. Continuing the example above, if you took the 40 MP image and downscaled it to 20 MP using Photoshop, and then compared that downscaled version to the image from the 20 MP camera, you would notice that the images now look very similar in terms of noise. This is because the downscaling process will average the values (brightness/color) of adjacent pixels together to create a single pixel in the smaller file, which means that the random brightness/color differences caused by the noise are smoothed out (technically this improves the signal-to-noise ratio, discussed in **Light & Noise** from page 62). This process is known as "pixel binning," and is a common practice to reduce noise at the cost of lower resolution in other areas of photography, including deep space astrophotography, and many scientific areas of imaging, such as x-ray photography.

Modern digital cameras have come a long way in handling noise and low light, and if you have good technique you will avoid having to deal with extremely harsh noise most of the time. Personally, I shoot with both low and high-density full-frame cameras. I use high-density megapixel cameras for daytime landscapes, and I go back and forth with high or low-density megapixel cameras for night landscapes. It's also worth noting that, because of the high number of individual images needed for some astrophotography techniques, sometimes using a lower pixel density camera is preferable not just because the images will have less noise, but also because the files are smaller and editing software such as Adobe Lightroom Classic and Photoshop will run faster while editing those images.

ASTROPHOTOGRAPHY SPECIFIC CAMERAS

Digital camera sensors are very sensitive to infrared (IR) light, so almost all digital cameras have an IR filter mounted in front of the sensor to block IR light. Otherwise, the camera would capture a very different-looking world.

However, red nebulae and other deep space objects emit IR light, so for deep space astrophotography it is often desirable to not have an IR filter or to have one that blocks all but the IR light from nebulae. This means that the nebulae will be more saturated red in appearance, and faint IR signals will show up more prominently.

There are many cameras for telescopes like this, but for traditional cameras there are models such as the Nikon D810A and Canon EOS Ra, both of which have an IR filter that allows the sensor to capture IR light from nebulae. With such cameras, objects like the Lagoon Nebula, Eagle Nebula and Orion Nebula will all pop with more red.

These cameras are intended for use when photographing deep space objects, but they work well for night landscapes too.

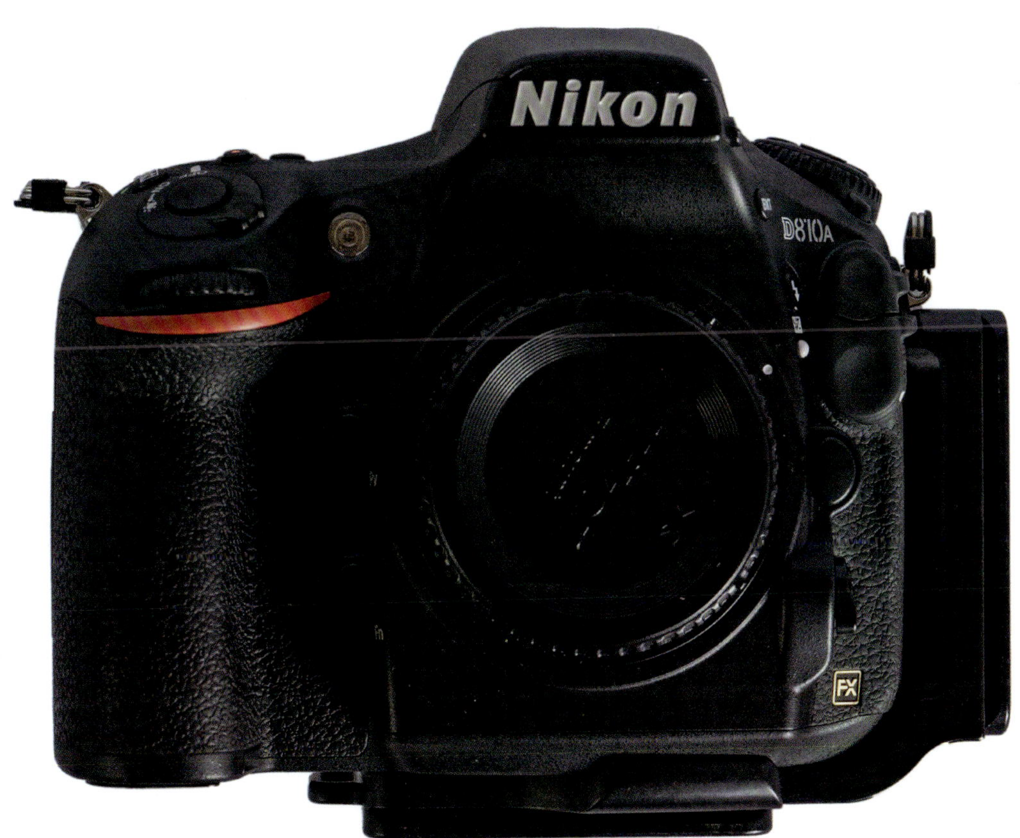

◀ My Nikon D810A with an L-bracket attached.

3.2 LENSES

The lens is arguably the most important piece of equipment you will need for night photography. A great camera paired with a bad lens won't help at all if the lens distorts stars so much that they look like UFOs. The camera is only as good as the lens being used. There are three main factors to consider in a lens for landscape astrophotography: Focal length, maximum aperture (lowest f-stop number) and aberrations.

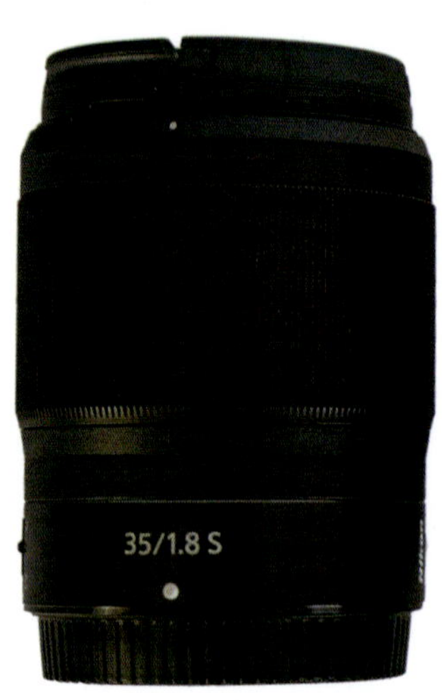

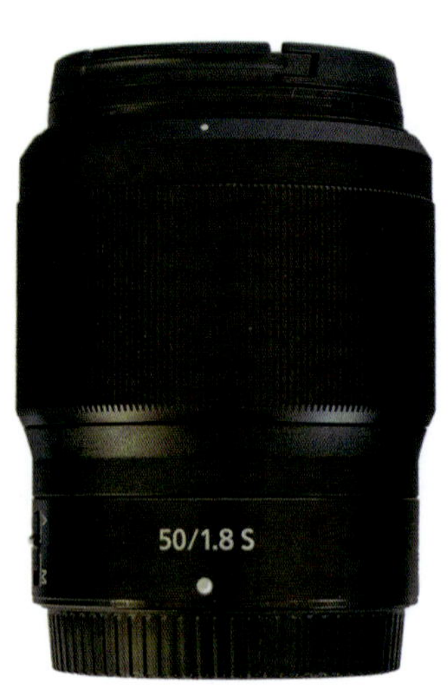

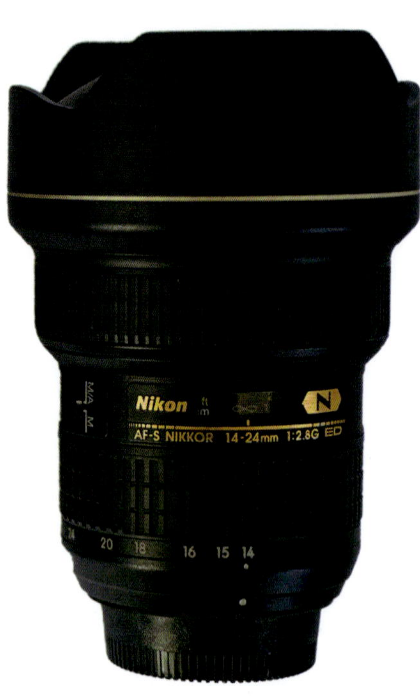

▶ Typical kit might include a 35mm and 50mm prime lens, and a 14-24mm zoom.

3.2.1 FOCAL LENGTH

The focal length tells you how wide or narrow the field of view will be when using that lens. Smaller numbers indicate a wider field of view, and larger numbers indicate a more narrow field of view. For example, a 24mm lens is wider than a 50mm lens, and 50mm is wider than 100mm.

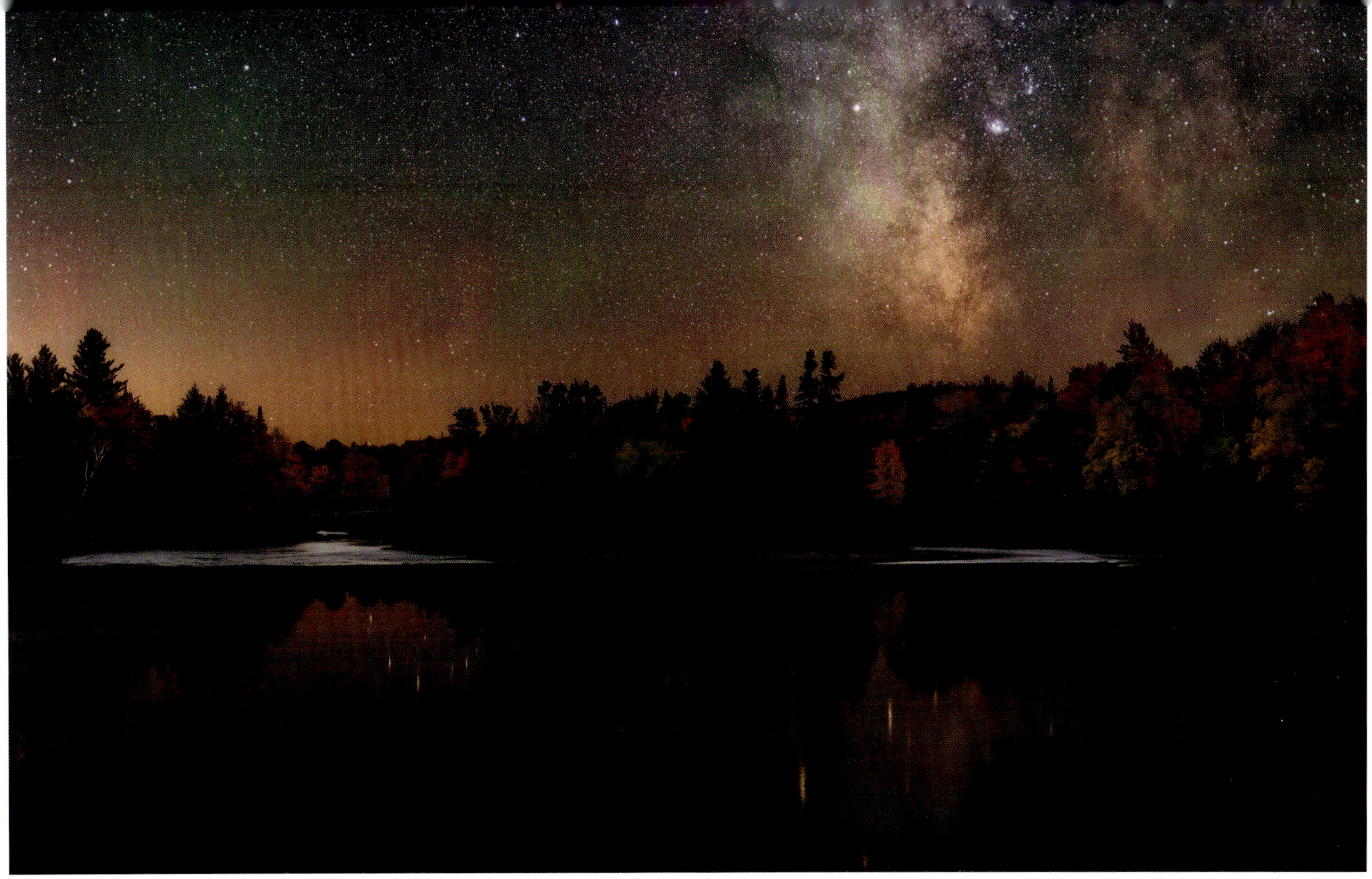

Super-wide-angle lenses are very popular for landscape astrophotography because they allow you to include a large amount of both the landscape and night sky in the frame at the same time. The preferred focal lengths for landscape astrophotography are 14-16mm on full-frame cameras, and 10-12mm on crop cameras. Why the smaller focal lengths on crop cameras? Remember from the previous section that crop cameras have a magnification factor, so a 10mm lens on an APS-C camera with 1.5x crop will actually have the same field of view as a 15mm lens used on a full-frame camera.

Longer focal lengths will have the opposite effect and will let you "punch in" on the Milky Way to really draw attention to the detail in the Galactic Core.

▲ Milky Way during fall in New Hampshire.

In this image, a 50mm lens was used to capture the Galactic Core of the Milky Way. The longer focal length makes it appear very large over the foreground.

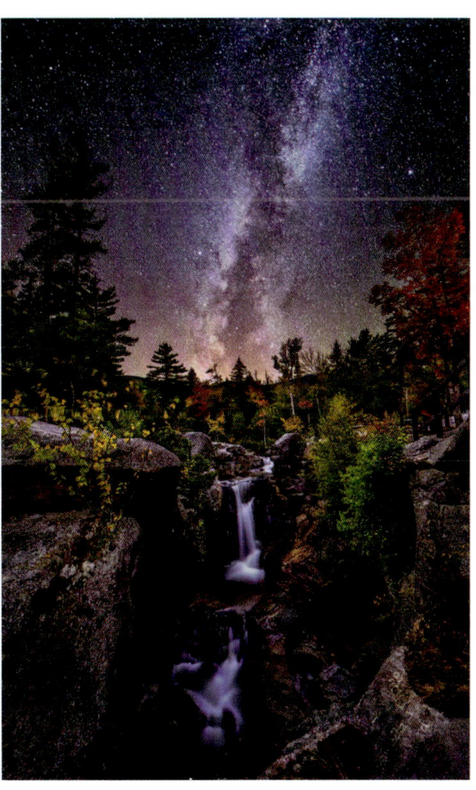

▶ Milky Way over Screw Auger Falls, Maine.

In this image a 14mm lens was used to capture a large amount of both the landscape and the sky.

3.2.2 APERTURE

A camera lens contains a diaphragm that controls how much light passes through the lens. The opening within this diaphragm is known as the aperture of the lens. The diaphragm is mechanical and can change the size of the opening, allowing for more or less light to enter. This allows for two things to happen:

1 Making the aperture larger lets in more light, but it also results in a more shallow depth of field. That is, a larger aperture indicates that less of the scene will be in focus.

2 Making the aperture smaller results in less light entering the lens, but it also results in a larger depth of field, meaning more of the scene will be in focus.

F-stop numbers are used to measure the physical size of an aperture. An f-stop is usually written with an "f/" preceding the number, for instance "f/2.8" indicates an f-stop of 2.8.

By going up one whole f-stop number you are halving the amount of light entering the lens, and by going down one whole f-stop number you are doubling the amount of light entering the lens. For example, f/4 lets twice as much light through the lens as f/5.6, four times as much light as f/8, and eight times as much light as f/11.

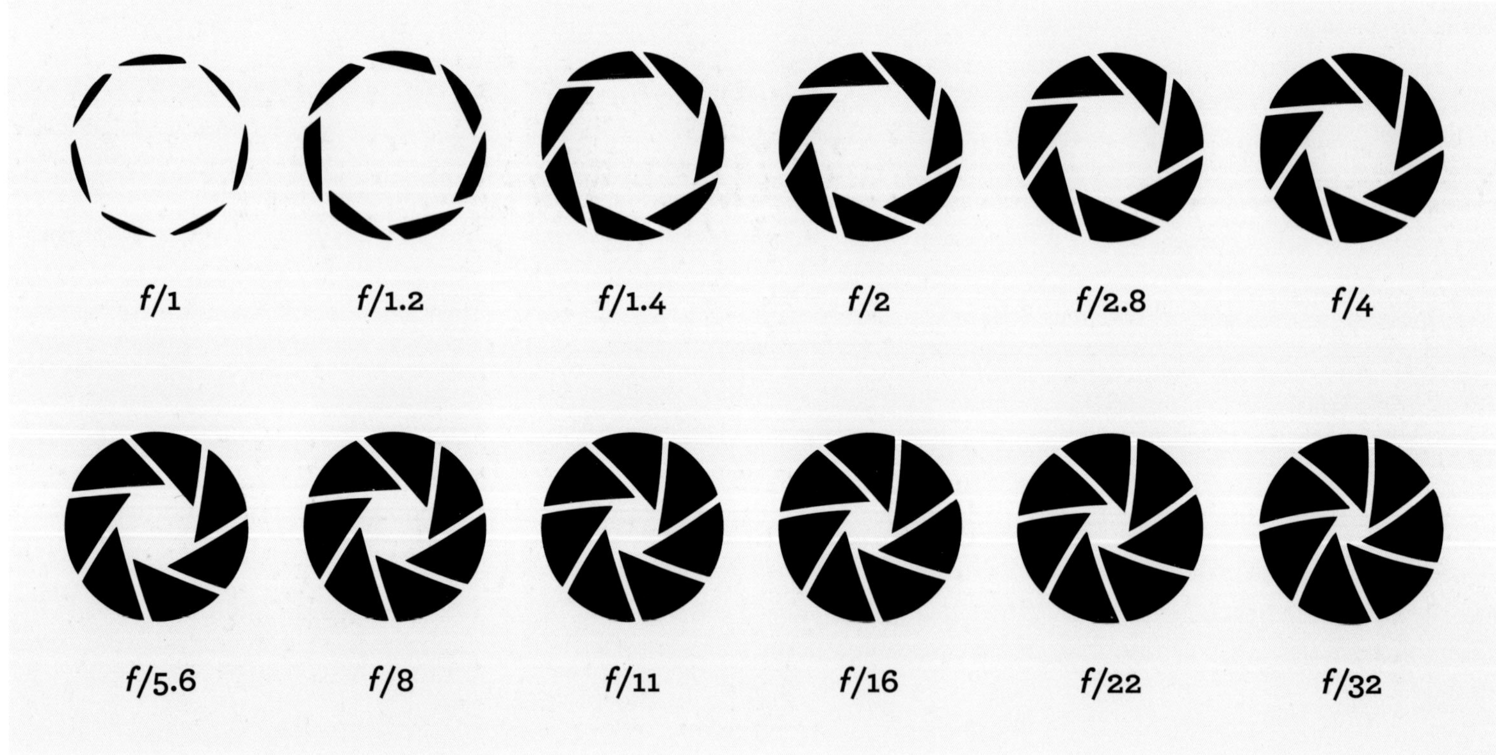

▲ Comparative size of apertures, from f/1 to f/32.

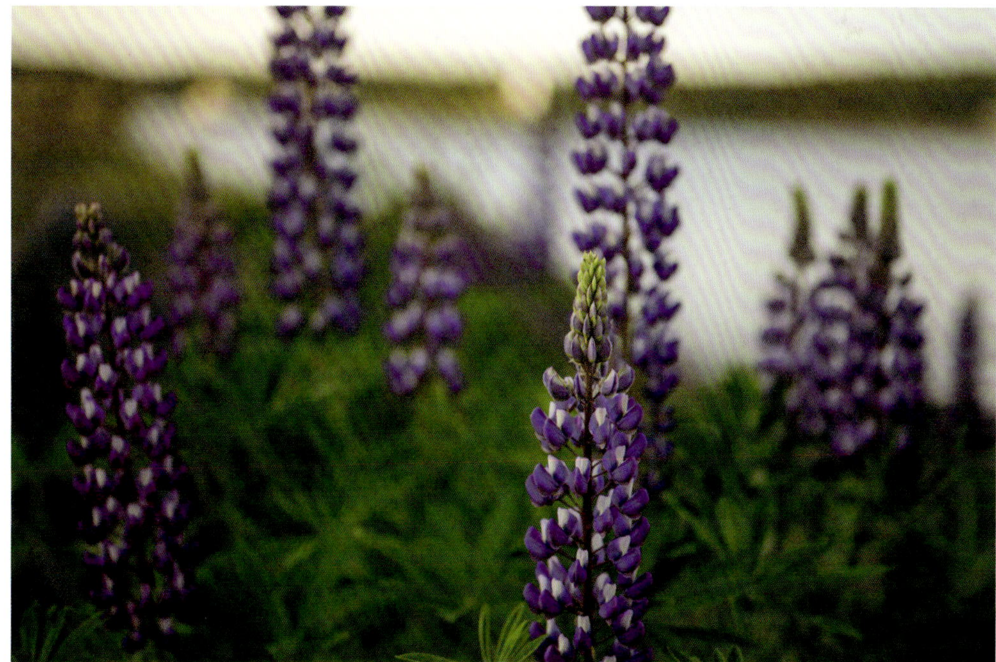

▲ Shot taken at 50mm, f/1.8, 1/1600 second, ISO 400. At f/1.8 the depth of field is very shallow.

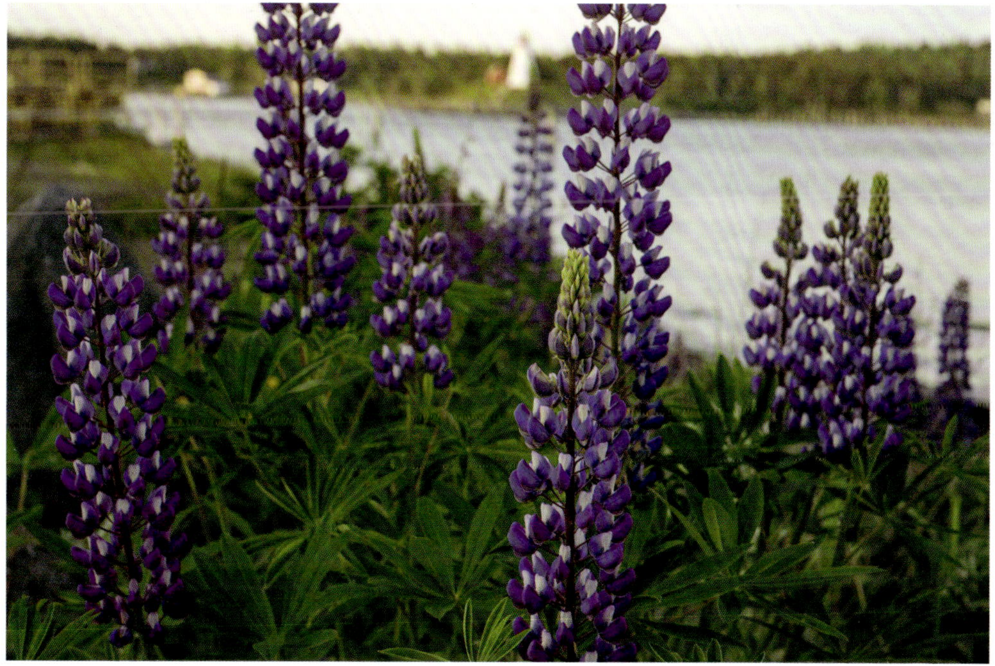

▲ Shot taken at 50mm, f/8, ISO 400, 1/100 second. At f/8 the depth of field is much greater, but a longer shutter speed is required to capture more light.

It's worth noting some commonly used terms here:

A fast lens is one that has a very wide maximum aperture, usually f/2.8 or lower. The term "fast" is used here because a wider aperture allows for faster shutter speeds, making it easier to capture fast action without significant motion blur.

Stopping down a lens refers to increasing the f-stop number to use a smaller aperture, letting in less light, and increasing the depth of field.

Opening up a lens means to use a lower f-stop number for a wider aperture, letting in more light and decreasing the depth of field.

For landscape astrophotography, where working in the dark is the name of the game, we want to capture as much light as possible. This is why lenses with a maximum aperture of f/2.8 (or even smaller f-stop numbers) are very popular.

So, you might think that you would always use the fastest (lowest f-number) lens possible, but that's not always the case. Lens aberrations are a significant factor to consider when picking a good lens and determining the best f-stop to use on that lens. Lens designers have to balance optical quality with the desire for a wide maximum aperture, and very wide-aperture lenses often have the worst aberrations of pinpoint sources of light, distorting the stars. Sometimes these distortions are tolerable, sometimes not. This brings us to our next section where we will look in more detail at lens aberrations.

3.2.3 LENS ABERRATIONS

Most lenses will have some amount of aberrations, which are issues with how the lens focuses light or distorts the scene. Some are not a problem for landscape astrophotography, but others will make your stars looks like UFOs or as if they have angel wings.

Chromatic aberrations are caused by the different wavelengths of light not all being focused at the same point, causing "color fringing." This occurs most often around high-contrast edges, and stars are most certainly high-contrast bright spots against a dark background. Lenses are a lot better at handling chromatic aberrations these days, and most Raw editors have chromatic aberration removal built in which does an amazing job of removing the color fringing, but you may still experience it with some lenses, and it will be most prominent with brighter stars. The fringing will usually appear magenta or cyan in color.

Comatic (or coma) aberration gets its name due to the comet-head-like shape that pinpoint sources of light exhibit with this kind of aberration.

Astigmatism aberrations cause points of light to be elongated. This stretching causes the stars to look like slits or slits with wings, depending on the strength of the astigmatism aberration.

These three aberrations can be reduced by stopping down the lens to a higher f-stop number. Remember that a higher f-stop means a smaller aperture, blocking more light rays from passing through the lens. Light rays that enter the lens from very oblique angles will cause more aberrations, so blocking more of them with a smaller aperture will reduce those aberrations.

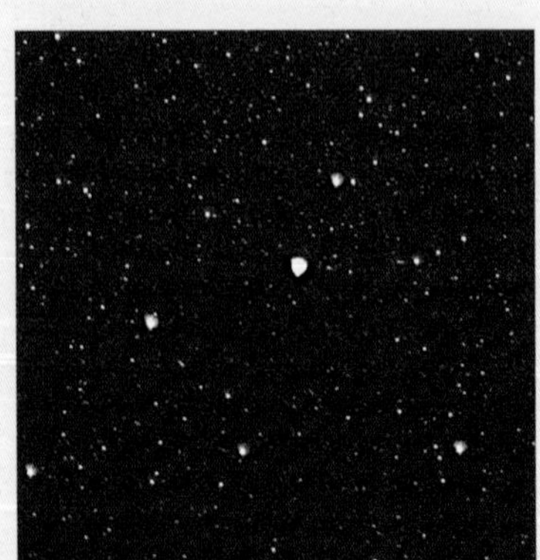

▲ An example of comatic (or coma) aberrations.

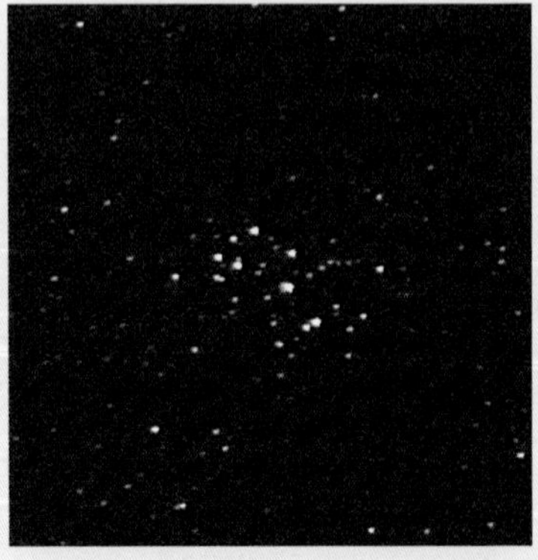

▲ An example of chromatic aberrations, which are also visible in the other examples.

▲ An example of astigmatism aberrations.

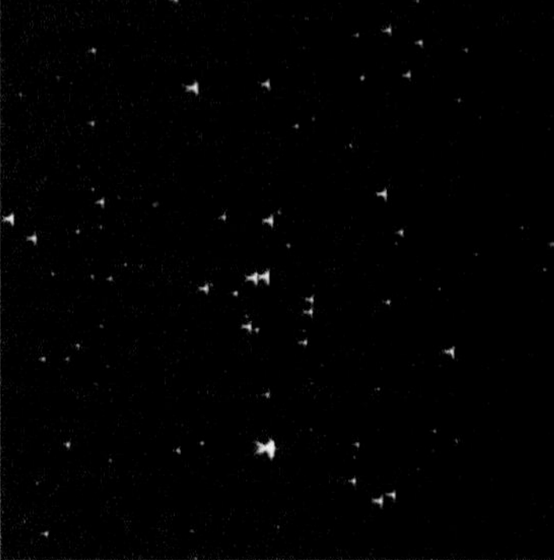

▲ Another example of lens aberrations. The stars look like birds!

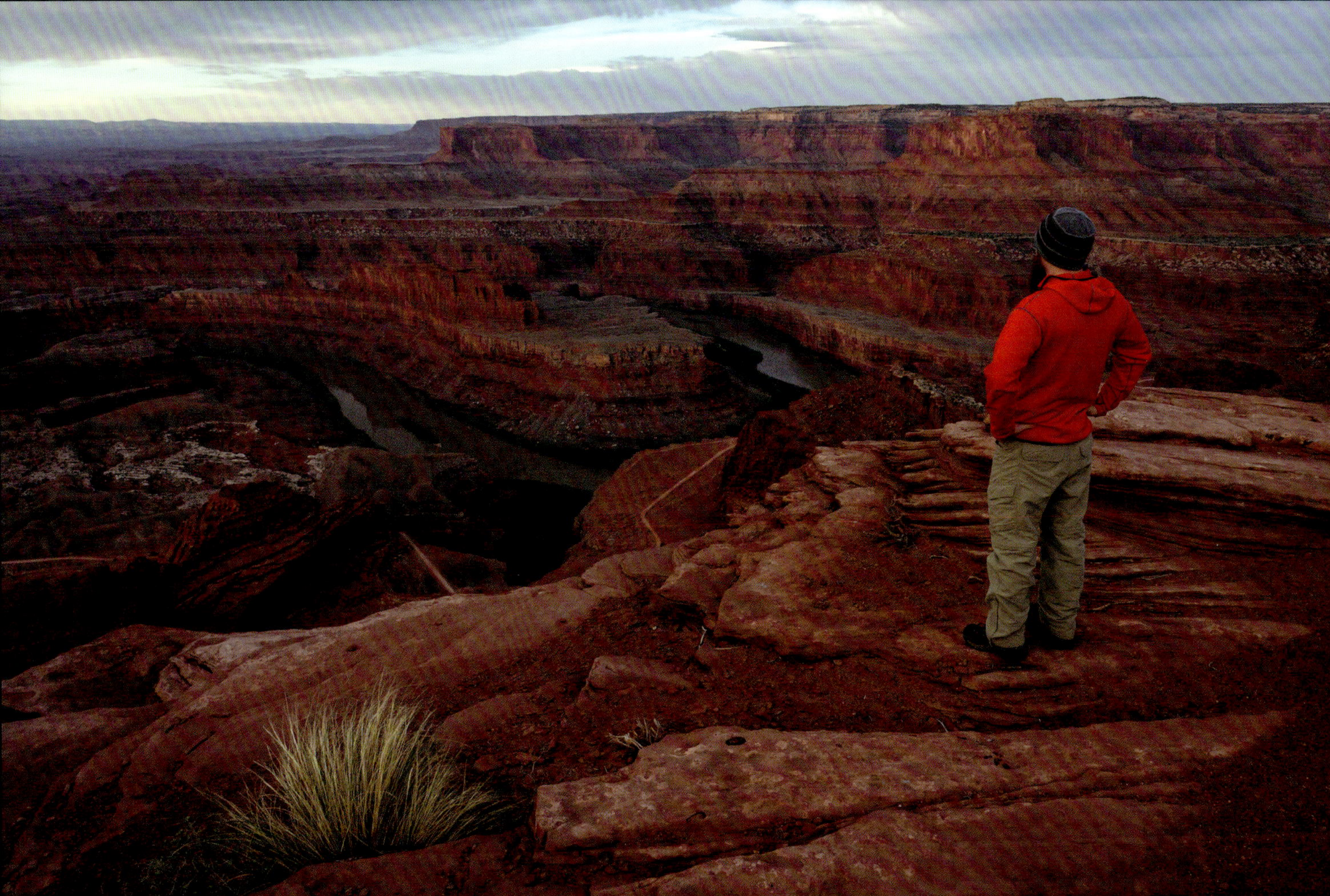

Lens distortion refers to the overall scene being warped in some manner, and it manifests in a few different ways.

Barrel distortion causes the scene at the center of the frame to look larger than at the edges of the frame. Pincushion distortion is the opposite, causing the center to appear smaller than the edges. Mustache distortion is a combination of the two, and gets its name from the fact that having both types of distortion causes straight lines to appear wavy. You'll often see a photo of a brick wall being used to illustrate a review of a lens; the straight lines in the brick wall are being used to demonstrate the distortion (or lack thereof) of the lens.

Unlike the other aberrations, distortion cannot be corrected by stopping down the lens. It is a permanent problem with the lens.

Wide-angle lenses, such as those favored for landscape astrophotography, often have quite a lot of distortion, but this is tolerated as it allows photographers to capture huge scenes in a single frame. However, the distortion does present problems that may have to be fixed in software. Distortion on rocks and mountains may not be too noticeable, but if trees or a building are leaning inward or outward, that is usually distracting. Such issues can be corrected in software by manually warping the image, either by warping the entire shot or by warping just the part of the image where the correction is needed.

▲ Despite standing up straight, I appear to be leaning backwards in this image because of wide-angle lens distortion that is made much more noticeable when pointing the lens up or down. We don't notice this type of distortion with rocks and many other features of nature, but it is noticeable with trees, people and buildings.

Vignetting causes the corners of the image to be darker than the center. This is due to the design of the lens and/or camera blocking some of the light coming in from those corners. Since less light is hitting the sensor in the corners, this can result in more noise in these areas due to the lower signal-to-noise ratio (see **Light & Noise**, page 62). This is the same reason that any dark area (shadow) of an image may seem to have more noise than the rest of the image. On bright exposures the corners likely won't appear to have any more noise than the rest of the image, but for the short exposures we use for the stars you will often find that strong vignetting on a lens results in noisy corners.

Many Raw editors have lens corrections built in that can be turned on or off. These corrections are for distortion, chromatic aberration and vignetting only. Astigmatism and coma aberrations cannot be fixed in a Raw editor, though I wouldn't rule out some AI software coming along eventually that can detect and fix stars that suffer from such aberrations. But before that happens, you can manually correct the worst issues by using the Healing Brush or Clone Stamp tools in Photoshop or your Raw editor, perhaps just trimming off the edges of the brightest stars to get them to look less like UFOs.

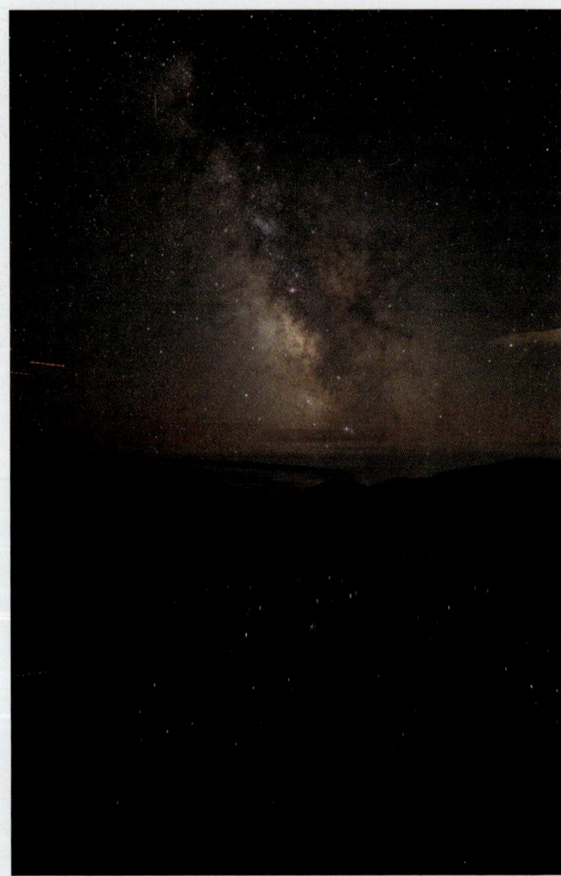

▲ An example of what an image may look like with lens vignetting.

▲ The same image but with the lens vignetting removed in Lightroom Classic. Notice how the edges of the frame are substantially brighter.

3.2.4 LOOKING FOR A GOOD LENS

The goal is to find a lens where aberrations of pinpoint sources of light (the stars in our case) are as minimal as possible, or at least acceptable to the point where it is just the brighter stars in the corners that may have some issues.

Many fast lenses that sound like they might be good for low-light photography end up not working well at all for photographing stars because of strong aberrations. A tempting f/1.4 lens may be horrible at capturing the stars until it's stopped down to f/2.8 or so, at which point you might as well just use a cheaper f/2.8 lens. (This is unless you have a need for a fast lens for other low-light photography subjects of course, such as concerts or fast action, something where pinpoint sources of light aren't an issue.) Always look up reviews of lenses before you purchase them to check out how they perform with pinpoint sources of light, and if you can't find this information in the reviews, then make sure you can return the lens. You can also borrow lenses to test them out before you purchase one of your own. Companies like **lensrentals.com** and **borrowlenses.com** can ship rental lenses to your door or vacation spot.

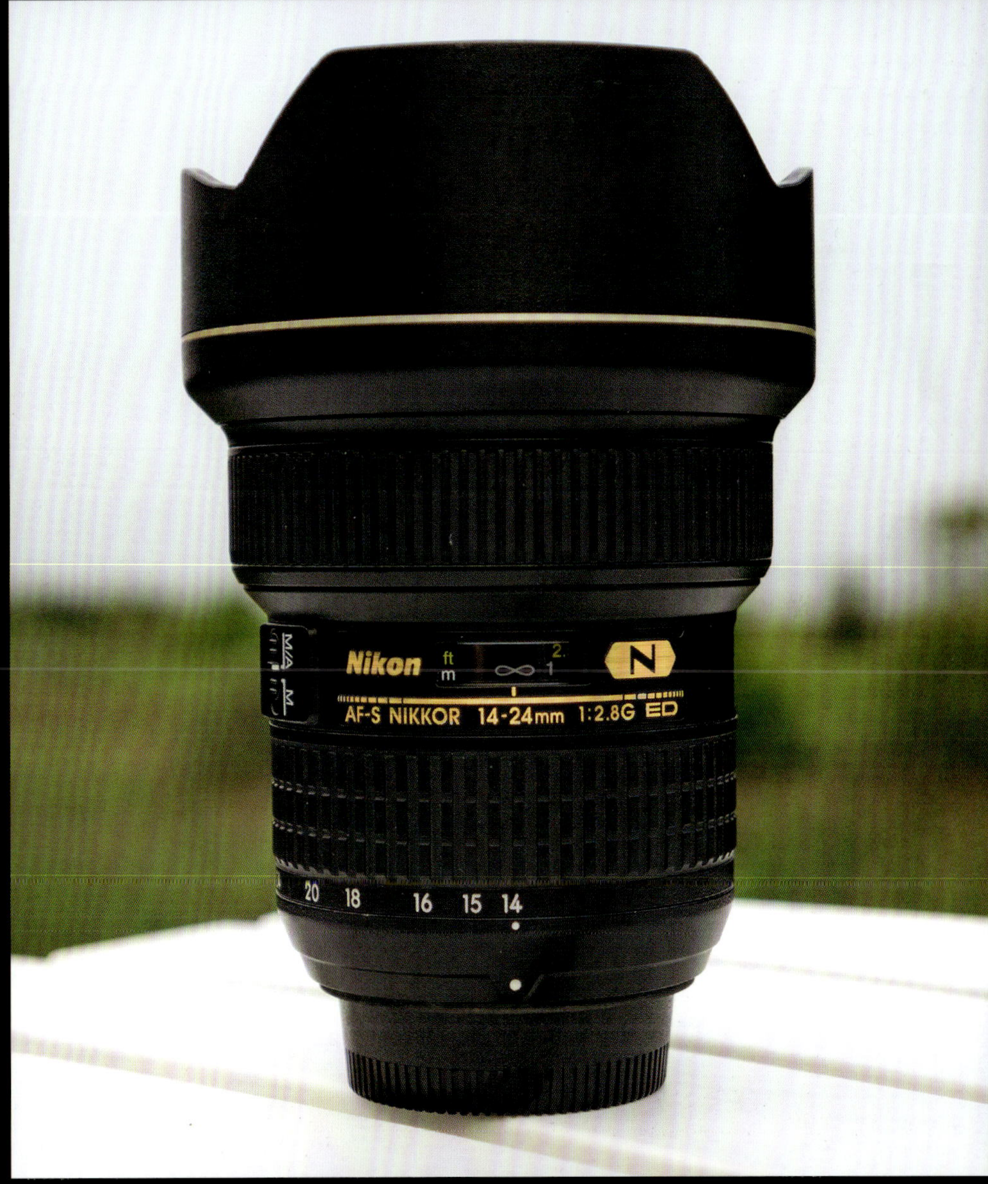

▲ The Nikon AF-S NIKKOR 14-24mm f/2.8 ED lens. A great ultra-wide zoom lens.

3.2.5 PRIME VS ZOOM

A prime lens has a fixed focal length, for example, 14mm, that cannot be changed. A zoom lens will allow you to use a range of focal lengths, for example, from 14mm to 24mm.

Prime lenses are often sought after for their higher quality optics and low f-stop numbers, but these days many zoom lenses are of amazing quality as well. In fact, for landscape astrophotography, prime lenses are often the ones that need to be stopped down to reduce lens aberrations that distort the stars, as mentioned previously. So for our purposes, prime lenses often don't live up to the hype or associated price tag. You'll likely be better off spending your money on a good-quality f/2.8 wide-angle zoom lens instead of a few primes.

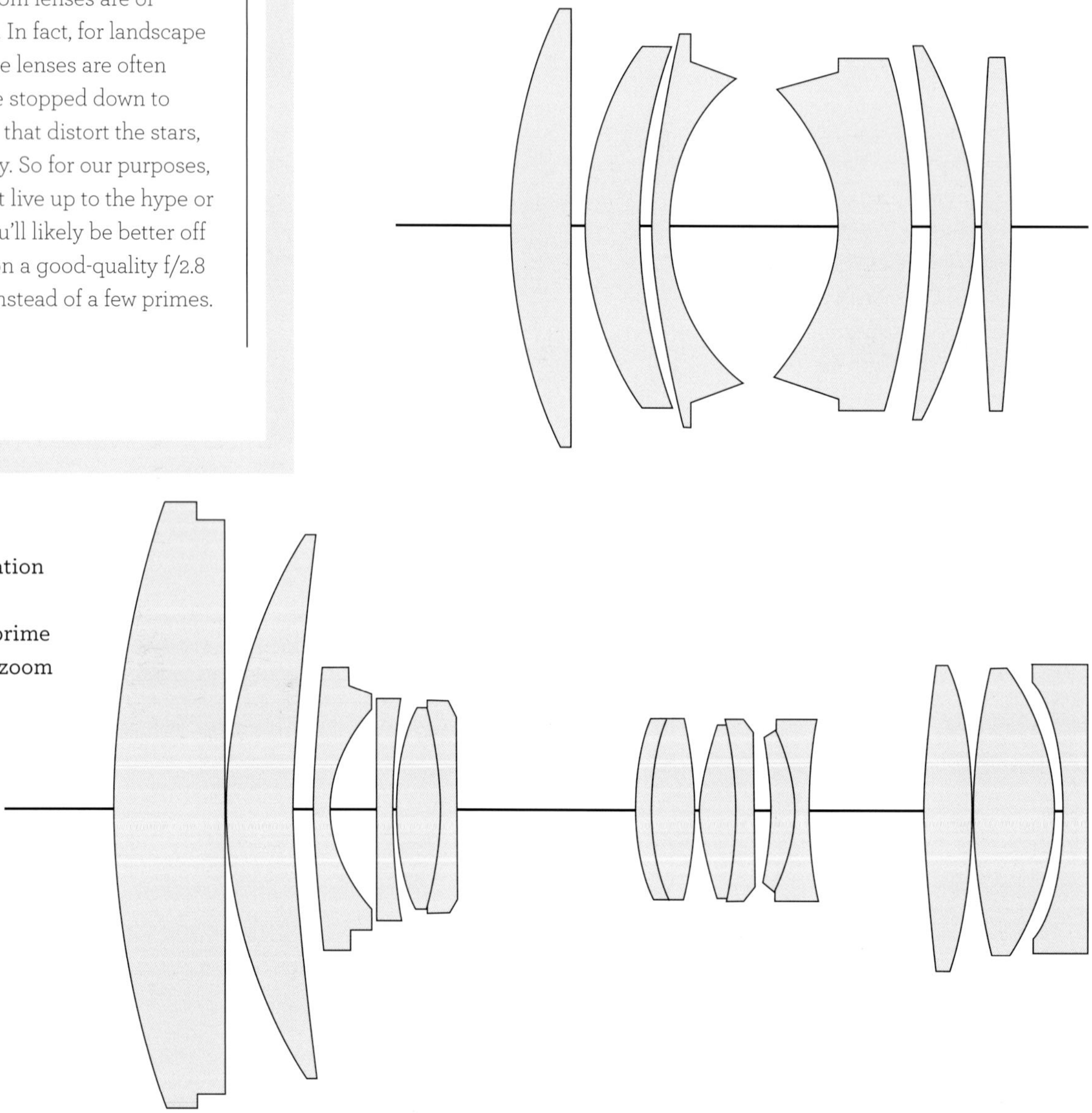

▶ A representation of the optical elements in a prime lens (top) vs a zoom lens (bottom).

3.2.6 LENS RECOMMENDATIONS

There are lots of lenses to choose from these days that are suitable for landscape astrophotography, but I will list some here that, as of this writing, are known to be good choices. This is by no means an exhaustive list, and it covers only ultra-wide prime and zoom lenses. There are also many other lenses with longer focal lengths available from various manufacturers that can also be used with great results.

Full-frame lenses can be used on crop cameras of the same brand most of the time, for example the Nikon 14-24mm f/2.8 lens can be used on a crop Nikon DSLR such as the D500. When using a full-frame lens on a crop camera, the field of view will change because of the smaller sensor on the crop camera. You can determine the equivalent focal length by multiplying the focal length of the lens by the crop factor of the sensor. For example, a 14mm full-frame lens used on a 1.5x crop factor DSLR would mean that the effective focal length is 21mm. In other words, a 14mm lens used on a crop camera would appear like a 21mm lens on a full-frame camera.

The Rokinon lenses in this list are also sold under the names Bower and Samyang, but they are the same lenses. These lenses are great because they are affordable and perform very well, however they are also known to have quality control issues. It is not uncommon to have to return a Rokinon lens once (or more) in order to get a good copy of the lens free from issues. The most common issue is with the lens elements not being centered properly, causing half of the frame to be soft when the other half is in focus. Always buy from a reputable store with a good returns policy.

FULL-FRAME DSLR OR MIRRORLESS CAMERAS
Nikon 14-24mm f/2.8
Canon 16-35mm f/2.8
Sony 16-35mm f/2.8
Sigma 14-24mm f/2.8
Tamron 15-30mm f/2.8
Rokinon (Bower, Samyang) 14mm f/2.8

APS-C DSLR CAMERAS
Tokina 11-16mm f/2.8
Tokina 11-20mm f/2.8
Rokinon (Bower, Samyang) 10mm f/2.8

APS-C MIRRORLESS CAMERAS
Zeiss 12mm f/2.8
Rokinon (Bower, Samyang) 12mm f/2.8

3.3 TRIPOD & BALLHEAD

A good tripod is a critical piece of equipment, yet it is one that is often overlooked. long exposures in the dark you need a sturdy tripod that you can use easily without of a headlamp. Do not economize here and get some special bargain travel tripod m out of plastic. If you're spending thousands of dollars on camera equipment, don't t this on a cheap set of sticks. Get a tripod that is solid and reliable.

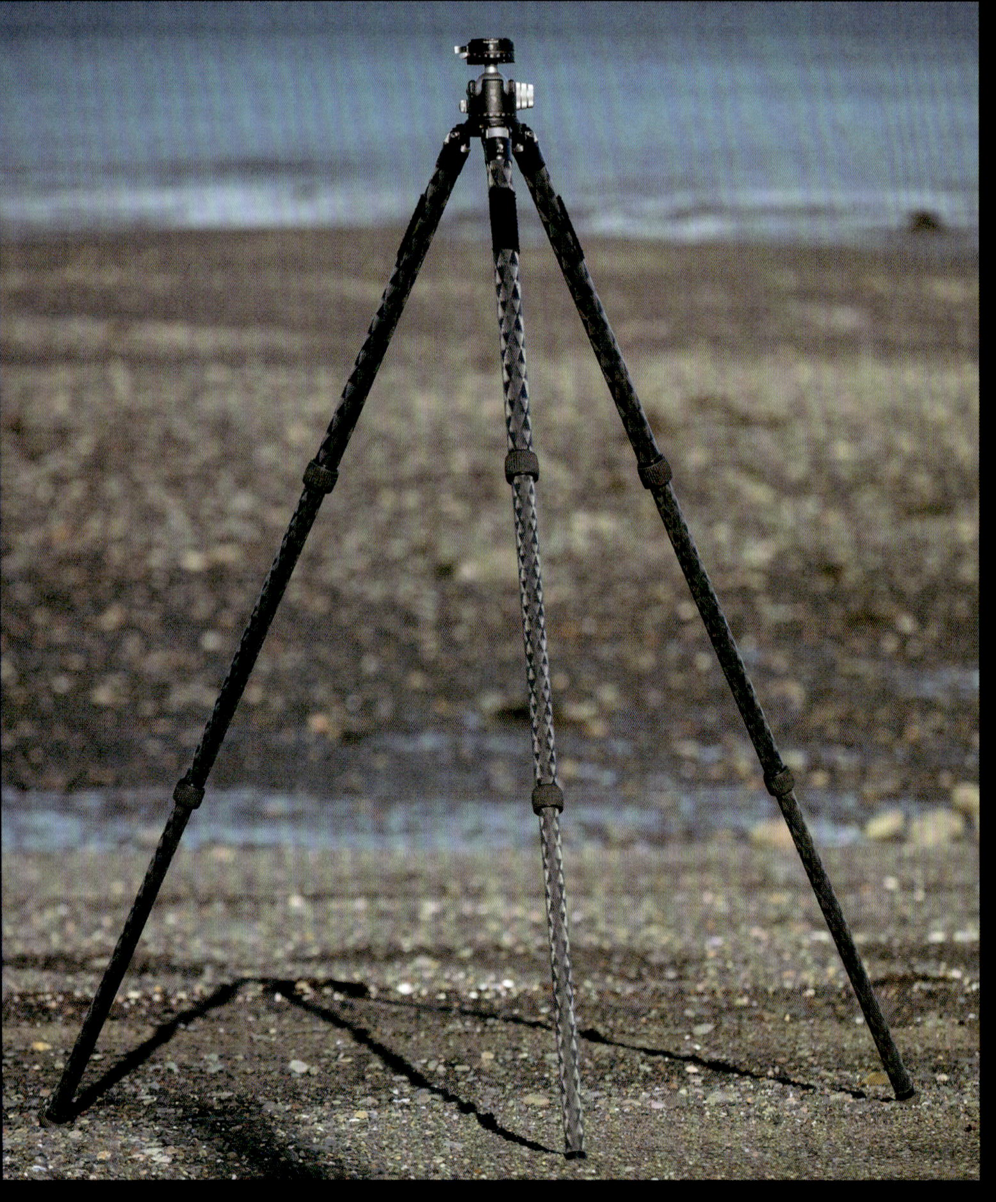

◀ A tripod with thick legs will be sturdy and allow you to operate the camera with less chance of you accidentally shifting the tripod between shots.

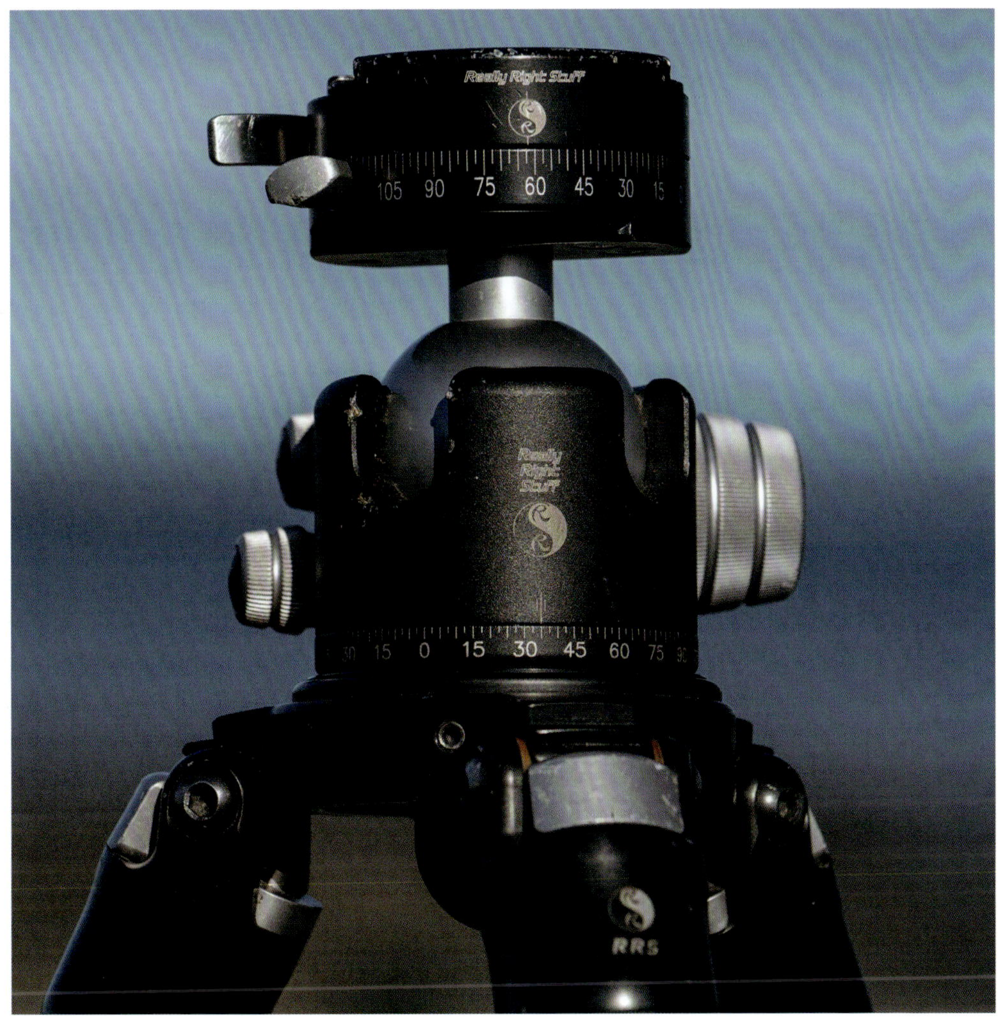

◀ My Really Right Stuff tripod and ballhead have taken a beating over the years, but both are still going strong.

Carbon fiber and aluminum tripods are very popular these days and for good reason: they are both strong and light. But be careful that you don't get something *too* light. If your tripod moves when you're adjusting your camera, that's a sure sign that your tripod isn't sturdy enough. You don't want to mess up your composition just because the tripod couldn't stay put when you were changing the shutter speed.

Established brands like Really Right Stuff, Gitzo and Manfrotto make great carbon fiber tripods. They may be pricey, but they are well made and durable. However, there are now quite a few smaller companies making very good carbon fiber and aluminum tripods that are more affordable. As of writing, these brands include 3 Legged Thing, Induro, Benro and Feisol, among others.

A good head is just as important as a good tripod and ballheads are the most popular for landscape photography of all kinds. They don't offer the ability to make small adjustments to a single axis like some heads, but their simplicity makes it easy to get setup and quickly change compositions. Just like with cheap tripods, a cheap ballhead is not worth the risk. Avoid any that are made of plastic and instead buy one made of metal. A ballhead needs to be easy to adjust and stay solidly in place when tightened, effortlessly supporting the weight of your camera and lens.

Again, as with tripods, there are lots of brands to choose from these days, with many affordable options available. Check out online reviews, and resist the urge to save money. If your tripod or ballhead fail after hiking for 4 miles in the middle of the night because some plastic piece gave way, you'll be wishing you spent the extra money on a higher quality piece of equipment.

I use a heavy-duty Really Right Stuff carbon fiber tripod and a Really Right Stuff BH-55 ballhead. The tripod has thick legs but is still pretty light. The BH-55 head is incredibly sturdy—it has taken quite a beating over the few years that I've had it, but remains as solid as a rock.

Do yourself a favor and buy a good tripod and head setup now instead of buying a cheap one and putting it off until later. I started that way, buying cheap tripods and heads and slowly upgrading them, only to be continually frustrated by them until I finally purchased high-quality gear.

the center of the tripod. It also means that when you change from a vertical to horizontal composition, you are changing more than just the photograph's orientation, because by moving the head up or sideways you are changing how the scene is viewed. You also need to level the camera each time you change orientation.

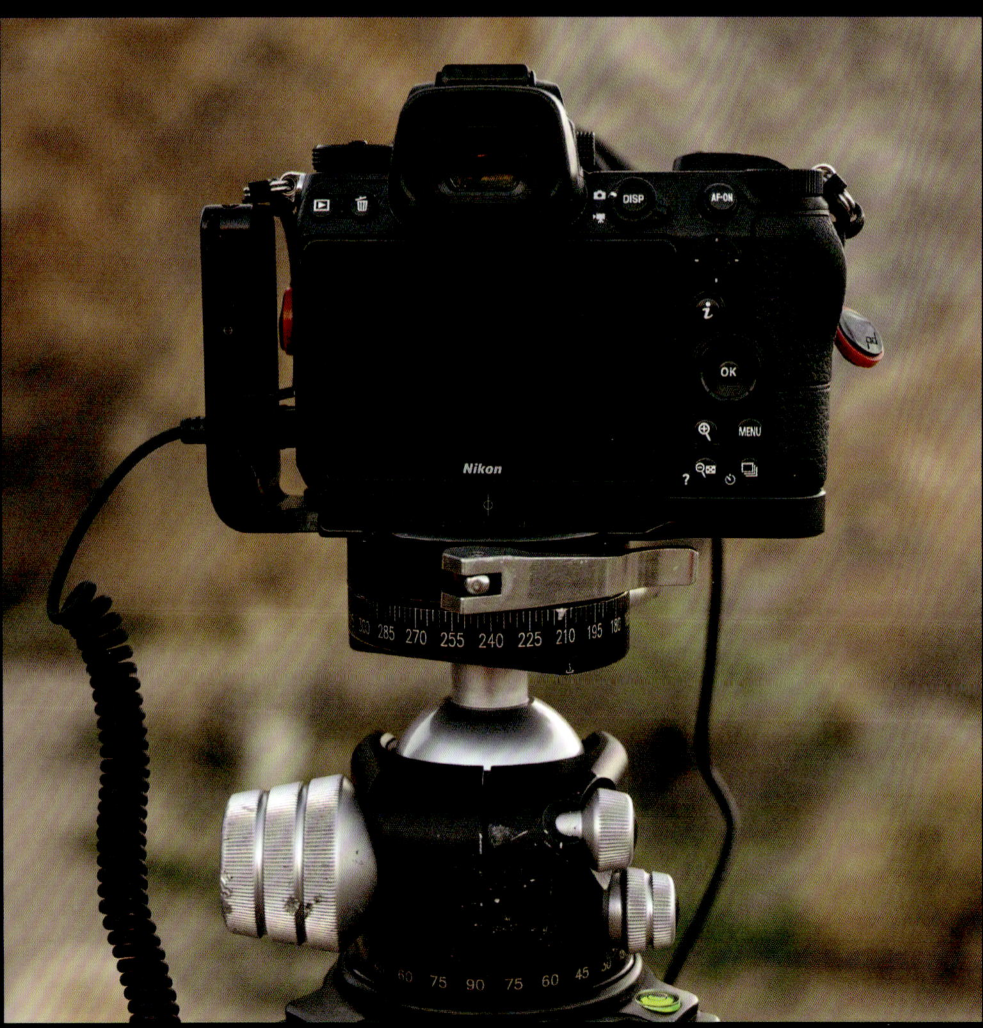

◀ Camera with L-bracket positioned horizontally.

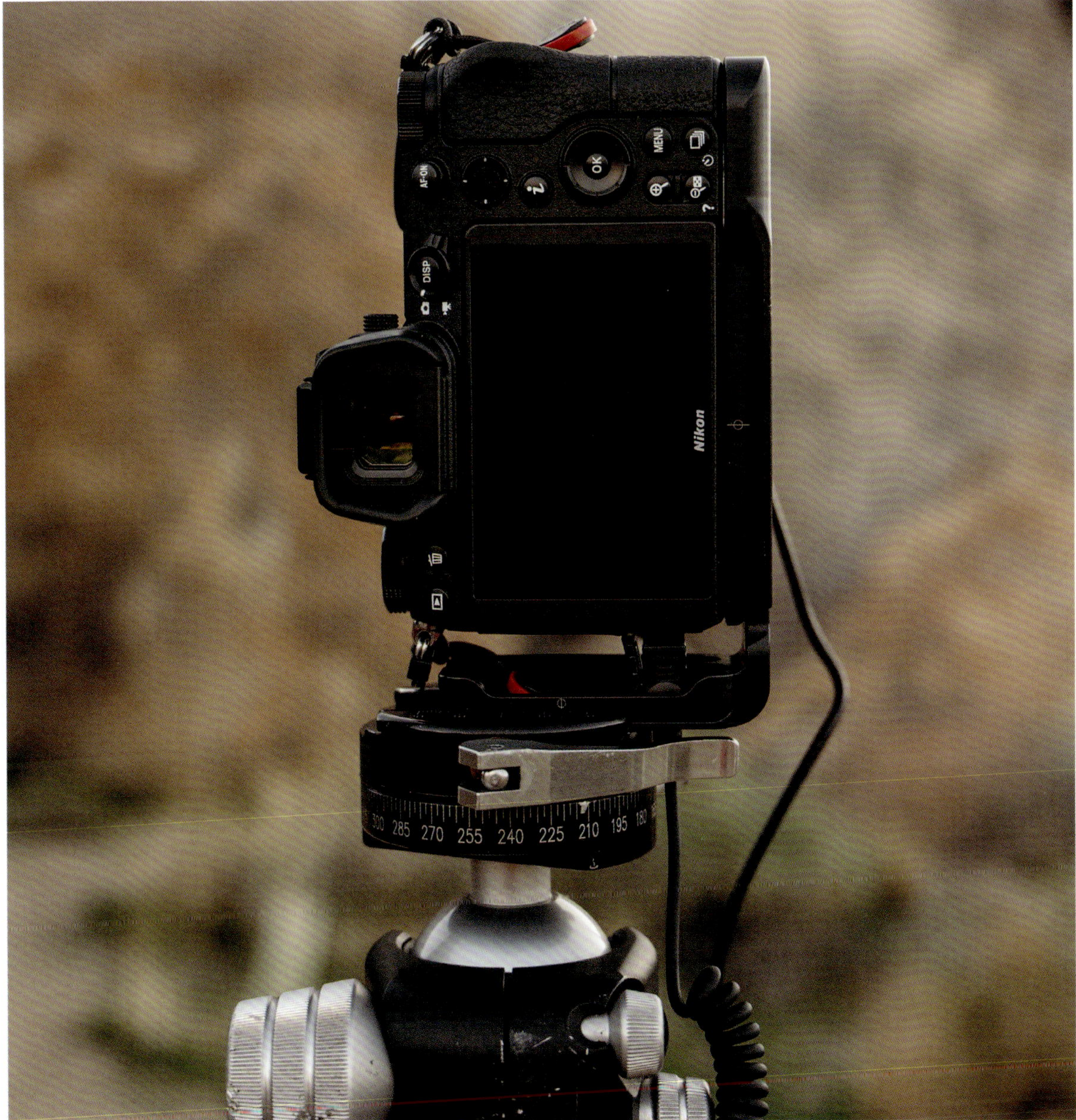

◀ Using an L-bracket, the camera's orientation can be easily changed without moving the tripod head and having to re-level the camera. Note how the shutter cable connection requires the camera to be mounted a little off center.

An L-bracket is, as the name suggests, an L-shaped tripod plate. It allows the camera to be attached horizontally like normal, but you can also remove the camera from the head clamp, rotate it 90 degrees, and re-clamp it to the head to quickly change to a vertical orientation. Once you level your camera in one orientation, it will be level in the other orientation, making switching between the two much easier. It also keeps the camera over the center of your tripod for a stable setup.

I consider this an essential piece of gear and I have an L-bracket attached to every one of my cameras. However, it can cause issues with accessing the ports on the side of your camera. Some L-brackets are adjustable so this is not as much of a problem, as you can slide the camera away from the bracket.

3.5 INTERVALOMETER

While all DSLRs and mirrorless cameras feature a Bulb mode that allows you to manually set an exposure time of longer than 30 seconds, and many also feature built-in intervalometers, the easiest way to program how many shots to take in a row, and how much delay between each shot, is to use an external shutter release or intervalometer.

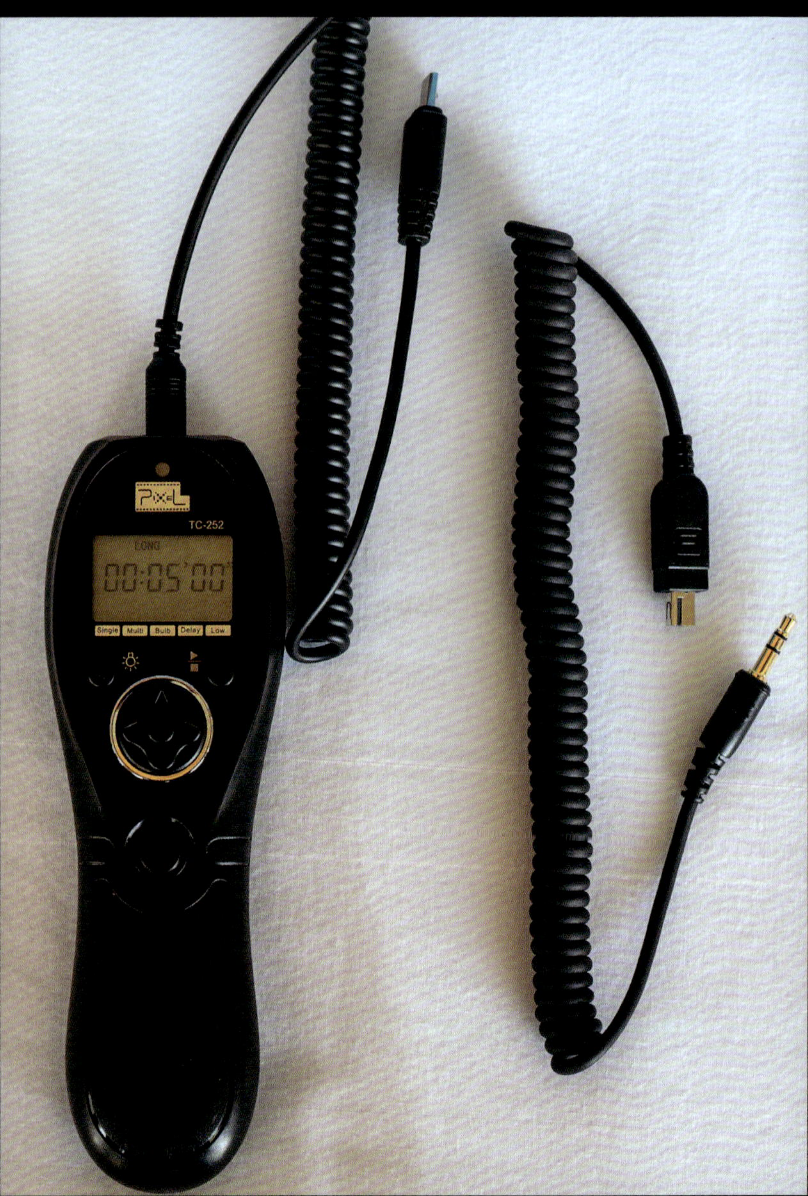

◀ A Pixel brand intervalometer with a spare cable.

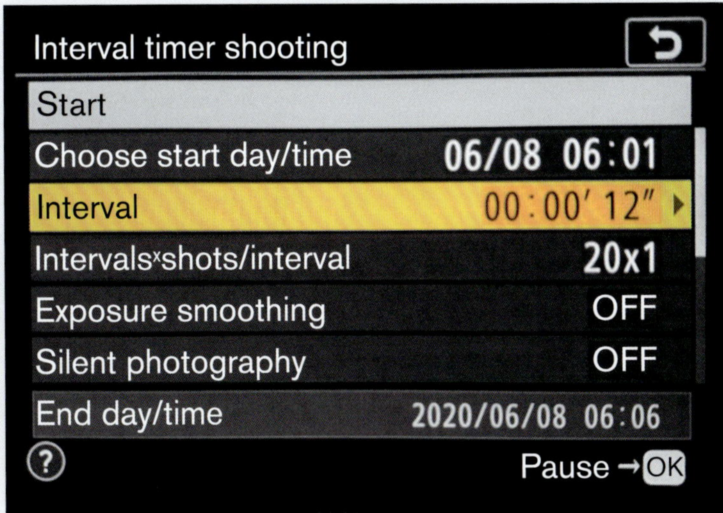

▲ The built-in intervalometer on some Nikon cameras.

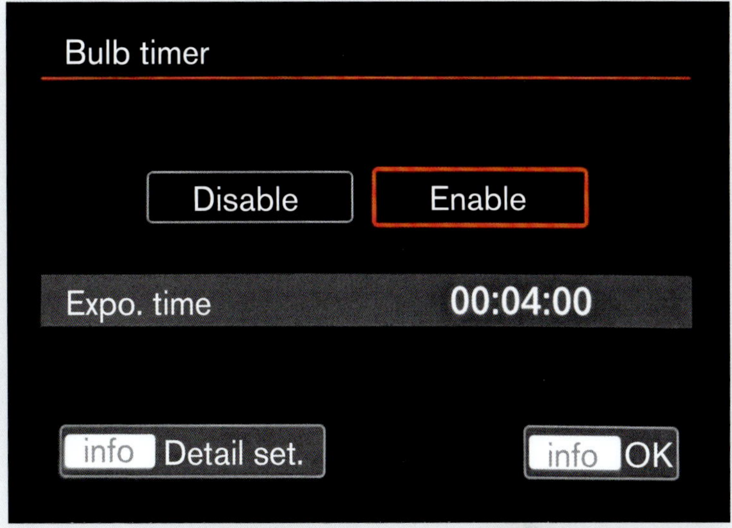

▲ The built-in Bulb Timer mode on some Canon cameras.

Before you look for an intervalometer or remote shutter release, check to see if your camera has one or both features already built-in. Many higher-end Nikon models include a built-in intervalometer, and many higher-end Canon models include a built-in intervalometer and/or bulb timer. The built-in bulb timer on such cameras is not just a Bulb mode, which almost all cameras have, but rather a setting that works in Bulb mode to allow you to enter a shutter speed longer than 30 seconds.

A remote shutter release will allow you to set the shutter speed to whatever you want it to be when your camera is in Bulb mode. To learn how to put your camera into Bulb mode, reference the manual as it will vary from camera to camera. On Nikon cameras this usually means rotating the shutter speed dial all the way past 30 seconds until it says "Bulb," and on Canon cameras there is usually a Bulb setting (shown as a "B") on the mode dial.

While the shutter speeds required to capture pinpoint stars are often less than 20 seconds, when you are shooting separate foreground exposures you will usually want shutter speeds that are much longer than 30 seconds, often many minutes in length depending on how dark the location is and whether or not you are adding artificial light to the scene. A remote shutter release and Bulb mode will allow you to do this. On a simple remote release you will only be able to have it on or off and you will need to use a stopwatch (or use your phone as a stopwatch). With an intervalometer, the process is easier because you can set exactly how long you want the shutter to be open.

An intervalometer also comes in handy when you are taking many photographs in sequence, as you would do if you are intending to stack them in software later (see **Star Stacking**, page 76).

There are many brands of intervalometers to choose from, but as far as wired ones go, the cheaper (sub $100) ones are pretty much all the same design, and unfortunately all suffer from the same weakness, where the cable will often break after a few months (or maybe years if you're lucky) of regular use. The wires inside the cable will often break where the cable attaches to the intervalometer body, rendering the entire intervalometer useless. You'll end up will either a non-functioning intervalometer, or one that functions intermittently, or a glitch where the camera always has the shutter open when the intervalometer is connected. It's for this reason that I recommend carrying a spare intervalometer, or purchase an intervalometer with replaceable cables and carry spare cables.

Wireless intervalometers are also available, including Bluetooth-enabled ones that consist of a device that connects to your camera's USB or remote shutter release port that is controlled via an app on your phone.

3.6 LENS HEATER

There's nothing worse than heading out for a long night of shooting at a beautiful spot that you've had planned for months only to have your shoot ruined by dew on your lens. You can try wiping it off, but it comes right back within a minute. You might be able to get some star shots in, but you'll be hard-pressed to get a long exposure for the foreground.

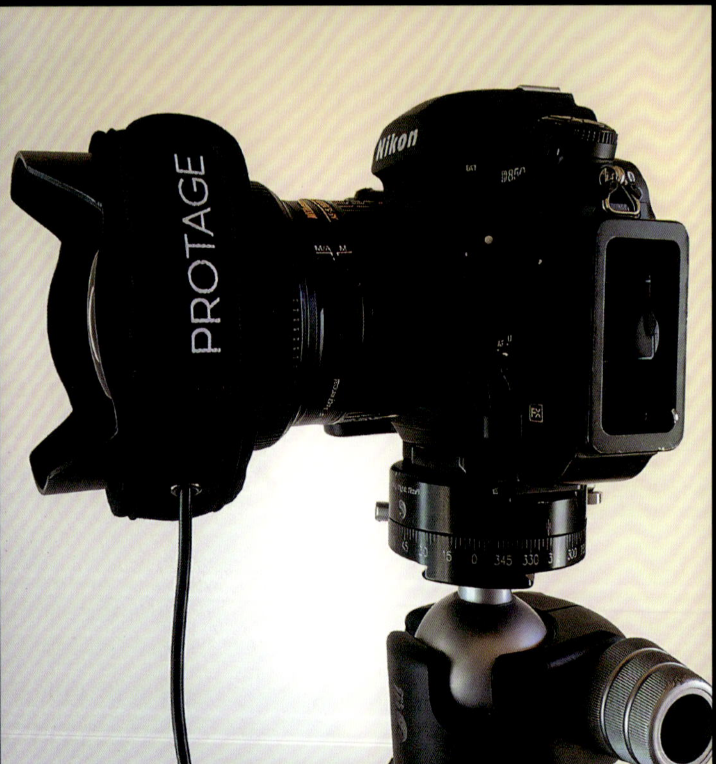

▲ A Protage lens heater wrapped around a Nikon 14-24mm f/2.8 lens.

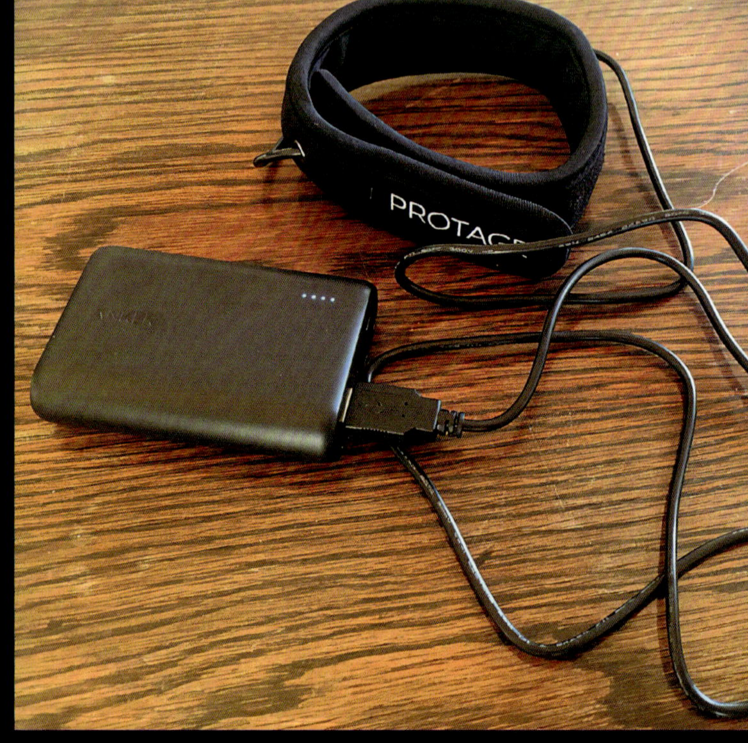

▲ The same lens heater with an Anker 10000 PowerCore USB battery pack.

This happens when the ambient temperature meets (or is close to) the dew point. When that occurs, moisture in the air will condense onto objects such as picnic tables, grass, the hood of your car, and most importantly, the front element of your lens.

There are a few ways to prevent this from happening. If it's windy, then there is little chance that you will have moisture settling on your lens. A lens hood can also keep the dew away, but super-wide-angle lenses that are popular for night photography do not have substantial lens hoods. The best way of keeping dew off your lens is to keep your lens heated.

One way you can heat your lens is to use chemical hand-warmer packets, attached to the lens with tape, rubber bands, or a sleeve designed for such a purpose. This may work, but you always risk the possibility of a packet being a dud, or there not being enough airflow to keep the packet warm. Conversely, too much airflow and the packet "burns out" really fast.

I prefer using an electric lens heater. It's like an electric blanket for your lens—the heater itself is an electric strap that wraps around the lens and connects to a battery for power. As long as it keeps the lens temperature above the dew point temperature, then you should be able to shoot dew-free. It's also cost-effective over buying a large stock of chemical hand warmers if, like me, you're out shooting at night frequently.

I prefer USB-powered lens heaters. My current favorite lens heater is made by Protage. You can find it by searching for a "Protage lens heater" on Amazon. For under $20, it's one of the cheapest but most useful pieces of camera gear you'll ever buy. There are also other brands of USB-powered lens heaters available, and it's likely more will hit the market in the coming years as night photography continues to grow in popularity and the demand for lens heaters increases.

You'll need a USB battery pack to power the lens heater, something with a minimum of a 10,000 mAh capacity rating. I use Anker 10000 PowerCore USB batteries, but any reputable brand should be able to offer something suitable. A 10,000 mAh battery pack should power a Protage lens heater for anywhere from 4–5 hours. Whichever battery pack you use, be sure to cover up the power LEDs if you can. They are often quite bright and can effect your night vision and possibly ruin the foreground of your scene.

I recommend carrying a spare lens heater and a spare battery. The spare battery in case you need more power to get through the night, and the spare lens heater in case your primary lens heater breaks. They do, after all, consist of wiring that you are bending constantly, and so they may break due to stress at some point.

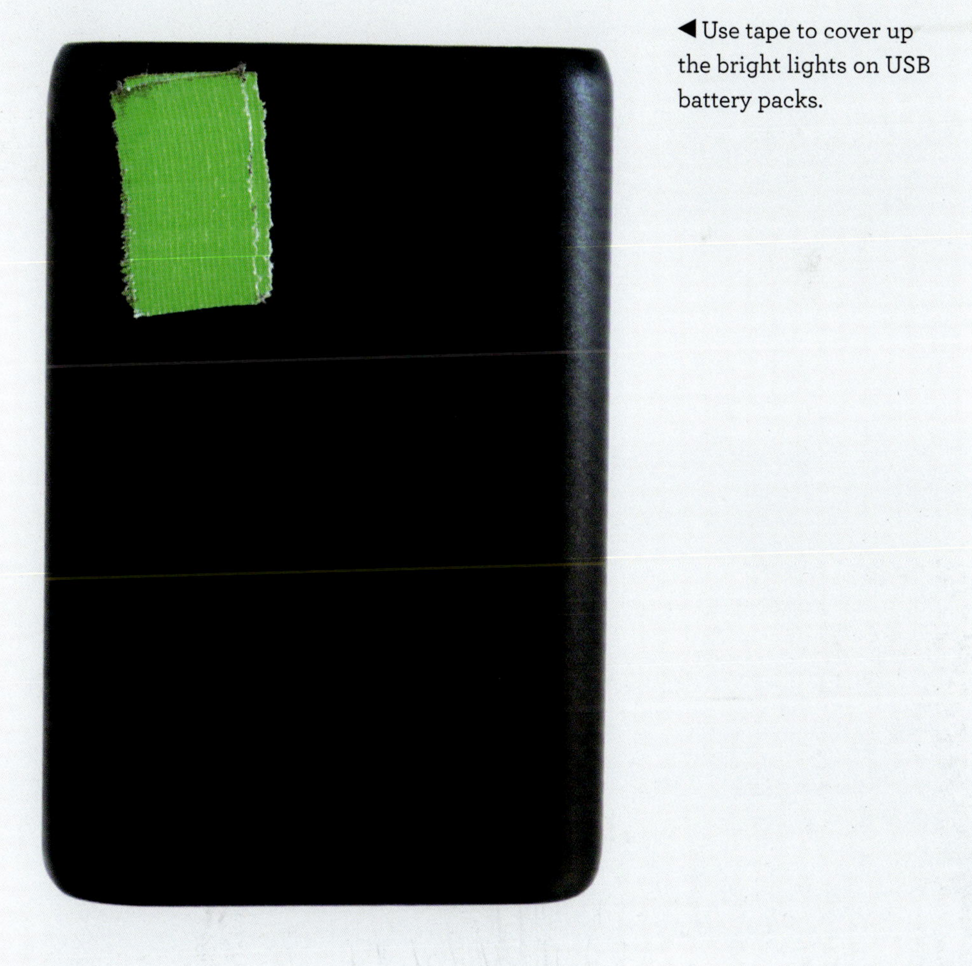

◀ **Use tape to cover up the bright lights on USB battery packs.**

3.7 MEMORY CARDS

Many of the techniques described in this book involve taking multiple exposures (often between 10 and 20) to be blended or stacked together later in software. This can result in a lot of photographs very quickly, especially if you're shooting different compositions throughout the night, or even just shooting the Milky Way at different angles as it moves through the sky. This means you'll want some spare memory cards, or at least one very large one (such as 32GB).

Make sure you download your photos from your memory cards daily, if you can. If you're camping and you don't have a laptop or Gnarbox (a portable backup device for your camera) with you to backup your photos, then using multiple memory cards and swapping them out at least daily is a good idea to avoid losing your entire camping trip's worth of photos if one card fails or goes for an unexpected swim in the ocean.

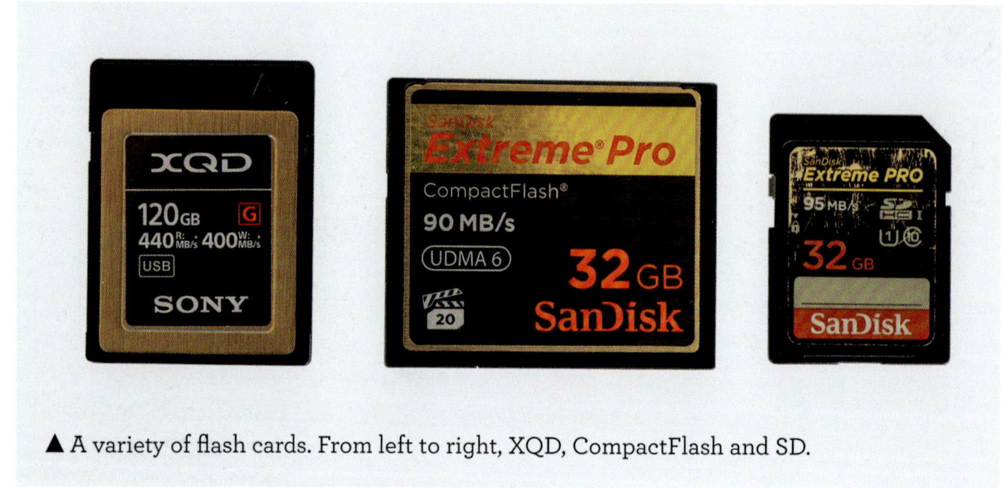

▲ A variety of flash cards. From left to right, XQD, CompactFlash and SD.

3.8 EXTRA BATTERIES

With all the photographs you'll be taking, and in particular the long exposures often needed for the foreground, you can quickly burn through a battery, so make sure to carry a few fully charged spares with you.

This is especially important if you are going to be out in very cold weather, which causes batteries to appear as if they are low on charge even though they aren't. If your battery seems to run out faster than usual on a cold outing, try putting that battery in a warm place, like a pocket, while you use a fresh battery in the camera. Then when that one "dies," you can swap it for the warmed-up battery. Keep all of your spares in a reasonably warm place.

3.9 HEADLAMPS & FLASHLIGHTS

When shooting at night, you'll need a headlamp with both white and red LED modes. The white mode is used for making your way out to your shooting location and any other time you need a bright light, while the red mode is for when you are setup and want to preserve your night vision (and the night vision of any others nearby). Red light doesn't interfere with night vision as much as other colors of light, and this makes it much less intrusive for you and those around you. Use your red lamp when you need to look for a button on your camera or intervalometer, or find something in your camera bag.

I also like to carry a small low-power red LED flashlight. This isn't necessary if you're out with no other photographers around you, but if you're with a group of people, or just near other photographers that you don't know, it's considerate to use a dim red light instead of a brighter red headlamp light when needed. This way you can look for camera buttons or dig around in your bag without getting red light in other people's photos. Believe it or not, what may seem like a dim red light on a headlamp is usually enough to ruin any foreground close to where the light is shining, so shine your red lamp away from what you and other people are shooting when shutters are open, and use a low-power red light when necessary.

The LRI Proton PRO is a pricey but compact flashlight that has a surprisingly bright white light for its size. More importantly, it has a very nice low-power red light (and you can increase its brightness).

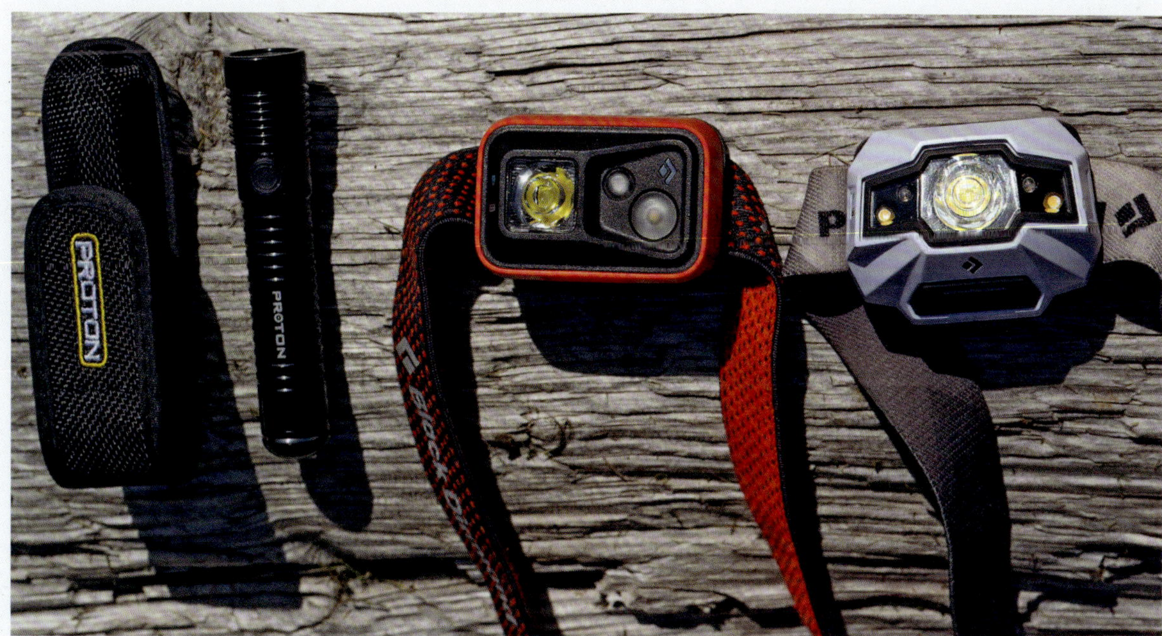

◀ A spare headlamp is always a good idea. It's especially useful if a friend joins you last minute and doesn't have their own.

Being comfortable outdoors means different things to different people. I almost never bring a chair with me and I routinely stand in the same spot for an hour or more waiting for long exposures, for the Milky Way to line up, or for the tide to be just right. You may or may not find that acceptable; you may desire a chair or a blanket to sit on. The danger there is that if you get too comfortable you may fall asleep and fail to get up when you need to adjust your camera. I speak from experience.

You should certainly plan ahead and check the weather forecast for the night that you will be out shooting. Bring appropriate clothing to keep warm, and bring some snacks and water. Dehydration can be a big problem, especially if you're out shooting in the dry desert air or at high elevations.

Even on the coast of Maine in the middle of the summer I will pack a fleece jacket, and often fleece pants and a down jacket. The ocean water is cold and it can make a huge difference to the temperature at night. I've held workshops in June where it dropped to the mid-30s Fahrenheit at midnight.

I almost always wear waterproof hiking boots; hiking trails may have some wet areas, and at many coastal locations I may need to cross some shallow water at the beach. They also provide warmth for those cold nights.

3.11 PERSONAL SAFETY

Given that night photography requires being out in the dark, possibly by yourself, it makes sense to consider personal safety.

EMERGENCY COMMUNICATIONS

If you're heading somewhere remote then having a buddy with you isn't a bad idea, but I shoot by myself in remote locations all the time, often in areas with very little or no cell phone service. So, for emergency purposes, I recommend carrying some sort of personal locator beacon (PLB), or a GPS unit that doubles as a PLB. These units can send out a distress (SOS) signal via satellite communications to alert the local search and rescue (SAR) team to come to your location as given by the GPS. Some units will also provide a way to send a quick text message (SMS) or email to anyone you configure in the settings (such as a significant other or family member). These messages can either be typed out manually or in simpler models you might have a few pre-configured messages, such as, "I'm okay."

I carry both a Garmin InReach Explorer+ that is a GPS, PLB and satellite texting device all in one, as well as an ACR Electronics ResQLink PLB. Why both? The InReach is very useful for texting my location/status to someone from anywhere in the world, as long as I have a reasonably clear view of the sky, but the ResQLink has a much longer antenna (coiled around the unit when not in use), higher power output and multiple frequencies for getting your SOS signal out of more concealed locations.

I highly recommend getting at least an InReach or similar device so that you have both a PLB and a texting device. I once had to use the InReach to text my emergency contact to call a tow truck when my RV broke down in the middle of Alaska in a spot where I had no cell service and very little road traffic. I also use the satellite texting just to keep in touch with loved ones whenever I'm out in the middle of nowhere without cell service.

WILDLIFE

As with any recreational activity that takes place in areas where you are sharing space with wild animals, it may make sense to carry a can of bear spray, depending on where you go, and maybe a whistle or small air horn. The whistle (or air horn) can be used to try to scare off a wild animal, but it can also be used to signal that you're in trouble. You can use it, for example, if you've gone out with friends but have become separated from the group and have hurt yourself. But, hopefully, you will never have to use them for any reason.

In some areas of dense grizzly bear territory, you may find that hiking in groups is required, or at least highly recommended, so check out the local regulations before you go somewhere known for bears. Give the ranger station (or similar) in that area a call, or check their website.

FIRST AID

It's always a good idea to have a small first aid kit with you whenever you're out hiking, even if it's just some bandages, gauze and ointment.

BE CAREFUL AND TAKE IT SLOW

Hiking through the woods, for example, with lots of exposed roots and rocks, can be tricky footing in the daytime, and it is of course harder in the dark, even with a headlamp. So take extra care getting around in the dark, and don't rush. Give yourself ample time to make it to your shooting location.

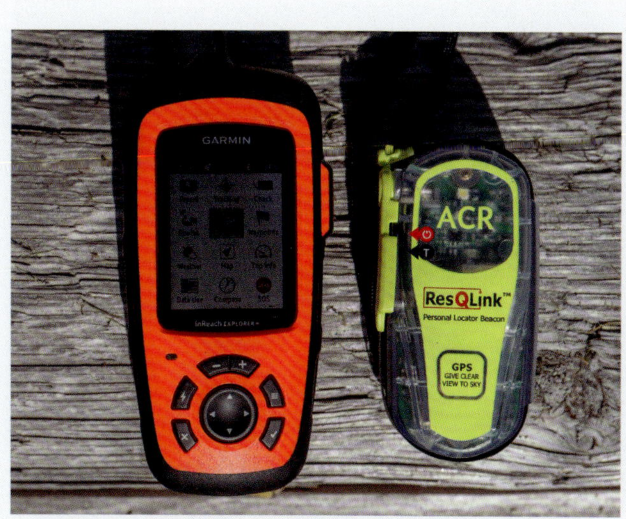

◀ Garmin InReach Explorer+ (left) and ResQLink PLB (right).

3.12 CALIBRATED DISPLAY

Whether you've spent a small fortune on your camera gear or you're using entry-level equipment, you're not going to know what your images really look like until you view them on your computer. In order to really be sure you're looking at your photos in their correct colors and brightness, it is essential to use a good-quality display and calibration device.

The technology in computer displays has come a long way, and now even some high-end laptops have screens capable of very good color reproduction.

While you can get by with a good laptop display, there's no substitute for a really nice large display. A large display of at least 24 inches (the diagonal measurement of the screen between opposite corners) will not only provide you with a larger view of your photos, it will allow for a less cluttered workspace when working inside of Adobe Lightroom Classic or Photoshop.

A better display will also provide better color reproduction, more consistent levels of brightness across the display, and better tolerance for side-angle viewing (meaning that colors and brightness don't shift dramatically when you change your angle of view).

DISPLAY CALIBRATION

A great monitor is only great if you keep it calibrated so that the colors are consistent and accurate. An uncalibrated display, or one that hasn't been calibrated in a long time, will not show your photos with accurate colors, and in the worst cases the colors will be so far off that they appear far more cool (more blue) or warm (more yellow) than they should be. This can effect how you edit your photos—you could end up editing your photo to be a lot warmer than you would otherwise if your display is shifted towards cooler colors.

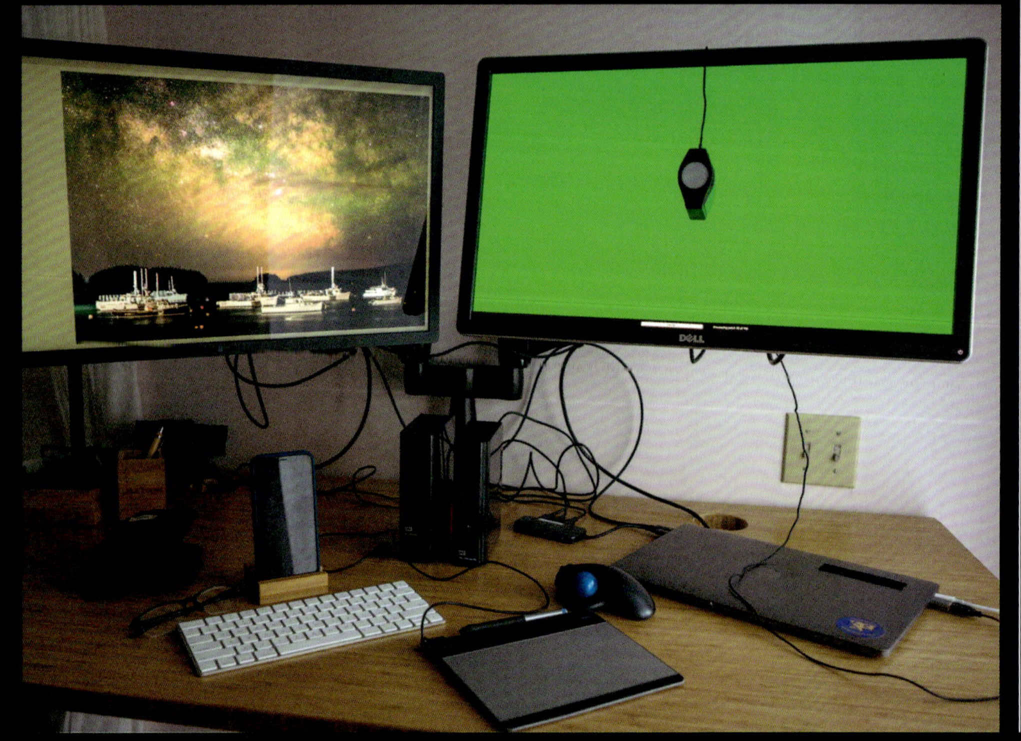

◀ Using the X-Rite i1Display to calibrate a monitor.

The calibration process is performed by using a hardware device that sits on your display in conjunction with software. The software shows colors on the display and uses the hardware device to measure the actual color being shown versus what it should be. This process should also walk you through setting the hardware controls of the display for correct brightness and color output.

The calibration process generates a color profile that your computer's operating system will use to accurately present colors on the display. In basic terms, this profile tells the computer that to show the color red, for example, it needs to send a certain signal (color value) to the display.

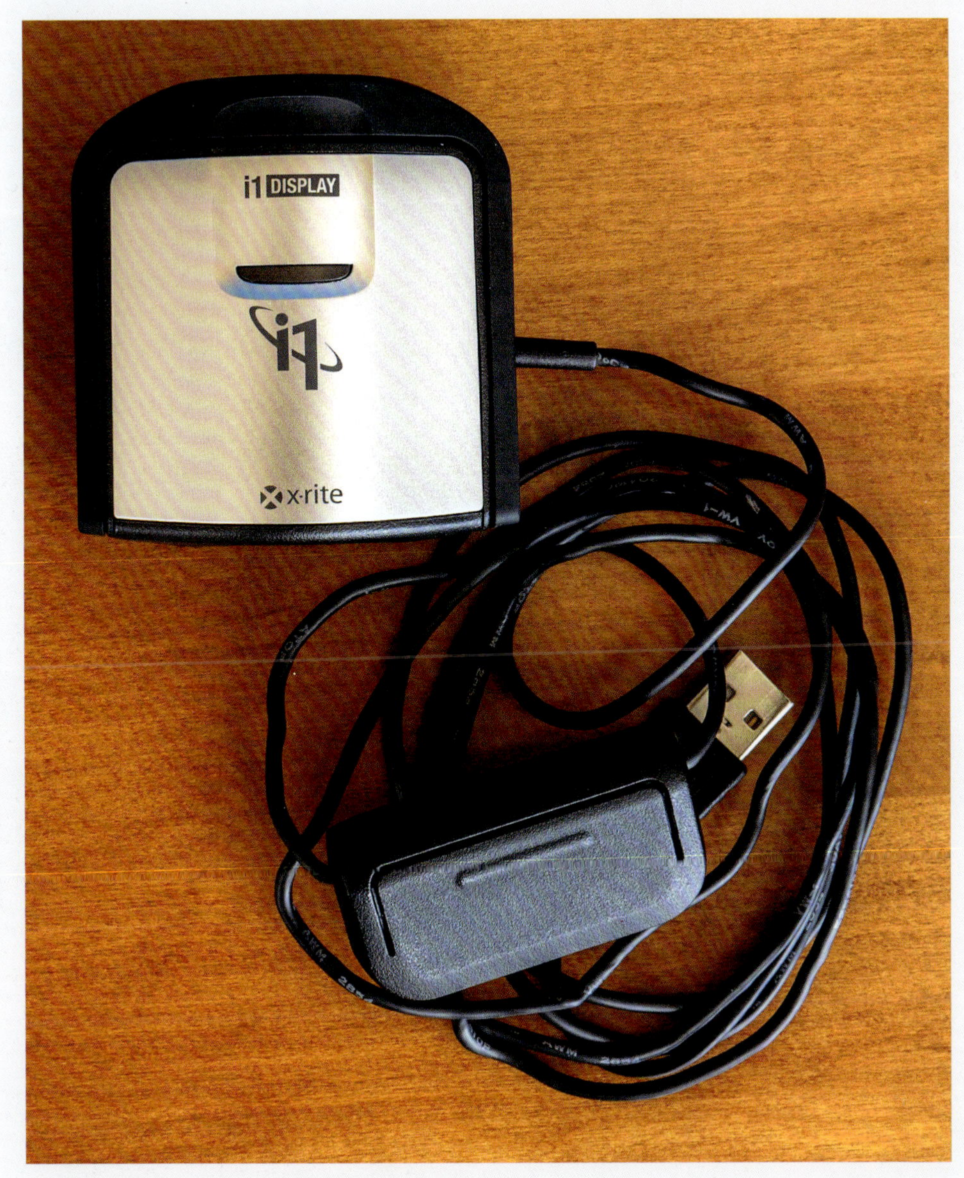

▲ The X-Rite i1Display calibration device.

As of writing, X-Rite and Spyder are the two biggest brands in color calibration devices. I currently use an X-Rite i1Display Pro. Whatever you get, make sure you use it on a monthly basis to keep your colors in check.

The white point used for calibration affects how the color white should appear on your display. For photography purposes, you should be choosing a white point of "D65" in the profiling software. It's likely this is already the default choice; D65 is the daylight setting and is the standard choice for calibration in the world of photography and general use.

Another incredibly important aspect of calibration is setting your display to an appropriate brightness level. This is the most common issue I see people facing in their editing, even if they are using a calibration device. If the display is too bright, then the photos will appear brighter than they actually are, and vice versa. This is also one of the biggest reasons a print will come out too dark, because the image is actually darker than you think it is. (To print you actually need to increase the brightness of an image in most cases, but the issue will be magnified if the photo is too dark to begin with.) Your calibration software should walk you through adjusting your screen to an appropriate level of brightness, which is usually 120 cd/m^2 (candelas per square meter). You may need to adjust the brightness further depending on how bright or dim the room is in which you are using the computer monitor.

On Apple computers you should also turn off "True Tone" for the display, as this will usually interfere with the calibration process. Turn it off and keep it off.

3.13 SOFTWARE

You will need a Raw editor such as Adobe Lightroom Classic, Adobe Camera Raw, ON1 Photo RAW, Capture One Pro, etc. in order to process the Raw files captured by your camera. A good Raw editor will also be able to catalog and organize your photos, making it much easier to find them years later.

For advanced editing, exposure blending and focus stacking, you will need Adobe Photoshop or a similar application, such as Affinity Photo. I highly recommend learning how to carry out these tasks in Photoshop. Your Raw editor may support some amount of blending, but it will likely not have the advanced masking tools needed to really fine-tune exposure blending and focus stacking.

You will also need specific software for star stacking (see page 170). On a Mac you can use Starry Landscape Stacker, and on Windows you can use Sequator.

There are a few other pieces of software you might require for specific purposes, such as noise reduction and panoramas, which we'll look at in the relevant sections. But your Raw editor of choice, Photoshop and a stacking program should be sufficient for general landscape astrophotography purposes.

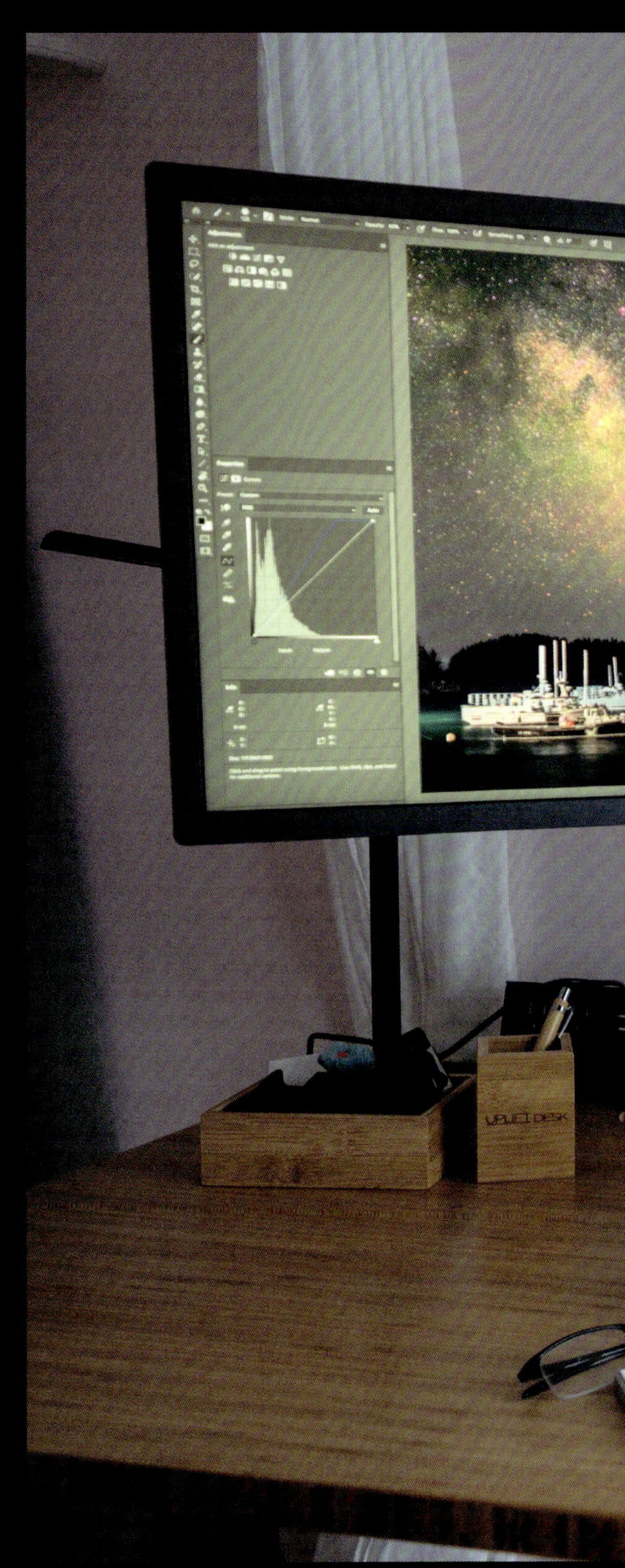

▶ Photoshop on my dual monitor setup. You certainly don't need two monitors for editing, but it makes it easy to spread out Photoshop's panels for easy access.

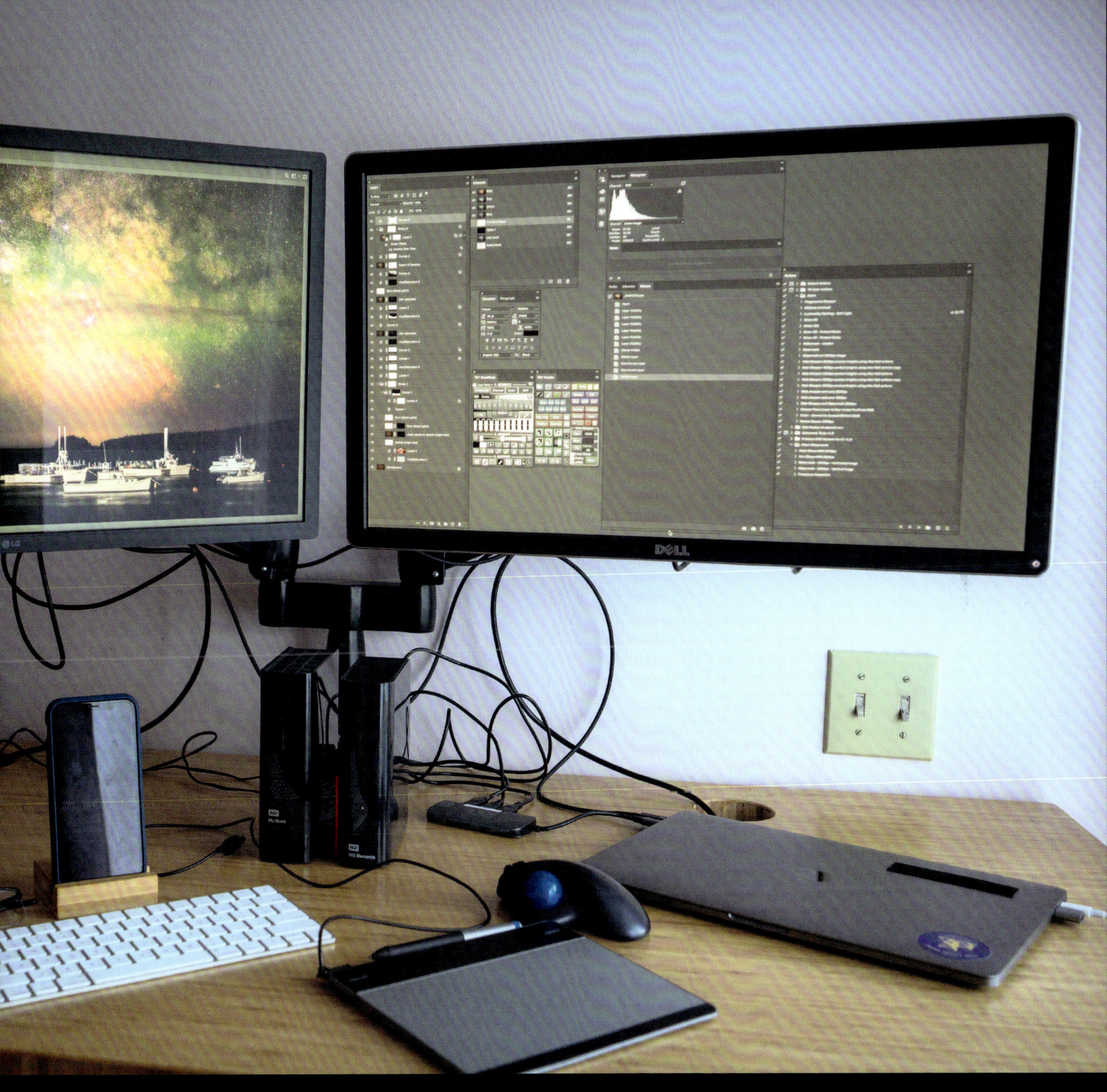
DELL
LG

BREAKING DOWN AN IMAGE

▶ This image captures the Milky Way rising over a rocky beach on the coast of Maine. This is the final edit that consists of separate sky and foreground shots blended in Photoshop.

Nikon Z 7 with the FTZ lens adapter using the Nikon 14-24mm f/2.8 lens at 14mm and f/2.8.

Sky: Star stack of 20 images, each exposed at ISO 6400 for 10 seconds.

Foreground: Focus stack of two images, each exposed at ISO 1600 for 600 seconds (10 minutes).

4

From camera gear to composition, camera settings and post-processing, there are a lot of "moving parts" that go into landscape astrophotography. Before we dive into the details of capturing and editing photographs, let's start by looking at a finished edit of a photo and break down the separate exposures that went into creating the final image.

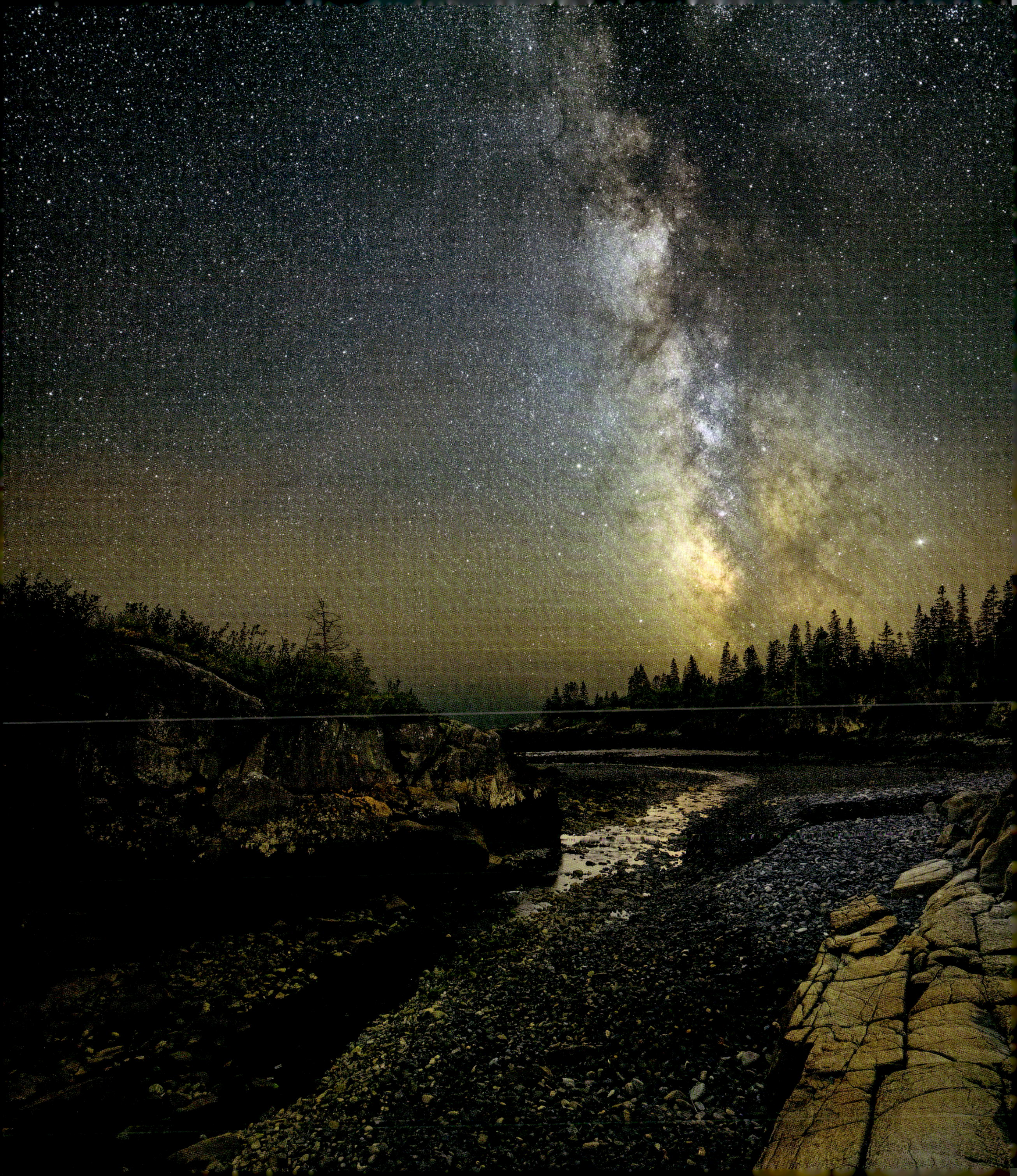

4.1 COMBINING EXPOSURES

▲ How the Raw file looks before any edits.

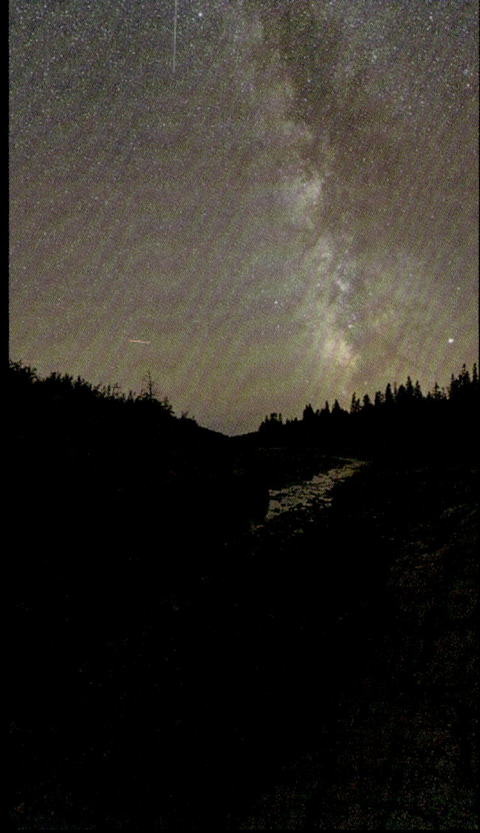

▲ With the exposure brightened.

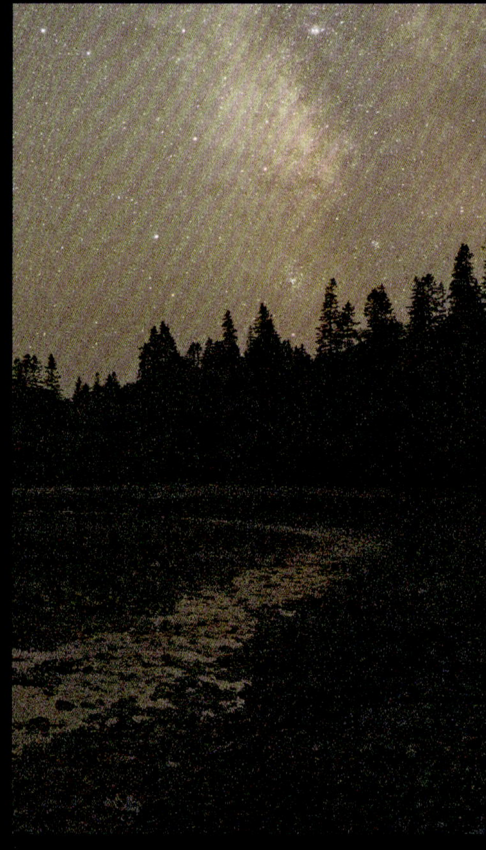

▲ A zoomed-in view of the same photo.

SEPARATE SKY & FOREGROUND EXPOSURES

Why do we need separate photographs? Why can't we just take a single photo of the scene and call it a day? There are a few reasons . . .

Earth spins on its axis at about 1,000 miles per hour (1,600km per hour) at the equator. The speed decreases as you go north or south away from the equator, but the effect on our viewing of the night sky is the same wherever you are on Earth—the stars appear to "move" through the sky over time, but in reality it is the Earth's rotation that causes the perceived movement. You may not notice it when you stand outside and gaze up at the stars, but if you look closely at the location of a particular constellation and then check it again a few minutes later, you should find it's now a little more to the west. Earth rotates towards the east, so everything appears to move towards the west.

This is great for creating images with star trails: open the shutter for a long time and you'll get an image capturing the stars moving through the sky with bright arcs or lines tracing their movement. But since we're interested in capturing sharp, pinpoint stars, we need to use a shutter speed short enough to prevent star trails. We'll get into the details of this in the section on **Shutter Speed** (see page 105), but for now it's enough to know that this means very short exposures considering how dark the night sky is. With a 14mm lens on a full-frame camera, you're limited to a shutter speed of about 10 seconds before the stars move enough to create trails. So what happens if we shoot a 10-second exposure in a dark location? We get something like the far left image above.

This was shot using a Nikon Z 7 with the FTZ lens adapter and the NIKKOR 14-24mm f/2.8 lens at 14mm, f/2.8, ISO 6400, 10 seconds.

The first image is how the Raw file looked in Adobe Lightroom Classic without any edits. As you can see, it's very dark. What if we brighten the exposure in Lightroom Classic? As you can see from the second image, the sky looks much better now. We can see detail in the stars and the Milky Way is already popping to life. But the foreground still doesn't look very good.

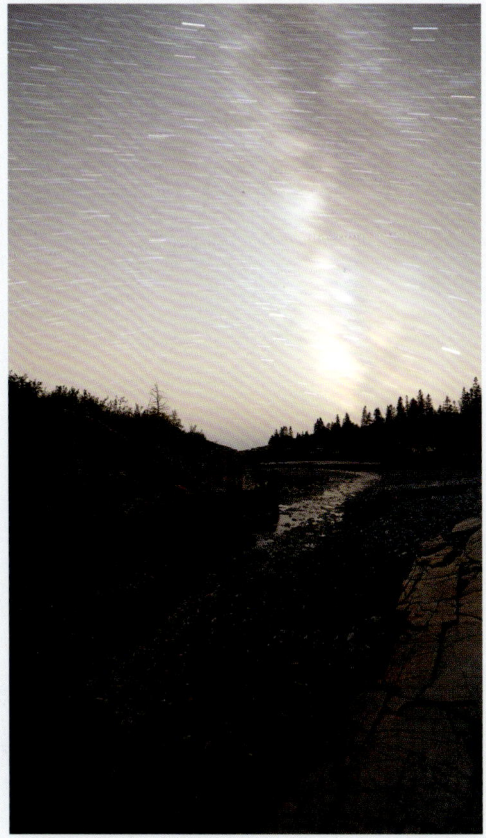

▲ Here is what a single 10-minute exposure looks like straight out of the camera.

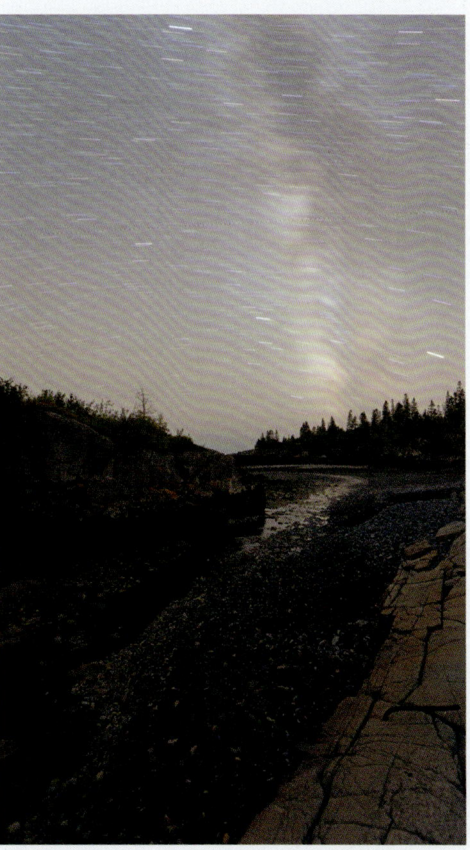

▲ With white balance and brightness adjusted and the lens vignetting removed.

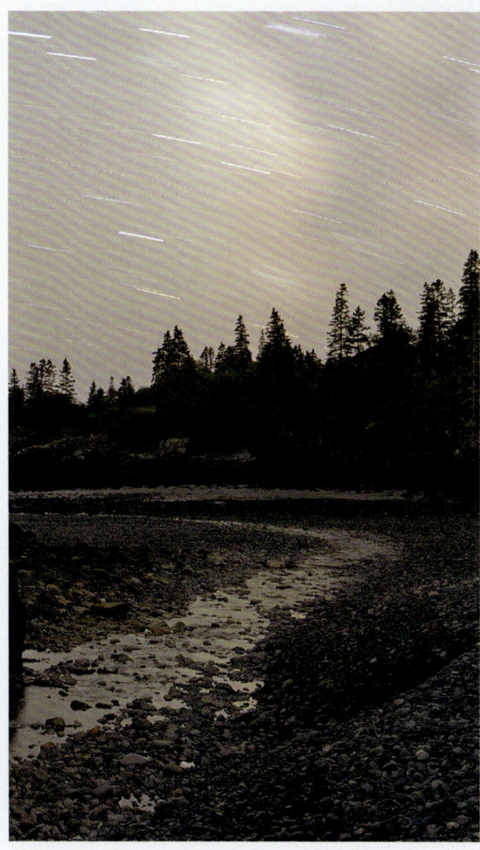

▲ A zoomed-in view of the same photo.

For a situation like this we need a way to have a brighter and less noisy foreground if we want to make a high-quality photograph. Noise-reduction software isn't going to save this foreground, it's just too dark and has too little detail. What we need is more light.

I could add artificial light to the scene to illuminate the foreground (known as "light painting," of which you can see an example on page 129), but I almost always prefer to use the natural ambient light of the scene.

To capture more light I will take at least one other shot of the foreground using a lower ISO and a longer shutter speed. The shutter speed needed will vary depending on the amount of ambient light on the scene; it could be 30 seconds or 10 minutes. In this location I chose a shutter speed of 10 minutes.

We will also cover foreground exposure times in more detail later (see page 107), but for now it's enough to know that a long shutter speed is often required for the foreground, and at this location 10 minutes at ISO 1600 worked very well; it was enough to capture detail in the foreground without a lot of noise.

BASIC ADJUSTMENTS

Now we can apply some basic adjustments in Lightroom to the the white balance and the brightness, and we can remove the lens vignetting. This leaves us with an image that now has a lot more detail in the foreground with considerably less noise. The stars have streaked significantly because this is a 10-minute exposure, however that's not an issue here as we are only going to use this exposure for the foreground in the final blended image. We can blend the sky and foreground exposures together in Adobe Photoshop using layer masking.

FOCUS STACKING

So, we now have a much better foreground image, but not all of the foreground is in focus within the entire scene. This particular foreground image was taken with the focus set to the stars at f/2.8. At 14mm on full-frame camera, there's a lot in focus at f/2.8, but not enough—the horizon (distant trees) and some of the distant beach is in focus, but the rocks closer to the lens are soft.

You always want at least one foreground photograph where the focus is set to the stars. This keeps the edges of the horizon in the same spot between the photographs, which makes it much easier to align and blend your images later in Photoshop.

The rocks toward the bottom of the frame start to get soft. In order to have those rocks in focus, we can take another photograph using the same settings except with the focus pulled in so that those rocks are sharp. Using a flashlight, you can light up the scene and use live view on your camera to see the foreground. Manually change focus until you have the rocks in sharp focus, or use auto-focus (just make sure to turn it off after using it so you don't accidentally change focus in the dark).

Alternatively you could also stop down the lens (use a higher f-stop number) for a greater depth of field, so you only have to take one shot to get the entire foreground in focus.

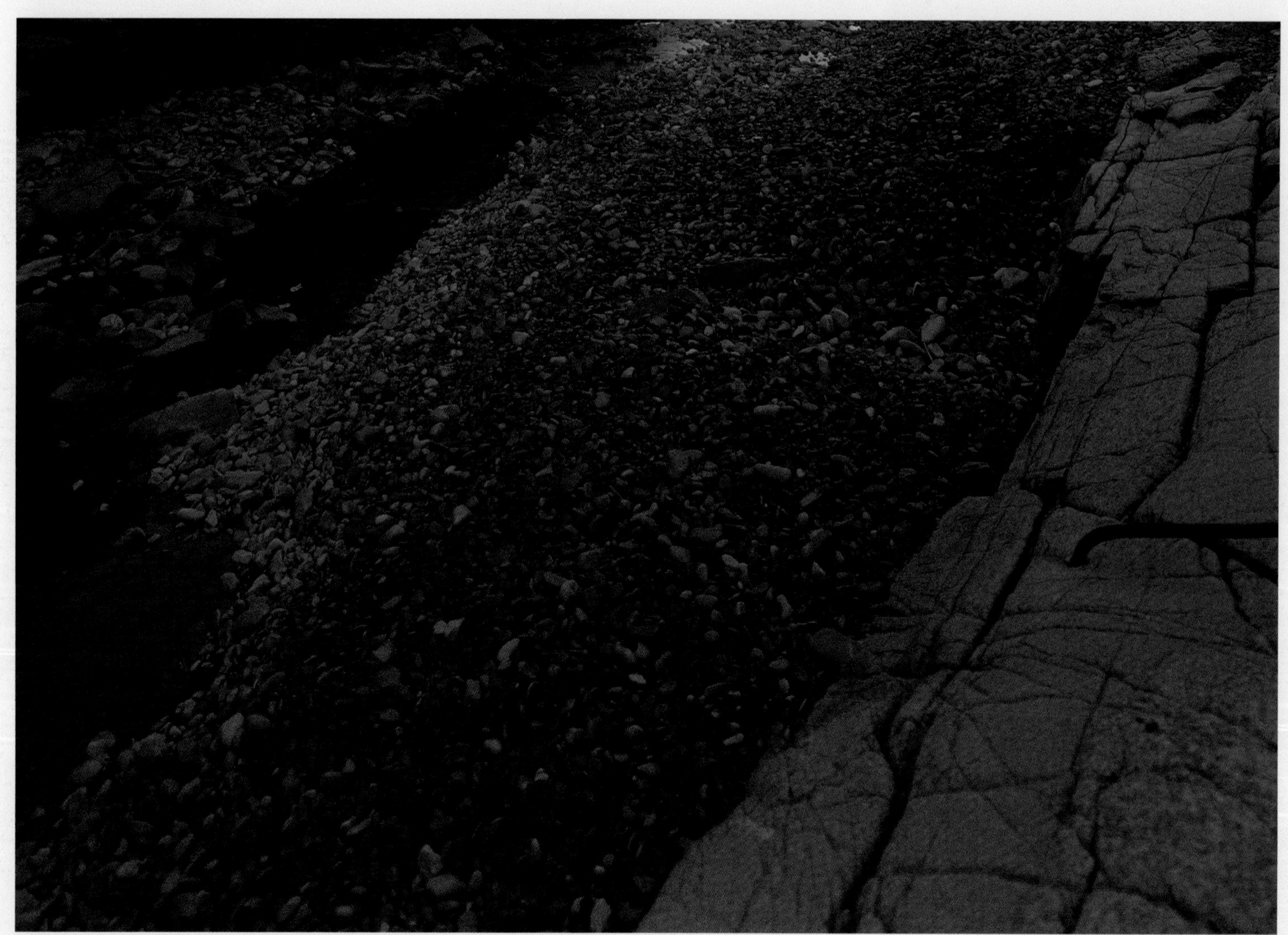

▲ Let's take a closer look at the foreground to see where the focus falls off.

However, this ends up dramatically increasing your exposure time. For example, I was using f/2.8 for the foreground at 10 minutes and ISO 1600, but let's say I used f/8 to get the entire foreground in good focus. For every additional full f-stop increment, the amount of light collected is cut in half, and f/8 is three stops down from f/2.8—counting down from f/2.8, the next full f-stop is f/4, then f/5.6, then f/8, so three full stops from f/2.8 to f/8. Dividing the amount of light collected by 1/2 for each of those three full stops means that the amount of light we collected in that 10-minute exposure at f/2.8 would be 1/8th the amount of light than if we used f/8. That would be way too dark to capture enough detail, so you would have to increase the shutter speed to make up for the loss of light.

So, if I was using f/8 and wanted to capture the same amount of light as I would have at f/2.8 for 10 minutes, I would need to increase the shutter speed by three stops, which means doubling it three times as 10 x 2 x 2 x 2 = 80 minutes. This is certainly possible, but now the risk of the image being ruined is much higher. You could accidentally bump the tripod, or a car could drive by, or another person could turn on their headlamp by accident, and so on. There are lots of reasons a long exposure could be spoiled in the dark, including the fact that it's easy to mess up a setting and end up with an unusable photo, and you wouldn't know that for 80 minutes. It could even be as long 160 minutes if you're using Long Exposure Noise Reduction, a camera setting to reduce hot pixels (see page 90) that takes a second exposure with the shutter closed in order to compare it with the original so the hot pixels can be mapped out.

You could make up for the lack of light by light painting your scene, which would mean you could use a much shorter shutter speed, but I prefer to use the ambient light available. In general, I will take multiple foreground exposures with the focus pulled in as needed. Sometimes I just need one foreground exposure, sometimes more; it just depends on the composition (i.e. how much depth you want in the image) and how far the foreground objects are from your lens.

PUTTING IT ALL TOGETHER

Once you have all the photographs you need for the stars and foreground, it's then a matter of using your Raw editor (such as Lightroom) to adjust the images. Possibly use a star-stacking program (discussed later on page 170), and then bring the sky and foreground photographs into Photoshop to blend them together using layer masking. This will give you a single image that has low noise and is in sharp focus from the foreground to the stars.

▼ The final edit that I ended up with for this photo.

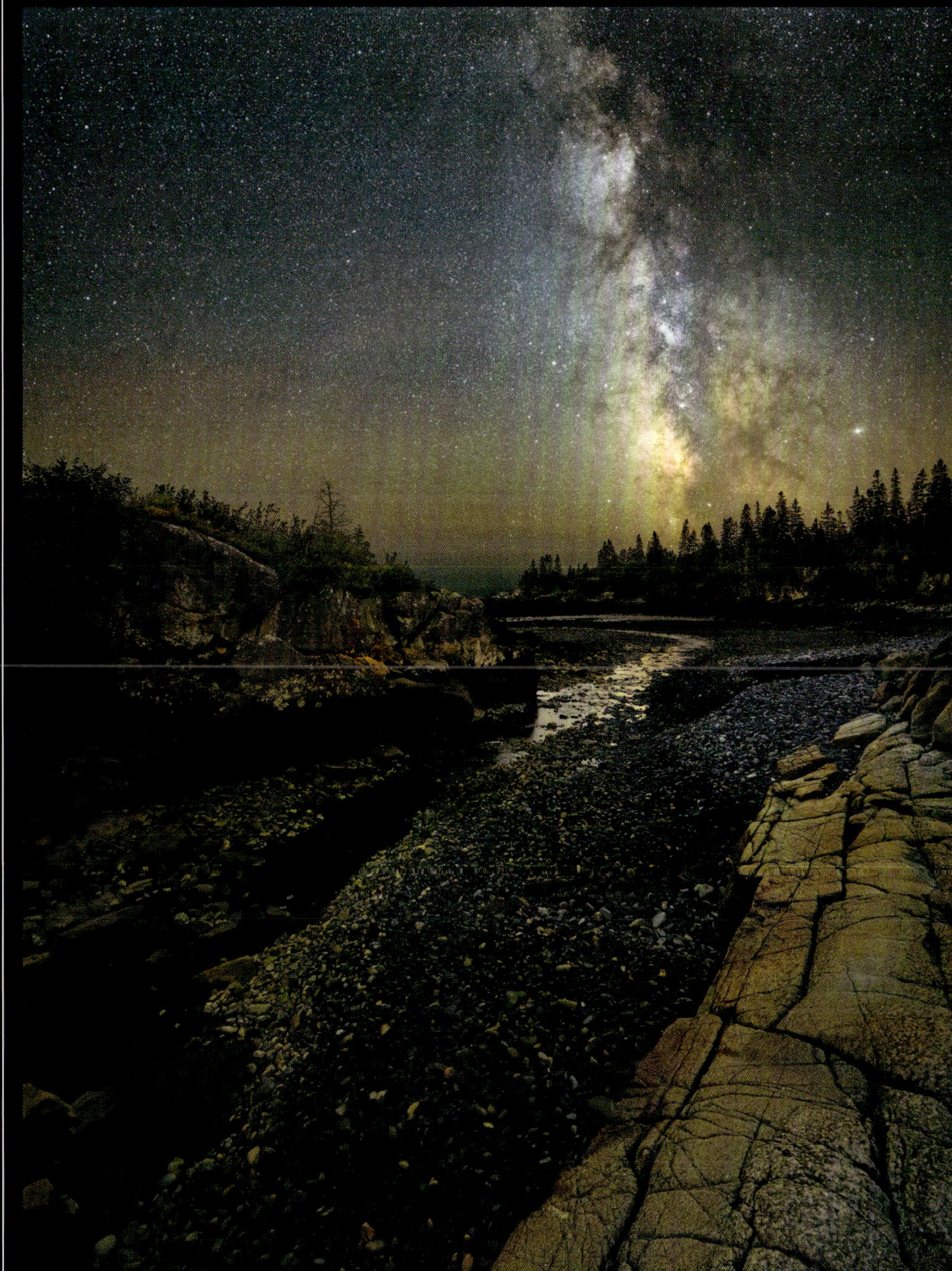

5

As seen in the previous chapter, capturing more light results in less noise. The more light you capture, the more signal you have that will drown out the various sources of noise inherent to photography. This is referred to as the signal-to-noise ratio (SNR). The higher the signal (the more light) the better the ratio, and the better the image quality.

The more we understand SNR, the easier it is to decide what camera settings and techniques to use to create images with a higher SNR, and thus retain more color and detail in our images.

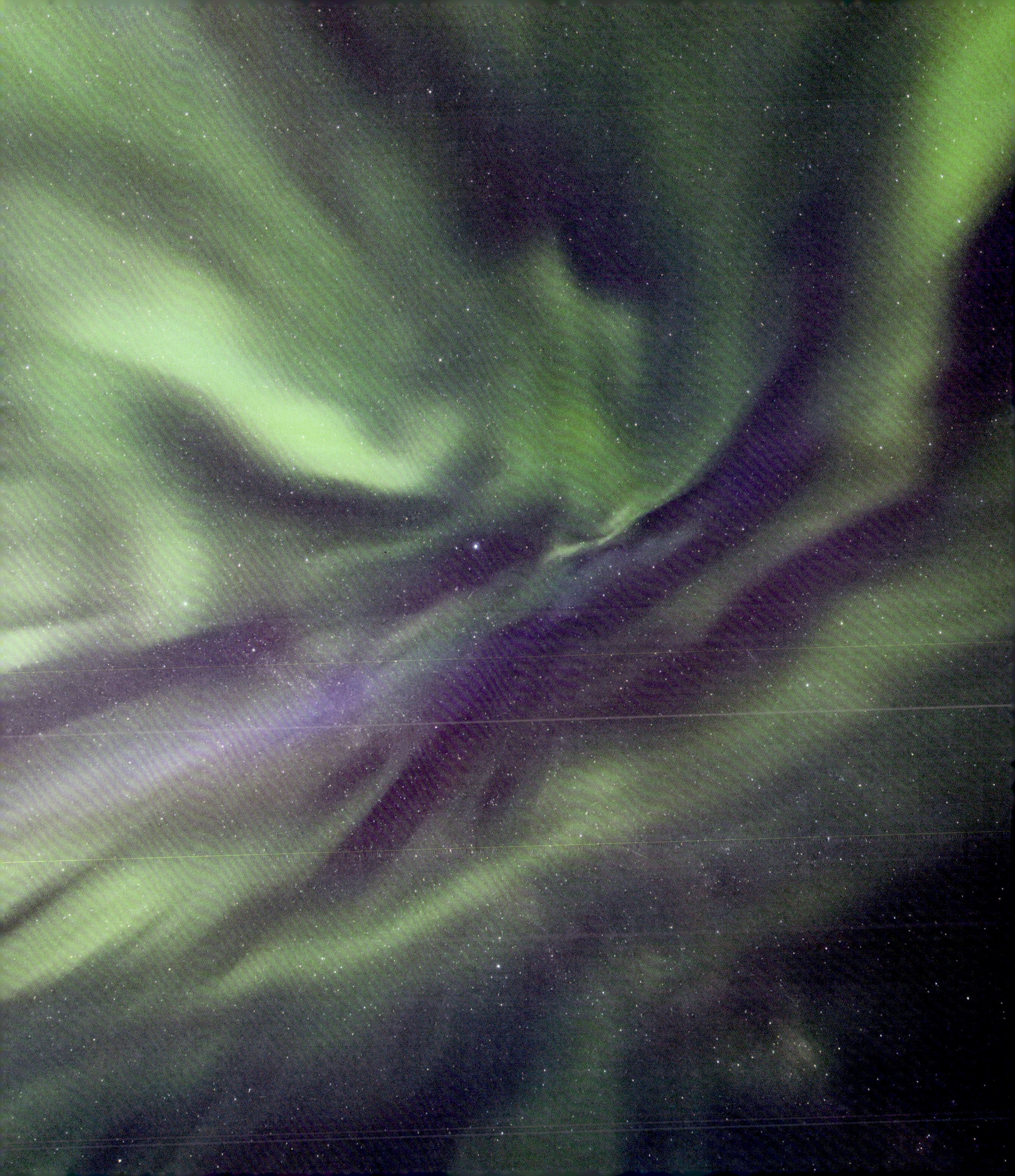

5.1 WHERE NOISE COMES FROM

Digital cameras work by taking photons (the particles of light) and converting them into electrons to create an analog electronic signal, which is then converted into a digital number used in the Raw file. Each pixel in your photo corresponds to a "pixel well" on the camera's sensor. These wells collect the photons for that particular pixel. In most modern digital cameras, the sensor is a CMOS type sensor which is covered by a colored filter array (CFA) that lets only red, green or blue light through to a single pixel well. The final full-color photo is created through interpolation of this data.

There are two main sources of noise in digital cameras—the lack of enough collected photons in the pixel wells to produce a high signal, and electronic noise that is introduced after the photons are collected on the sensor and processed by the camera's electronics. For most styles of photography, the former is the predominant source of noise in images, but for astrophotography (or any very low-light photography) both sources can play a large role in creating noise.

LIGHT IS NOISY

While a primer on quantum mechanics is well beyond the scope of this book, it is important to understand how light works in order to appreciate where most noise originates. Lightwaves are made up of discrete packets of energy called photons. A beam of light hitting your eye or a camera sensor is not a completely unbroken constant stream of energy, it is actually a fragmented and random collection of photons. A photograph is essentially a sample of these photons over a two-dimensional area, with each pixel well sampling a very small part of that area. The amount of photons that arrive at the sensor for a given shutter speed varies from one shot to the next. The chance of collecting the same number of photons in a particular pixel well between two shots of the same scene with the exact same camera settings is incredibly unlikely. This is true even for adjacent pixel wells capturing light from the same part of the scene—they will capture a different number of photons, resulting in random and varying levels of brightness for those adjacent pixels.

This source of noise is known as "shot noise," which is the most common source of noise in photography, and it is the nature of all light. Light, it turns out, is noisy all by itself.

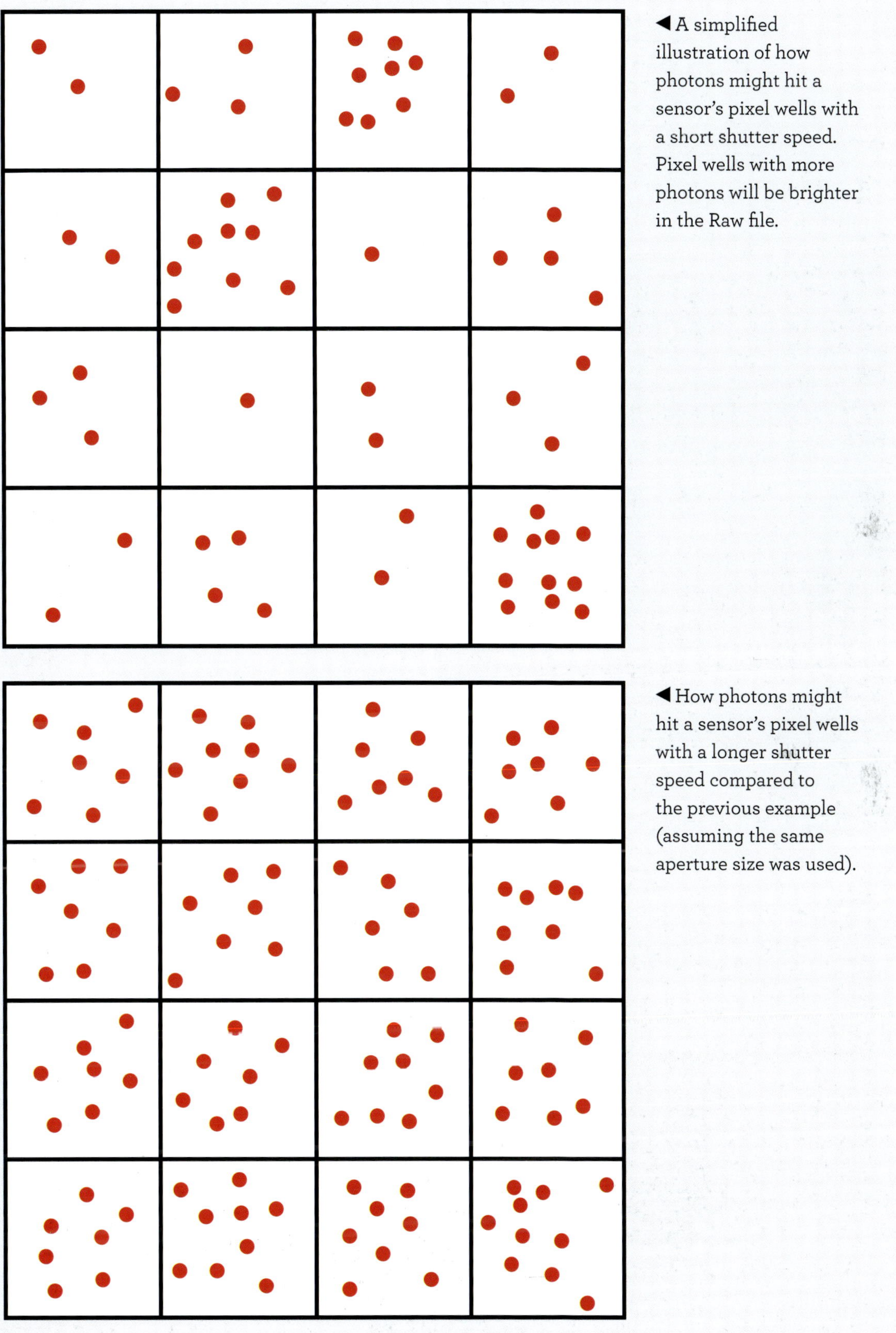

◀ A simplified illustration of how photons might hit a sensor's pixel wells with a short shutter speed. Pixel wells with more photons will be brighter in the Raw file.

◀ How photons might hit a sensor's pixel wells with a longer shutter speed compared to the previous example (assuming the same aperture size was used).

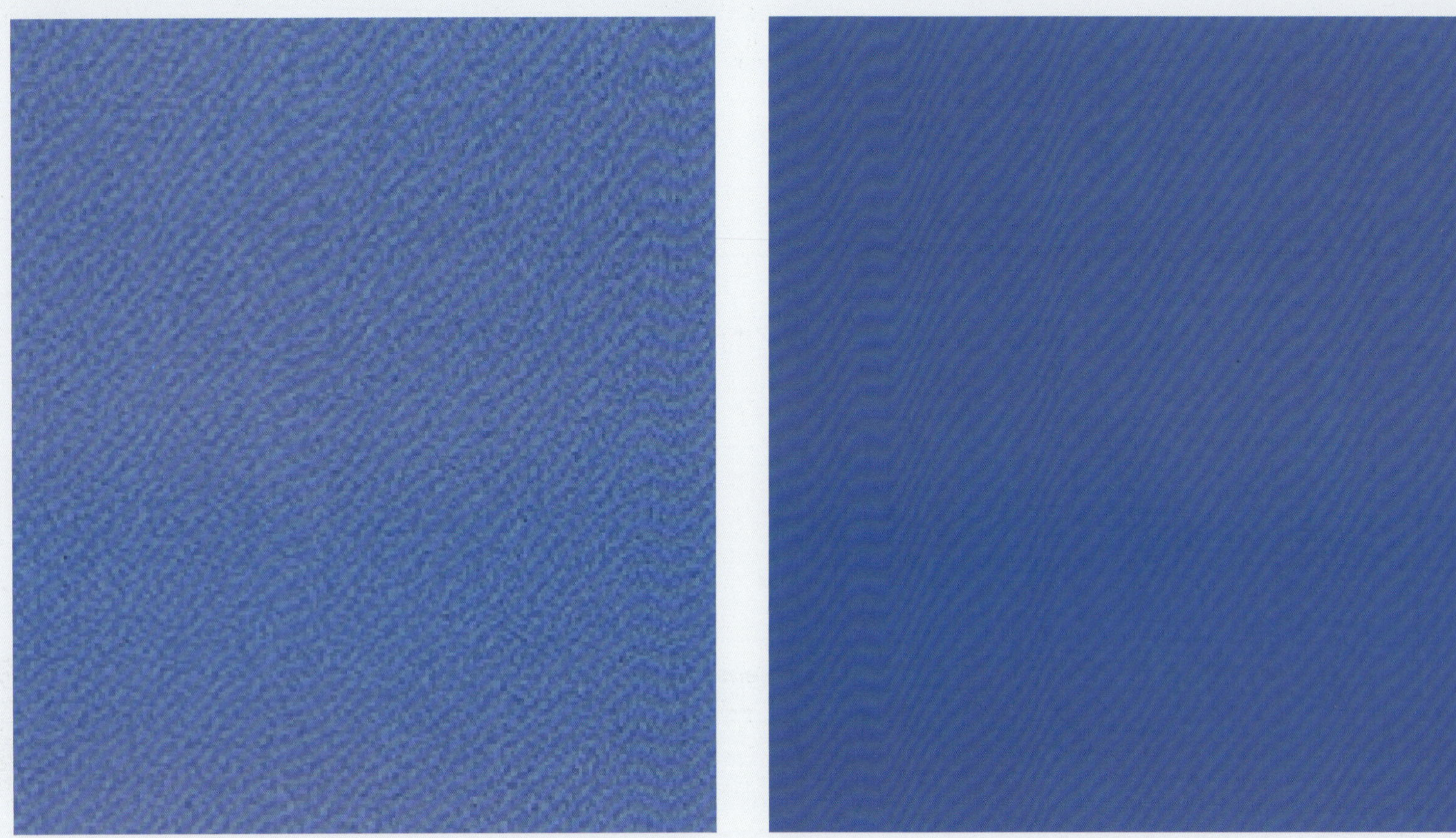

▲ Notice how the image on the left (1/8000 second) has varying brightness levels across the pixels. This is shot noise in action.

SHOT NOISE

Shot noise is most visible in a photograph in the shadow (dark) areas where less light has been captured, but it can even be found in what would normally be a smooth blue sky if the amount of light captured isn't enough to genererate a high signal-to-noise ratio (such as if a short shutter speed and/or a small aperture has been used). A low SNR will result in more visible shot noise.

For example, consider the two images above of a bright blue sky. They were captured with a 50mm lens at f/1.8 and ISO 64. The image on the left was captured with a shutter speed of 1/8000 second, and the image on the right used 1/500 second. In Adobe Lightroom Classic, I brought the exposure slider for the image on the left up by four stops (the difference between 1/8000 second and 1/500 second) so that it matches the brightness of the image on the right. The images have both been cropped to the same small section of the original so that we can easily see the noise at the pixel level.

▼ Here is another example, this time a cropped section of a night sky image at f/2.8, ISO 6400 and 10 seconds. Note that the noise seen here is still caused by shot noise, and this "grain" is often what people think of when using high ISOs, although it is not actually caused by the ISO, but rather the fact that the shutter speed was so short (and/or aperture so small) that a low amount of light was captured resulting in a low SNR. A high ISO can introduce some noise, as we will discuss next, but it is not the source of noise in this example.

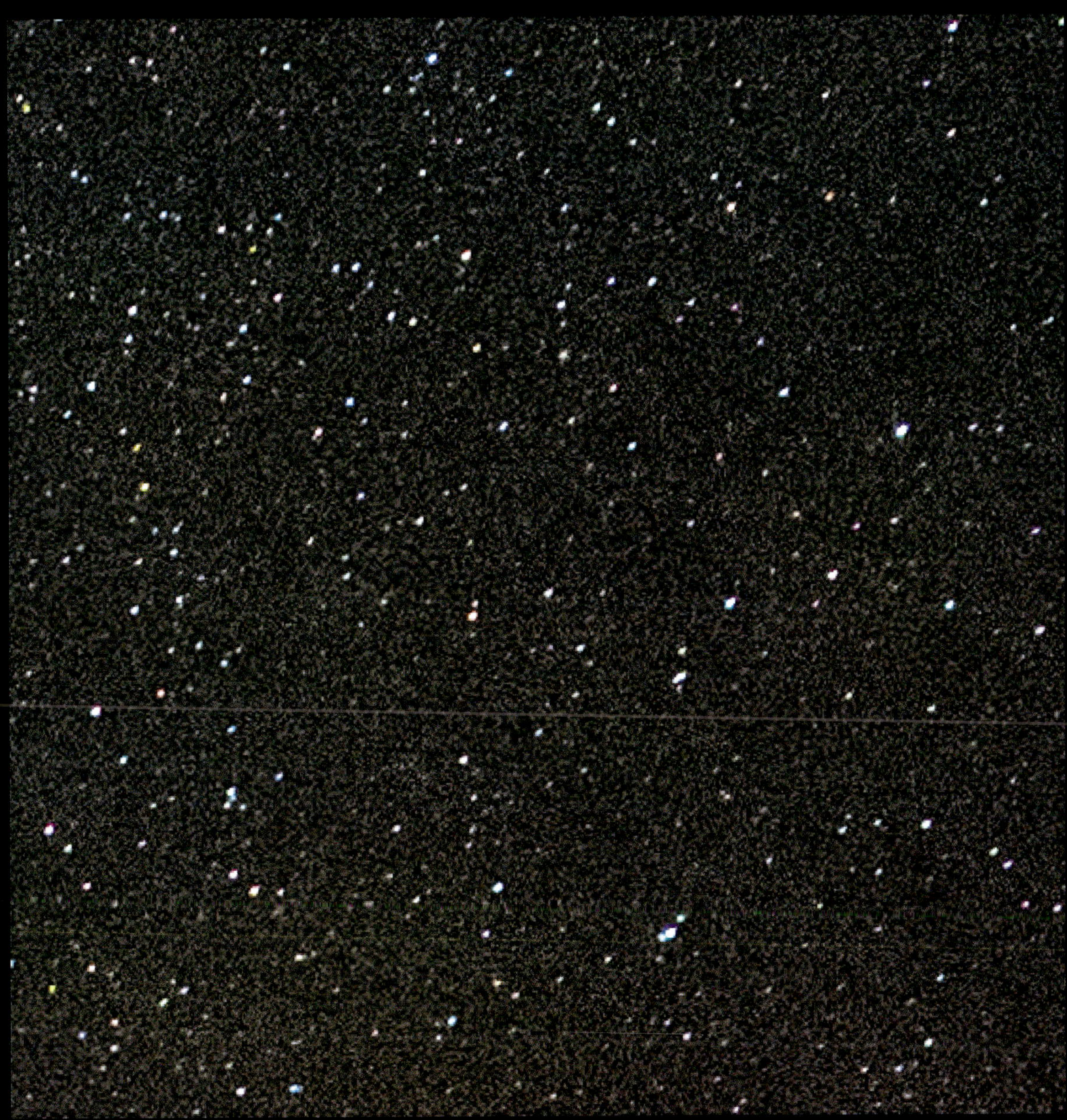

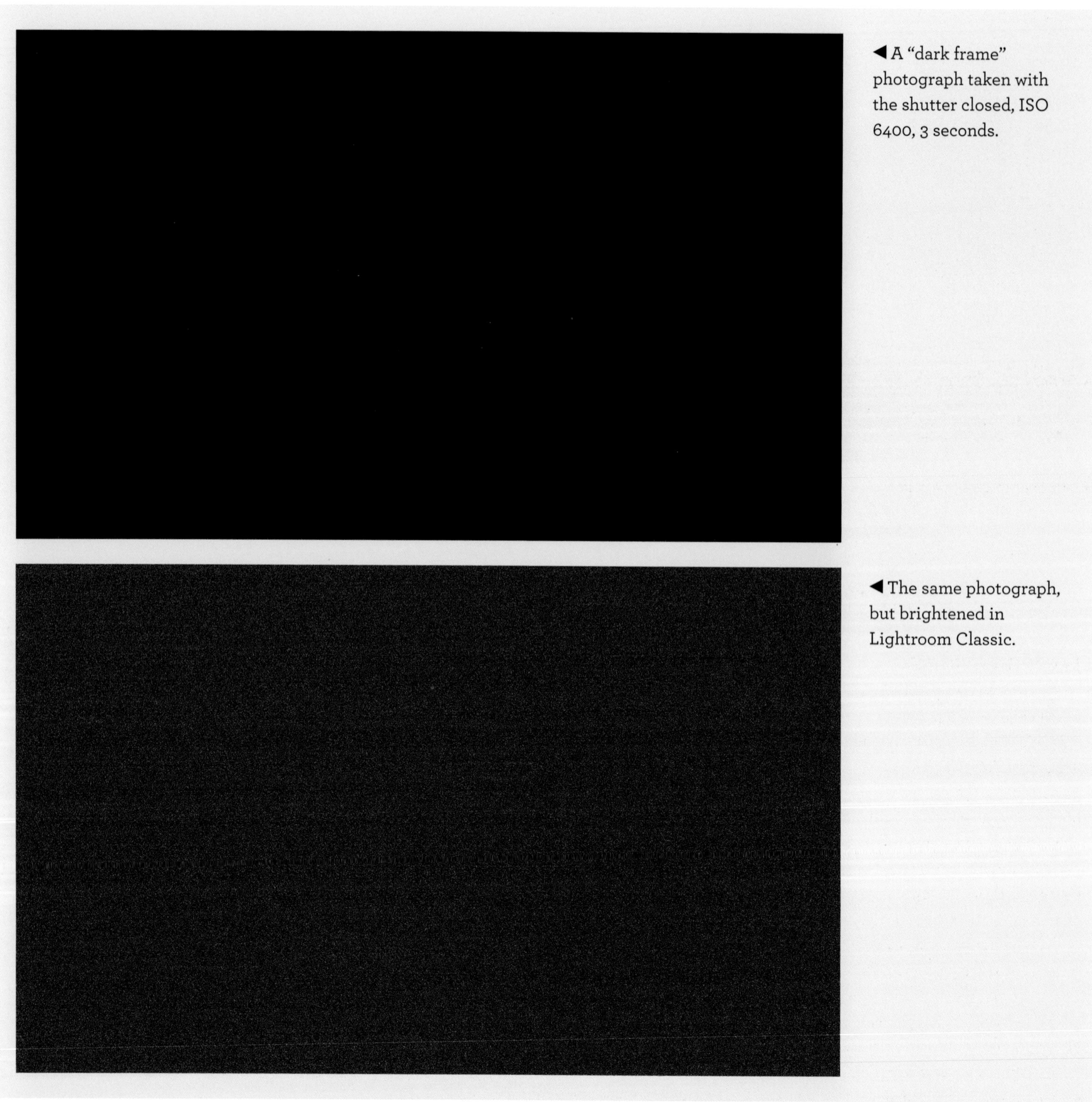

◀ A "dark frame" photograph taken with the shutter closed, ISO 6400, 3 seconds.

◀ The same photograph, but brightened in Lightroom Classic.

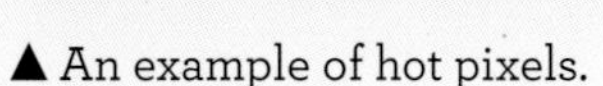

▲ An example of hot pixels.

▲ An example of magenta amp glow running along the edge of the frame.

ELECTRONIC NOISE

Noise can also creep in when a pixel well doesn't collect enough photons to create an electronic signal substantially higher than the inherent random background signals in the sensor and camera electronics. If you take a photo with your lens cap on and then brighten it in your Raw editor, you will not see an empty image devoid of any color or noise. What you'll likely see is a lot of colorful pixels. Since there was no light hitting the sensor with the lens cap on, all these colorful pixels are coming from the electronic noise, a part of how the camera reads the data from the sensor and converts it into a digital file. Even when a pixel well captures no photons, there will still be some background signal making its way through the camera electronics and into the final image.

Electronic noise can show up in other ways as well. On some cameras, using a very high ISO can introduce noise, often resulting in "hot" pixels that appear as bright dots in the image; "amp glow" that can appear as a strong magenta color along the edges of an image; or bands of strong color running through the image. The amount of electronic noise will vary from camera to camera, and many modern cameras are now able to vastly reduce electronic noise.

We don't notice this noise normally in most types of photography because a well-exposed photo will capture enough light to drown out the background noise. However, astrophotography is a different beast and we are dealing with low signal levels (low numbers of photons) while shooting in the dark. Thus, astrophotography is particularly sensitive to both electronic noise and shot noise.

Heat is one of the many enemies of the night photographer (along with clouds and a foggy lens), because heat causes cameras to produce more electronic noise. So, if you're shooting in Death Valley in the summer when it's 100 degrees Fahrenheit, you might notice a lot more hot pixels compared to a cool night in the mountains.

image. The amount of light captured is controlled by your f-stop and shutter speed. The longer the shutter speed, the more light is captured. A smaller f-stop number means a larger opening in the aperture of the lens, meaning more light will get through.

The ISO control won't let you capture more light, but you can use a higher ISO to amplify the signal from the pixel wells. This boosts the signal we care about above the electronic noise. It's an oversimplification and isn't always 100 percent true, as any electronic noise added before the amplification will also be increased, but in many low-light situations a higher ISO is necessary.

So we know that more light is better, but this poses a problem—the short shutter speeds required for pinpoint stars (or at least small star trails) don't allow us to capture much light in the dark, resulting in a low signal-to-noise ratio, and thus a lot of noise. So how can we capture more light in this situation?

For the foreground, it's simple, as we've seen in **Breaking Down an Image**, page 58; just take separate foreground photographs with longer shutter speeds and blend them with a separate sky photo in software.

▶ Cliffs overlooking the Bay of Fundy.

This shot consists of three exposures blended to achieve the widest depth of field. All shots were taken with the Nikon D850 and Nikon 14-24mm f/2.8 lens at 14mm. The sky is one shot at ISO 25,600 for 20 seconds, and the foreground is made of two exposures, one at ISO 1600 and f/4 for 60 seconds during blue hour to get the very close shrubs in focus, and one at ISO 1600 and f/2.8 for 16 minutes in complete darkness for the background cliffs and water.

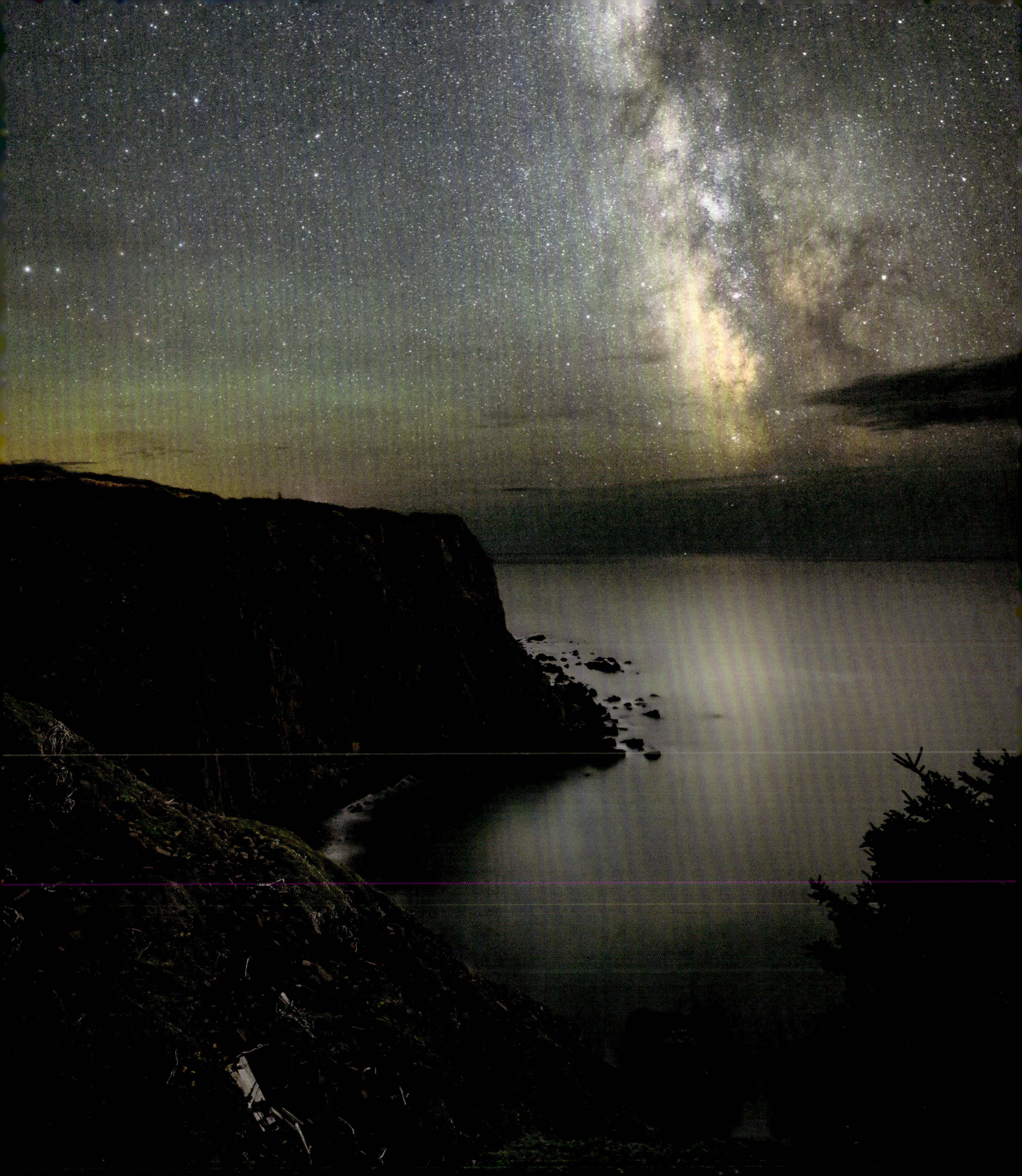

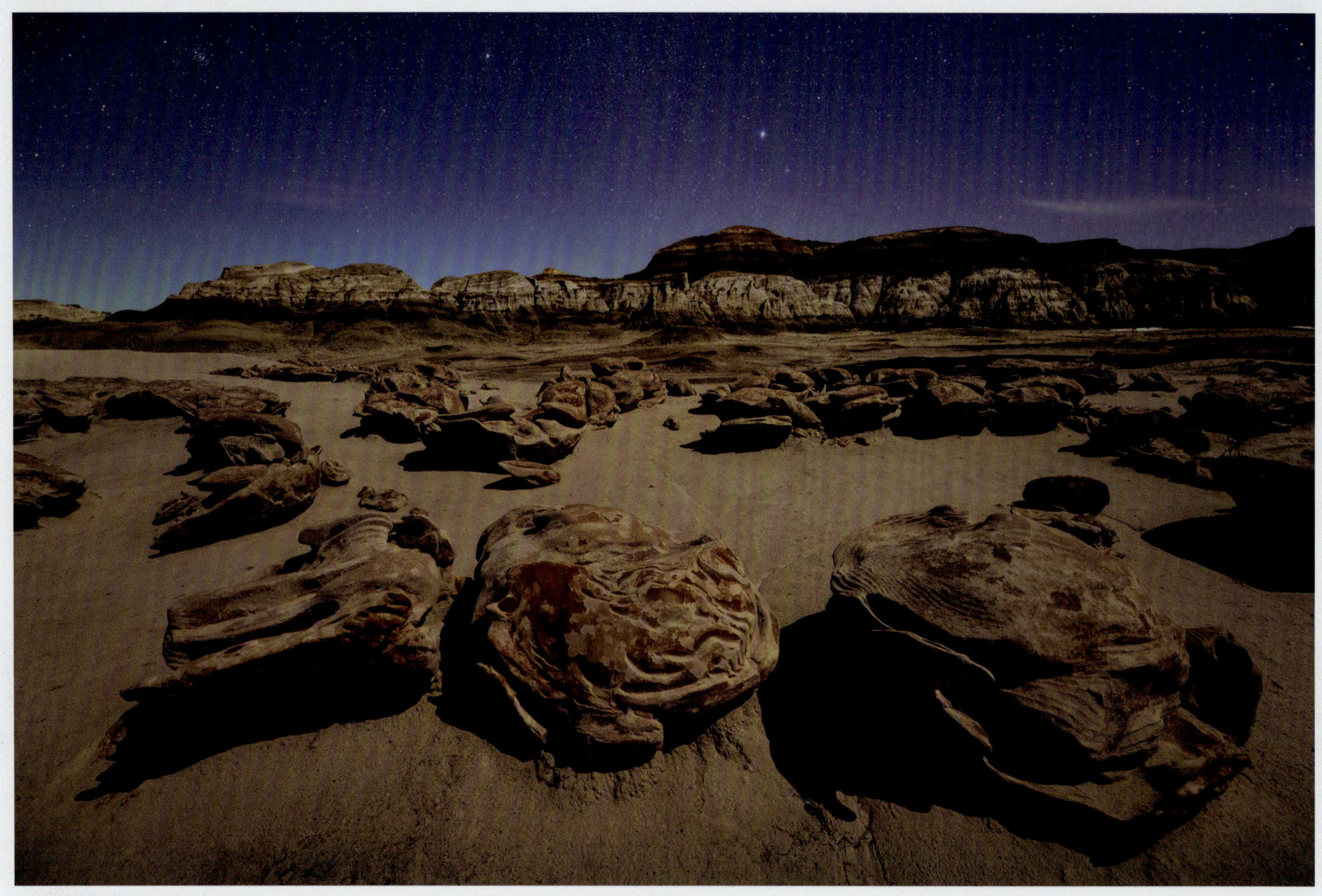

DEALING WITH NOISE

For the sky, we have a few options:

1 Live with the noise from short exposures and possibly use noise-reduction software.

2 Capture multiple exposures and use star-stacking software to create a single image that's an average of all them for low noise.

3 Use a star tracker (see page 80) to keep the camera moving with the rotation of the Earth, allowing for much longer shutter speeds. This can also be combined with star stacking.

There are also a couple of other techniques you can use for dealing with electronic noise.

1 A "dark frame" is a photograph you take with the lens cap on (likely many of these photos). You can use this to remove electronic noise from the "light frame" (or frames), which are the normal images of the scene. You can do this with particular software programs (including Starry Landscape Stacker and Sequator; see page 170).

2 A cooled camera will produce less electronic noise because the sensor and other electronics are kept at a lower temperature, which reduces electronic interference and errors introduced when reading photons from the sensor.

For landscape astrophotography, it's not essential to use dark frames or a cooled camera. However, if you get into deep space astrophotography, both of those things become much more important for keeping noise at bay.

◀ A moonlit night at the Alien Eggs in the Bisti Wilderness of New Mexico. This group of rock formations goes by many names—"alien eggs," "cracked eggs," "the egg factory," "the hatchery," the list goes on. Whatever you call them, they are pretty darn interesting!

Nikon Z 7 with FTZ lens adapter and NIKKOR 14-24mm f/2.8 lens at 14mm, f/2.8 for all shots.

Sky: Star stack of 20 exposures for pinpoint stars and low noise, each at 8 seconds and ISO 1600.

Foreground: Focus stack of two exposures, each at 30 seconds and ISO 800.

5.3 SINGLE EXPOSURES

The easiest method for dealing with noise in the sky is to just, quite literally, deal with it. Depending on how dark the sky is where you're shooting, and your shutter speed and aperture, the amount of noise visible in the sky may or may not be heavily distracting. Taking single photographs is certainly the easiest way to get into and start enjoying landscape astrophotography.

In a single photograph you can use a longer exposure for the sky that will cause a small, but manageable amount of star trailing —the longer exposure will capture more light and thus have less noise, with the trade-off of longer star trails. For example, on a full-frame camera with a 14mm lens, you may need to use a shutter speed of 10 seconds for reasonably pinpoint stars, but if you doubled the shutter speed to 20 seconds you'd get a little bit of star trailing and twice as much light, so a higher SNR resulting in less noise.

Noise-reduction software can also be used to decrease noise, although it can be easy to go too far with it, destroying stars and making the sky look plasticky and pixelated. But noise-reduction tools are getting better all the time.

How much star trailing and noise you can tolerate is going to be a personal decision based on your own style and how you display your photos. If you're only sharing them on social media and/or websites, then the low-resolution of the images that are used for such platforms will easily hide a significant amount of noise and star trailing. But if you are making reasonably large prints, say 12 x 18 inches (30 x 45cm) or larger, then the noise and star trailing will become more visible. Ultimately, what is more important than noise or star trailing are your skills in composition and editing. A photo with a beautiful composition that has some star trailing and lots of noise will easily be more dynamic and visually appealing than a photo of a boring composition that is technically well executed with low noise and pinpoint stars.

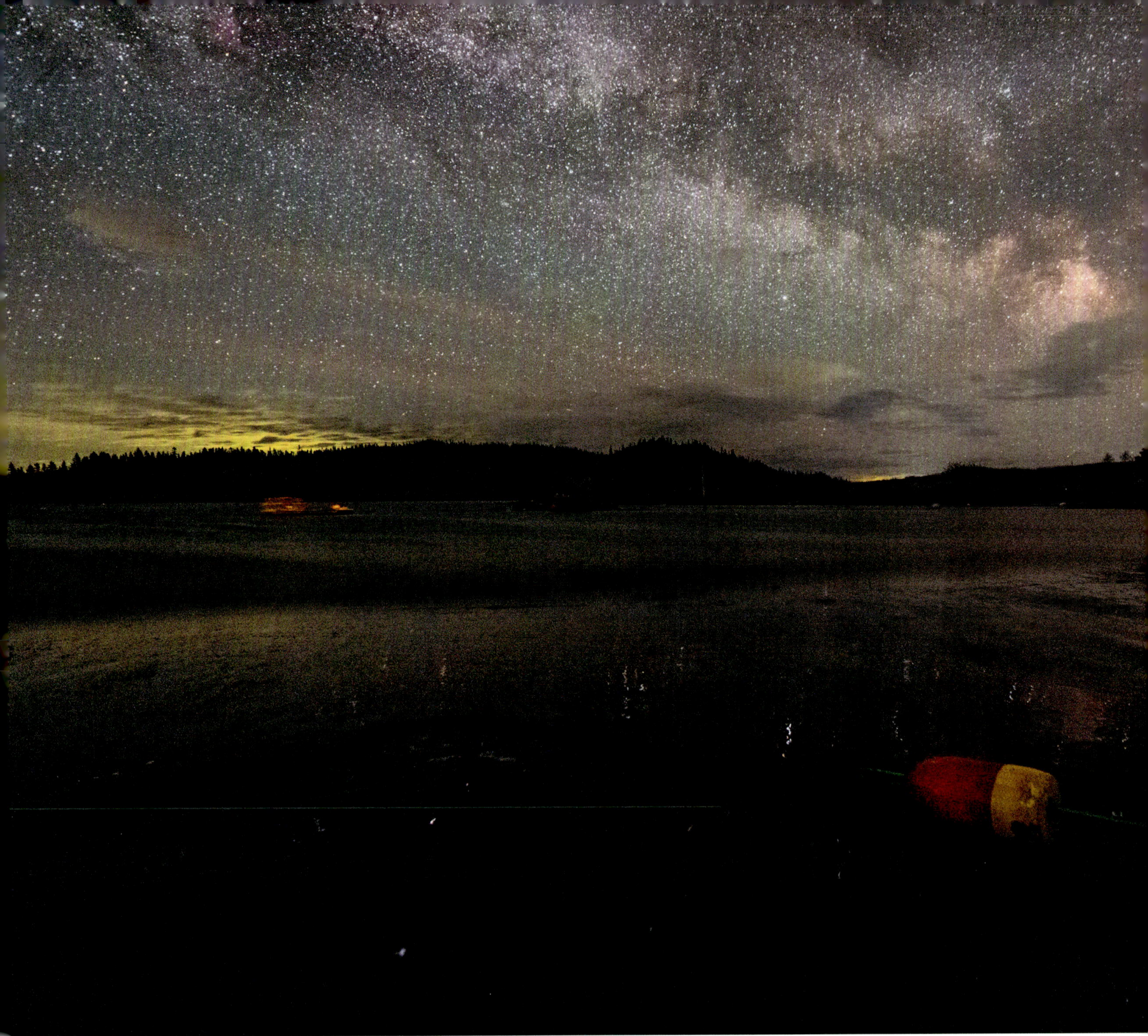

The above image is a single exposure from my Nikon D810A and NIKKOR 14-24mm f/2.8 lens at 14mm, f/2.8, ISO 3200, for 20 seconds. There was just enough light from a distant street lamp behind me to illuminate the foreground enough to capture detail in just 20 seconds. Since I had the focus set on the stars, the foreground is out of focus. There is noise throughout the image, and some small amount of star trailing. However, when the image is used at small sizes, like in this book, or on social media, you don't notice those imperfections. This would easily make a nice 8 x 12 inch (20 x 30cm) print, or even larger if you don't mind the out-of-focus foreground and noise becoming more visible. The small star trails wouldn't even be a big deal in a print of 20 x 30 inches (50 x 76cm) or larger.

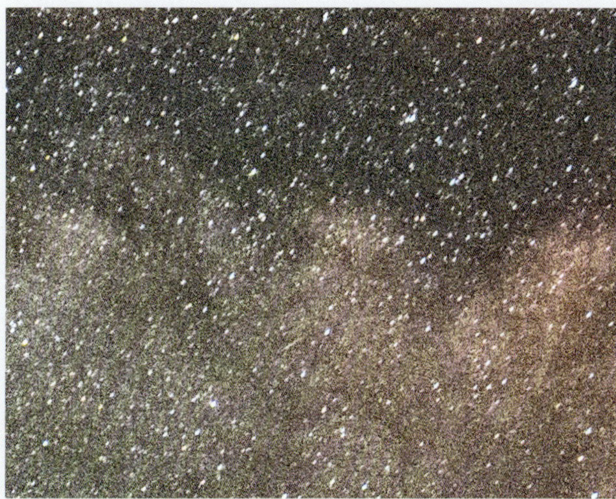

◀ A close-up of the small star trails and noise.

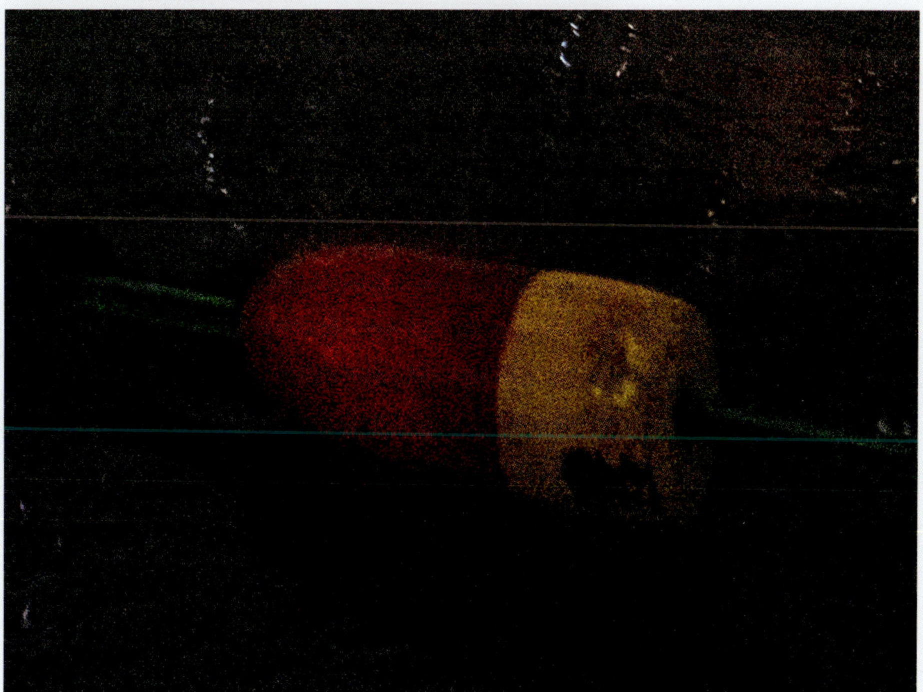

▲ A close-up of the somewhat out of focus and noisy foreground.

5.4 STAR STACKING

Star stacking is a technique that involves taking multiple photographs of the stars (sky), and then aligning them in software to create an image that's an average of all of them, so that the noise is reduced. Shot noise is random from image to image, so blending many photographs produces a much smoother (less visibly noisy) result. When using short shutter speeds to capture pinpoint stars, the result is a photo with both pinpoint stars and low noise—the best of both worlds.

This technique is used regularly in deep space astrophotography and other areas of imaging to improve image quality.

Star stacking requires specific software, which will be discussed in the **Editing** chapter (see page 170). These programs separate the sky from the foreground, so that you don't end up with a blurry foreground.

When you are taking images for star stacking, you can use a shutter speed as fast as needed for sharp, pinpoint stars, and an ISO high enough to boost the signal above the background noise. You can also use a higher f-stop number on your lens, which in many cases will improve the look of the stars by sharpening them more and reducing aberrations. Using a higher f-stop reduces the amount of light being captured, but you can simply just take more exposures to use in the stack to reduce the noise.

As a general rule of thumb, ISO 3200 and f/2.8 are good settings to start with. Your shutter speed will depend on the focal length of your lens and the size of your camera's sensor, which all make a difference to how long the shutter can be open before the stars appear to trail. (See **Shutter Speed**, page 105.)

Once you have your shutter speed figured out, take 10 to 20 photographs with your focus on the stars. I recommend 10 to 20 because the more images, the less noise there is in the stacked result, however there are limited gains after a while. It takes four times the amount of light to cut the shot noise in half, so assuming a constant shutter speed, 20 photographs will have less visible noise than 10 photographs, but it would take 40 photographs to halve the amount of shot noise from 10 photographs. I personally find 20 shots at 10 seconds each works very well for pretty clean skies. If you have to take shorter exposures because of your focal length, you may want to take more of them. It's all about the total accumulative amount of time that your shutter is open. If you take 20 photographs at 10 seconds each, that is 200 seconds of light. The total amount of exposure time is called the "integration time," a term you'll hear more often with deep space astrophotography.

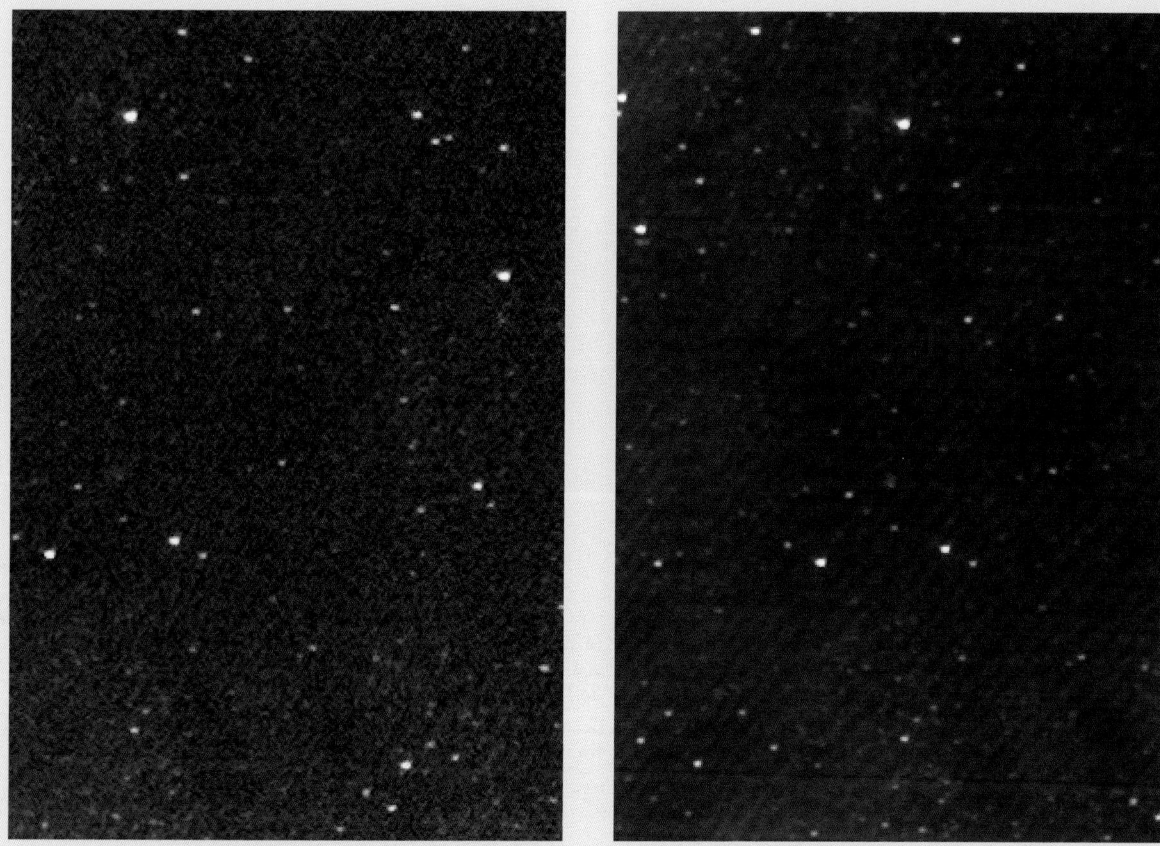

▲ An example of a single 10-second shot (left) compared to a star-stacked result of twenty 10-second shots (right). Notice how much less noise is visible with star stacking.

You might be wondering if this means that you could simply skip a separate foreground exposure, since the integration time for your sky exposures equals a much longer total shutter speed. In fact, this is true if the foreground is extremely bright and you can capture lots of good detail in a single exposure of 10 seconds or so, such as when there is a lot of artificial light hitting the scene or during twilight. But if the only ambient light is starlight or weak artificial light, the foreground most likely won't reflect enough photons for enough detail to be captured in exposures as short as 10 or 20 seconds, leading to a black, featureless foreground as seen in **Breaking Down an Image** (see page 56). In those cases, a separate foreground photograph is necessary, and even if there is enough ambient light for star stacking to produce a useful foreground, you may still need additional photographs for focus stacking.

Another benefit to star stacking is that any airplane and satellite trails in your sky images will almost always be removed by the stacking software. Since the airplane and satellite trails are in different places in each shot relative to the stars, they will be "kicked out" of the final result by the stacking algorithm. This applies to hot pixels as well (except when using a star tracker, explained next)—since the hot pixels will appear in a different spot in each image after alignment, the averaging process will be able to tell they are not stars.

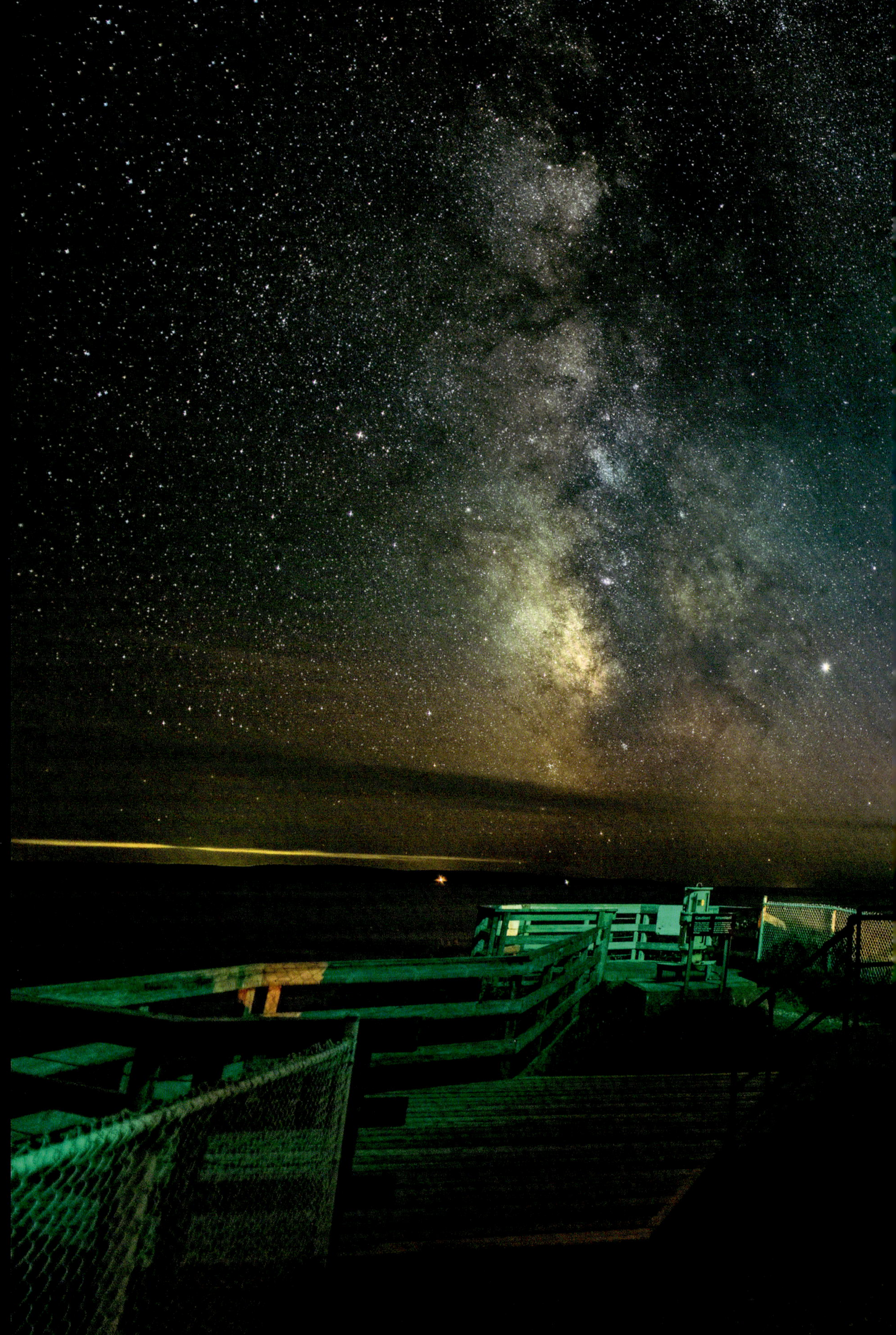

▶ At Cape Enrage Lighthouse there was so much ambient light that I didn't need a separate foreground shot for a low-noise foreground; my sky exposures had enough foreground detail that the stacked result looked good. However, I should have taken at least one separate foreground shot with the focus pulled in for the rocks, as they're a bit soft.

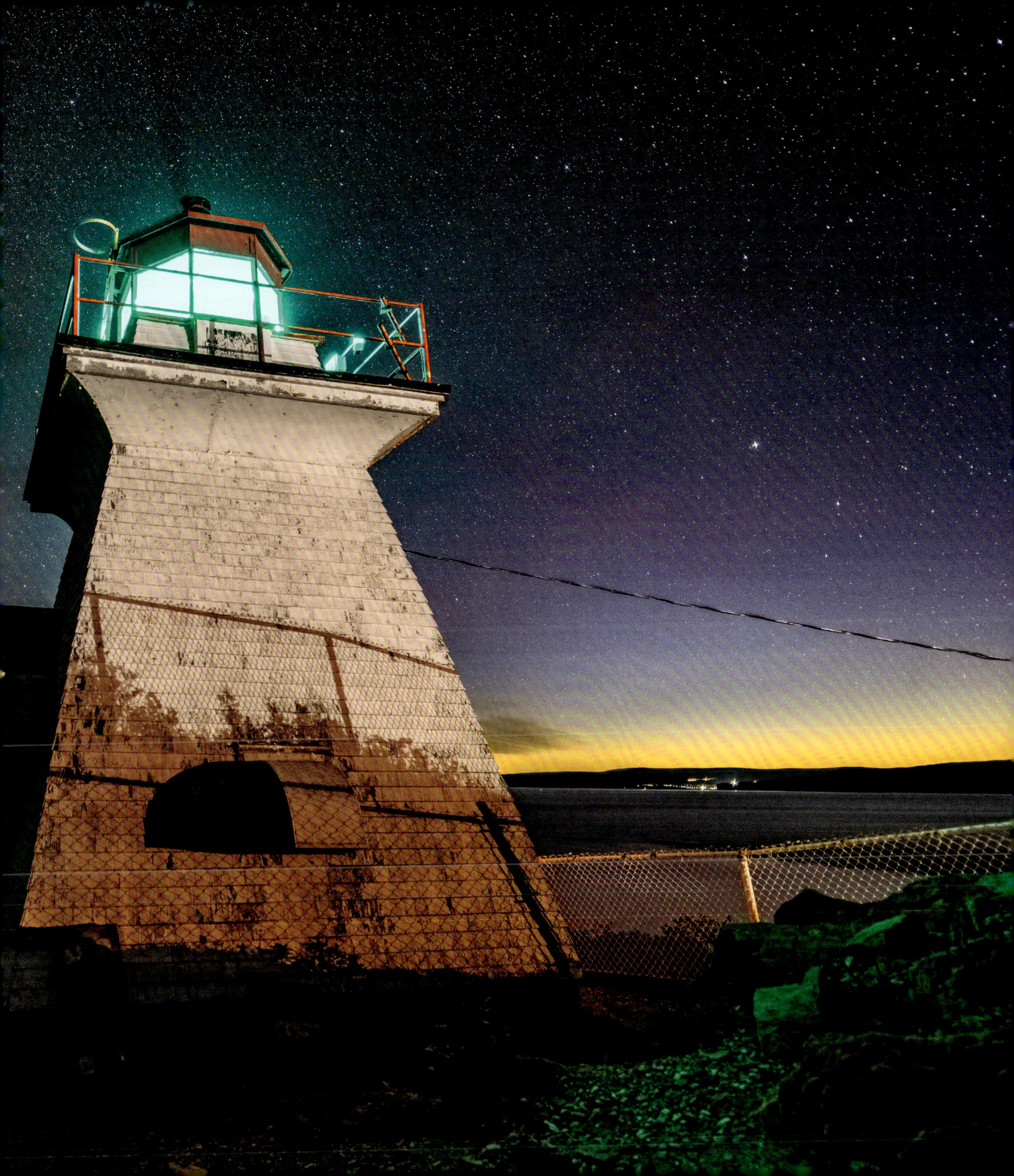

5.5 USING A STAR TRACKER

Mounted between your camera and your tripod, a star tracker is a device that moves the camera with the rotation of the Earth so that the camera can follow the stars without causing star trails. This allows for much longer single exposures, capturing lots of light and thus getting a higher signal-to-noise ratio than you could get with a single exposure (before the stars would trail). Star trackers are mostly used for deep space photography, but they can be used for landscape astrophotography too.

In order to properly track the stars, a star tracker needs to be aligned with Polaris (aka the North Star) when shooting in the Northern Hemisphere, or Sigma Octantis when shooting in the Southern Hemisphere. This aligns the tracker with Earth's axis of rotation. The tracker can then rotate the camera slowly in the same direction as the Earth rotates on its axis.

To align the tracker you need to be able to have a clear line of sight to Polaris or Sigma Octantis. If trees, mountains, clouds and so on are obscuring that view for you, you can generally get away with using a compass and your latitude to align the tracker if you're using a wide-angle lens. Many tracker mounts will have an elevation adjustment with latitude markings—set this to your current latitude, and point the tracker north, and you are generally aligned well enough for wide-angle astrophotography. This is because a wider angle of view will capture smaller star trails than a narrower field of view, so even if your alignment is not precise you can use a tracker with wide-angle lenses.

The longer the focal length, the more accurately your tracker will need to be aligned in order to take long exposures without capturing star trails. There are phone apps that can help you align the tracker without seeing the stars, but they are only so accurate.

Every time you move your tripod, you will need to re-align the star tracker. This makes changing compositions complicated. This is particularly challenging if you're frantically changing your composition in order to capture a reflection or the tide level just right, before it changes.

Since the tracker moves the camera, the foreground will be blurred, making blending a separate foreground exposure with the star exposure more complicated.

However, both of the above issues are made easier by using your star tracker in a location with a clear view of the sky down to the horizon, and blending that with your foreground exposure in software. That way you can use your camera normally (without the tracker) to capture your foreground.

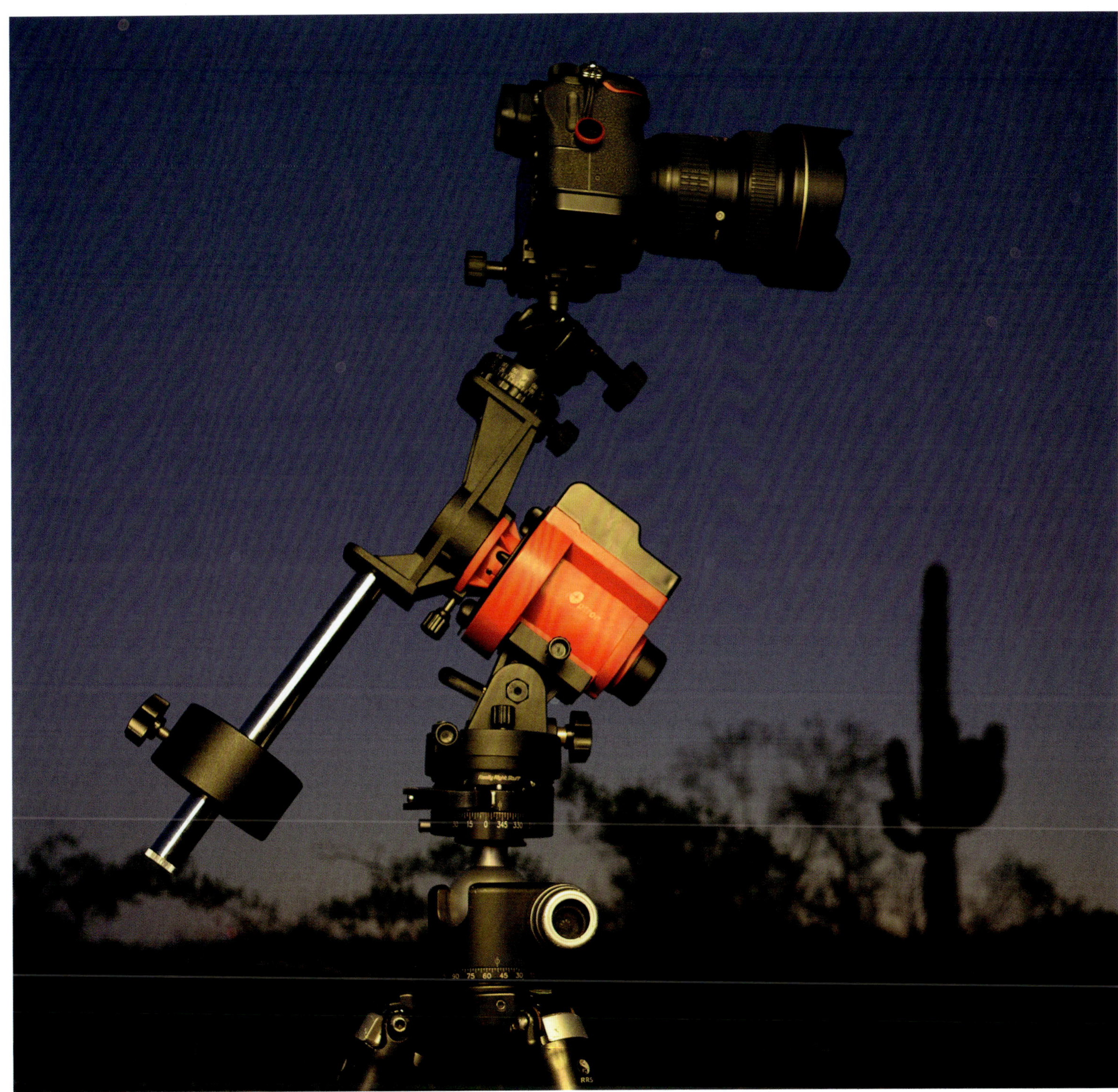

▲ The iOptron SkyGuider Pro with my Nikon Z 7 camera and 14-24mm lens.

▲ A close-up of a single photograph taken with an iOptron SkyGuider Pro with Nikon Z 7 and NIKKOR 14-24mm lens at 14mm, f/2.8, ISO 250, 200 seconds. Notice how the stars are pinpoints and there is low noise in the sky, but the foreground is blurred because the tracker was moving so it could follow the stars.

▲ Close-up of the star-stacked result of 20 exposures, each at 14mm, f/2.8, ISO 5000, 10 seconds. I had to boost the ISO to compensate for the short shutter speed, otherwise the signal would have been buried in the electronic noise (though I could have used ISO 1600 or so to protect the stars from overexposing, this was just for testing). Notice how the noise after stacking is the same as in the single photograph taken using the tracker, and the foreground is not blurred.

Using a tracker, you can easily get exposures of the stars that are multiple minutes in length without star trails, capturing tons of light, and thus more detail and less noise. However, if you don't use a tracker and instead take multiple short exposures and combine them in star-stacking software (as mentioned in the previous section on **Star Stacking**), the result will be very similar to an image taken with a star tracker and a much longer shutter speed.

For example, if you use a star tracker with a 14mm lens at f/2.8 and capture a 200-second exposure without star trails, you could compare that to 20 exposures of 10 seconds each that were then stacked in software, and the results would be very similar to each other—both would have pinpoint stars and low noise. This is because the end result of star stacking is essentially the same as a long exposure of the same accumulated length of all the exposures in the stack. You are capturing the same amount of light, whether you split it up into multiple exposures or capture it all at once in a single exposure.

(As a side note: technically, the noise will not be quite the same, as you will have more electronic noise to deal with when stacking, but the added electronic noise is often so minimal that it doesn't make a difference.)

This is the biggest reason I personally don't use a star tracker for wide-angle landscape astrophotography—the added complexity just isn't necessary to get pinpoint stars and low noise. Additionally, using a tracker means carrying around an extra piece of equipment when hiking, and possibly extra batteries, or at least remembering to charge the tracker's internal battery. So while a tracker makes capturing more light an easy task once it's set up, it creates other issues.

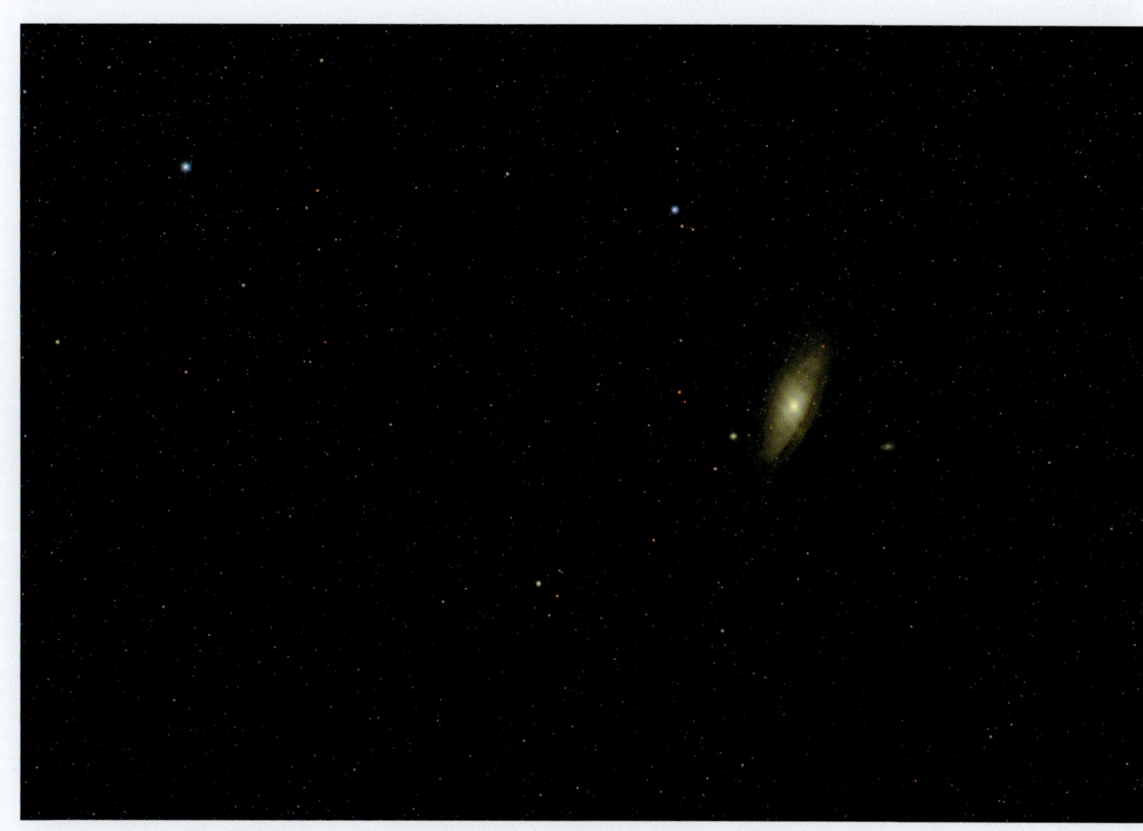

◀ The Andromeda Galaxy. Nikon D810A and Nikon 70-200mm f/4 lens using a star tracker. This photo is the result of star-stacking 62 photographs that were shot at 200mm, f/5.6, ISO 6400, 12 seconds. I was using a very small, lightweight star tracker that didn't really support the weight of the camera and lens, so I was limited to 12 seconds before the stars started to trail. Combining star tracking and star stacking I was able to capture a total of 744 seconds of light. I stopped down the lens to f/5.6 to sharpen up the stars a bit.

LONGER FOCAL LENGTHS

However, it's a different story with longer focal lengths. The longer the focal length, the quicker the stars will appear to move in a short amount of time, and this means that if you're not using a tracker you may end up having to take a ridiculous number of very short exposures for star stacking.

On top of that, the object will be moving quickly through the frame, making it difficult to keep the object where you want it in the frame without tracking.

Even when using a tracker, you may still want to use the star-stacking technique, i.e. take multiple exposures while using the tracker to combine later in software. This enables you to capture even more light before the stars start to trail, and it will also get rid of airplanes and satellites, as those objects will be removed during the averaging process since they change from one frame to the next —the same reason that airplane and satellite trails are removed when star stacking without having used a tracker. If you use just one photograph with a tracker, then any airplane or satellite trails will need to be removed manually in software.

If your tracking is perfect and the stars don't move at all between frames, then you will not get the benefit of hot pixels being removed during the stacking (unless the software is good enough to notice and remove them with fancy algorithms, but they aren't always caught this way). Since "stuck" hot pixels will be in the same place from frame to frame, it is hard for the software to tell if it is a star or a hot pixel. This is where dark frames come in handy—the software can use dark frames to identify where the hot pixels are and remove them.

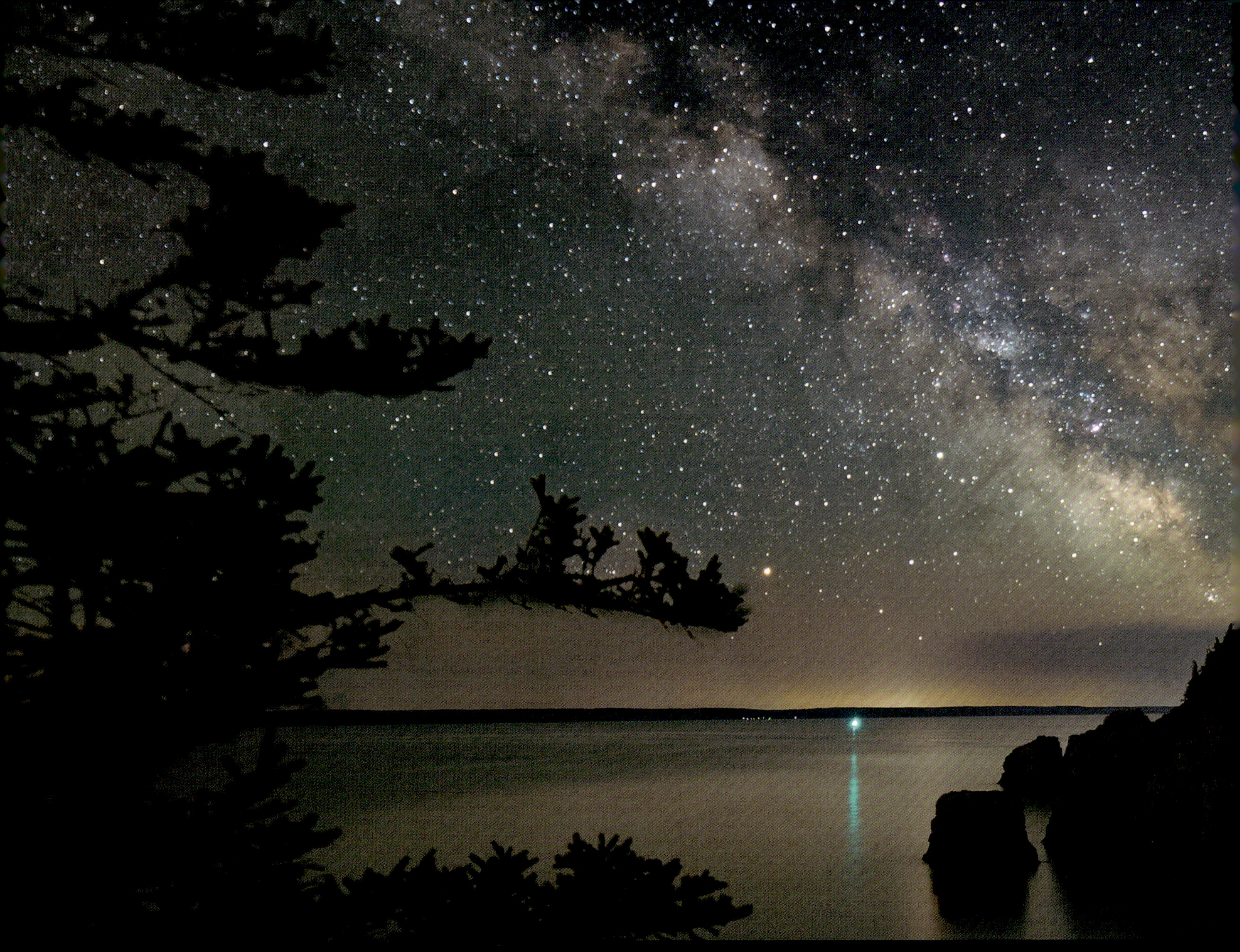

6 CAMERA SETTINGS

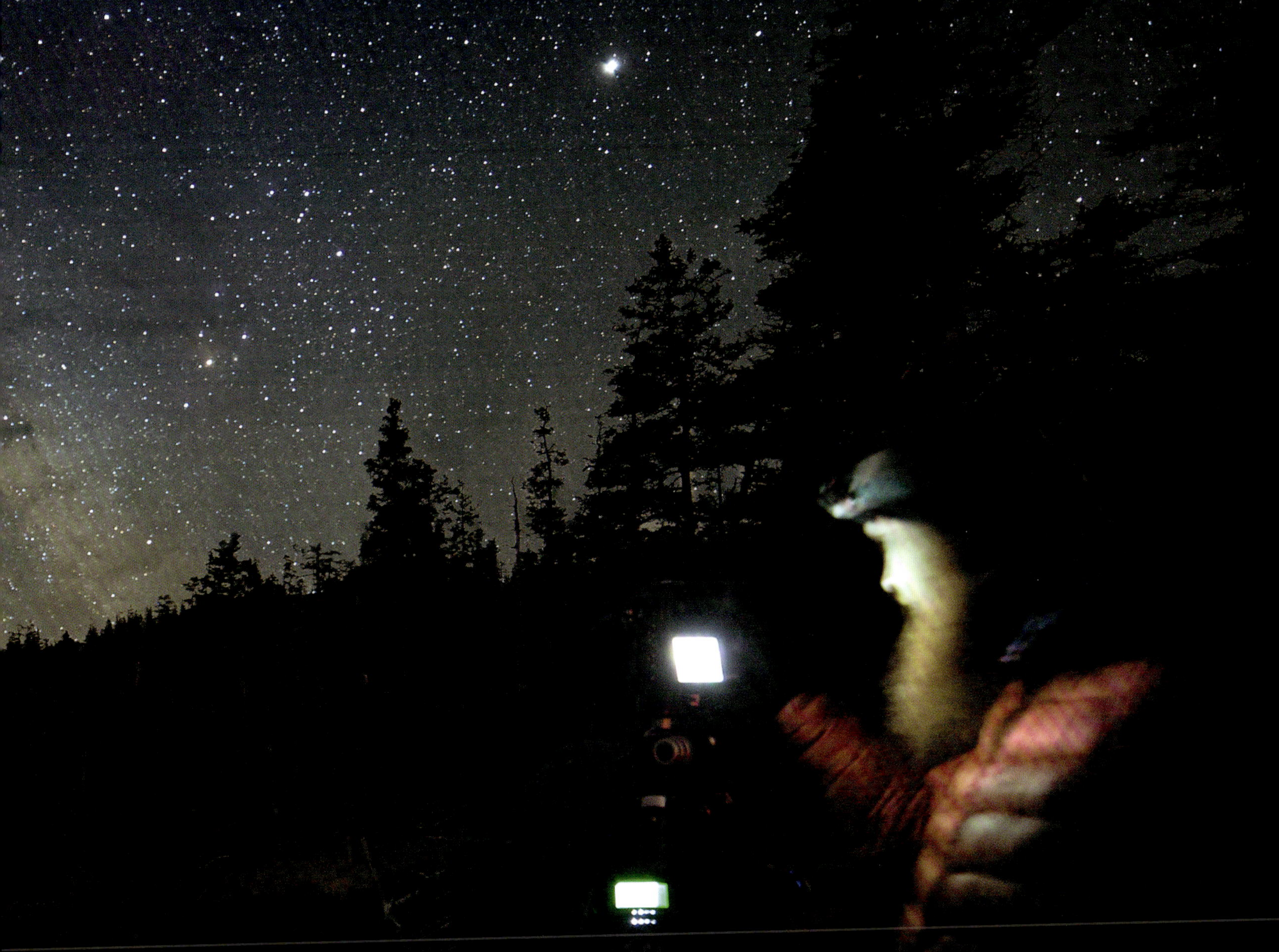

Before we jump into exposure settings (f-stop, ISO and shutter speed), we need to cover some other camera settings, both basic and advanced. Some of these you may already be very familiar with, but others are not mentioned often and may be entirely new to you. They are all important and knowing how these settings affect your images, whether the Raw file or the preview file, will help you in all aspects of digital photography, as many of them can cause issues when used incorrectly or inappropriately.

▲ Yours truly adjusting settings on my camera while photographing the Milky Way. Photo by Eric Tirrell.

6.1 SHOOT RAW

You should always shoot in Raw mode, as this will enable you to get the highest quality image out of your camera, and give you the most flexibility when editing your images. Make sure that your camera isn't set to "lossy" Raw compression, as this will result in a degradation in image quality. Set the Raw compression to "lossless" compression for no impact on image quality. "Uncompressed" Raw is not necessary and is just a waste of space. Lossless compression means that the data is compressed into a smaller file without any loss in image quality.

Also make sure you are using the highest bit-rate setting supported for you camera's Raw files. This is usually 14-bit. Some cameras allow you to select 12-bit to save space, but at the cost of image quality.

Most cameras have lossless compression and 14-bit configured by default for Raw files, but double-check your camera menus to make sure they haven't been switched by accident. Reference your camera's manual to find out where these settings are located in the menus.

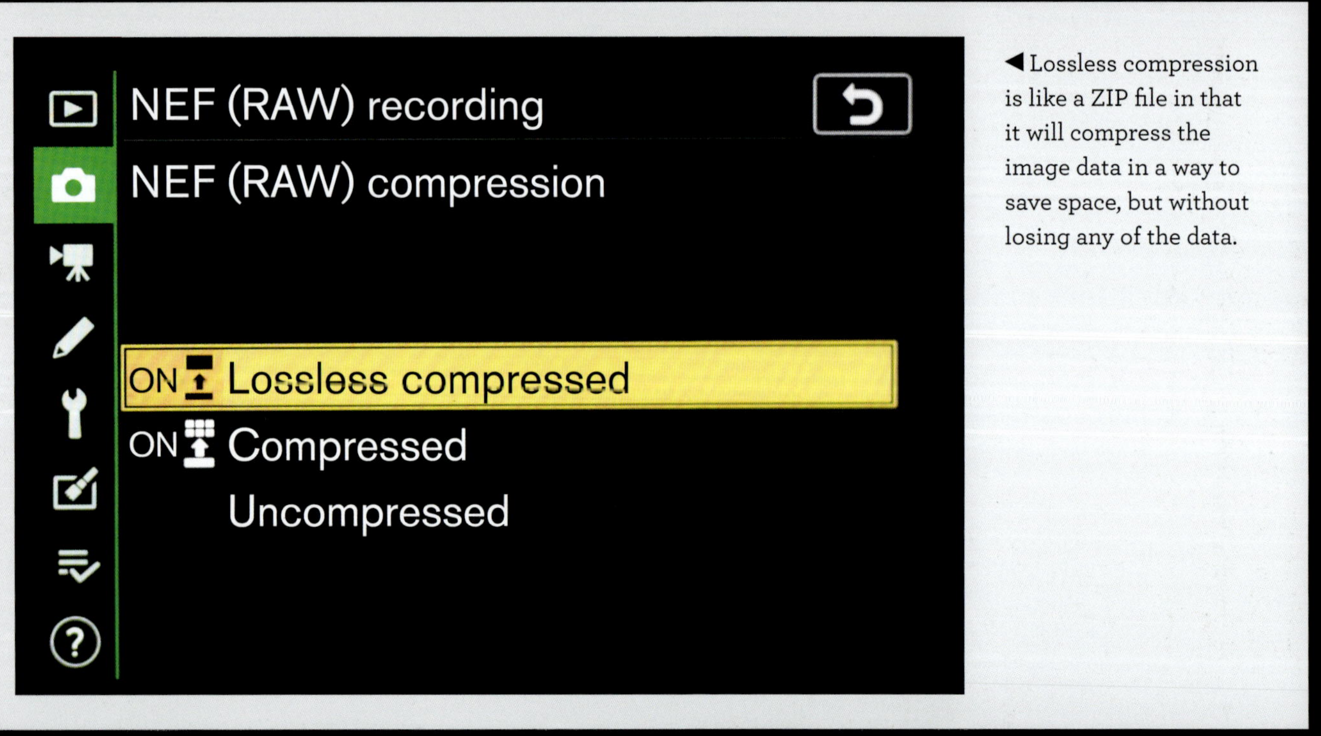

◀ Lossless compression is like a ZIP file in that it will compress the image data in a way to save space, but without losing any of the data.

6.2 WHITE BALANCE

When shooting in Raw mode, white balance is really just metadata that tells the camera or editing software how to render the colors in the image, and it can be completely altered in your Raw editing software without affecting image quality. However, the white balance affects your camera's histogram, so if the white balance is way off, the histogram won't be as accurate. Therefore, if you're using the histogram to check the exposure of the image, then it's worth paying this some attention.

Generally speaking, you can leave your camera on Daylight White Balance (5500–6500K). If that's too garishly yellow, you can use between 4000K and 5000K, but again it won't have any affect on your ability to edit your Raw file later. A white balance of Tungsten (incandescent; 3000K) is often suggested, but that is generally overwhelmingly blue, and the true color of the dark night sky is not blue. We'll look at these decisions more when we discuss color balance in the **Editing** chapter (see pages 176–9).

Your time in the field is better spent finding a good composition instead of worrying about a white balance setting that is ultimately meaningless when you start editing (assuming you are shooting Raw, which you should be).

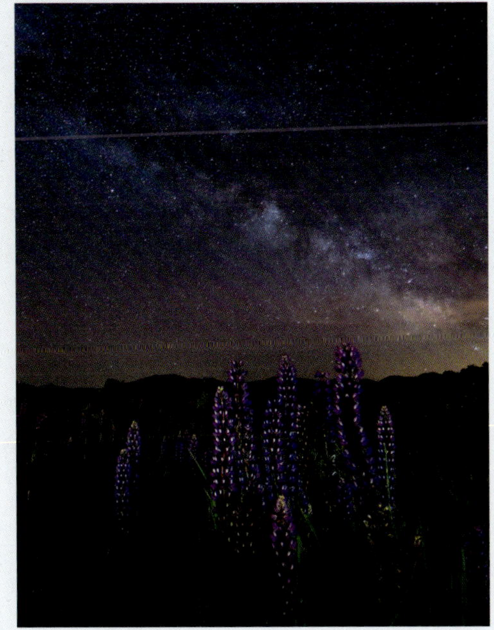

▲ Cool white balance.

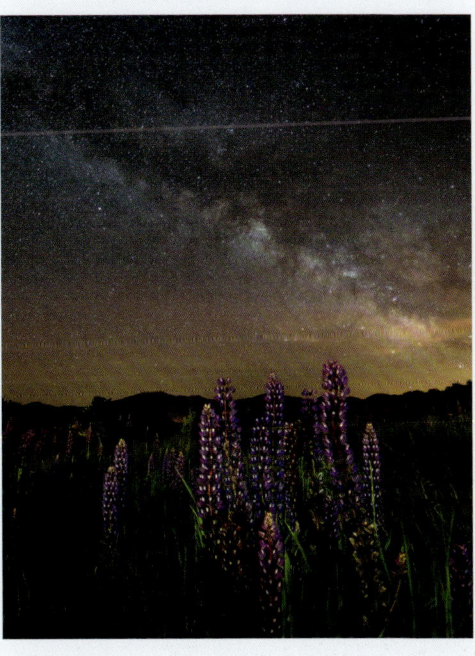

▲ Between cool and warm.

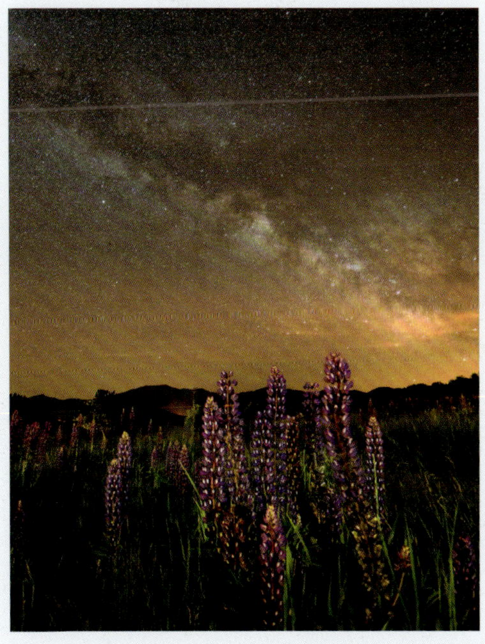

▲ Warm white balance.

6.3 CONTROLLING THE IMAGE REVIEW

When you shoot Raw, your camera generates a small JPEG file that is embedded in the Raw file, and that JPEG is what you see when you review your images on the rear LCD of your camera (and in the electronic viewfinder of mirrorless cameras). It's important to remember that some camera settings will affect the accuracy and usefulness of the JPEG preview image.

PICTURE CONTROL / CREATIVE EFFECTS

An often overlooked setting is the "Picture Control" or "Creative Style" mode (it might be called something different on your camera), which controls what creative adjustments are applied to the preview JPEG. There are usually options like Neutral, Standard, Landscape, Portrait, Vivid and so on. I highly recommend that you set the mode to Neutral, as any other setting (even Standard on some cameras) may apply too much contrast to the JPEG preview image, which will make it hard to see detail in dark night-time photos. The most obvious example of this is when you shoot a 10-minute exposure of a foreground that looks pitch black in the image review. This most likely means that you're using a creative effect that is applying too much contrast and crushing the shadows.

VIGNETTE & LENS DISTORTION CONTROL

Most digital cameras offer settings to correct lens vignetting and lens distortion (often called "Lens Corrections" in the menus). Again these apply to the JPEG preview image, but not the Raw file. I usually turn these off so that I can get a better idea of what the Raw file will look like. However, as you'll often want to correct any lens vignetting in post, you might want to turn this setting on to see what your image looks like with the vignette reduced.

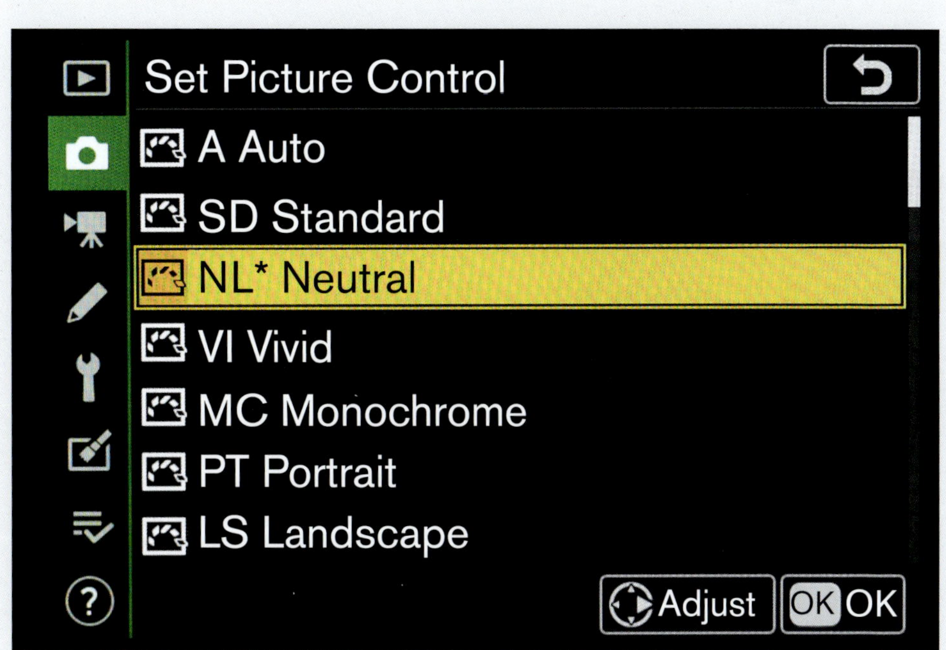

▲ On Nikon cameras, the creative effects you can apply to JPEGs in image review are found in the "Picture Control" menu.

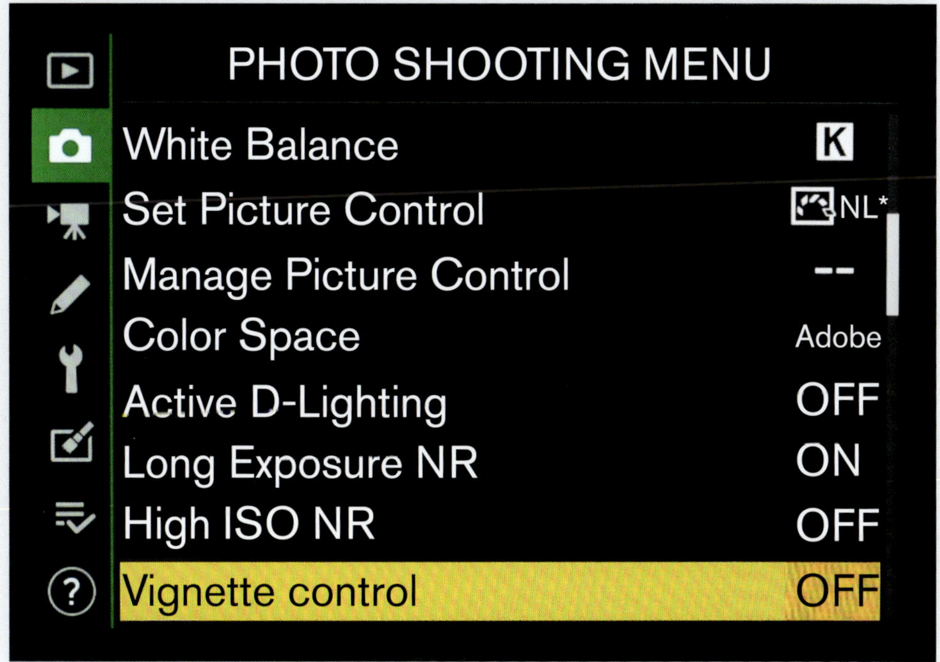

▲ On Nikon cameras, many of these settings are in the Photo Shooting menu.

ROTATE TALL

I recommend turning the "Rotate Tall" (or similar) playback feature off. Otherwise, vertical images will be rotated on the camera's rear LCD screen to appear upright when the camera is horizontal. When you're shooting a vertical image with your camera mounted to your tripod in that position, it makes much more sense to have the photos appear upright without having to rotate the camera.

HIGH ISO NOISE REDUCTION

This is one of those settings that easily confuses people. This setting only affects JPEG files, including the preview that you see on the back of your camera when shooting Raw. You do not need this setting turned on, it has no affect on Raw files. Disable it so you can see a truer version of your image when previewing it on the camera's LCD. Set it to "Off" instead of "Low," "Medium" or "High" (or any similar settings that your specific camera may have).

COLOR SPACE

This is another confusing setting, because just like High ISO Noise Reduction, the Color Space setting in your camera only affects JPEG files and the preview you see on your camera. It has no affect on Raw files. Set it to Adobe RGB, instead of sRGB, for better-looking JPEG files and previews. Adobe RGB is a larger color space than sRGB, and thus capable of better color reproduction. But ultimately, this setting is not important for your Raw shooting.

Some cameras are more prone to hot pixels than others, and they are more common in images taken with long exposures and high ISOs.

In order to eliminate hot pixels, most digital cameras have a "Long Exposure Noise Reduction" feature built in that can be turned on and off as needed. When enabled, after taking a picture, the camera will automatically take another picture with the same exact settings, only with the shutter closed so that no light enters the camera. This second image is known as a "dark frame" because it is a black image, but it's not just black, it will contain hot pixels and noise from the camera electronics. The camera then uses this black frame to subtract out the hot pixels from the original image before writing out the final Raw file. This is known as "dark frame subtraction".

While it's generally a good idea to have this enabled, it does mean that your exposures will take twice as long because of the dark frame. In cases where you don't have that kind of spare time—for example, if you need to move onto another composition or if the Milky Way has now lined up into the position you want and you have to move onto your star shots—you may decide to turn it off and deal with removing the hot pixels in software.

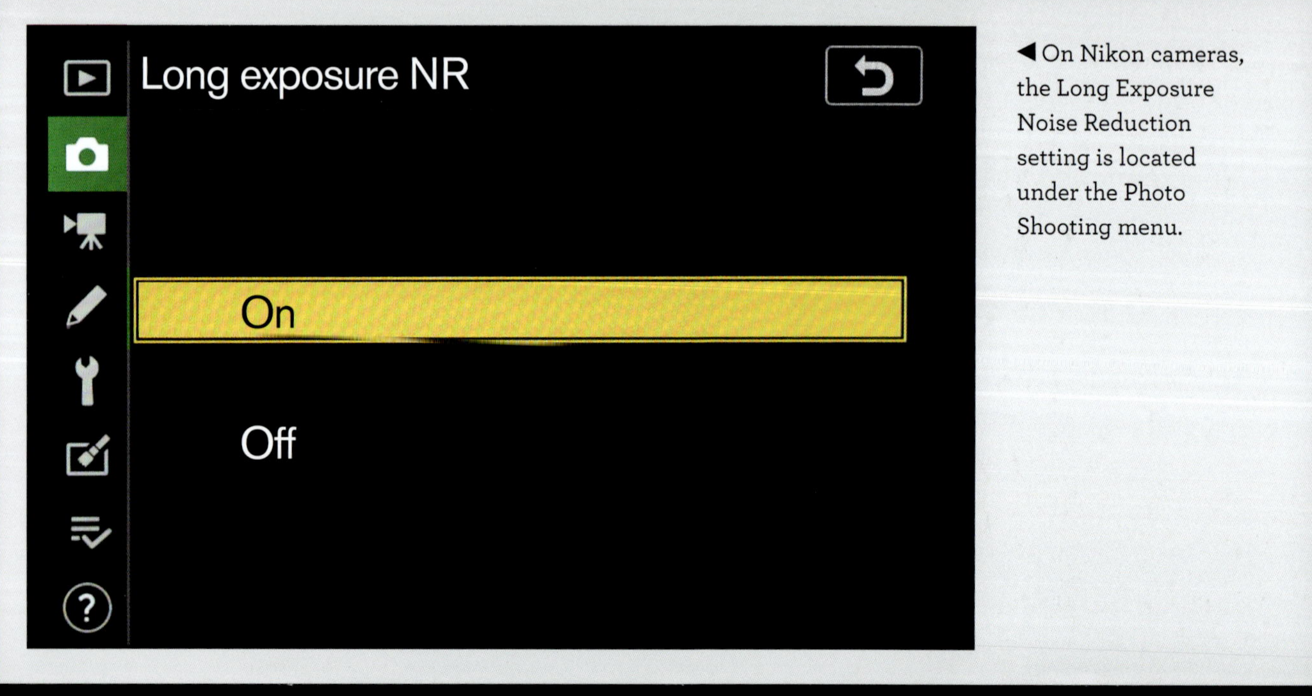

◀ On Nikon cameras, the Long Exposure Noise Reduction setting is located under the Photo Shooting menu.

6.5 EXPOSURE DELAY & MIRROR LOCK-UP

There's always a chance that the shutter or mirror can cause a slight vibration in the camera and blur the shot. This is especially true with slow shutter speeds, where any movement of the camera will show up as motion blur.

For this reason, I almost always have a delay configured in my camera so that the exposure is taken after the shutter and/or mirror have been opened for at least a second.

On Nikon cameras you can enable this through the Exposure Delay setting — reference your camera's manual to find out what this feature may be called on your model. Some DSLRs only have a Mirror Lock-up mode, where the mirror flips up with the push of the shutter button, and the next push of the shutter causes the actual exposure to be taken.

6.6 OTHER SETTINGS

There are a few other settings or features that your camera may have that are worth noting.

Virtual Horizon Make sure you know how to get into this mode as it makes leveling your camera at night much easier. It gives you a virtual level on your camera's LCD. Not all cameras have this option.

Turn Off Auto-Focus Make sure you disable Auto-Focus at night so that you don't accidentally change focus by hitting the focus button. You'll almost always be using Manual focus in the dark. You can always enable Auto-Focus as needed.

Disable Extra Lights You might want to cover up or disable any extra lights on your camera, especially when out with other photographers. I use gaffer tape to cover up these lights.

Turn Down Monitor Brightness Your eyes and fellow photographers will thank you if you turn down your monitor brightness at night. You can always turn it up temporarily to see the preview image better, but your night vision (and the night vision of those around you) will be affected by a bright LCD, not to mention it will take away from your enjoyment of the dark sky.

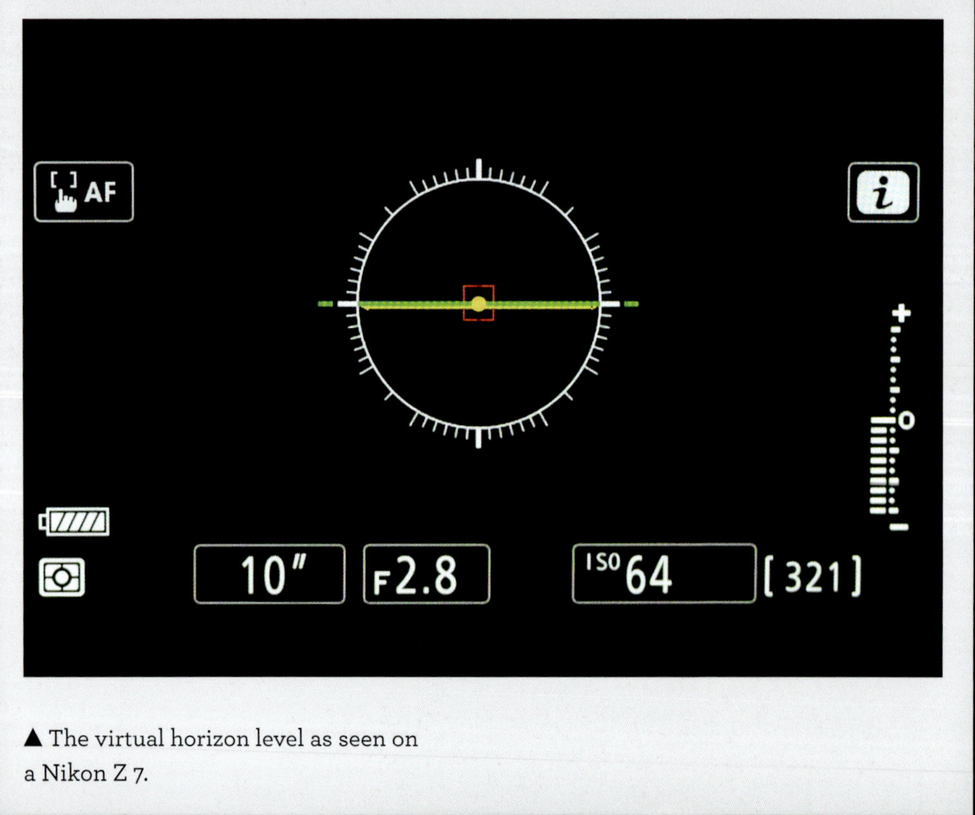

▲ The virtual horizon level as seen on a Nikon Z 7.

▶ The Milky Way during twilight on the coast of Maine.

Nikon D850 with NIKKOR 14-24mm f/2.8 lens at 14mm, f/2.8 for all shots.

Sky: Single photograph, ISO 12800, 20 seconds.

Foreground: Focus stack of four shots for depth of field, all taken at ISO 3200 and shutter speed of 2 minutes.

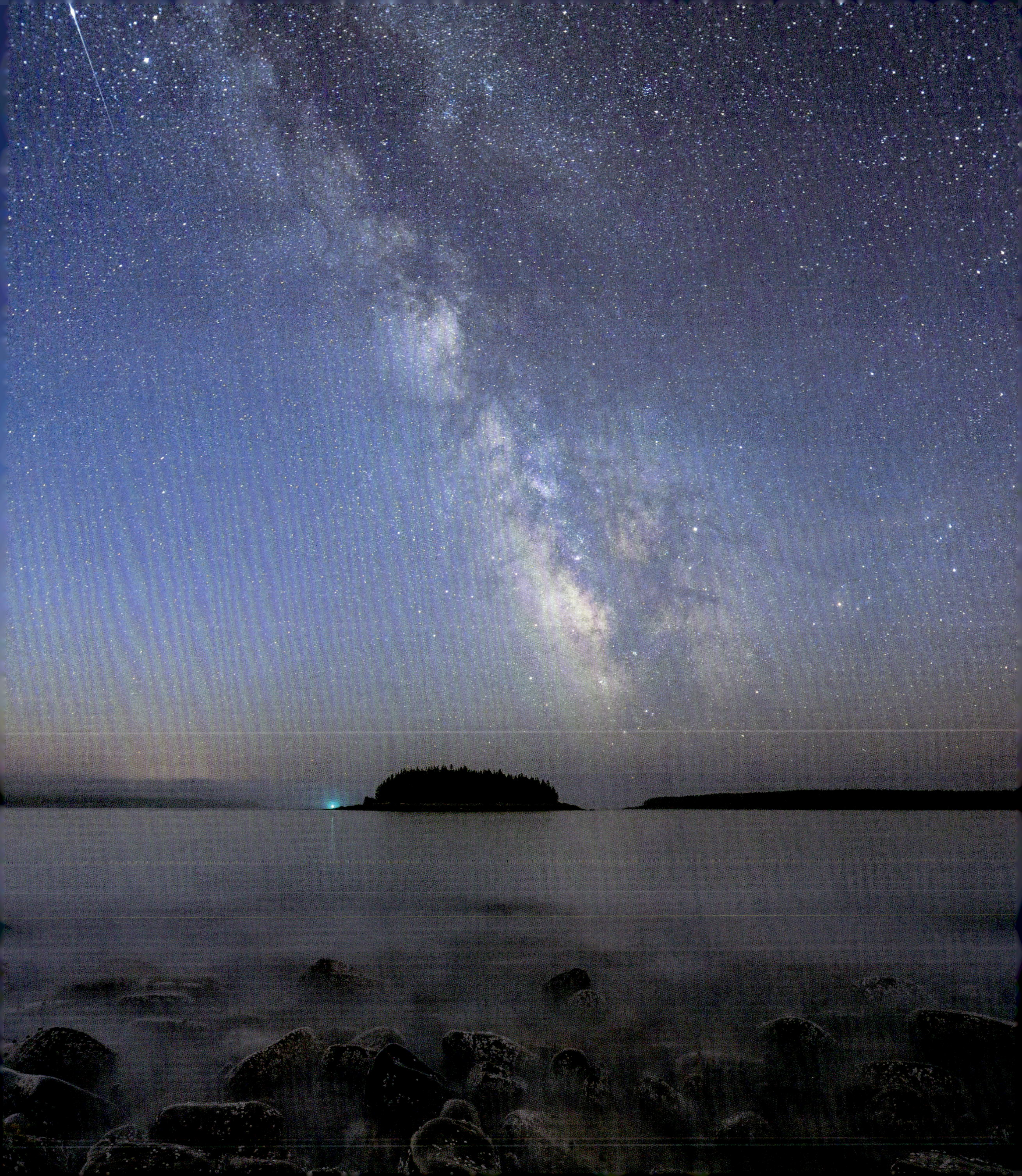

7

EXPOSURE SETTINGS

The Milky Way, flanked by Mars and Jupiter, reflects in the water on a mudflat.

Nikon D850, Nikon 14-24mm lens at 14mm, f/2.8.

Sky: Star stack of seven shots for low noise and pinpoint stars, each at ISO 6400, 10 seconds.

Foreground: 20-second exposure taken less than two minutes before I took the photographs for the sky. The tide was going out, and on the mudflats it goes out really fast, so the 20-second shot had more water in the foreground on the mudflats, and the reflection of the stars was better.

7.1 THE BASICS

If you're just getting your feet wet with landscape astrophotography and you don't want to deal with the more complicated techniques of star stacking and using separate foreground images, then exposure settings are pretty simple: Use the fastest aperture on your lens (often f/2.8 for lenses popular for night photography), ISO 3200 (lower ISOs will protect star color but it will be harder to see the results on the camera's LCD; higher ones will make it easier to see what you're getting), and a shutter speed of 10–30 seconds. Try those and see how your image looks. If it's way too bright, use a shorter shutter speed and/or a lower ISO. If the stars are trailing too much, use a shorter shutter speed. Take test shots with different exposure settings and see what works. Make good use of the image review on your camera's LCD screen; zoom in and see how the stars and foreground look. Don't get too caught up in the details at first, it is not hard to figure out a good exposure in the dark with patience and practice.

▶ Reflection at high tide on a calm night on the coast of Maine.

A single photograph taken with my Nikon Z 7, with FTZ lens adapter and Nikon 14-24mm f/2.8 lens at 14mm, f/2.8, ISO 3200, for 30 seconds. The foreground is not in good focus, there is a lot of noise throughout the image, and the stars are trailing, but these things are not noticeable in small prints or when sharing the image on websites or social media.

Just remember that without a separate foreground photograph, your foreground is likely to be very dark, noisy and/or out of focus, depending on where you're shooting and how far away the foreground is from your lens. A more distant foreground will be sharper when the focus is set on the stars, and an area with more ambient light (for example, a beach with a nearby a lighthouse, or a mountain lit up by a nearby town) will have more light hitting the foreground. You can shine a light on your foreground — often referred to as "light painting — to make it brighter (see page 132 in the **Lighting** chapter for details).

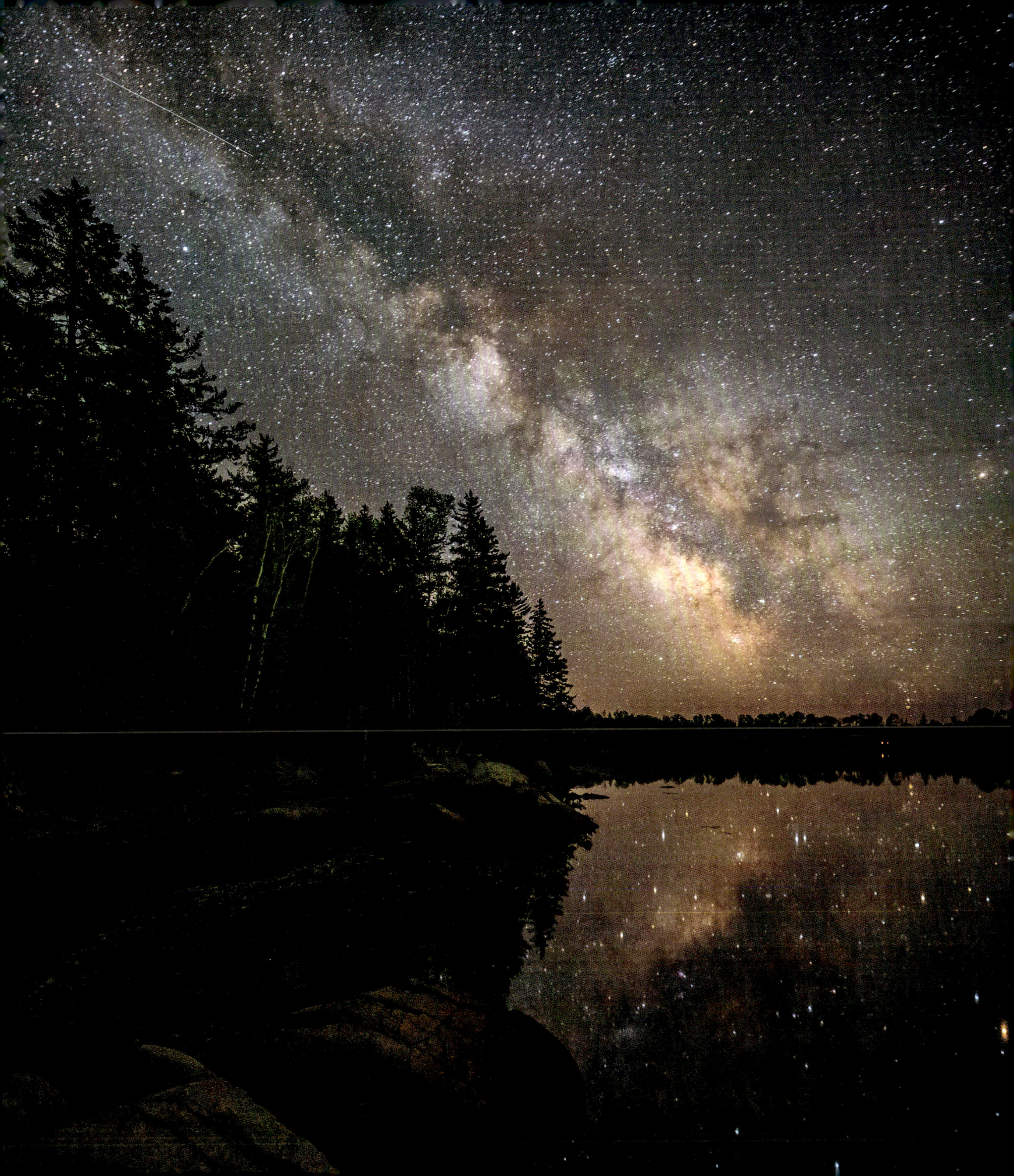

7.2 THE HISTOGRAM

You've probably seen this graph before, whether on your camera's rear screen or in image-editing software. This graph is called a histogram, and it provides a visual representation of the distribution of tones in an image.

The left end of the histogram represents pure black, and the right end of the histogram represents pure white. We can further break down the histogram into thirds, with the left third considered the "shadows," the middle third considered the "mid-tones," and the right third considered the "highlights."

The bottom of the histogram represents no pixels having that tonal value, and the top represents many pixels having that tonal value. The tall peaks you see in a histogram indicate a lot of pixels with a certain tonal value in an image. So a peak close to the left edge of the histogram would indicate a lot of very dark pixels in the image; a peak in the middle indicates that there are a lot of medium-brightness (mid-tone) pixels in the image; and a peak toward the right end of the histogram indicates that there are a lot of very bright (highlight) pixels in the image.

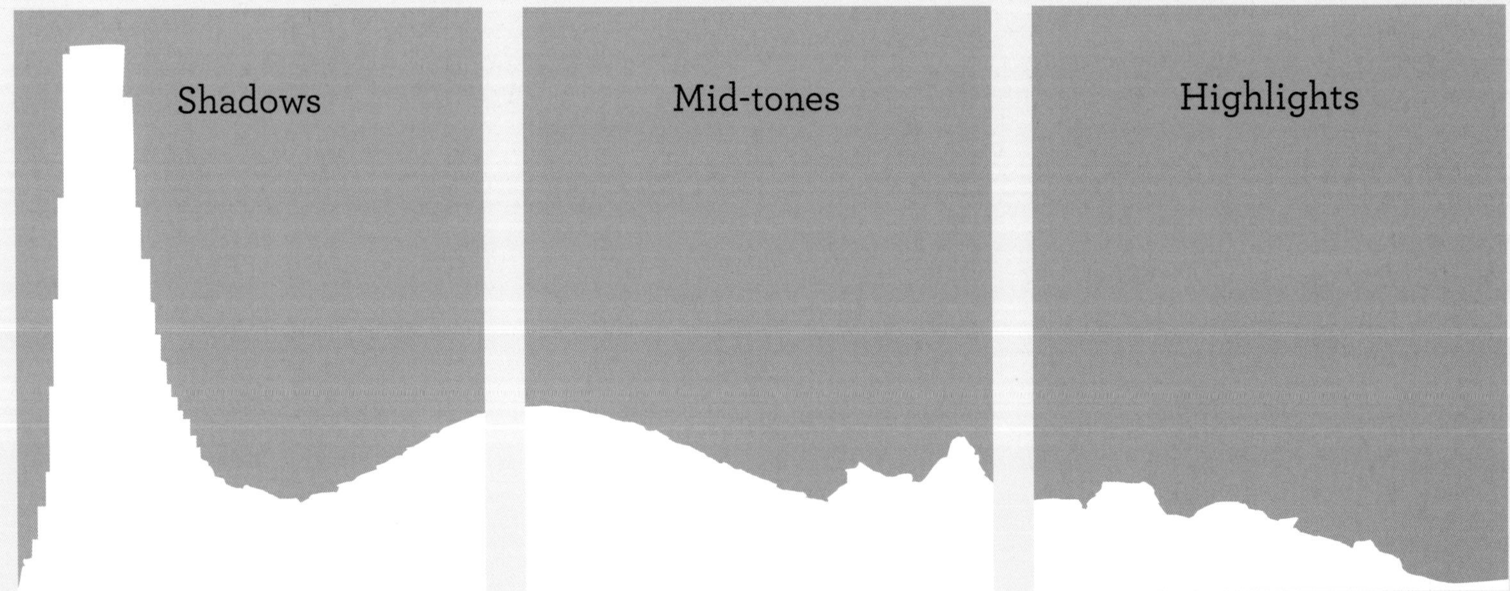

▲ This histogram indicates that there are some very dark pixels in the image it represents, but mid-tones and highlights are also present.

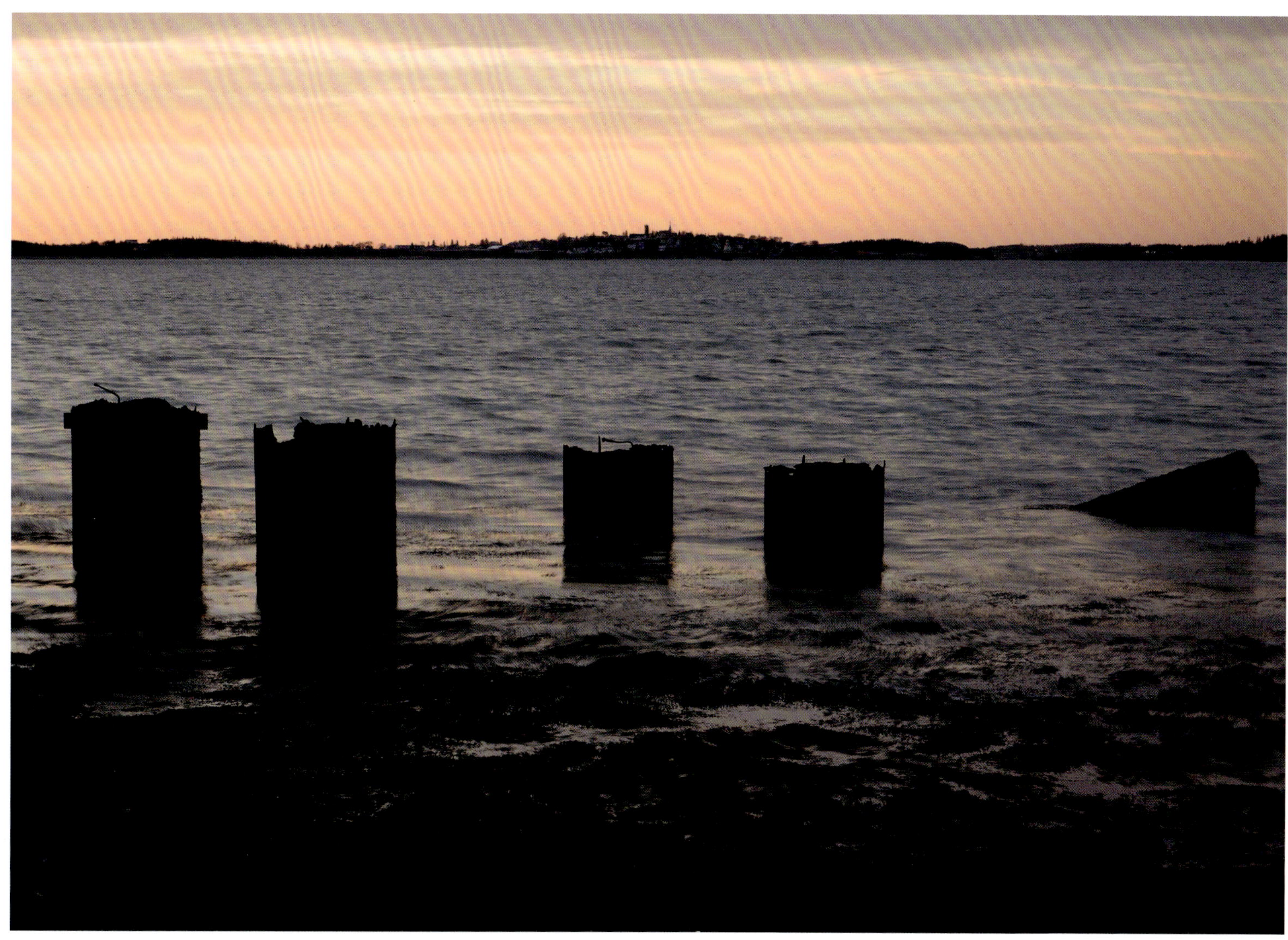

▲ The histogram opposite is for this image.

Ok, so what's the point of the histogram?

Surely you can look at the image itself and judge how bright it is, right? Well, not always. If your camera screen or computer display are too bright or too dark, you will not be able to accurately judge the tones in the image. This is particularly important when taking pictures of the dark night sky, when you might adjust the brightness on your camera's LCD and turn it up high in order to see the image. This might make the image appear bright when it's not. However, the histogram will always tell you what's really going on in an image.

More importantly, the histogram will tell you if your image is "clipping" in the blacks or whites. A pixel is "clipped" if the histogram scale juts up against the left (pure black) or right (pure white) end of the frame. In a pure black pixel no light has been collected, or the signal (the electronic translation of photons into a digital image) has not been amplified enough to relate what little light was collected. In a pure white pixel either too much light has been collected or the ISO has amplified the signal to pure white.

For landscape astrophotography, it is important to know if the sky photographs are too bright, thus clipping many stars and whatever planets might have been visible to white. We also want to know if the foreground photographs are too dark, which would cause the shadows to clip to black. You can use the histogram to judge these issues.

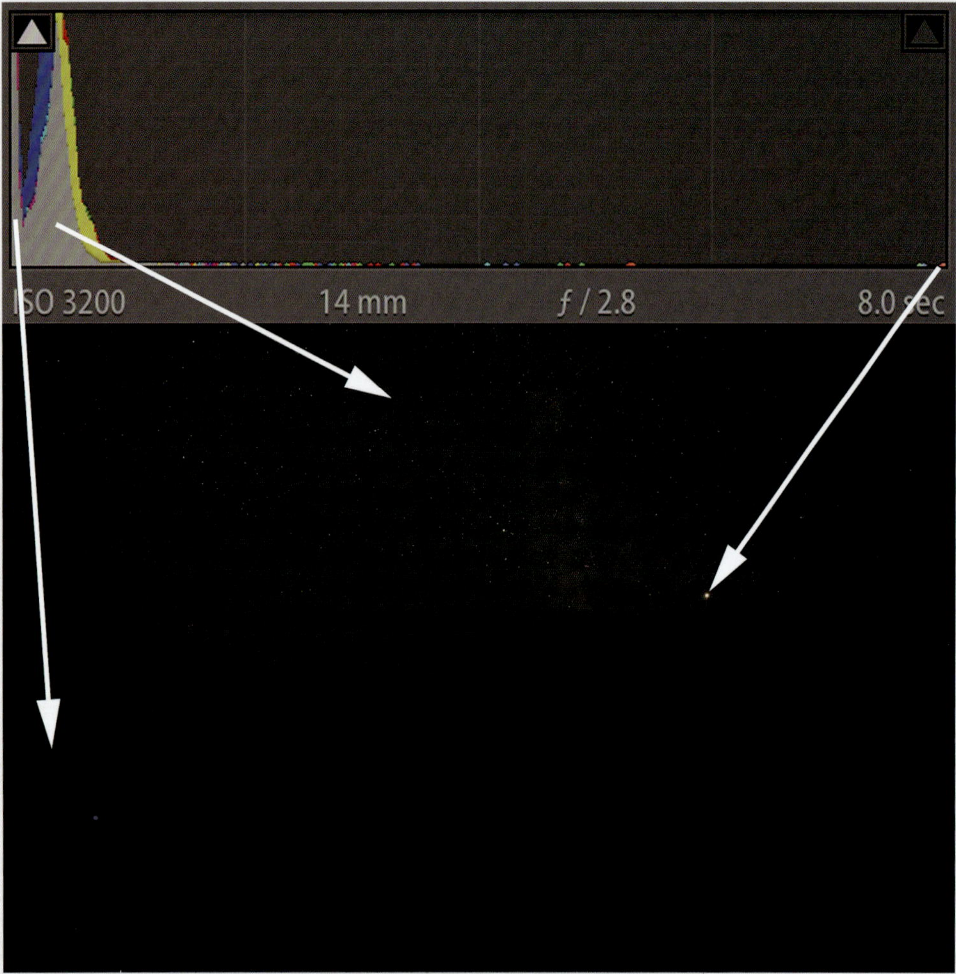

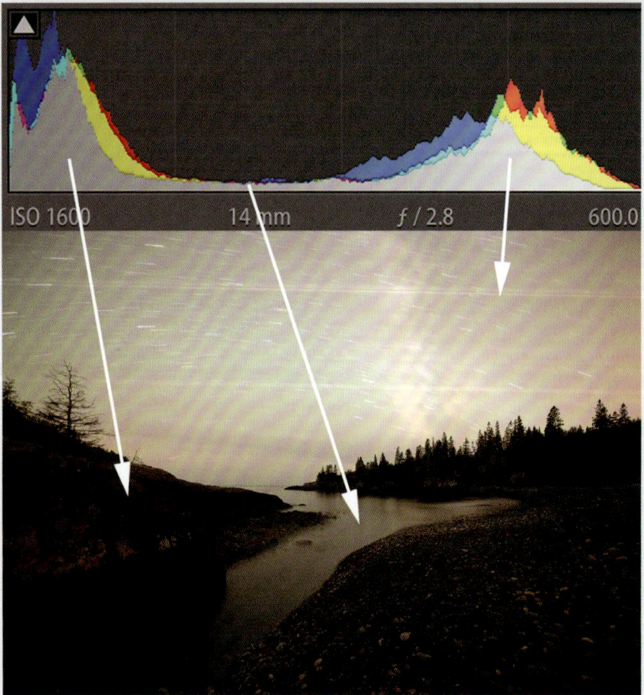

▲ This is a sky image to be used for star stacking, captured at 14mm, f/2.8, ISO 3200, 8 seconds.

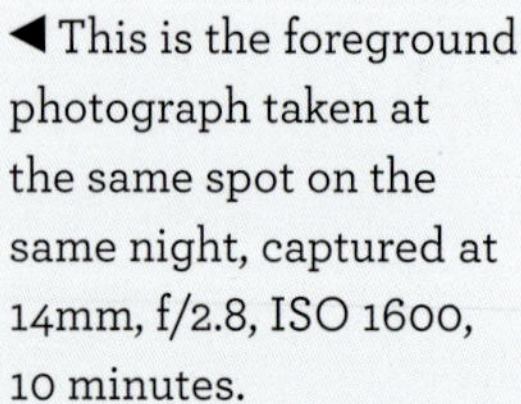

◀ This is the foreground photograph taken at the same spot on the same night, captured at 14mm, f/2.8, ISO 1600, 10 minutes.

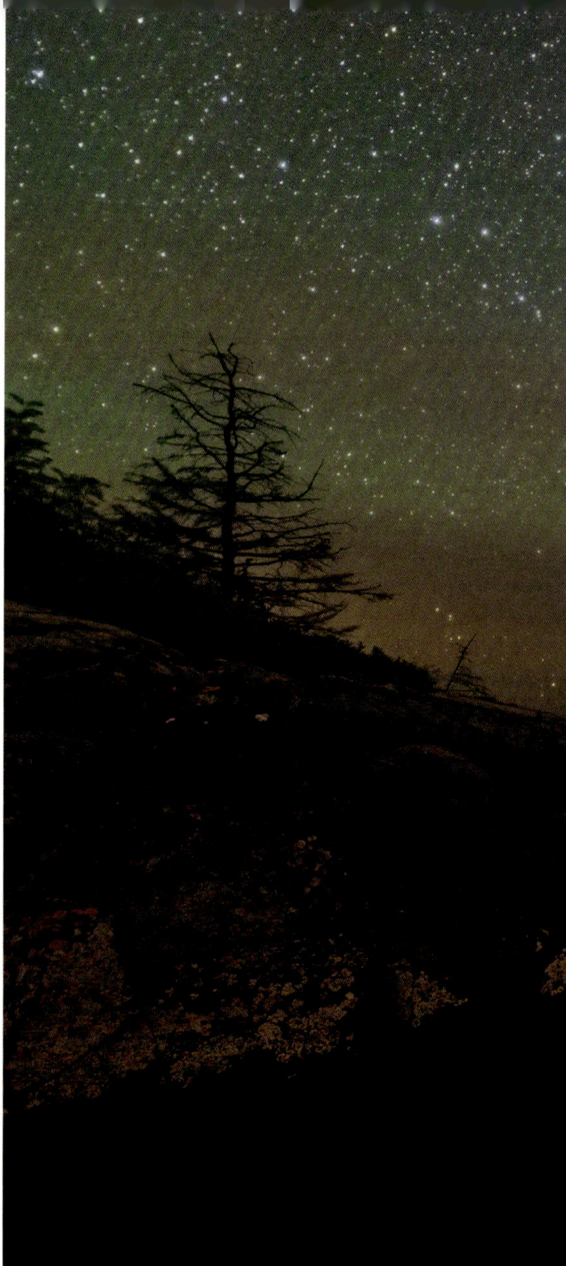

The image at the top left of the page is an exposure to be used for star stacking. It is incredibly dark, but there is still detail in the sky. There is a hump against the left edge of the histogram which indicates a part of the image is basically clipped to black. This hump must correspond to the foreground, since it is the darkest part of the image. In this case, it isn't a problem, because we will be replacing the foreground with a separate, brighter foreground exposure in editing.

The big peak to the right of that is the brightness level of the sky. It is certainly

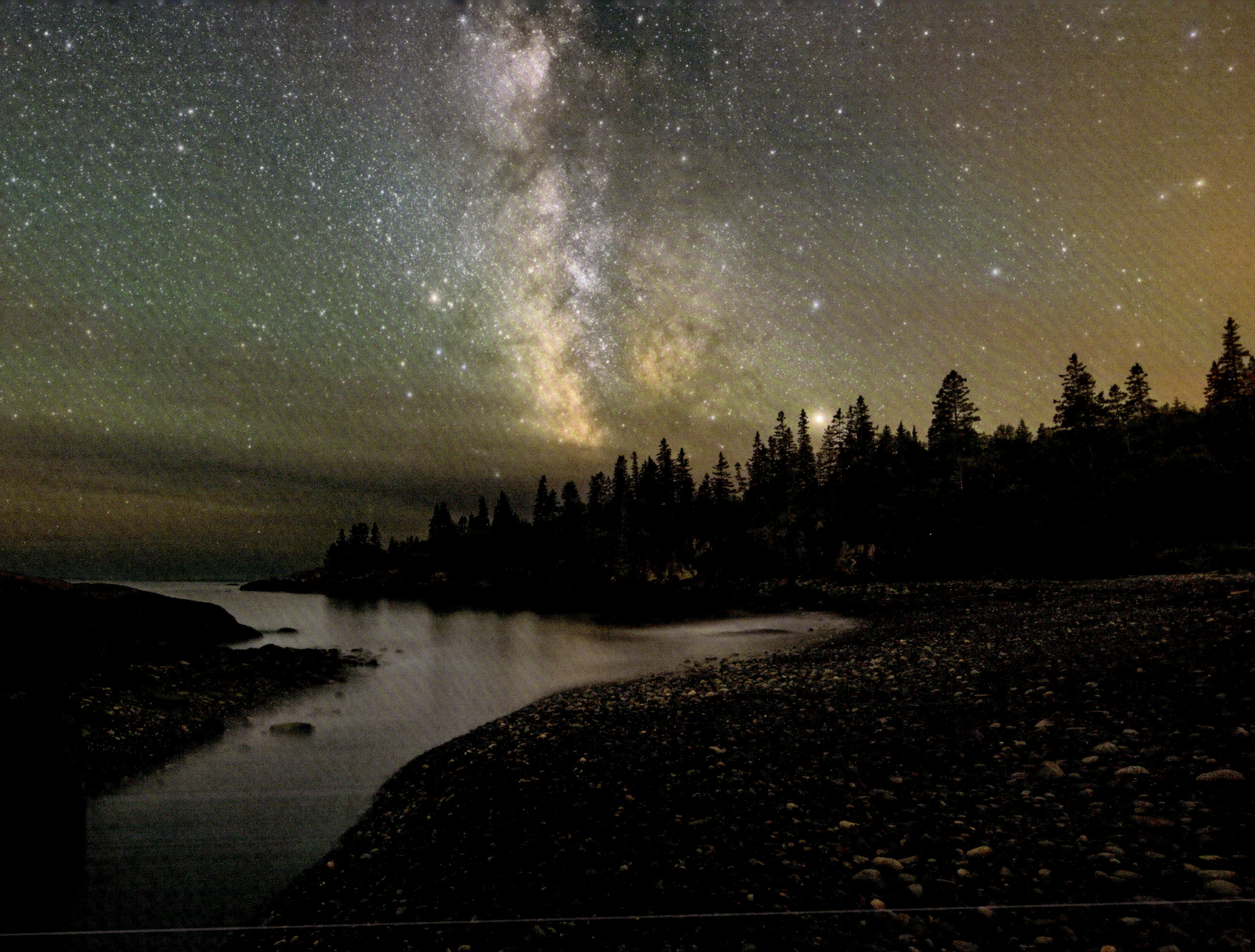

dark, but since it is not pushed up against the left side of the histogram, we know that it is not clipped to black. The tiny bumps across the bottom of this histogram represent the brightness of various stars, with the bump at the right edge indicating that Jupiter (the bright spot right above the trees) is probably clipping to white, which is fine, since it is much brighter than the rest of the sky.

In the histogram of the foreground (left), the peaks on the left again correspond to the foreground brightness. It's dark, but we can see that it is not pure black, so detail is retained. Some of the darkest spots of the foreground may still be clipped to black but that is normal and not a problem. The peaks on the right side of the histogram indicate the brightness of the sky, which we don't need to care about in this photograph because the sky will be replaced in editing. The "valley" between the two peaks on the histogram corresponds to the mid-tones of the water.

▲ This is the final edit after star stacking, exposure blending and creative edits. As you can see, there was plenty of detail in the sky even though the images it was based on (like the one opposite, top) appear to be very dark.

7.3 MANUAL MODE

Manual mode, usually indicated by an "M" on your camera's mode selection dial or menu, is the only mode you can use at night. There simply isn't enough light for the camera to make an intelligent decision when in any of the other modes that rely on some amount of automation, and with the techniques needed to minimize star trailing and capture separate foreground photographs, you'll need to choose all the f-stop, shutter speed and ISO settings yourself.

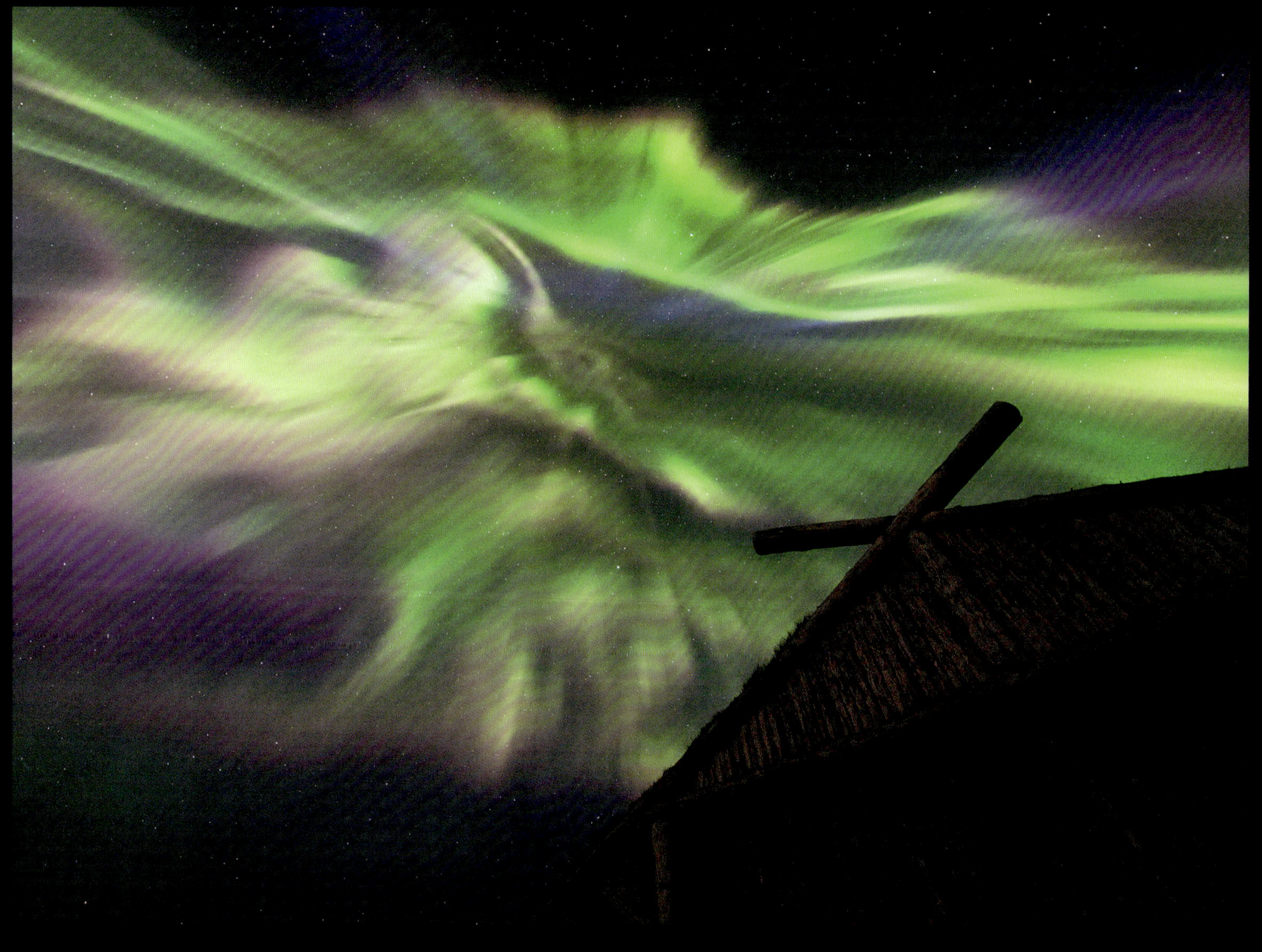

7.3.1 F-STOP

Generally speaking, using the maximum aperture (lowest f-stop number) of your lens is always desirable when shooting at night because it lets the most light in with minimum movement in the image. But you may need to adjust it based on your lens's performance and whether you're taking an exposure of the stars or the foreground.

STARS

The f-stop you use for star exposures is ideally going to be the lowest f-stop number that produces acceptably sharp stars with minimal aberrations. The definitions of "acceptably sharp" and "minimal aberrations" are subjective and entirely up to you. If you're only going to post online and/or make small prints, then a slight softness or distortion in the stars isn't going to show up too much. You want to balance capturing as much light as possible using the lowest f-stop you can get away with, without losing too much quality.

If you're just getting started, you can use whatever that lowest f-stop number is on your lens—you'll most likely be happy with the results at small sizes. However, if you zoom in on the stars, you may see a different story—one that includes stars that look like flying saucers or an undiscovered planet with rings. These are caused by lens aberrations (see page 34).

On most ultra-wide-angle lenses, such as the Nikon 14-24mm f/2.8, Canon 16-35mm f/2.8 or Rokinon 14mm f/2.8, you will get good results at f/2.8. The stars may not be perfect around the edges of the frame, but overall the images will look great.

However, with many ultra-fast lenses of any focal length, particularly f/1.4 or faster lenses, the stars often have strong aberrations at f/1.4 (or the lowest f-stop number). These can often be reduced substantially by stopping down to f/2 or f/2.8. Test your lens on a starry night to see how it works and what you find acceptable.

Don't get frustrated if the lens captures some star aberrations around the edges or corners of the frame—this is pretty normal, even with very expensive lenses. But if you've got flying saucers throughout your entire frame, then you may need to stop the lens down or look for an alternative.

◀ Nikon D810A, 14-24mm f/2.8 lens at 14mm, f/2.8, ISO 12,800, 2 seconds.

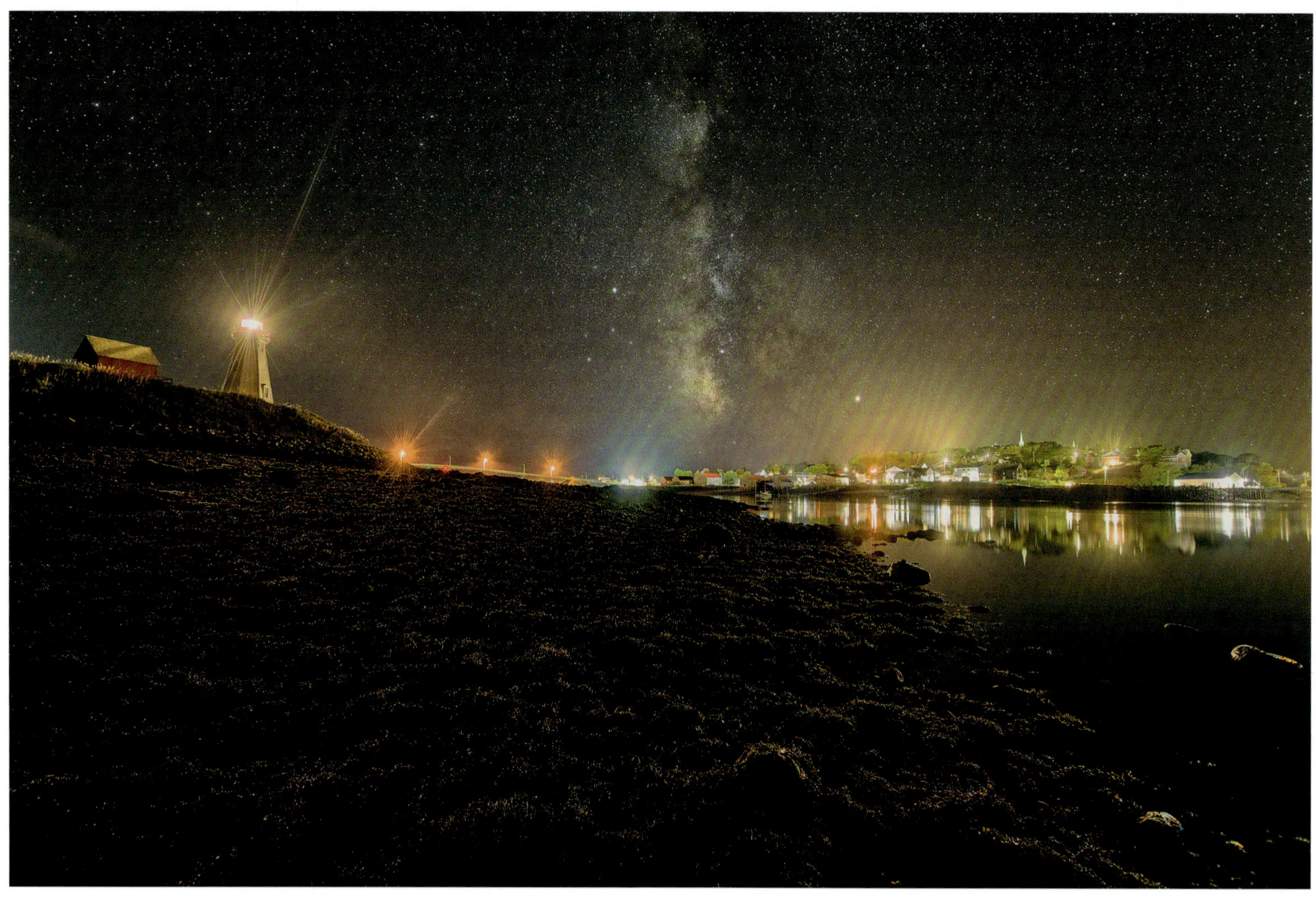

FOREGROUND

For foreground photographs you can often use the lowest f-stop for your lens, letting in the maximum amount of light. This will allow you to use a shorter shutter speed, although we're still talking often a minute or more. But that's pretty quick in the dark!

If you are focus stacking your images, you may want to consider using a higher f-stop number for a wider depth of field. This will require a longer shutter speed but fewer photographs to achieve optimum focus.

If you are introducing artificial light (i.e. light painting, see page 132) or are in an area with a lot of ambient light, then you may be able to use a high f-stop (for example, f/5.6 or f/8), getting pretty much the entire scene in focus.

▲ Looking back at the town of Lubec, Maine, from Campobello Island, New Brunswick . The lighthouse in the foreground is Mulholland Point Lighthouse on Campobello.

I wasn't sure if this shot would work, given all the lights from downtown Lubec, but it did.

Nikon Z 7 with FTZ lens adapter and Nikon 14-24mm f/2.8 lens at 14mm, f/2.8 for all shots.

Sky: Star stack of 20 exposures, each at ISO 3200 and 8 seconds.

Foreground: There was so much ambient light from the town lights that I was able to use the foreground from the star-stacked result for some of the image. I used another shot at ISO 400 for 2 minutes with the focus pulled in to capture the seaweed in the foreground in focus, and one more shot at ISO 400 for 10 seconds for the town lights since they were blown out in the star-stacked result at ISO 3200.

The flares from the lighthouse and bridge lights are from the lens.

7.3.2 SHUTTER SPEED

The length of time you open the shutter will depend on a few different factors, in particular which details you are trying to capture.

Before we dive into details, I want to briefly summarize the main considerations so you can quickly reference this in the future:

If you are star stacking your images, use 10-second or shorter shutter speeds for your sky exposures. If you are using a single exposure for your sky, then keep the shutter speed to 30 seconds maximum. (I prefer no longer than 20 seconds to keep the star trails minimal.) And if you are taking separate exposures for the foreground, then start with a shutter speed of 1 minute and go up from there until you're happy with the level of detail and noise. In very dark areas, I often use shutter speeds as long as 10 minutes for foreground shots. Onto the details!

STARS

In this book we look at capturing pinpoint stars, or at least minimizing star trails so that they still appear to look like stars instead of hot dogs when printed large.

You may have heard of the "500 rule," which says that to get the shutter speed for sharp stars, you divide 500 by the focal length of your lens (or the 35mm full-frame equivalent), with the result being the shutter speed for minimal star trails. However, this rule is outdated when it comes to modern high-pixel-density sensors and the very large prints that can be produced these days. For example, for a 14mm lens on a full-frame camera, 500 / 14 = 35.7 seconds. But a 35-second exposure at 14mm would be way too long. You can reduce the rule number to 400 or 300 for better results, but the best way to calculate your shutter speed is to use an algorithm that was designed for just this purpose.

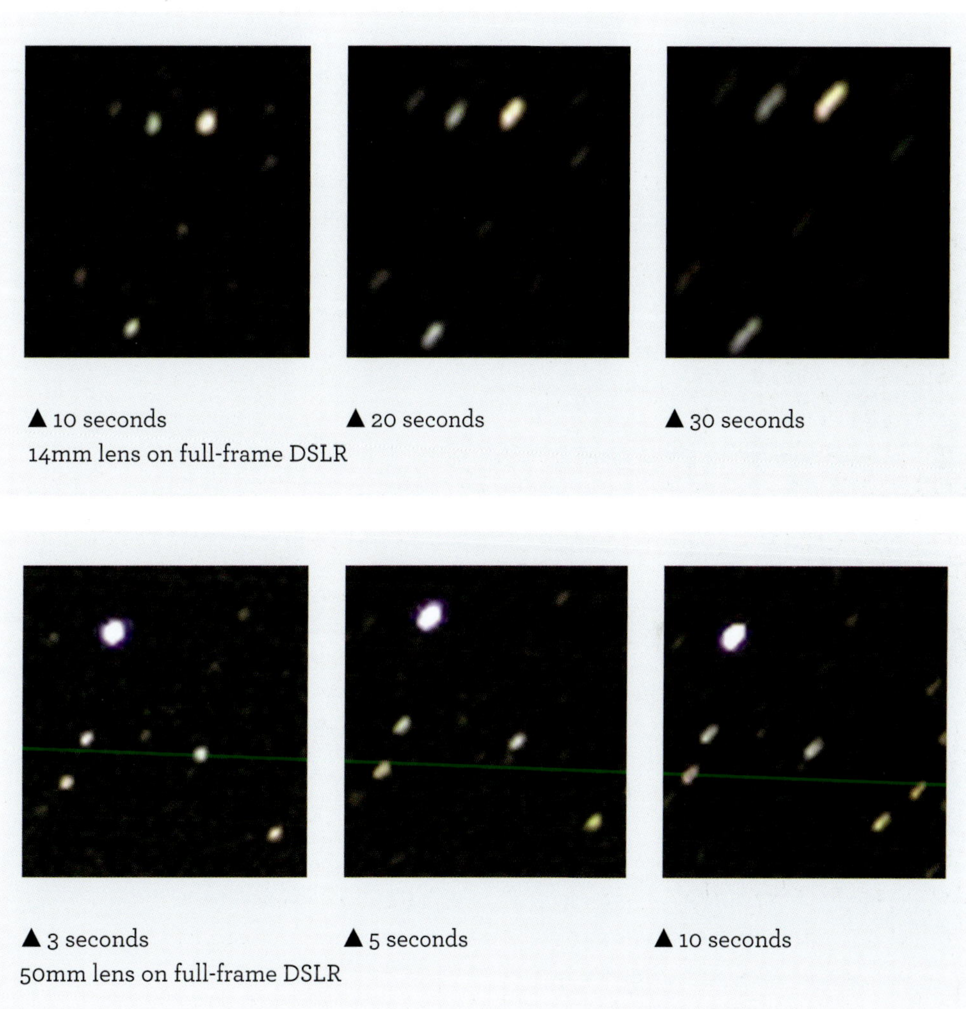

▲ 10 seconds ▲ 20 seconds ▲ 30 seconds
14mm lens on full-frame DSLR

▲ 3 seconds ▲ 5 seconds ▲ 10 seconds
50mm lens on full-frame DSLR

SPOT STARS TOOL IN PHOTOPILLS

The Spot Stars tool in the PhotoPills app, available for iOS and Android devices, is an easy way to make this calculation. PhotoPills is an amazing app with an enormous number of useful tools — we cover the "Planner" feature later in the **Planning** chapter (see page 142).

Below is an example of using the Spot Stars tool in PhotoPills on an iPhone: I have entered a focal length of 14mm, an aperture of f/2.8, and chosen my camera (Nikon Z 7) from the list of cameras. The setting at the top with an icon that looks like a crooked Y is the "minimum declination" of the stars to be captured in the composition you have in mind. This means the smallest number of degrees away from the celestial equator (or the projection of the Earth's equator into space) that you plan to have in your shot. Stars will appear to trail less the farther they are from the celestial equator. This is not terribly important for wide-angle lenses since we are capturing a huge portion of the sky, so leave it at "0" to get the most aggressive shutter speed calculation for pinpoint stars.

The setting at the far right at the top that looks like a cluster of five stars lets you choose a "Default" or "Accurate" limit of star trailing for the algorithm. If you choose "Accurate," as I did in this example, you will get a shutter speed that will produce spot stars, or very close to it. If you choose "Default," then you will get a longer shutter speed that is double the "Accurate" value. This longer shutter speed will still give you fairly sharp stars but they will visibly trail a little bit. If you want to print big with reasonably pinpoint stars and if you are star stacking your images go with "Accurate."

If you are taking exposures for a panorama, it's likely you will not be star stacking them, as it would take a long time to capture and process that many star stacks, considering 10 or so frames (taken by panning the camera on the tripod head) are required for a panorama. In this case, use a longer shutter speed (the one given by "Default" or even a little longer) to sacrifice a little star trailing for a higher signal-to-noise ratio.

In the lower half of the screen you will see the values for the "NPF Rule" and the "500 Rule." Use the NPF Rule, which is based on a mathematical formula created by Frédéric Michaud for the Société Astronòmique du Havre. The acronym represents the variables in the formula, where N stands for aperture, P for pixel density and F for focal length.

Even with a calculation given to you by a tool like this, it's important to take test shots and see for yourself how the stars look. Maybe you can push the shutter speed to something a little longer and still get sharp stars for large prints. For example, the Spot Stars tool tells me that approximately 8 seconds (7.73) will produce pinpoint stars when using a focal length of 14mm on my Nikon Z 7, but in practice, I find that I can use 10 seconds and get good, sharp stars.

Below is a simple chart with a list of shutter speeds for sharp stars and barely noticeable star trails at some common focal lengths. If you're using a focal length not listed in this table, you can simply round up or down to the nearest listed focal length. If you want more accurate shutter speeds for pinpoint stars, you can break out PhotoPills, as outlined here, or any other spot star calculator. PhotoPills is good for this task because you can use the Spot Stars tool on your phone without an internet connection—great for those times when you're in a remote area in the middle of the night.

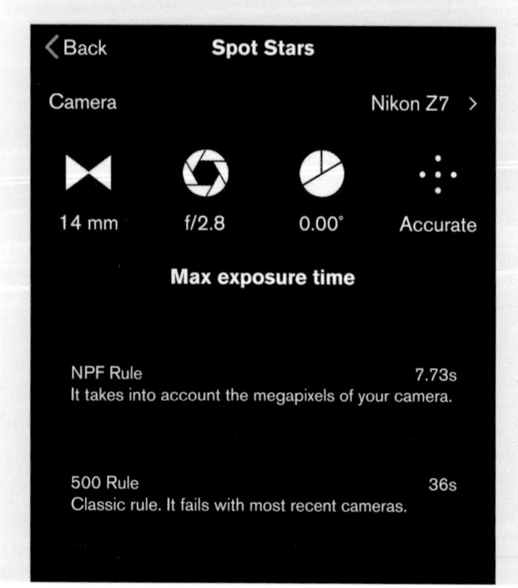

Focal Length	Pinpoint Stars	Very Small Star Trails
10mm	12 seconds	25 seconds
14mm	10 seconds	20 seconds
20mm	7 seconds	14 seconds
24mm	6 seconds	12 seconds
35mm	4 seconds	8 seconds
50mm	3 seconds	5 seconds

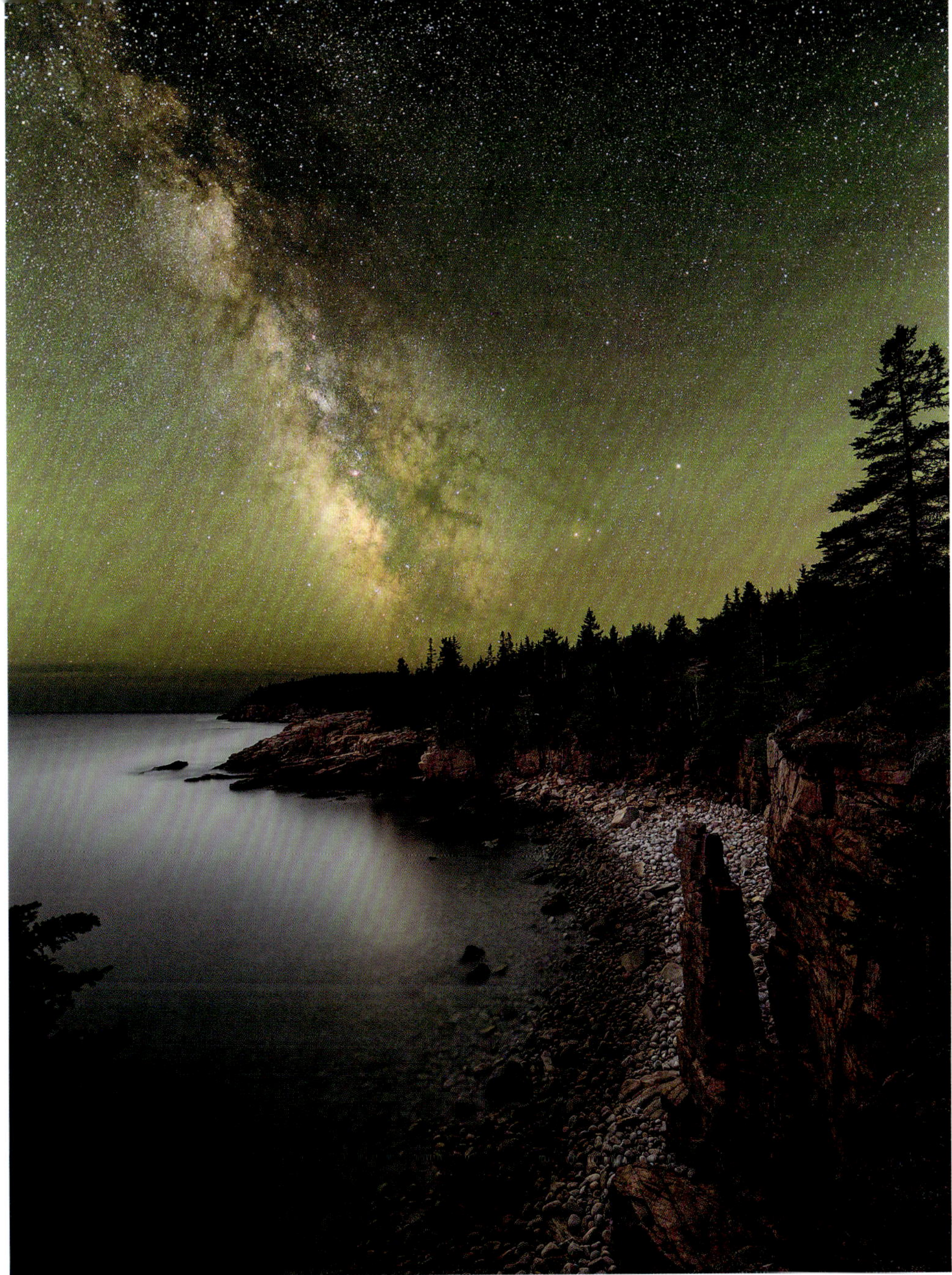

▲ Acadia National Park

Nikon D810A with Nikon 14-24mm f/2.8 lens at 14mm and f/2.8.

Sky: Star stack of 10 shots, each at ISO 12800 and 10 seconds.

Foreground: Focus stack of two shots, each at ISO 1600 and 15 minutes.

FOREGROUND

If you are shooting separate foreground exposures for exposure blending and/or focus stacking, then you can use a much longer shutter speed than you can for the sky to collect much more light in a single image. Don't worry about the sky being really bright and the huge star trails that will be captured in a very long exposure, the sky will be replaced with the result from your star-stacked shots later.

A general rule of thumb for dark areas is that you will need a shutter speed of at least 1 minute to capture enough light to show detail in the scene, but that will vary widely depending on the f-stop you're using and how much ambient light is hitting the foreground. You may find that you need as long as 10 minutes in some areas where the foreground has a lot of shadow from cliffs, or trees, and so on.

When blending sky and foreground exposures, one thing to keep in mind is how noisy each image is. If the sky (even after star stacking or tracking) has a lot more noise than the foreground, or vice versa, then the blend won't look realistic. As much as it might make sense to capture 30 minutes of light for the foreground, the blend might look better with a 10, 5, or even 1-minute exposure. You could even the noise out in the blend by using noise-reduction software on the sky, or adding noise to the foreground (see page 186), but you will save time in the field and in software by not going overboard with the foreground shutter speed.

So how do you calculate the best shutter speed to use for your foreground exposures? The best thing you can do is find what works for you by trial and error. With proper technique in the field and in software, you can get by with a lot more noise than you might think.

In dark areas I often find myself using foreground shutter speeds up to 10 minutes. But if I'm shooting a panorama that requires 10 or more frames, 10 minutes per frame (or twice that if you're using Long Exposure Noise Reduction) is just too long. In these cases, I'll often use a shutter speed between 1 and 4 minutes per foreground exposure. This results in more noise in the foreground, but it tends to match the noise in the sky better, since I will not be star stacking the sky shots when making a panorama, for the reasons mentioned.

7.3.3 ISO

The ISO should be the last thing you adjust, after you know what f-stop and shutter speed to use for the shot, whether it is the sky or the foreground you're exposing for. The f-stop and shutter speed control how much light is coming into the camera, and the ISO simply determines how much to amplify (brighten) that signal. Essentially, you want to use an ISO that isn't so high that it severely overexposes most stars, but at the same time it needs to be high enough to increase the signal above the electronic noise of the camera (see page 69).

SKY EXPOSURES

For the most part, you'll probably never need an ISO higher than 3200 for sky exposures. Going higher will make the image much easier to see on your camera's LCD screen, but at the cost of overexposing stars and thus losing color in the stars. However, if you're using super-wide-angle lenses most of the time, star color will be hard to see anyway as the stars will be such tiny dots. I will often use an ISO of 6400 or higher for sky exposures just so the image is easier to see on the camera preview, although this is probably just out of habit more than any real necessity.

The ISO may need to be adjusted based on your f-stop and the ambient brightness of the scene. The brighter the scence, the lower the ISO you'll need. If you're shooting during twilight or beneath a bright moon, then you may not need anything above ISO 400 or 800.

▶ **Acadia National Park.**

Nikon D810A with Sigma 50mm f/1.4 Art lens.

Sky: Star stack of 10 shots at f/1.4, ISO 12800, for 3 seconds each.

Foreground: Single ISO 12800 shot at f/2 and 4 minutes. I accidentally left the ISO at 12800, normally I would have used ISO 1600 for the foreground. The high ISO didn't ruin the photograph, it was just really bright, so I darkened it in editing.

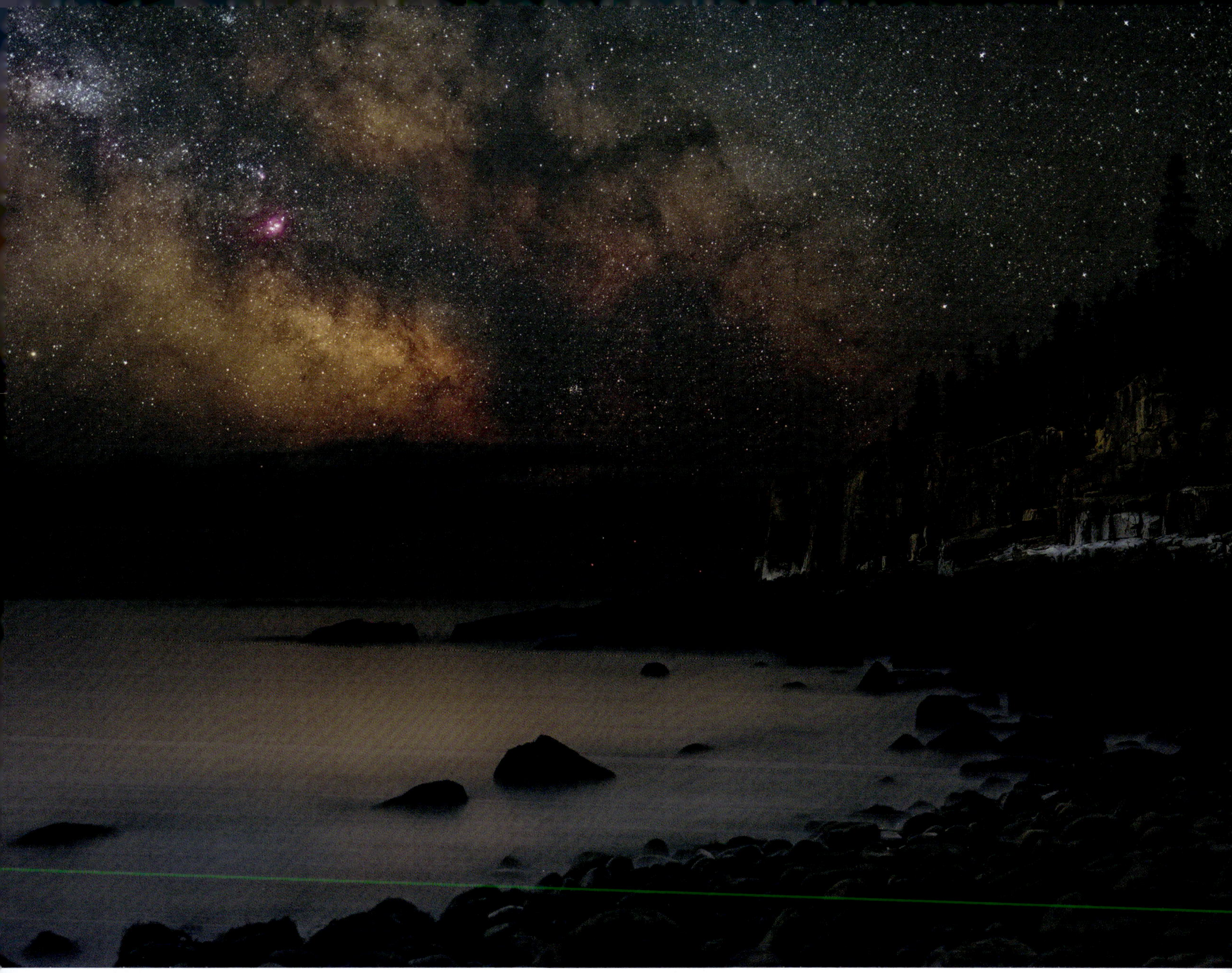

FOREGROUND EXPOSURES

When shooting separate foreground exposures, I often use ISO 1600 in very dark areas. If your shutter speed is at least 1 minute long, then an ISO of 1600 will most likely be as high as you need to boost the signal above the electronic noise, but it may not be enough to see what the exposure looks like. If the histogram is bunched up toward the left end then you're in danger of clipping the foreground to black, so use a higher ISO (amplifying the signal above the background noise, but not reducing shot noise) or a longer shutter speed (increasing the captured signal and lowering shot noise).

Also double-check that your camera's Creative Effect mode is set to "Neutral"—any of the other settings could increase the contrast of the preview JPEG so much so that you can't see anything in the dark areas.

You may find that you need to use ISO 3200 or even 6400 to see the foreground. Or you may need to use a much lower ISO to keep the scene from overexposing if you're shooting during twilight or with lots of ambient light.

8 WORKING IN THE DARK

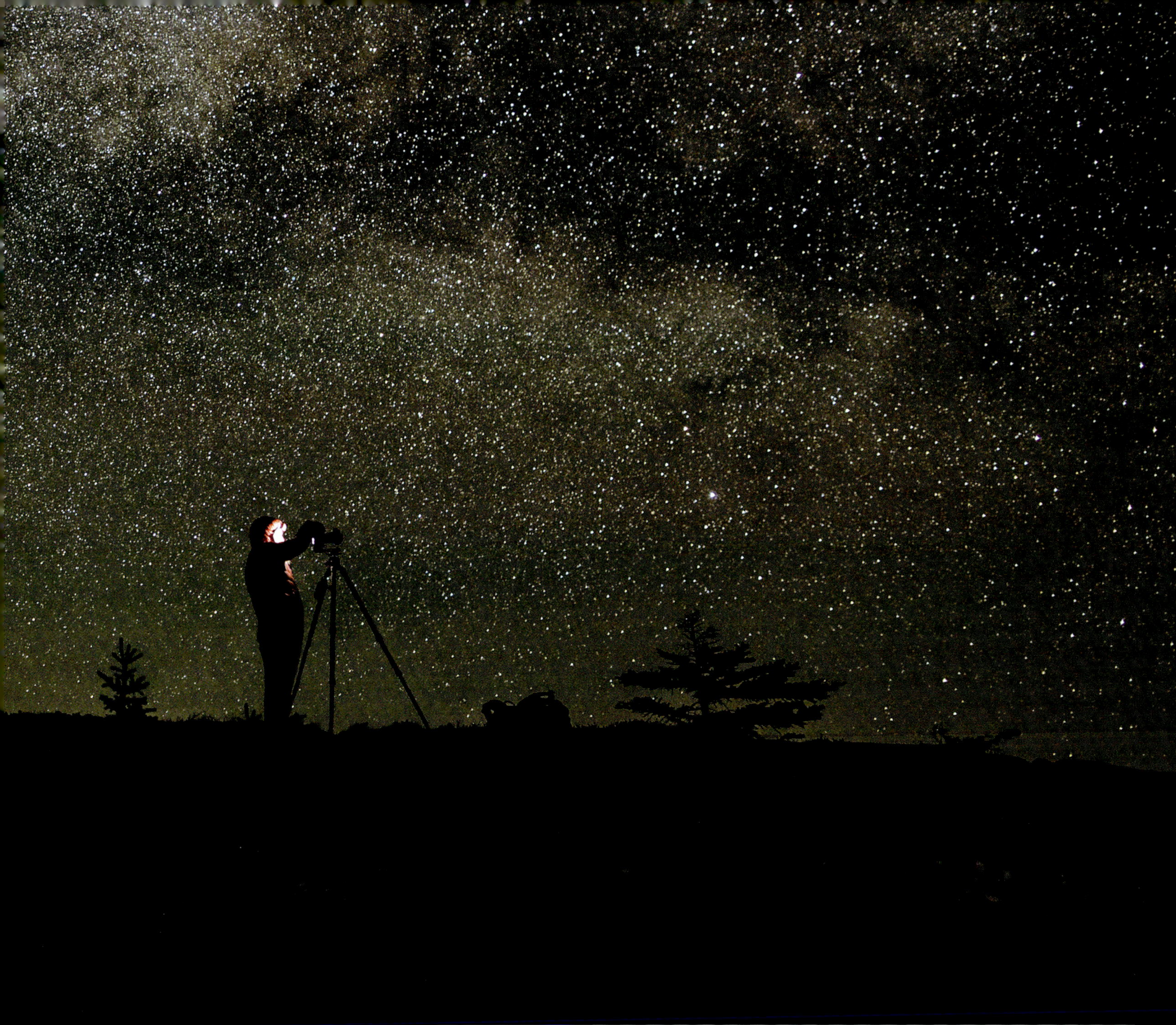

Operating your camera in the dark brings its own set of challenges, as you may imagine, but with some practice and patience you should get used to it and eventually become so comfortable you'll barely need to turn on your headlamp.

In this chapter we'll look at ways to make adjusting your camera settings in the dark a little easier.

▲ Another beautiful night out under the stars, adjusting the settings on my camera. Photo by Eric Tirrell.

8.1 CAMERA CONTROLS

Adjusting your camera controls in the dark is fairly straightforward if you can turn on your headlamp so you can see what you're doing. This is perfectly fine if you're shooting alone or with a friend and you're both in sync. However, if you're in a group or there are other photographers in the area, chances are someone is going to have their shutter open when you need to turn on your headlamp. In these situations, you should coordinate with others before you turn on your lamp. In my workshops, people will generally ask, "Is anybody shooting?" to see if it's okay to turn on a light.

The best way to overcome the challenges of operating your camera in the dark is to get used to where your camera buttons are through muscle memory, so you don't need to turn on your light to find them. If you shoot in the dark regularly, make it a point to avoid using your headlamp and force yourself to get used to finding the buttons by feel. Eventually, you'll hit them spot on almost every time.

Of course, sometimes you'll need your light for other reasons, such as finding something in your camera bag, checking your lens for dew, and so on. In these situations, make sure you ask the others around you when you can turn on your lamp.

A low-power light can be a real lifesaver, something dim enough that it won't affect the foreground of other people's photos, and just bright enough to allow you to see your camera or inside your bag. The small Proton Pro flashlight mentioned in the **Gear** chapter is a good choice—its adjustable red LED starts out at its dimmest level when you first turn it on, and it allows you to find camera buttons or check your lens, and so on, without affecting anyone else with a bright light. Just make sure you face away from the scene and cover the bulb with your hand when turning it on to make sure you get into red mode successfully without disturbing anyone. You can then carefully shine the light directly at what you need to see without it casting light on the foreground.

On a related note, make sure that any bright lights on your camera, or your intervalometer, or lens heater battery pack, and any other electronics are all either disabled or covered with tape or something similar. I use gaffer tape, which has a light adhesive that easily unsticks and doesn't leave residue on most things (unless you leave it on for a long time). This protects both your night vision and your foreground. You would be surprised by how much the dim red LED of an intervalometer or battery pack can illuminate the foreground if you're not careful. (Fun fact: a gaffer is an electrician/lighting technician on a movie set.)

▶ Workshop students under the stars.

Nikon Z 7 with Nikon 14-24mm f/2.8 lens.

Single image at 14mm, f/2.8, ISO 6400, 30 seconds.

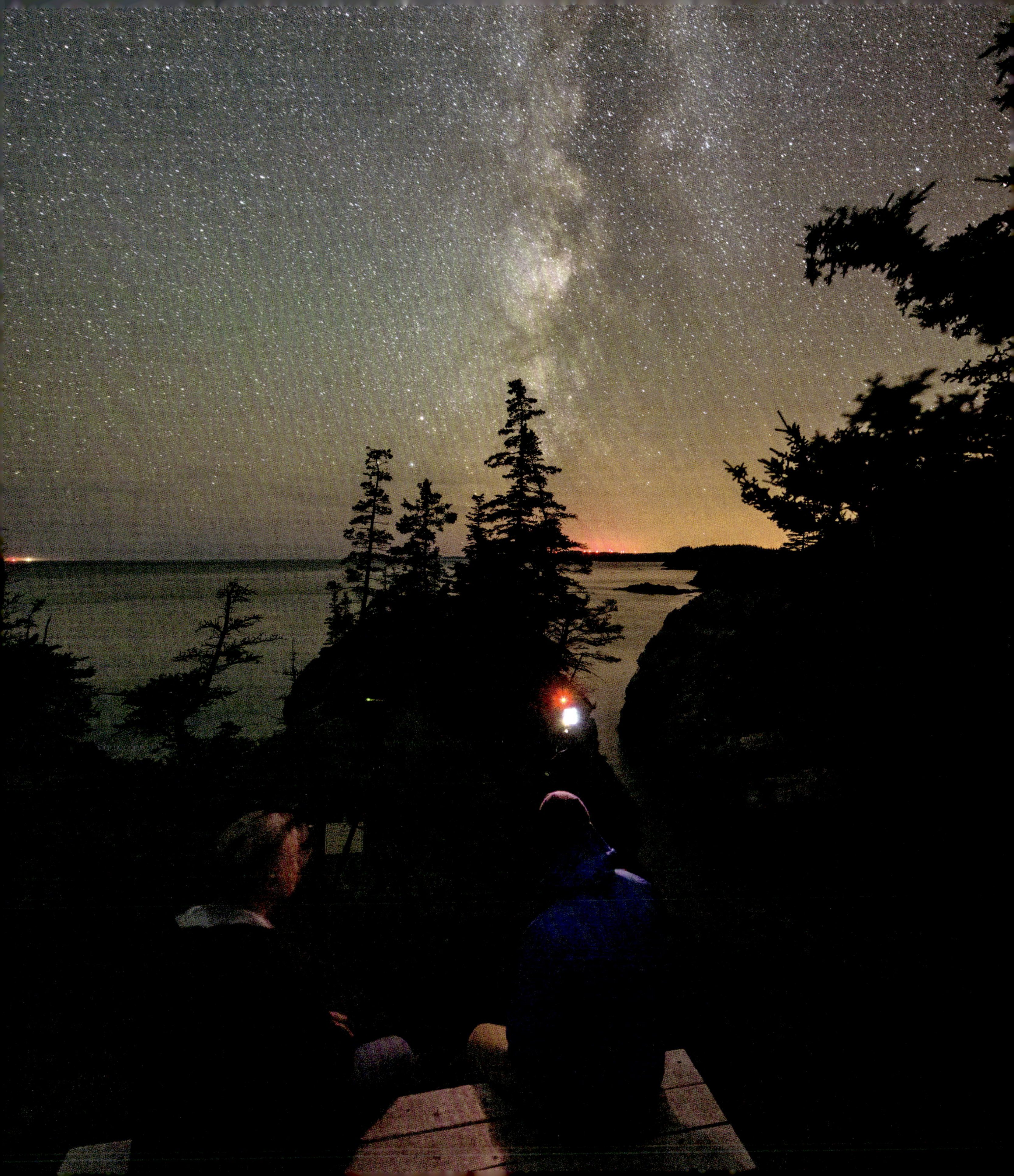

8.2 FOCUSING

You might be wondering how you are supposed to focus in the dark. This is definitely tricky, but there a few ways you can achieve the correct focus for your lens in low light.

First off, you'll need to make sure your lens and/or camera are in Manual Focus mode. You can't use Auto-Focus for the stars, and if you have Auto-Focus enabled you might accidentally hit the Auto-Focus button (or accidentally half-press your shutter to engage it, depending on your camera), throwing your lens out of focus. You may want to temporarily enable Auto-Focus to focus on the foreground with a flashlight, but always turn it off after doing so.

For the stars, on an ideal lens you could set the focus ring to the Infinity mark and the stars would be in perfect focus. But, this is often not the case and you should never rely on the Infinity mark unless you've tested it already on that particular night. Temperature, humidity and age can cause a lens to focus differently over time. Even if your brand-new lens has sharp focus on the stars at Infinity you should still double-check it every time you go out.

FOCUSING DURING THE DAY

Something I recommend to anyone getting started with landscape astrophotography is to find Infinity Focus on your lens during the day. Pick a location where you can see something very far away on the distant horizon and get it in sharp focus, either using Auto-Focus or Manual Focus in live view. Take test shots and zoom in on the preview image to make sure the object is truly in focus. It may be difficult to get good focus on distant objects; humidity or air temperature differences between you and the object can make it appear soft and fuzzy, so keep trying.

Once you've found a good focus on a faraway object, make a note of it somehow—jot it down or mark the focus ring on the lens with a grease pencil or tape so you can get back to that exact focus mark. You can even tape the ring down with gaffer tape so it won't move.

All being well, the stars should be in focus when subsequently using the lens at that focus mark. Always take test shots when you're shooting at night and zoom in on the preview image to see if the stars look sharp.

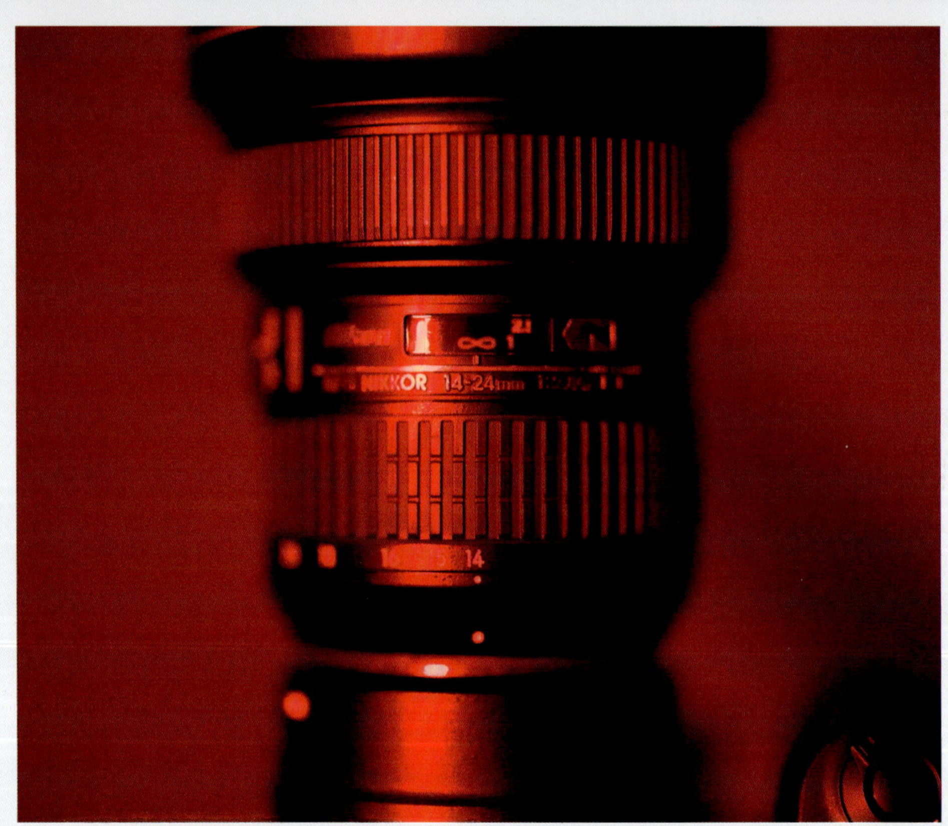

▲ Set the focus ring to Infinity to start, and if using a zoom lens, set the zoom ring to your desired focal length. Don't forget to use your red headlamp to preserve your night vision.

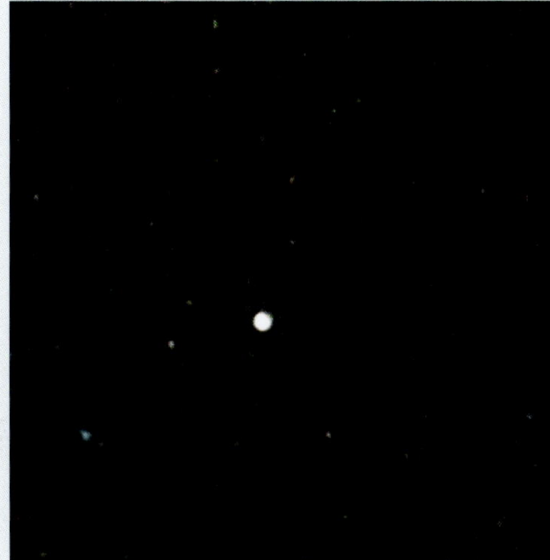

▲ Slowly turn the focus ring to get small, in-focus stars. An in-focus star should be as small as possible.

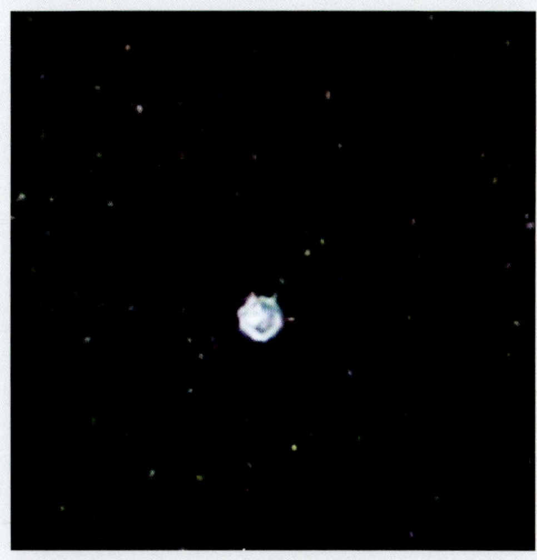

▲ An out-of-focus star will look bigger and softer.

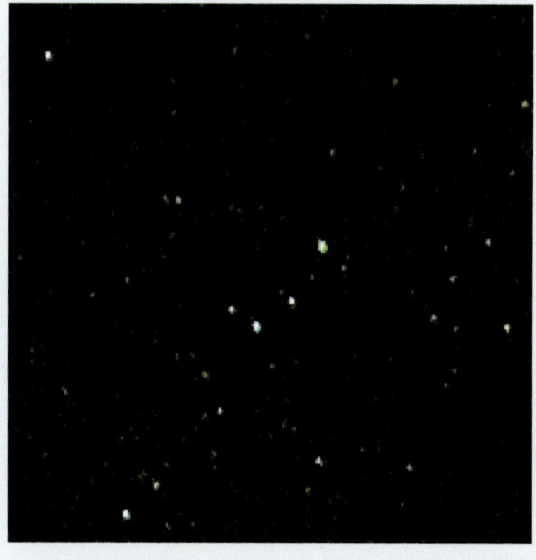

▲ In-focus stars should look something like this.

Note that the bright small specks in these images are from electronic noise and not other stars.

USING LIVE VIEW

In order to see what you're doing, you will likely need to learn how to get the stars in focus using the live view on your camera. Here is a step-by-step process for how to do this:

1 If you are using a zoom lens, first turn the zoom ring to your desired focal length. Often what is in focus for one focal length will be out of focus for another focal length.

2 Turn the focus ring to the Infinity mark. If the lens is focused too closely, then any stars in live view will be impossible to find because they will be too blurry.

3 Set your ISO to the highest it will go, and open the aperture as wide as it will go on your lens (the smallest f-stop number).

4 Turn on live view so that the rear LCD (and/or electronic viewfinder for mirrorless cameras) displays a live feed from the sensor. During daylight this will show your whole scene, but at night it will be difficult to see anything but the brightest stars.

5 Try to find a bright star near the center of the frame. It is critical that the star is close to the center of the frame, otherwise lens distortions that are most visible around the edges or corners of the frame can make it impossible to get good focus. And if you do get a star in focus in a corner, then the center might be out of focus. If you cannot find any stars at all, then double-check that your focus ring is at or near Infinity. If it is and you're still having trouble, make sure your lens cap is off.

6 Once you've found a suitable star, turn the focus ring until the star is as sharp and small as you can get it. The exact appearance of the star will vary from lens to lens. When you think you've got it, take a quick test shot with a shutter speed of 5 or 10 seconds. When the exposure is complete, go into Image Playback mode and zoom in on the stars to see how they look. If you notice any blur or distortions, go back into live view, change the focus a bit, and take another test shot.

7 Once you have the stars in focus, it is a good idea to take note of the markings on the focus ring (as mentioned on the opposite page). If you have no intention of changing focus for the rest of the night (for instance, if you don't plan to focus stack your images) then taping the focus ring down with gaffer tape isn't a bad idea to keep it from being moved by accident.

It may sound like a lot of work, but most of this process is very fast. Finding a star in live view is the hardest part. But with practice, it will come very quickly to you.

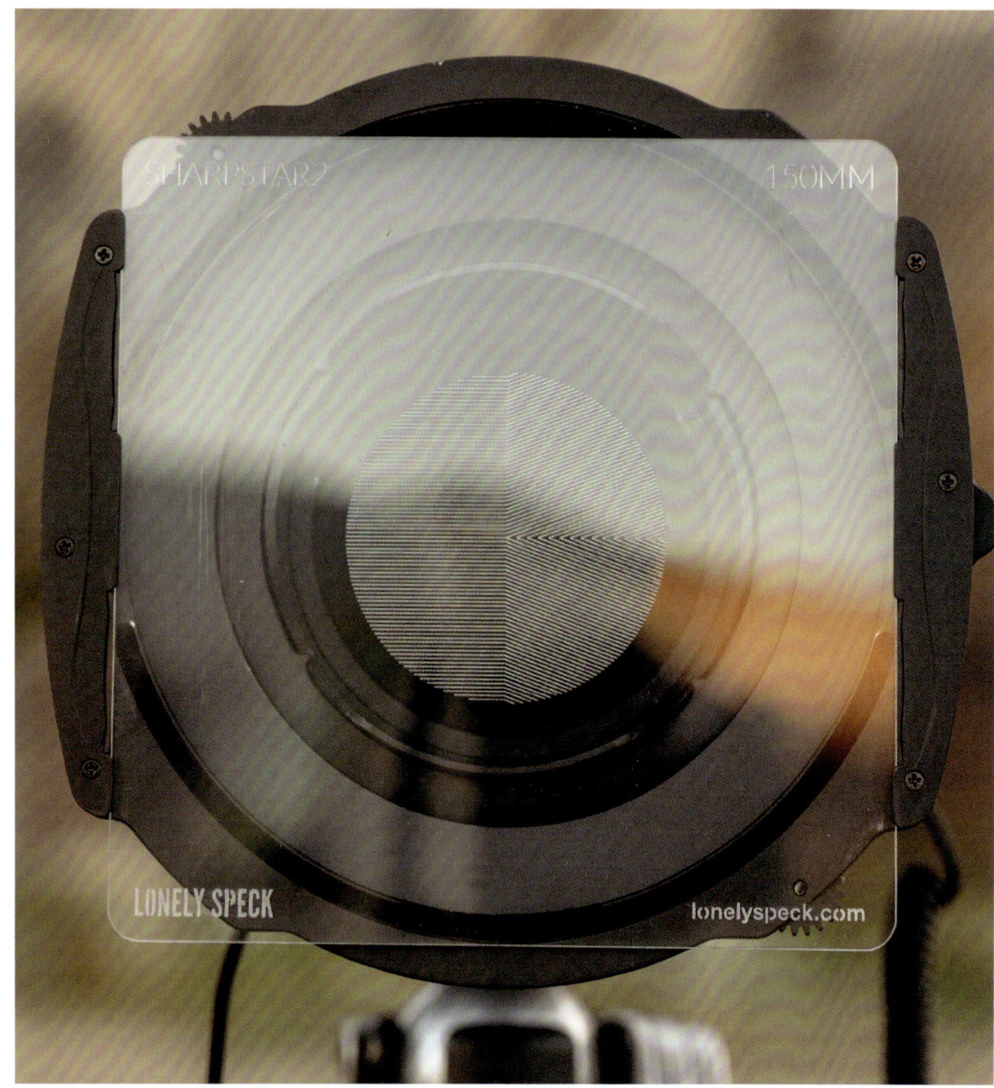

▲ The SharpStar mask from Lonely Speck works with all lenses.

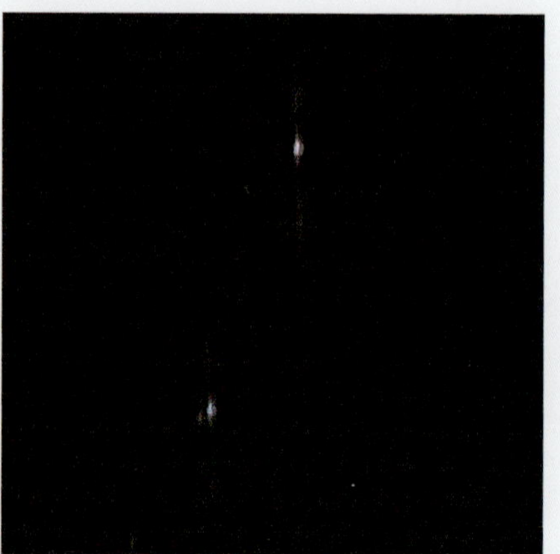

▲ Soft or off-center diffraction spikes indicate the stars are out of focus.

▲ Sharp and centered diffraction spikes indicate the stars are in focus.

USING A BAHTINOV MASK

If you're having trouble getting stars in focus, then you might want to try using a Bahtinov mask. A Bahtinov mask is a type of filter that sits in front of your lens, and by using diffraction it will create spikes on stars. If the spikes are sharp and central, then you know you have the stars in focus. They are particularly useful on telescopes or long lenses where you can easily see stars and adjust the focus in live view, but on wide-angle lenses you may not be able to see the diffraction spikes in live view because the stars are so small. In this case, try to find the focus using the live view method outlined previously on page 115, then take a test shot with the Bahtinov mask and check the diffraction spikes in your image review. If the diffraction spikes are not sharp and centered on the stars, then keep going back between using live view to find your focus and taking test shots until they are.

Most Bahtinov masks are made for telescopes or long focal length lenses, but the SharpStar mask from Lonely Speck (**lonelyspeck.com**) works with all lenses and is available in various sizes.

8.3 TEST SHOTS

When working in the dark, you'll frequently need to take test shots. They are very handy for checking what your composition looks like, or whether the stars or foreground are in focus. Since they are not going to be your final images, you don't have to worry about noise or star trails.

Set the ISO to at least 6400 (or possibly higher to really see your composition in a dark area), use the widest aperture (lowest f-stop number), and a shutter speed of at least 5 seconds. This way you can see what your camera sees, make an adjustment to composition or focus, and take another test shot to see how well the change worked.

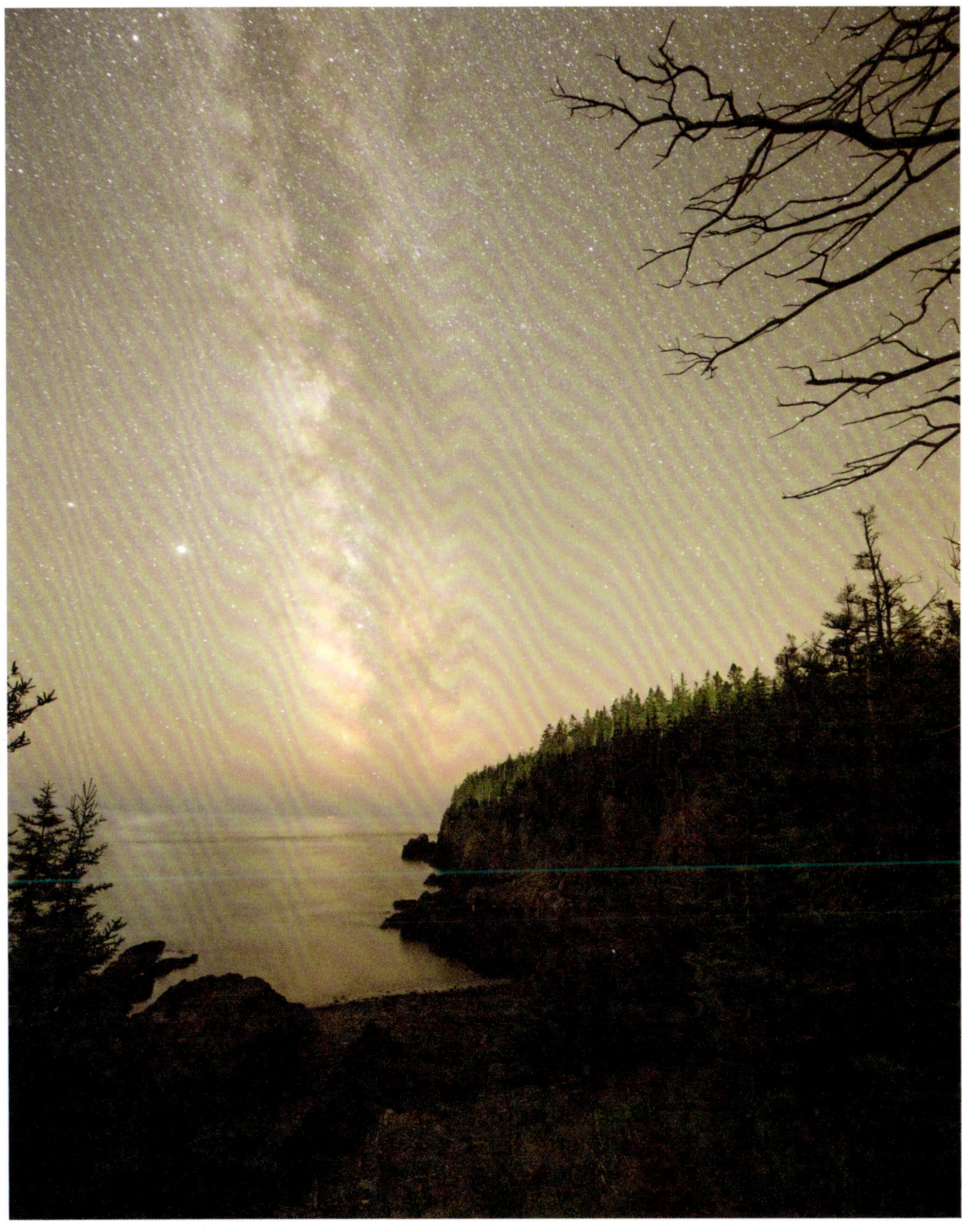

▶ A 30 second test shot at ISO 25,600 and f/2.8 lets me see what the scene looks like in a very dark location. This is a "throwaway" shot, so the quality of the image is not important.

COMPOSITION

9

The Milky Way makes for a great compositional element when paired with all sorts of landscapes. You can use the leading lines of a river or rock formation to draw the viewer through the frame, and often times just placing the Milky Way over any beautiful foreground works well, but there are some basic compositional rules to remember that will help you out.

▶ River gorge on the Bay of Fundy.

When the Milky Way is straight up and down it works well for vertical shots. In this river gorge, the vertical Milky Way complements the canyon walls.

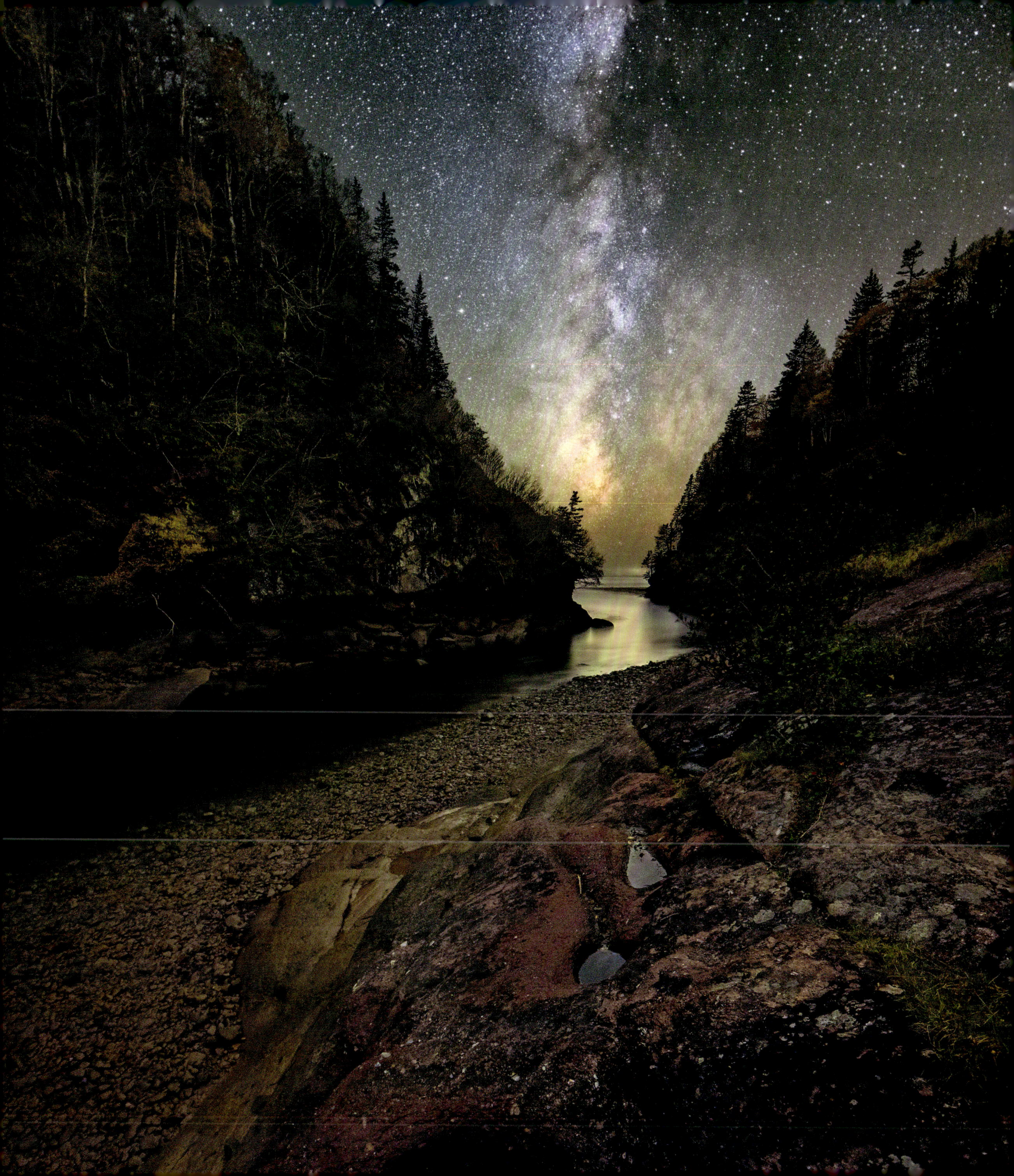

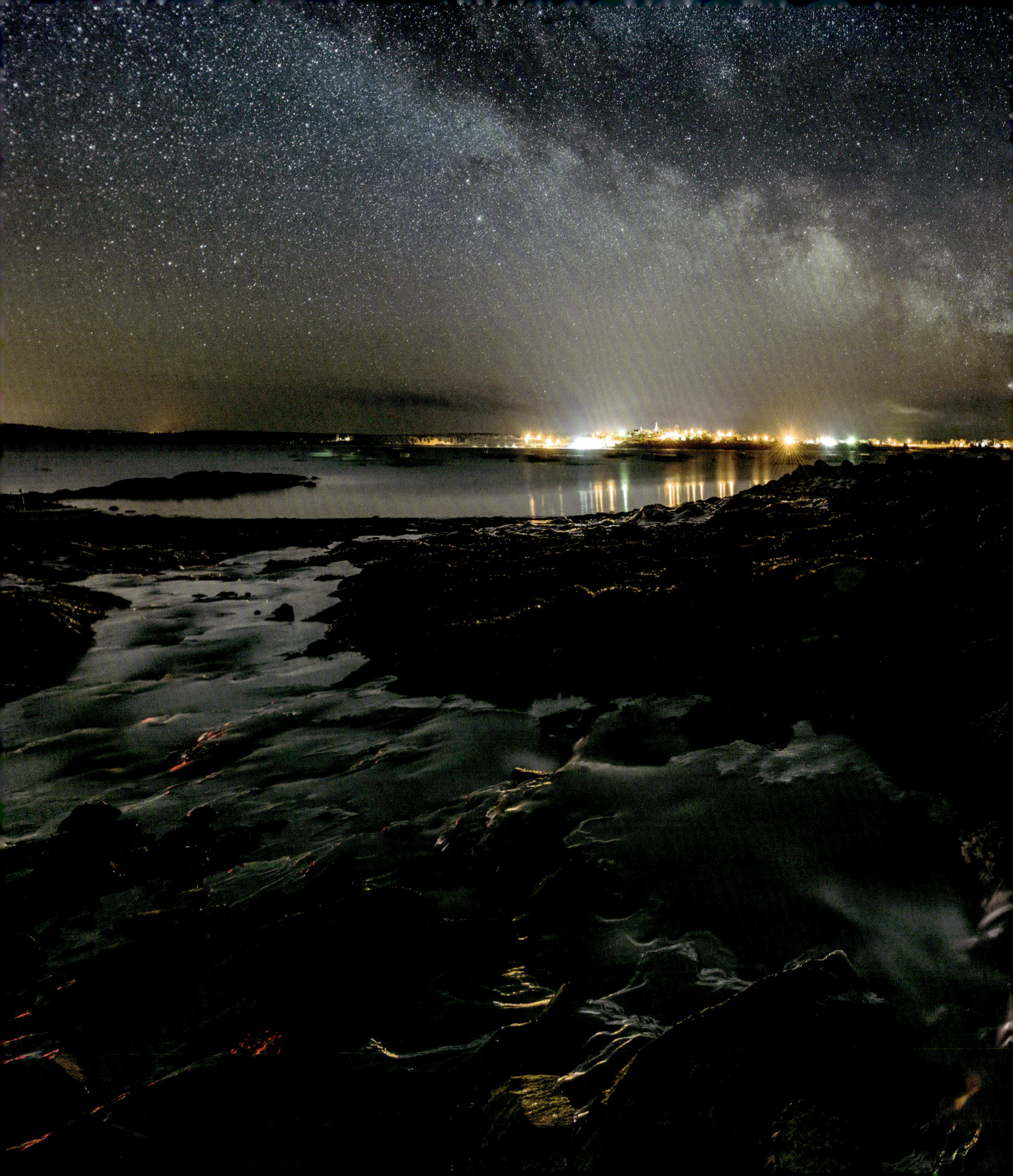

IT'S MORE THAN JUST THE SKY

Landscape astrophotography is, in essence, about capturing the stars over a landscape. It's tempting to just place the Milky Way above the silhouette of trees in the very bottom part of the frame for an easy shot. If you can shoot that in your backyard, it's a good composition to use to get the basics down, but try to use the Milky Way in some way to complement the foreground.

Chances are, any location that's good for sunset or sunrise shots in landscape photography will also be a good place to capture the Milky Way, provided that the Milky Way will be visible over the desired foreground at some point in the year (see the **Planning** chapter from page 134).

MILKY WAY ORIENTATION

When the Milky Way arc is low in the sky it works well in horizontal (landscape) compositions. When the Milky Way is more upright it works well for vertical (portrait) compositions. But those are just guidelines, you can certainly shoot in whatever camera orientation works for the scene.

Panoramas are easily achievable when the Milky Way is arcing low in the sky, which means you don't have to tilt the camera up to capture more of the sky. More details on panoramas are covered in the **Milky Way Panoramas** chapter (see from page 150).

◀ Milky Way over the town of Lubec, Maine, on a frigid night in February. When the Milky Way is laying low in the sky it works well for horizontal shots.

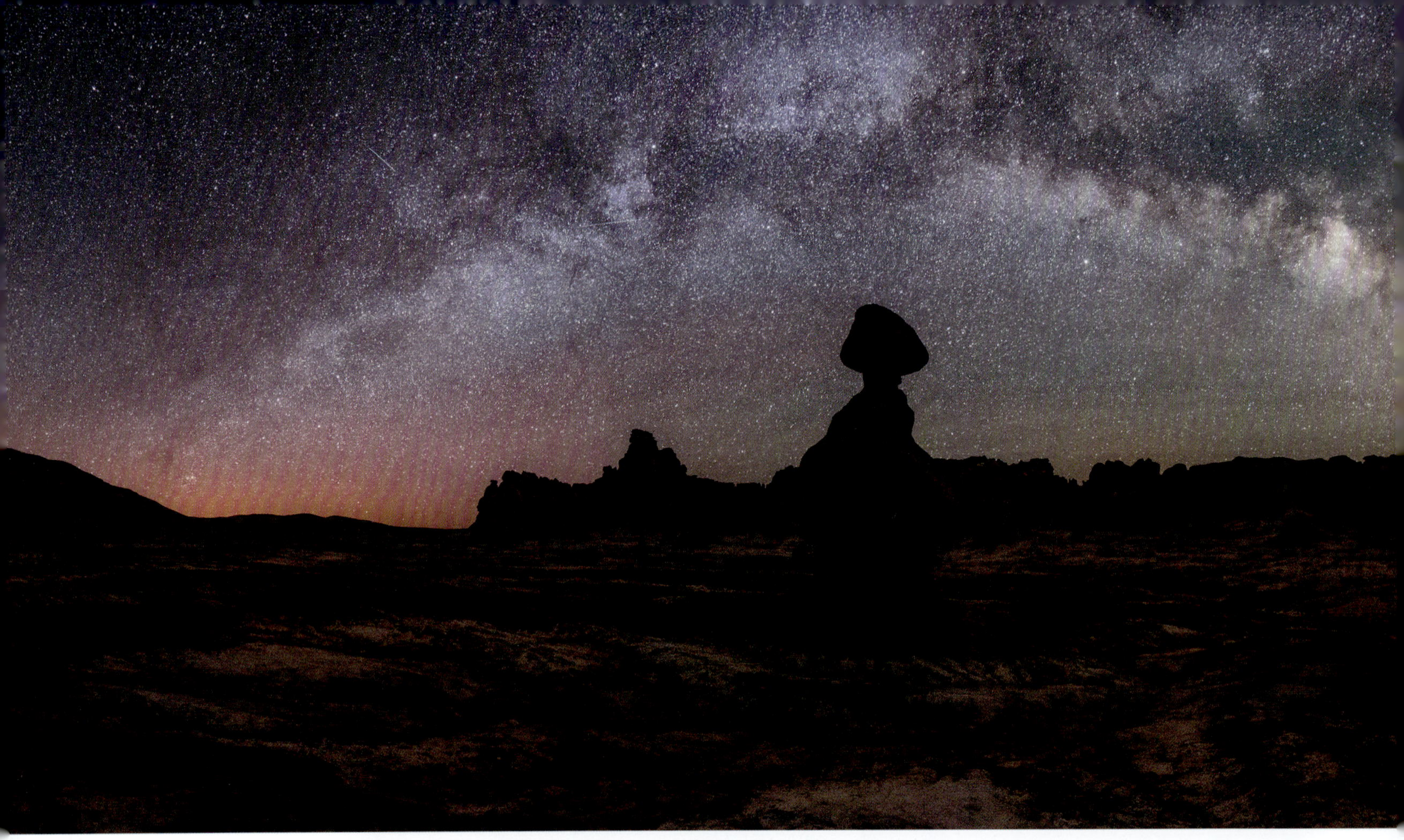

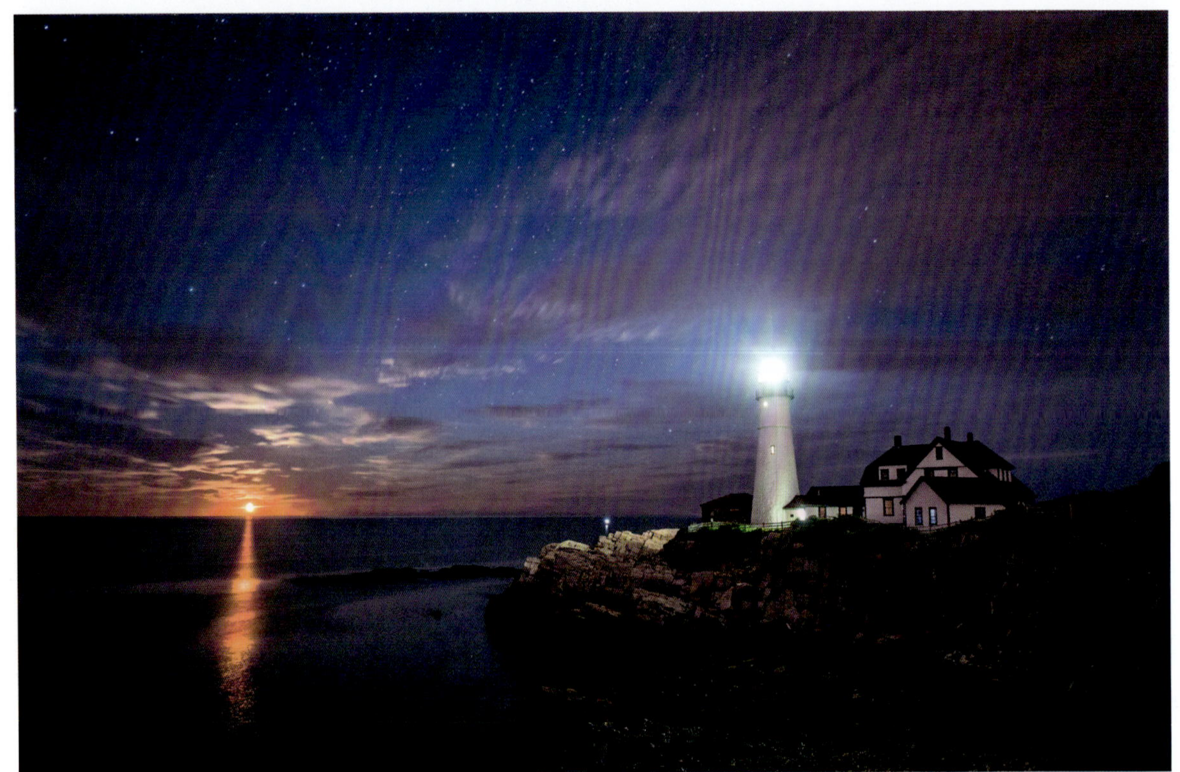

▶ The moon rises next to Portland Head Light in Maine. The moon appears orange when it is low in the sky because the light coming from the moon (which is reflected sunlight) is shining through a lot of atmosphere, just as the sun appears orange/red when it is low in the sky—this is Rayleigh scattering at work. A thin layer of clouds caught the moonlight, making it seem almost like a sunrise, only the stars would not be visible if the sun was up.

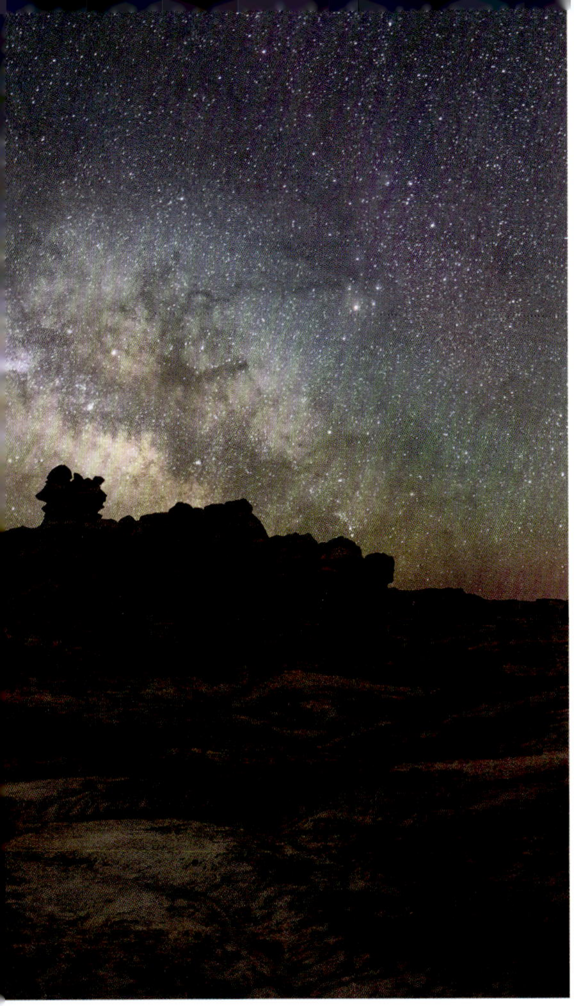

◀ A single-row panorama of the Milky Way in the desert of Utah. The left side of the frame is facing north, and the red glow is from the northern lights, which were so strong that night that they were faintly visible that far south.

▼ Acadia National Park in Maine. A calm night on a lake or pond is great for mirror-like reflections.

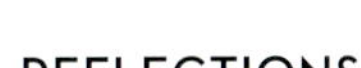

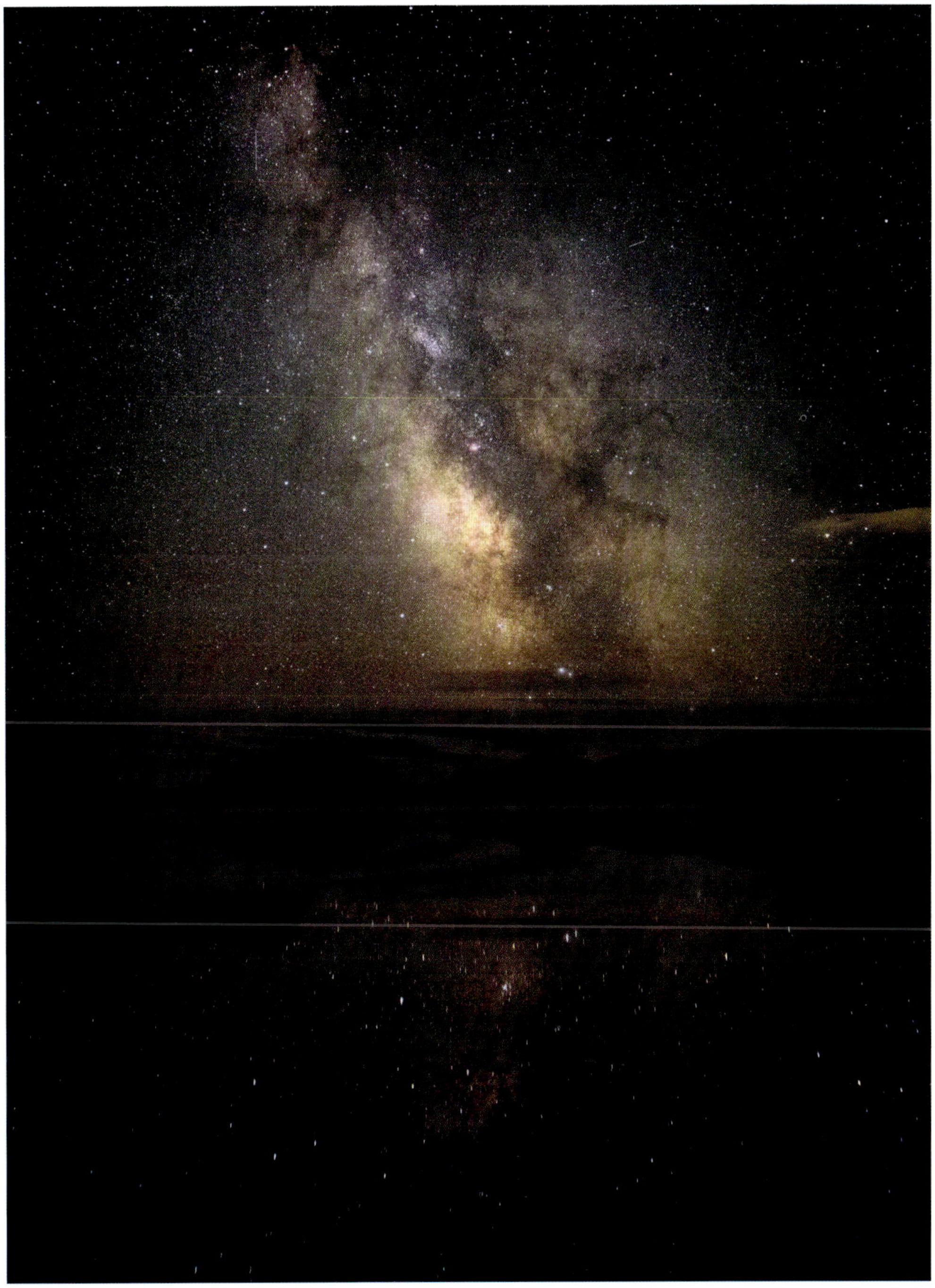

REFLECTIONS

It's possible to capture reflections of the stars in any calm section of water. In more turbulent water, you can still often capture the glow of the Milky Way's Galactic Core in a reflection. Seeing that glow on the water in person can be quite the experience.

A windless night at a pond or lake is a great place to capture mirror-like reflections of the Milky Way. In smaller sections of still water you can capture parts of the Milky Way or maybe just a few bright stars.

FRAMING THE MOON

When it's high in the sky, even a crescent moon can really wash out the sky, but when just above the horizon, a moon of any phase can add a nice element to the composition without washing out the entire sky. You'll get a nice orangey glow from the moon when it is just rising.

▶ Yours truly standing under a rock arch on the Bay of Fundy, with a headlamp shining at the camera for effect.

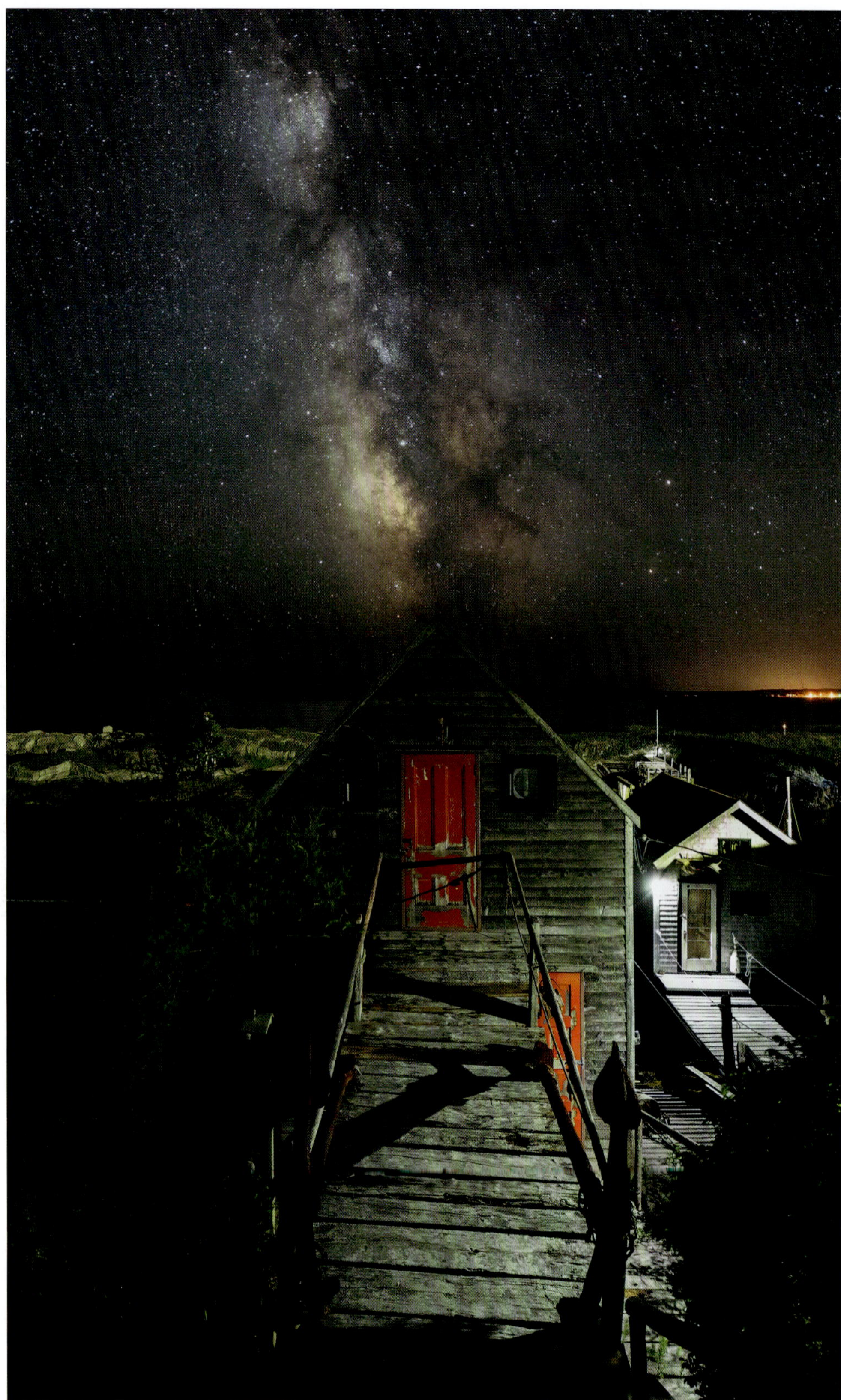

▲ The Milky Way over a fishing shack in Nova Scotia.

FOREGROUND SUBJECTS

Lighthouses, old barns, a rusted truck in a field—these can all make for interesting foregrounds that add context to your images.

Sometimes you might find yourself at a spot with a great view but no interesting foreground. An easy way to add some interest to the foreground is to place yourself, a friend, a tent, etc., into the scene.

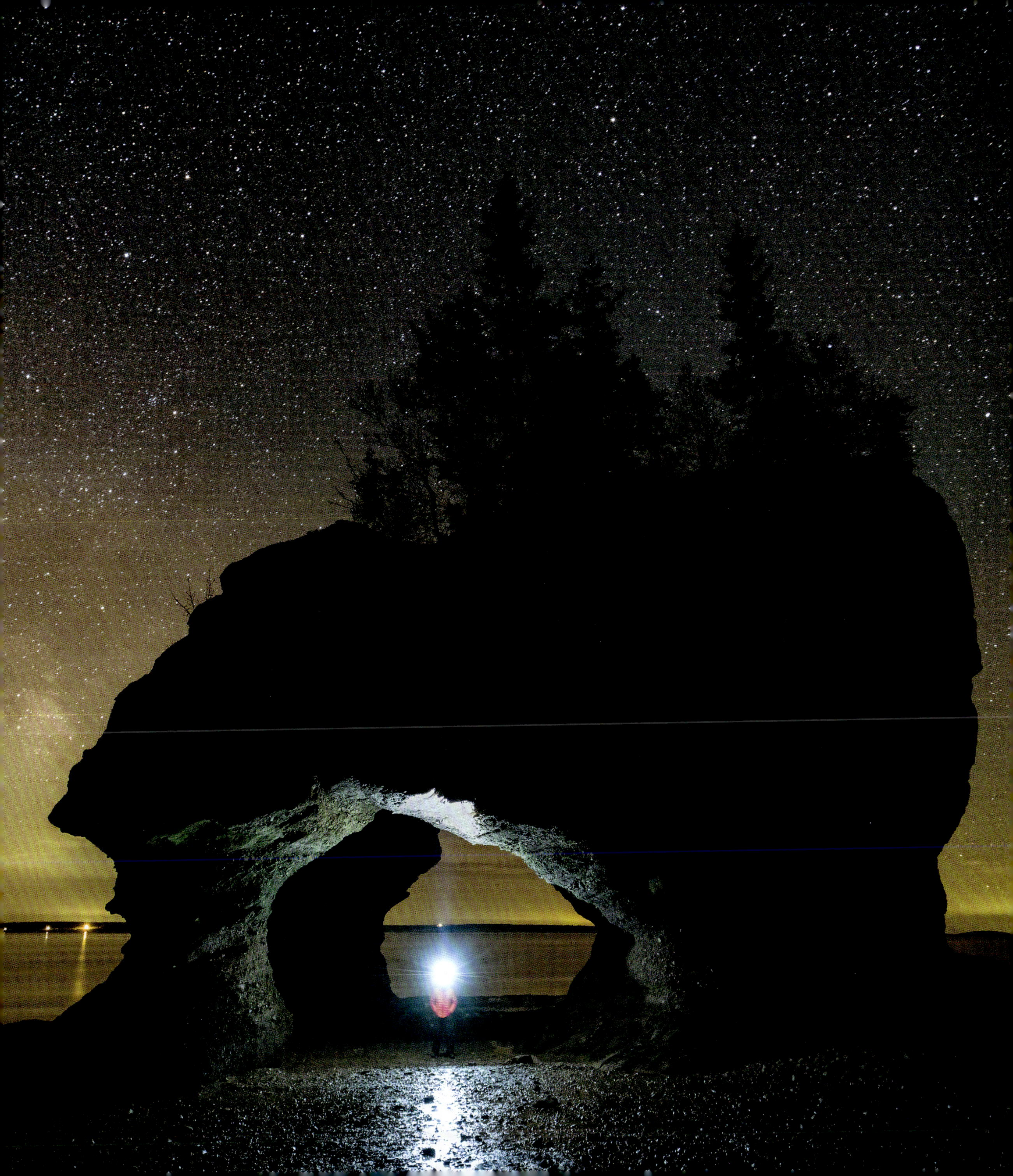

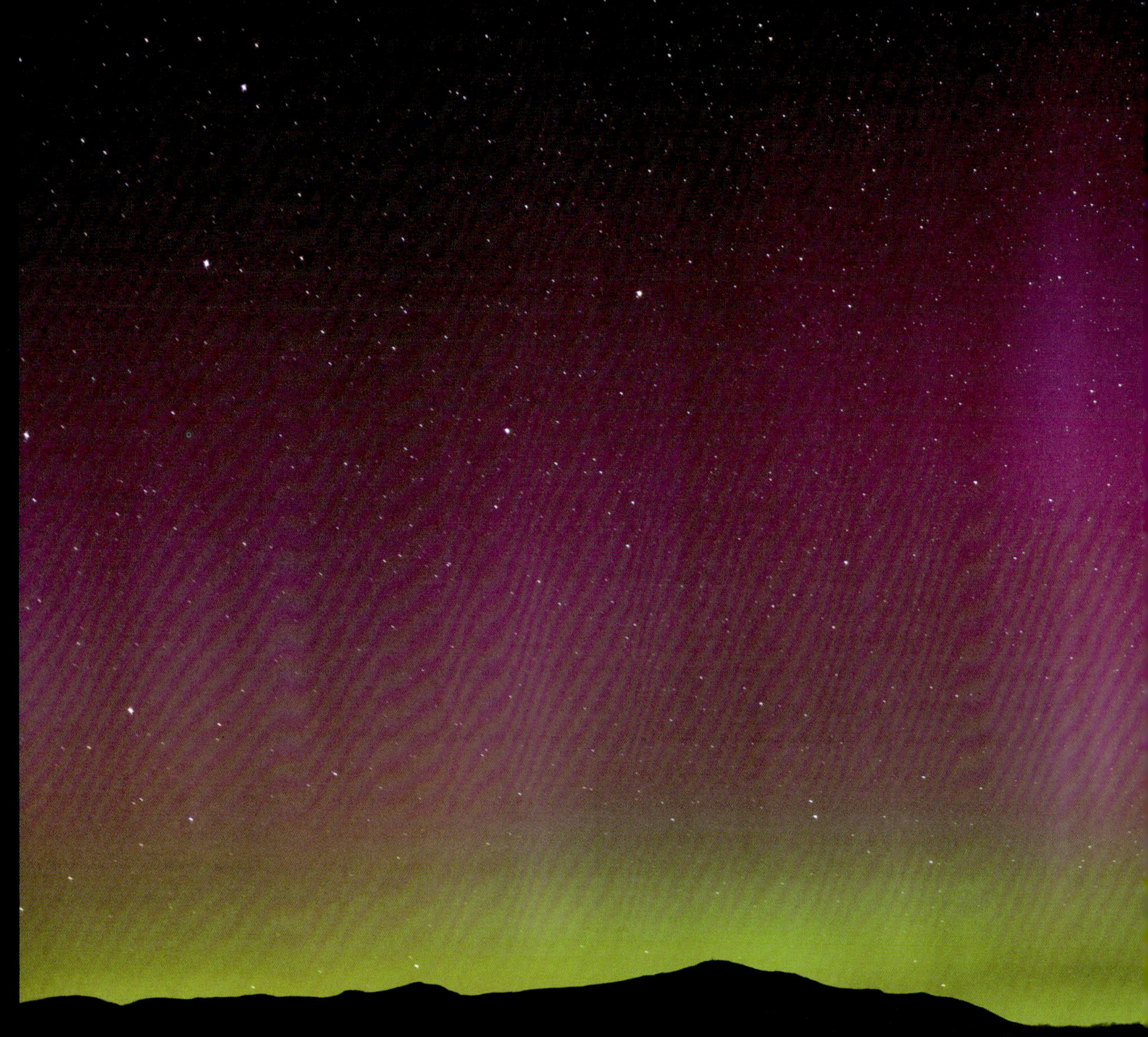

▶ In this photo I was photographing the northern lights over the White Mountains of New Hampshire with some friends. We had a stunning view but the foreground was just dirt and grass, so fellow photographer Jim Salge set up his tent and used his headlamp to light up the inside while we all took pictures. It made for a great composition.

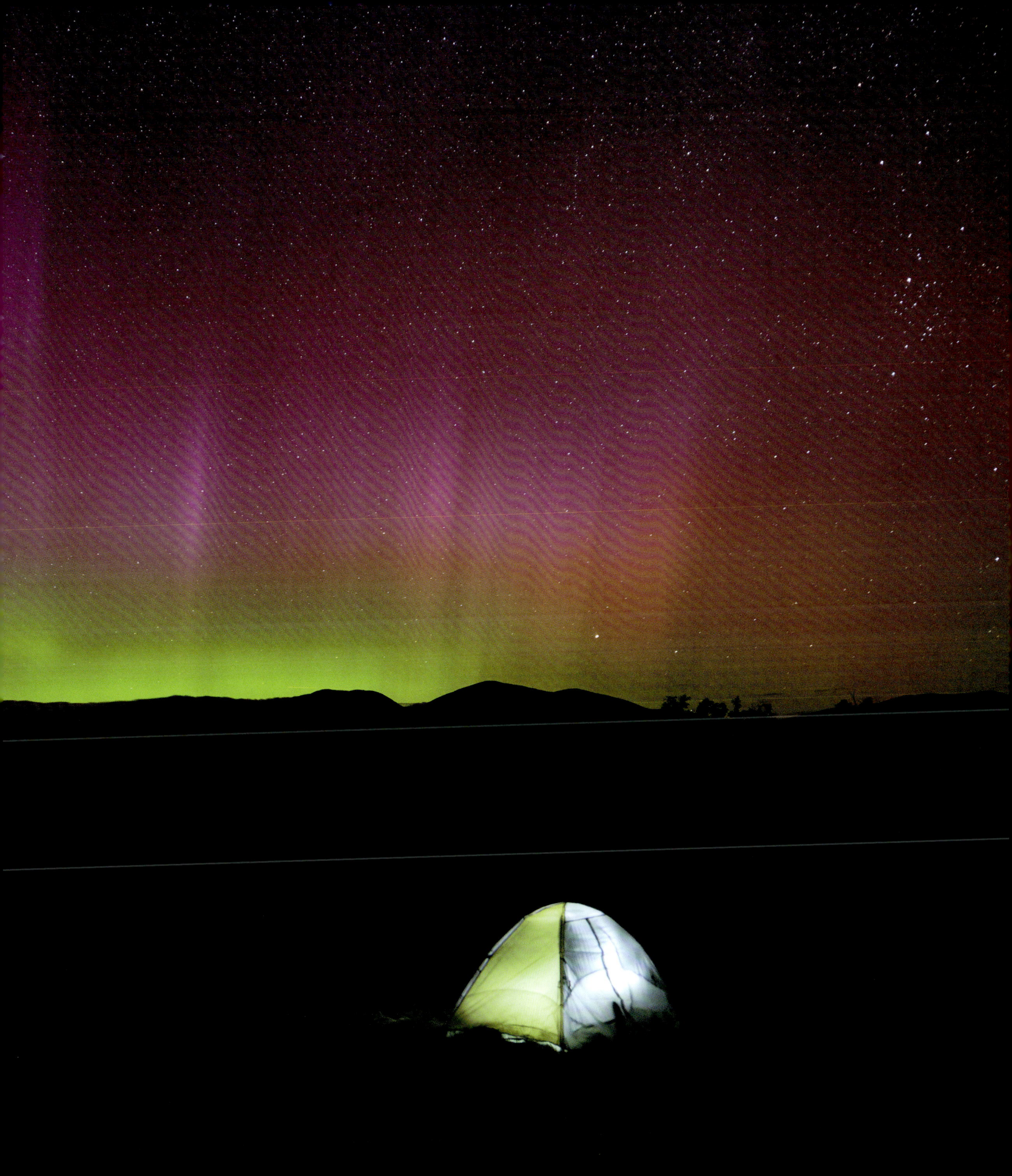

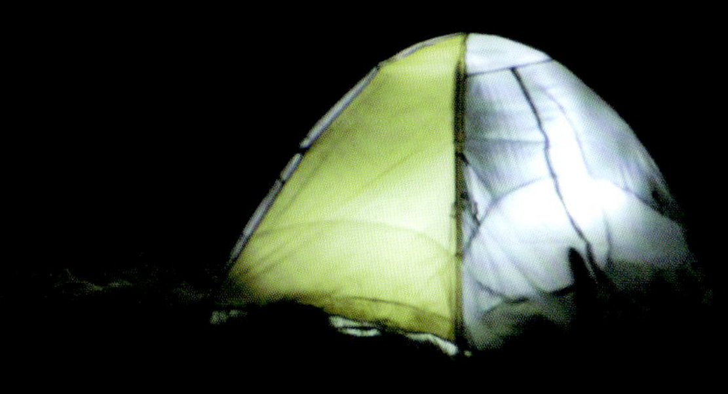

LIGHTING

10

▶ Lupine field in New Hampshire.

In this photo, I used a flashlight with a halogen bulb to light up the foreground field of lupines (this is called “light painting”). The halogen bulb has a warm color, and I used a lens cloth over the light to diffuse the beam for a softer effect, avoiding really harsh shadows. I waved the flashlight over my head during each exposure.

This is one of my earlier images of the Milky Way, and it shows my previous editing style of using a much bluer sky, resulting in a purple Milky Way. I probably wouldn’t do that these days, but I have not re-edited this image because the color balance of the sky and the foreground go nicely together, however “wrong” the sky may be.

Nikon D800E and Nikon 14-24mm f/2.8 lens.

This photo is made up of a single shot for the sky using 14mm, f/2.8, ISO 2500, 25 seconds, and four shots for the foreground, each at 14mm, f/2.8, ISO 1000, 60 seconds. Each foreground image used a different focus distance to get the entire scene in focus (known as “focus stacking”).

As we’ve discussed in previous chapters, landscape astrophotography that aims to capture pinpoint stars requires short exposures for the sky, causing not much light to be collected from the foreground unless there is a lot of ambient light at the location. In dark locations you’ll need some way of getting light in your foreground, whether that means using a longer shutter speed or adding light.

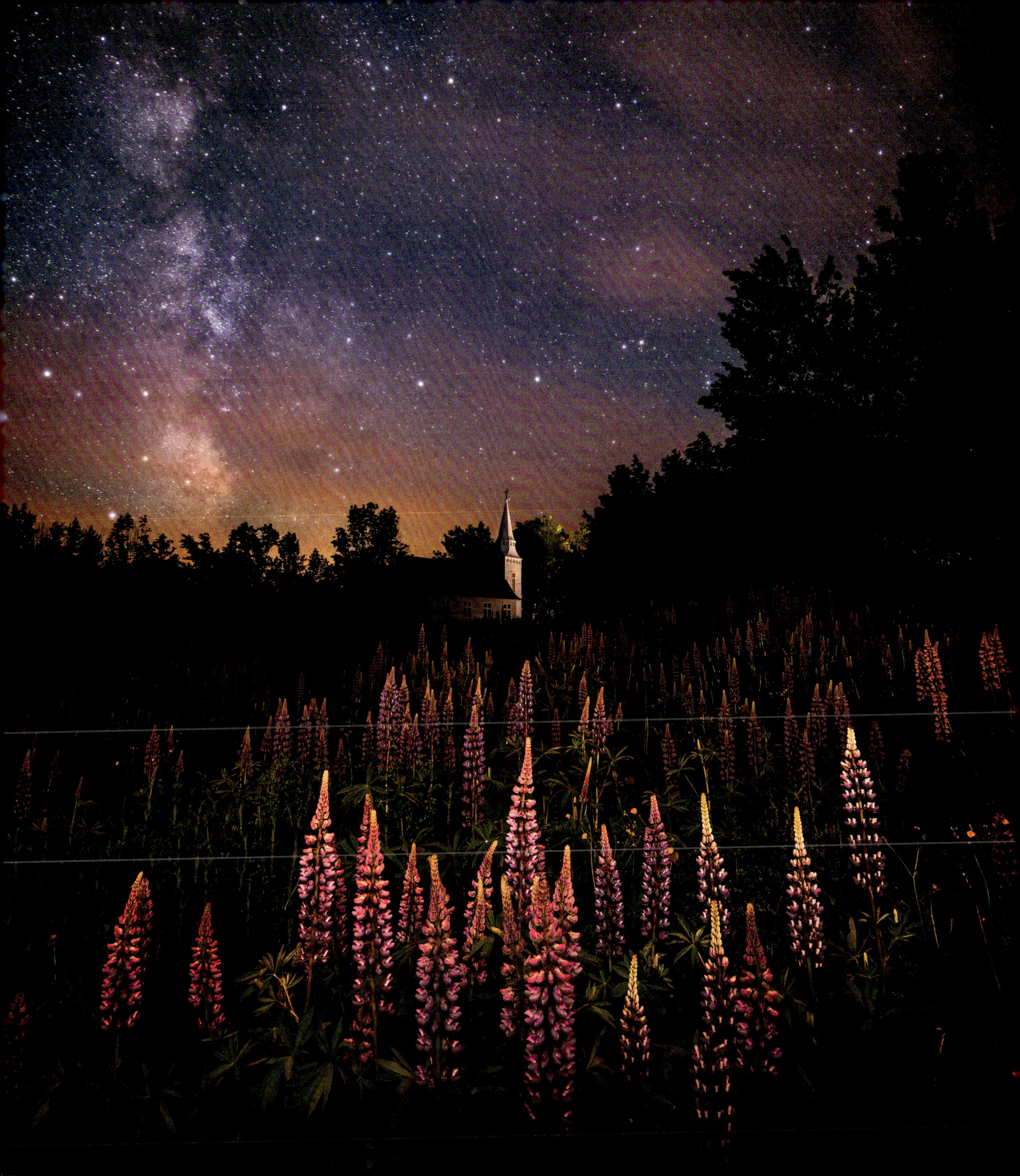

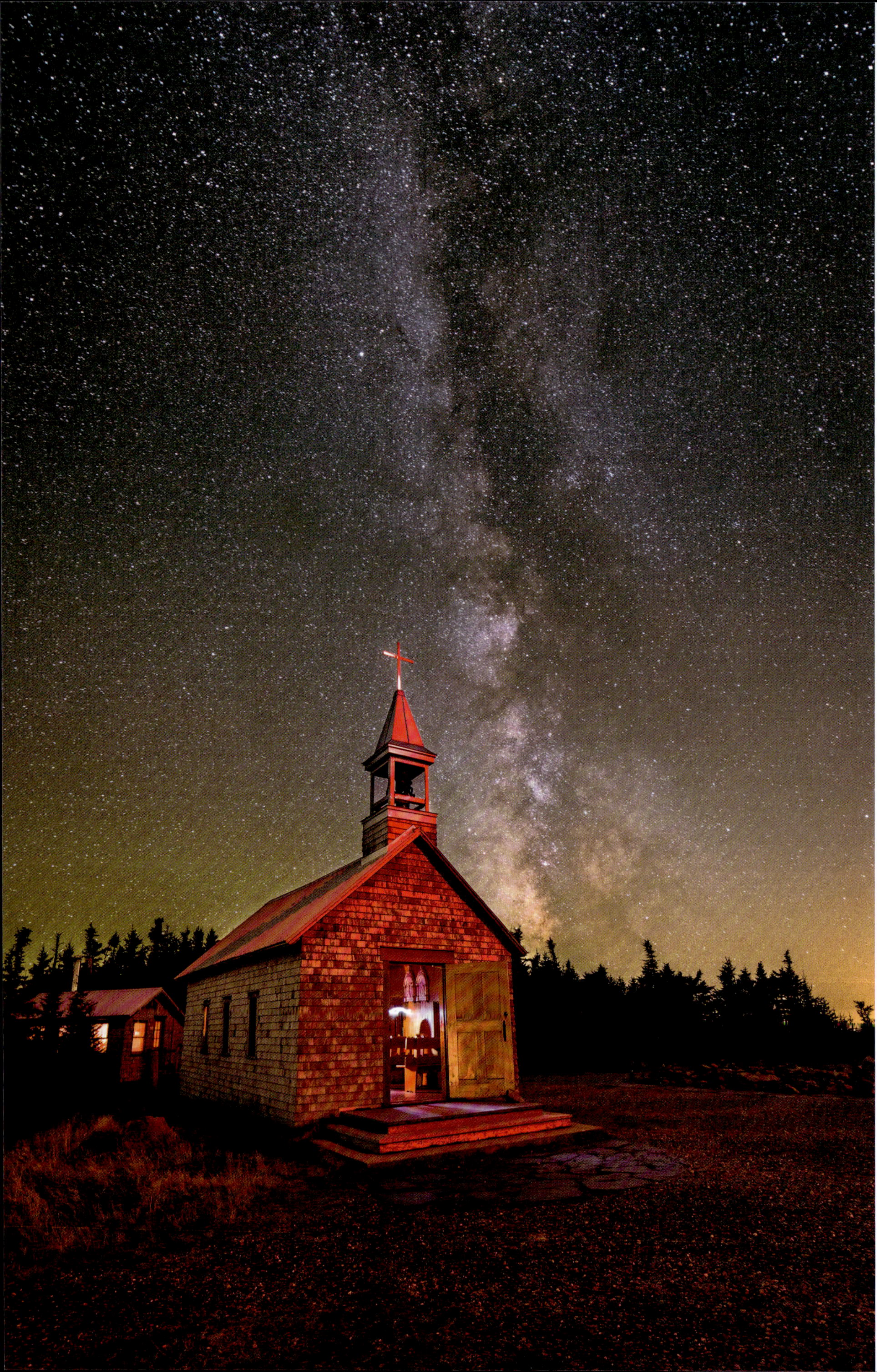

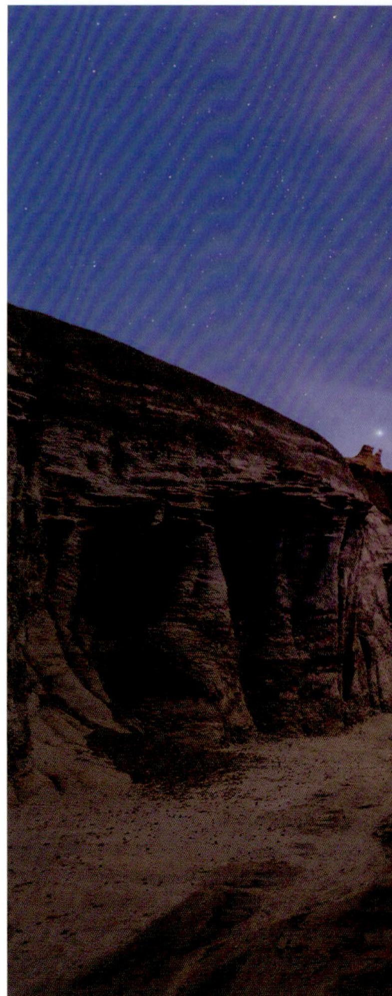

▲ The landscape in the badlands of the Bisti Wilderness of New Mexico during twilight with the moon (just above frame) lighting up the foreground. The Orion constellation can be seen in the upper left of the frame.

◀ The ambient light on this small chapel on a mountain in Quebec was provided by the red light of a giant antenna tower behind me.

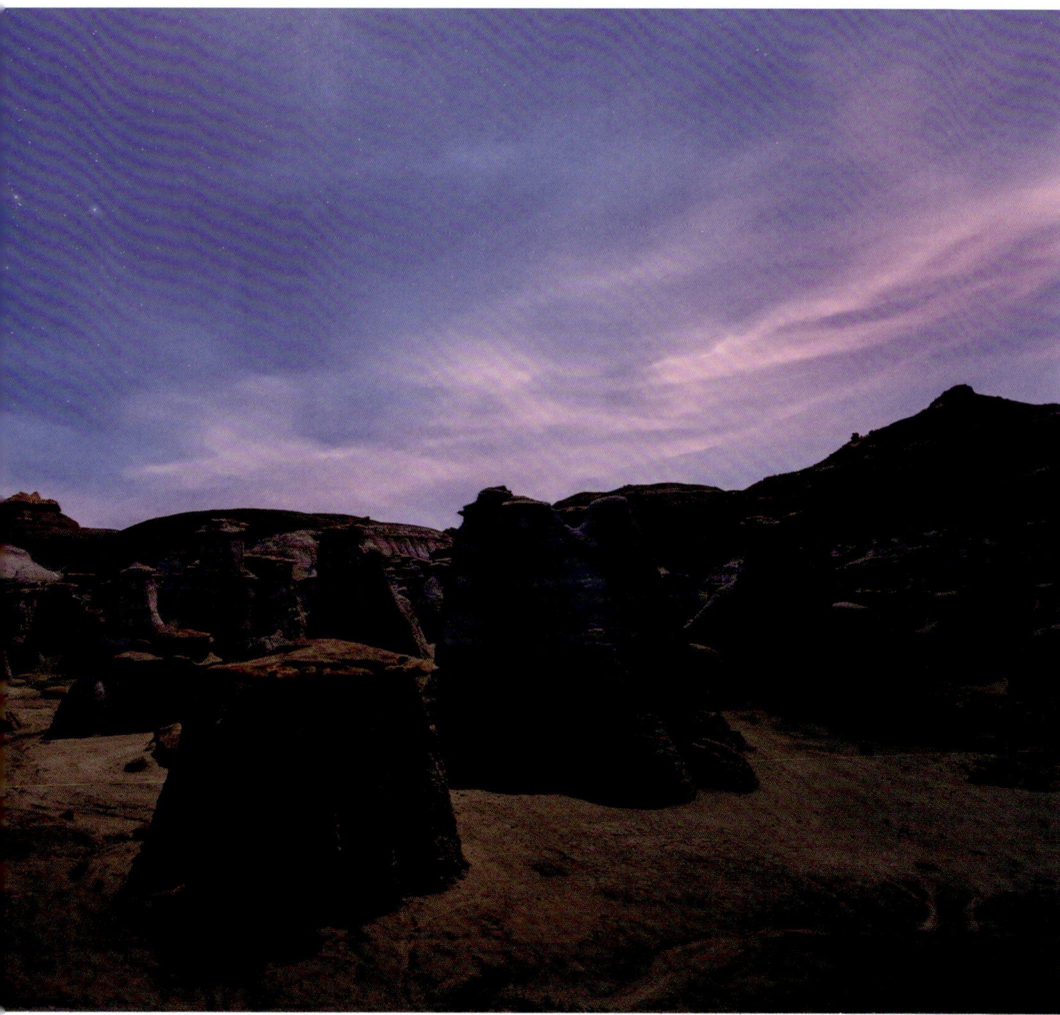

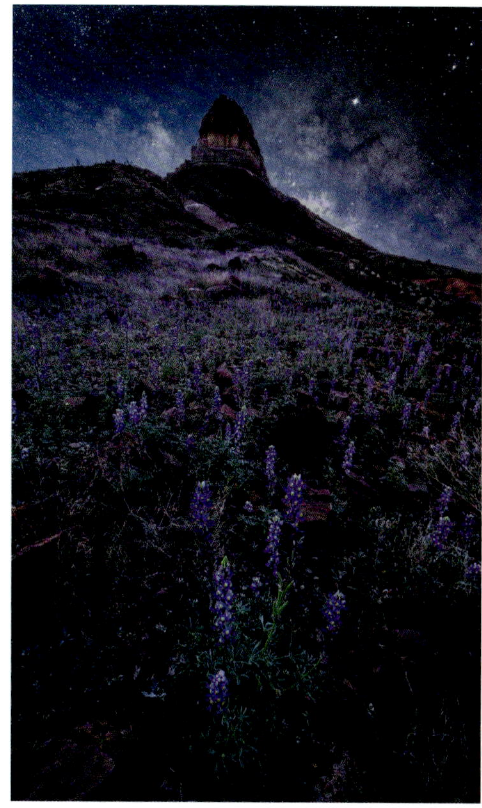

▲ The Milky Way during blue hour with bluebonnet flowers in Big Bend National Park. In this case, both the sky and foreground photographs that make up this image were taken during twilight (blue hour).

AMBIENT LIGHT

My preference for foreground lighting is to use whatever ambient light is available. This could be starlight in a dark location, or bright light from a lighthouse, or perhaps the light from buildings or a nearby town. A nearby source of light pollution can add a surprising amount of light to your foreground.

In a very dark location with little ambient light, I will use a longer shutter speed for my foreground shots. Shutter speed suggestions for this purpose are covered in the **Shutter Speed** section of the **Exposure Settings** chapter.

Most of the photos in this book have separate foreground photographs that use only the ambient light available at the location.

MOONLIGHT

Shooting under a partial moon low in the sky that's positioned behind you or to the side of your scene can be a very effective way of getting some dramatic lighting on your foreground, enabling you to use shorter shutter speeds for the foreground. With enough moonlight, you could also use a higher f-stop for more depth of field in a single shot without requiring a very long shutter speed.

BLUE HOUR (TWILIGHT)

Blue hour is the period of twilight where the landscape takes on a very blue tone, with very soft shadows. This can be a great time to take your foreground shots if you've planned far enough ahead to know exactly where you want to be for your Milky Way shots. Similar to moonlight, the amount of extra light on the landscape during twilight allows you to use a shorter shutter speed and/or higher f-stop for your foreground shots.

One thing to remember when shooting twilight foregrounds is that they will not look exactly as they would under starlight with a long exposure. You can correct the blue colors in post-processing so that your foreground looks more like a dark night scene, but shadows that would not appear under starlight will look out of place with a dark sky Milky Way shot blended in that was taken during darkness.

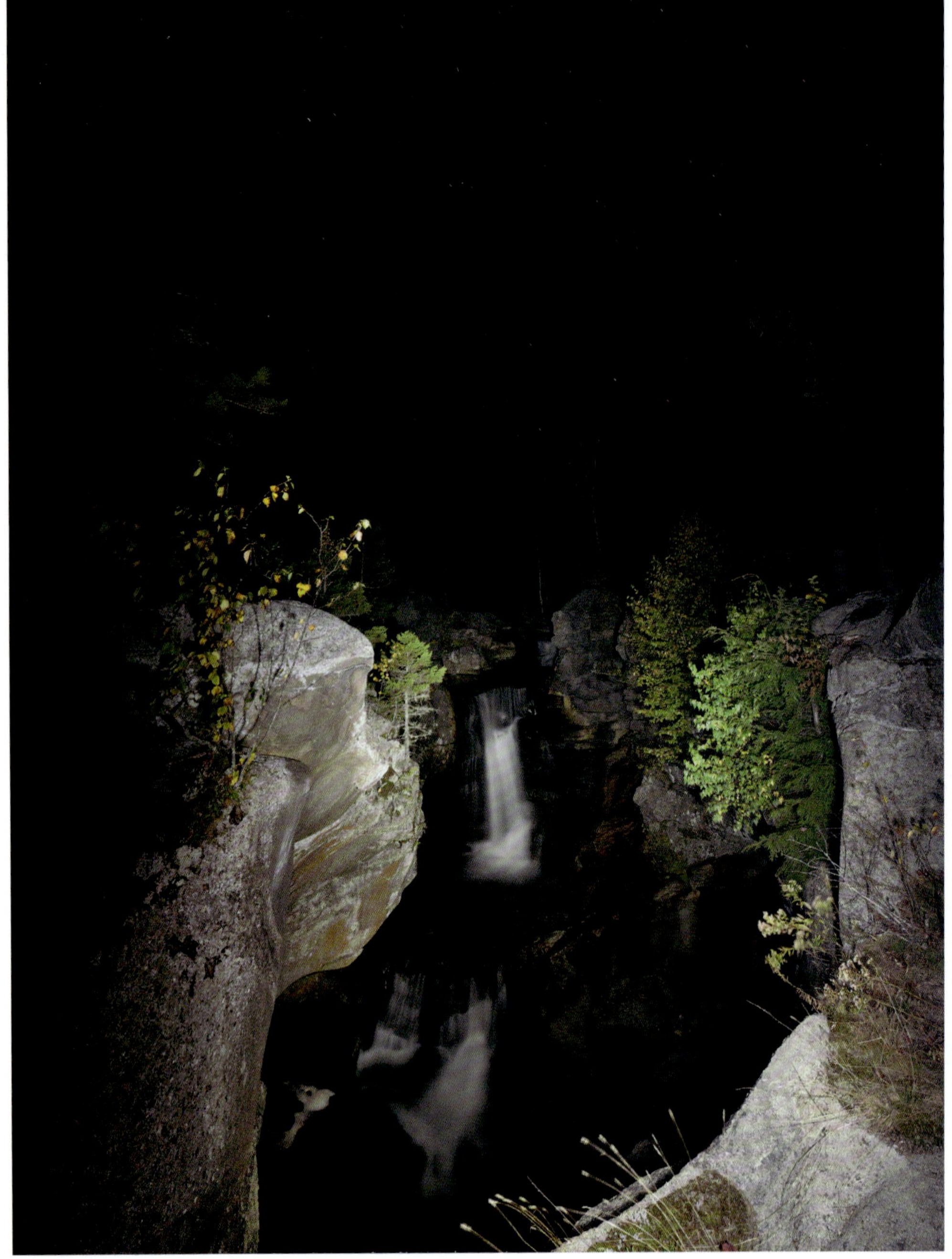

▲ I tried light painting this gorge, but I didn't like the results. It created too many harsh and unnatural shadows that wouldn't be there under a dark sky.

ARTIFICIAL LIGHTING

If you don't want to wait for long exposures, or you want to highlight certain objects, you can add your own light to the scene with artificial lighting. However, be aware that using lights can ruin other people's enjoyment of the night, and is in fact illegal in some parks. I encourage you to use ambient light whenever possible.

LIGHT SOURCES AND FILTERS

There are many light source options available, including flashlights of all kinds and LED light panels that offer continuous low-level lighting.

If you're using an LED light source, it's a good idea to either buy a warming gel or get an LED panel that can change colors. Regular LED light is sometimes too blue for lighting up a landscape or building, and a warmer color of light will often look nicer.

You'll also want some way to diffuse the light to a softer, broader beam that provides move even lighting. For a flashlight this could be as simple as using a lens cloth to cover the light, while LED panels should come with diffuser filters or have compatible filters available for purchase.

TECHNIQUE

Light panels can be placed on light stands or tripods, leaned against rocks, or held by hand, and they can be placed out of frame facing the foreground.

A flashlight can be used to paint light onto your scene by holding it in your hand and moving it around the scene or just specific foreground objects. Be sure to move the light around to avoid harsh lighting in just one spot.

DRAWBACKS AND PROBLEMS TO AVOID

The technique of light painting can work well in situations where you have a primary foreground object, such as a rock formation, and you want to light it up, but for a scene with a lot going on in the foreground it might be difficult to light up the entire scene without it looking harsh or taking in a huge amount of light. Flooding a scene with uncontrolled light is what I call the "car headlight problem" because it can often look like a car was parked behind the camera with its high beams blasting onto the scene. This results in harsh shadows that you wouldn't see at night, very uneven lighting, and bright, ugly highlights on wet rocks and water.

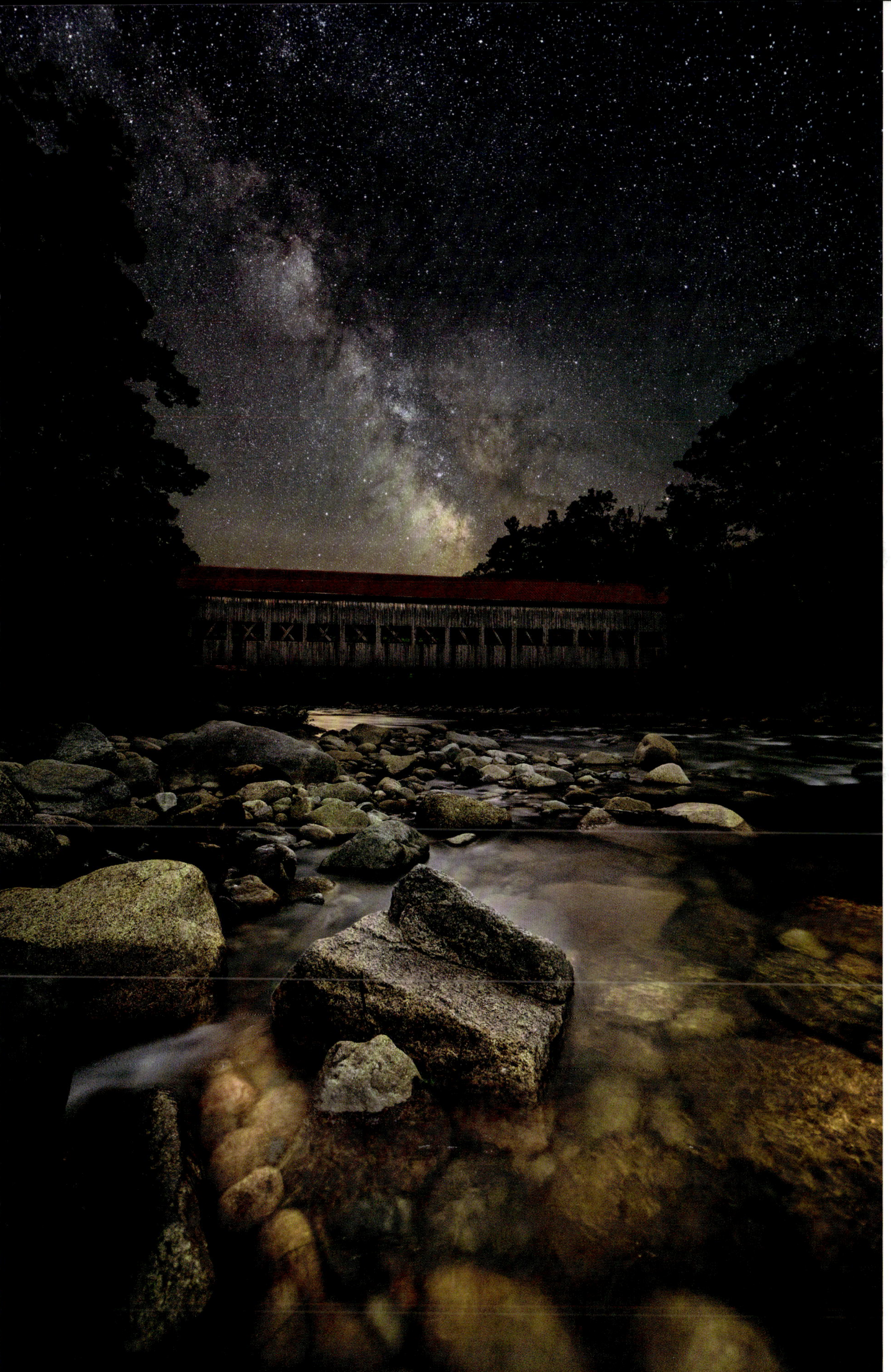

◀ New Hampshire.

Here is an example of an image made with light painting. I used a halogen flashlight with a lens cloth diffuser to light up the foreground rocks and water, giving them some definition and a nice glow. I also light painted the bridge, without diffusing the light since it was far enough away that this wasn't necessary. While the technique worked on the bridge, it appears a bit flat because the light was head-on. Lighting from the side achieves better definition. However, lighting up a fairly distant object is not something I can recommend as it will be a nuisance to anyone else in the area trying to enjoy the night. These days I don't use such techniques and prefer long exposures to capture the ambient light.

PLANNING

11

So you have the gear and knowledge to shoot Milky Way landscapes, but how do you know when and where the Galactic Core will be visible? You don't want to just show up to your favorite location only to find out the Milky Way isn't visible that time of year, or that it's not visible over the foreground you were hoping to use. This is where planning tools come in handy.

▶ Hopewell Rocks on the Bay of Fundy.

As I knew where the Milky Way was going to be, I was able to plan this shot in daytime and be confident that it would work when I came back at night.

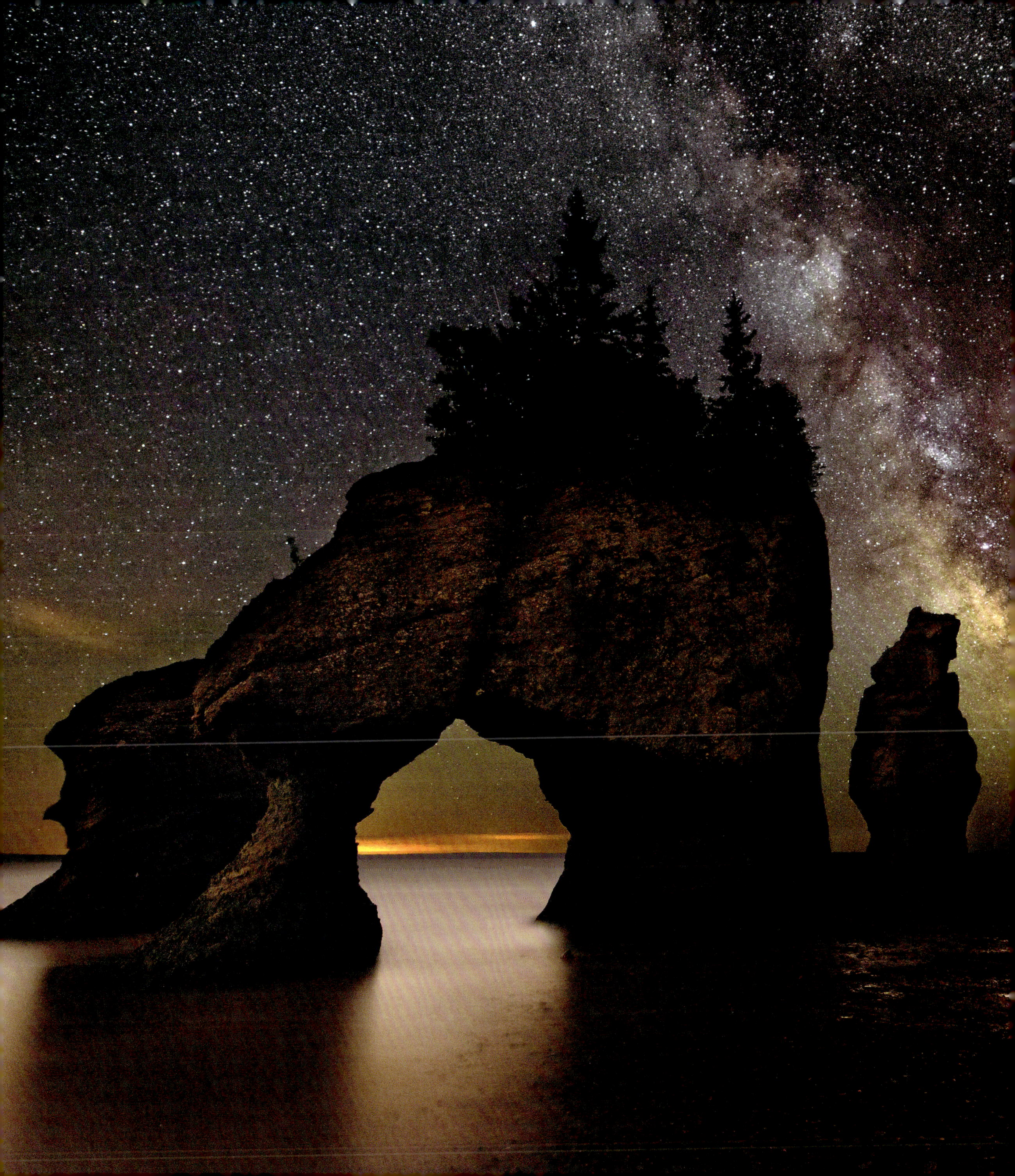

11.1 ASTRONOMY BASICS

If you know the basics of our view of the cosmos you'll be better able to use the advanced planning tools available for astrophotography. Understanding how celestial objects move across the sky according to your location and the hemisphere you are in will help you to envision photo opportunities. It will also help you to use the planning tools available to fine-tune your compositions.

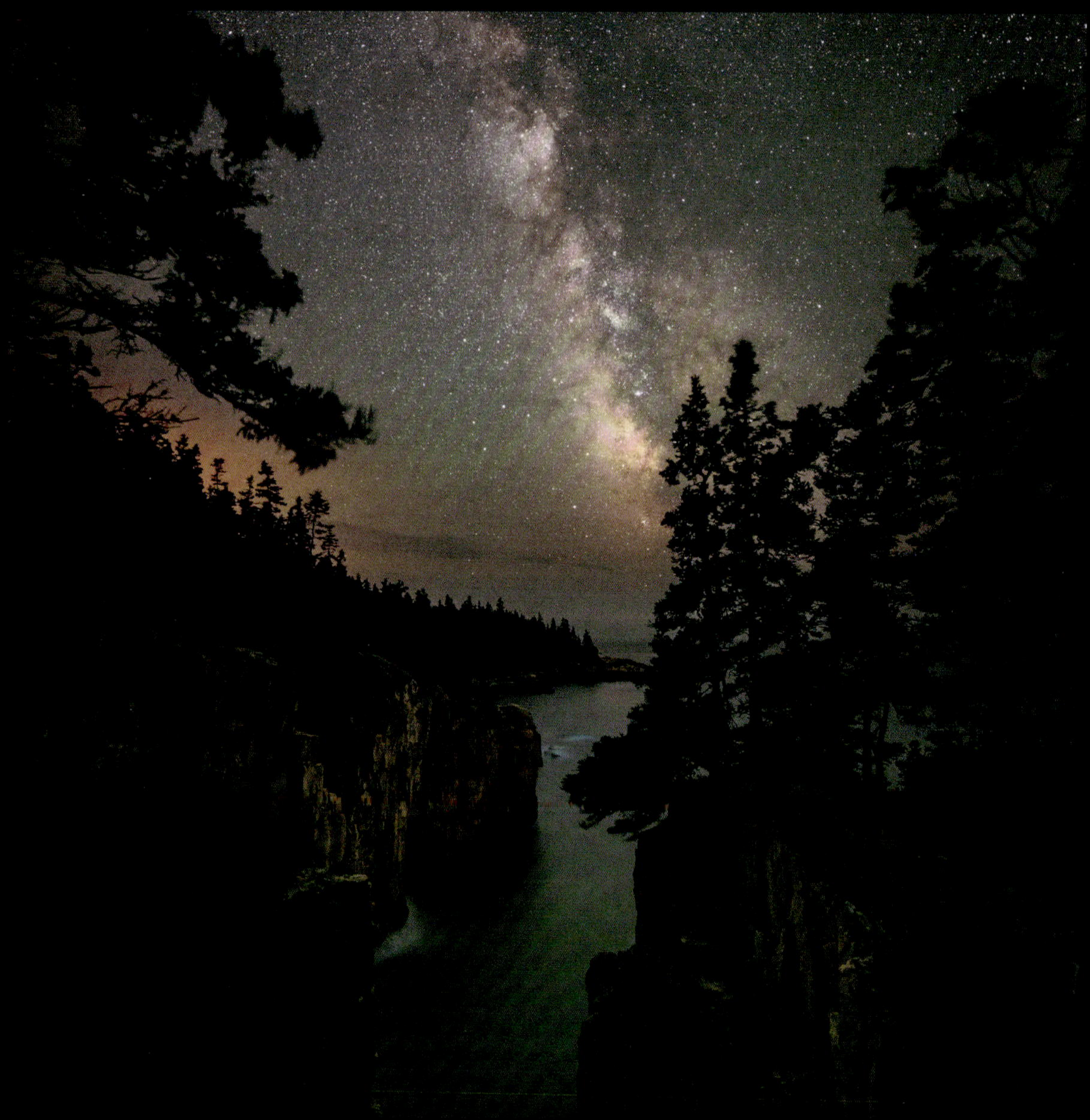

◀ Acadia National Park.

In the Northern Hemisphere, the Milky Way is vertical by the summer.

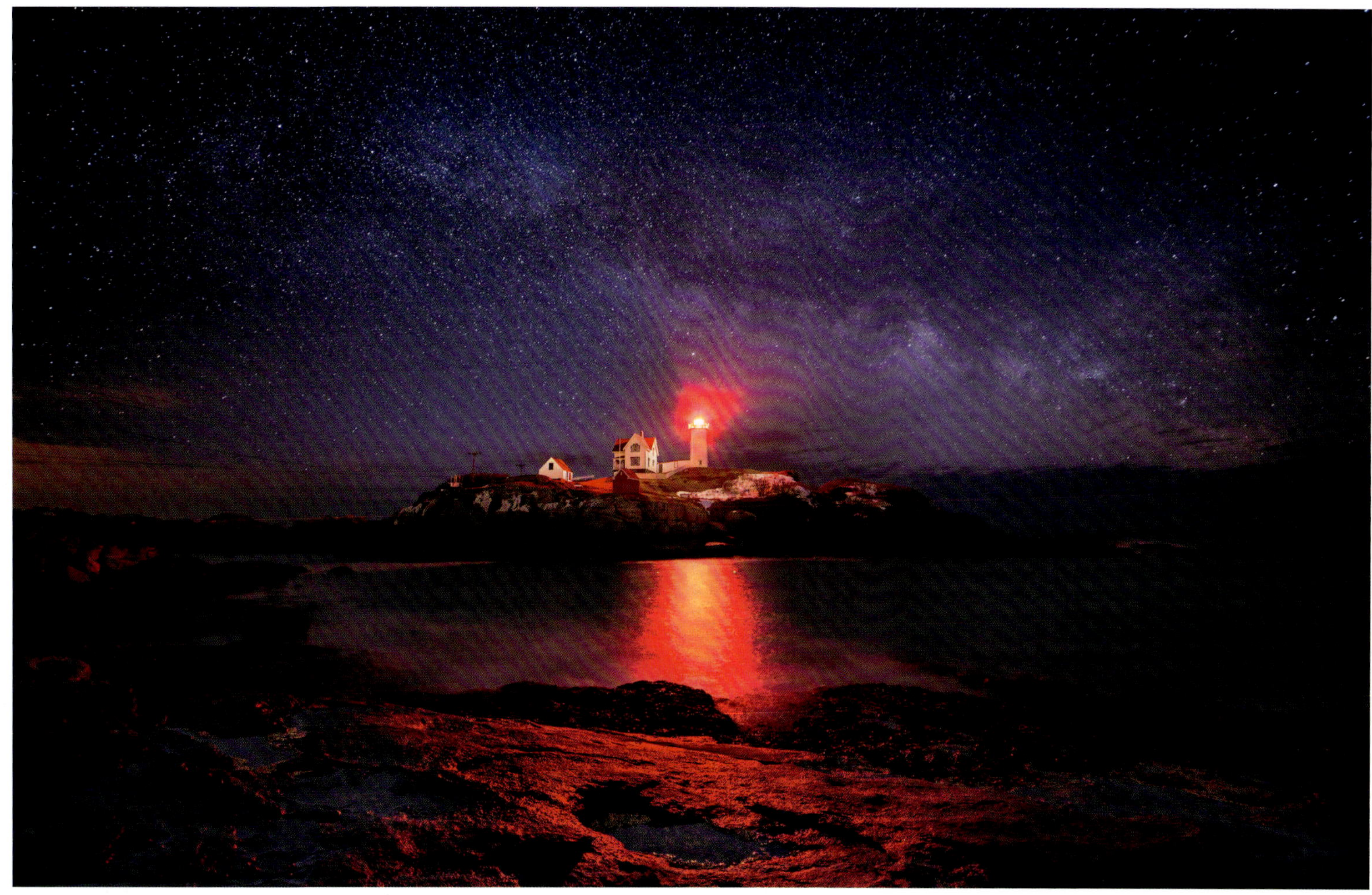

▲ Nubble Lighthouse.
In the Northern Hemisphere, the Milky Way is low on the horizon early in the year. This is another early Milky Way image of mine when I was pushing the color balance toward blue, resulting in a purple Milky Way. As technically inaccurate as the sky color may be, I haven't re-edited this photo to change the color as I like the dreamy mood it creates.

THE MILKY WAY

The location and angle of the Milky Way's Galactic Core in the sky will change throughout the year, and it will be different in the Northern and Southern Hemispheres. The Milky Way orientation can even vary within a hemisphere depending on how far north or south you are.

NORTHERN HEMISPHERE

In the Northern Hemisphere, the Galactic Core of the Milky Way is visible late in the night starting in February; it fades from view early in the night in October; becoming completely hidden below the horizon at night until the following February. The Galactic Core may technically be above the horizon briefly late in the night in January or early February, and early in the night in November, but it is so brief and so close to the horizon you won't see much of it during those times. The time of year when the Milky Way is visible is often referred to as "Milky Way season" by photographers.

The Milky Way will lay fairly flat early in the year and will be in the south east, with the core in the east and the rest of the Milky Way arcing northward along the horizon. As the year goes on, the Milky Way will move to the south and south-west and rise more and more vertically until it is straight up and down in mid-summer, with the core eventually dropping below the horizon and the rest of the Milky Way arcing to the north.

The Galactic Core is always close to the horizon in the Northern Hemisphere, but the further south you go, the higher above the horizon it will be.

The following chart can be used as a guide to when the Milky Way will be visible in the Northern Hemisphere. These times are approximate and are based on a location of 45 degrees north. The times will vary a bit the further north or south you are from there. Use a planning app such as PhotoPills to determine the exact times for your desired shooting location, and don't forget to take the moon's position and phase into consideration.

SOUTHERN HEMISPHERE

Things are a little different in the Southern Hemisphere. Being south of the Equator means you will see the Galactic Core much higher in the sky compared to views in the Northern Hemisphere. This allows for some very different compositions. By the middle of the year (winter in the Southern Hemisphere), the Galactic Core is directly overhead in the middle of the night.

MOON PHASE

It is a misconception that only the night of the new moon is a dark, moonless night. In fact, each month there are at least two weeks around the new moon where some of the night (if not the entire night) will be dark and moonless. Check the moon rise and set times for your shooting location.

▶ This photo was taken in Bolivia by Yuri Beletsky and shows the high elevation that the Galactic Core can reach in the Southern Hemisphere.

CHART OF MILKY WAY CORE VISIBILITY BY MONTH FOR 45 DEGREES NORTH LATITUDE

Month	Visible As Early As...	Visible Until...
January	Not Visible	–
February	4am	5am
March	2am	5am
April	1am	4am
May	11pm	3am
June	10:30pm	2am
July	10:30pm	2am
August	10pm	1am
September	8:30pm	11pm
October	7:30pm	9pm
November	7pm	7:15pm
December	Not Visible	

CHART OF MILKY WAY CORE VISIBILITY BY MONTH FOR 45 DEGREES SOUTH LATITUDE

Month	Visible As Early As...	Visible Until...
January	3:30am	4am
February	1:30am	5am
March	11:30pm	6am
April	9pm	6am
May	7pm	6am
June	7pm	6:30am
July	7pm	6:30am
August	7:30pm	5:30am
September	9pm	4am
October	10pm	2am
November	10pm	12am
December	Not Visible	

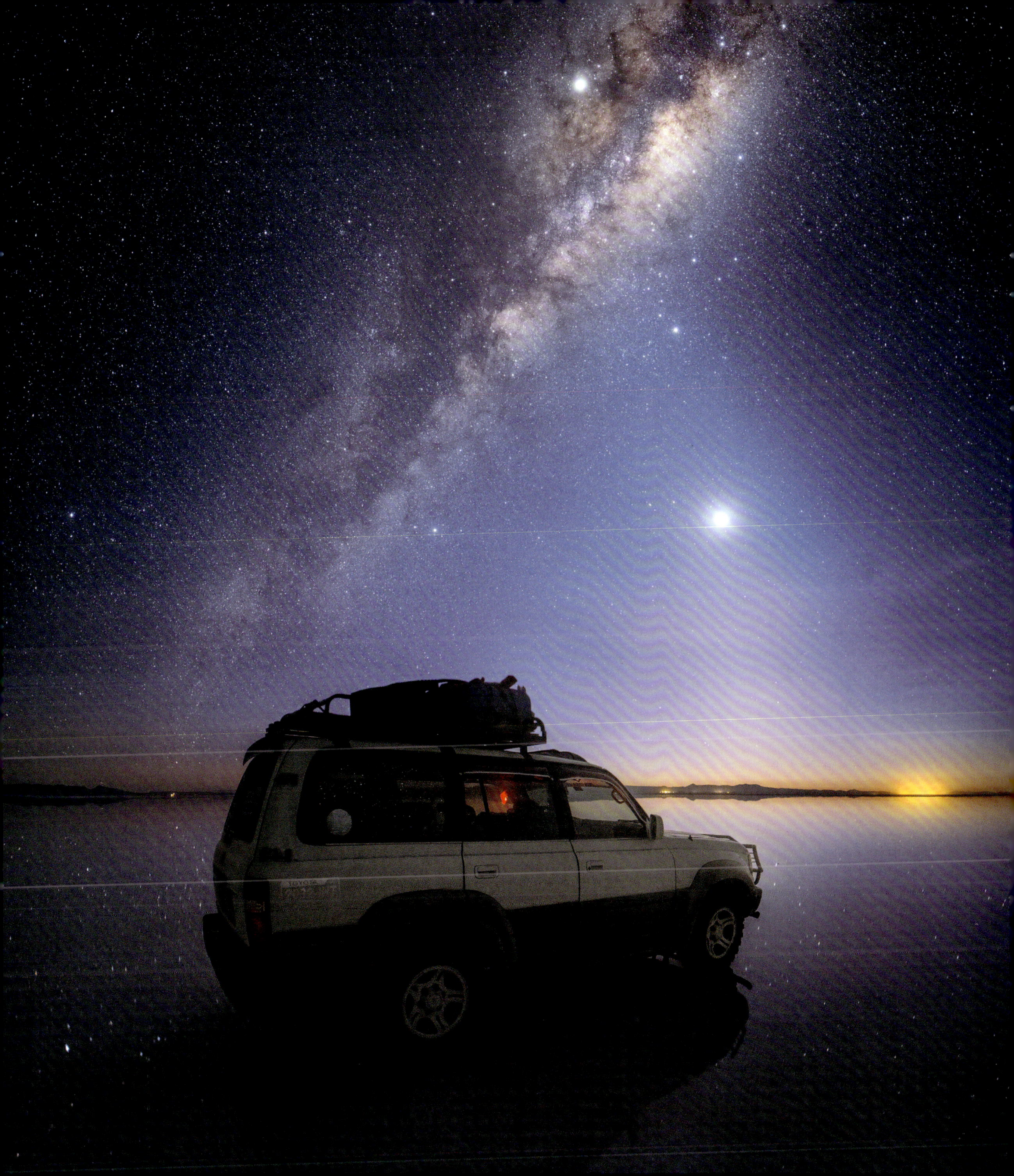

11.2 STAR MAP PROGRAMS

There are a variety of star map software applications available that help with visualizing the night sky and where certain objects, like the core of the Milky Way, the Orion Constellation and so on, will be in the sky on any given night of the year at any location on Earth.

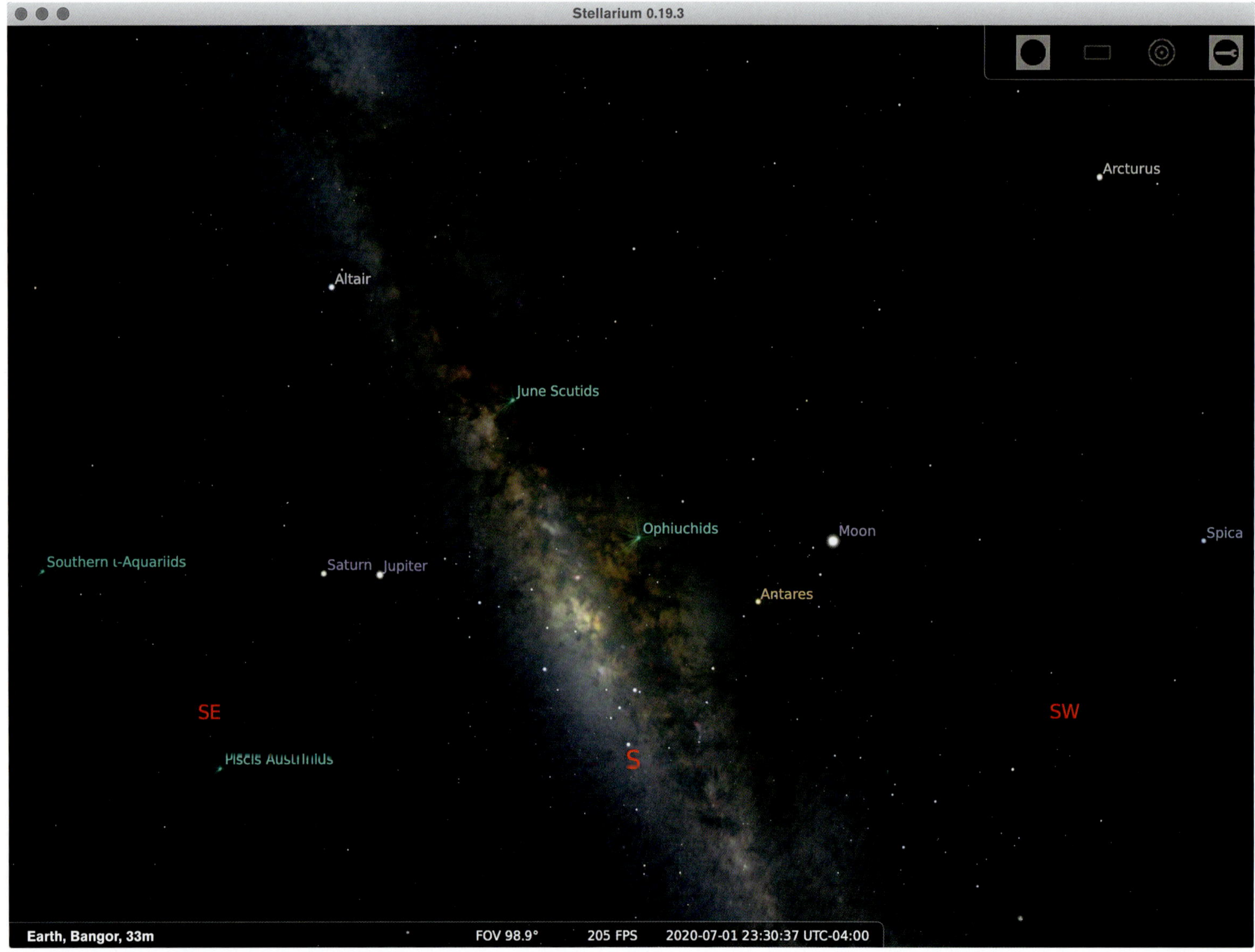

▲ The free computer program Stellarium is useful for a variety of planning needs.

A phone or tablet app such as PhotoPills is the best way to plan a shot of the Milky Way anywhere on the planet, which we'll cover in the next section, but before we do that, let's look at some general apps for shooting the night sky.

Stellarium, available at **stellarium.org**, is a free program you can download onto your computer. This is a very feature-rich program that can be used for everything from finding where the Milky Way will be on a particular night to knowing how a deep space object will look framed up at a specific focal length. It also contains information about different stars and deep space objects. Try clicking on a star or object and you should see a window pop-up with details on that subject.

For smartphones and tablets, there are a ton of star apps available, depending on your phone's operating system (iOS or Android), including a mobile version of Stellarium. Among these are SkySafari, Star Walk, and Planets.

Most of these mobile apps all support virtual reality, allowing you to hold the phone up while outside and see a map of where the stars and planets will be at any time of night. Alternatively, you can turn on Live mode to see where they are at that very minute from your location. This is handy at night so you can know, for example, whether that really bright star-like-thing in the sky that you don't remember seeing in that spot before is actually one of the planets in our solar system.

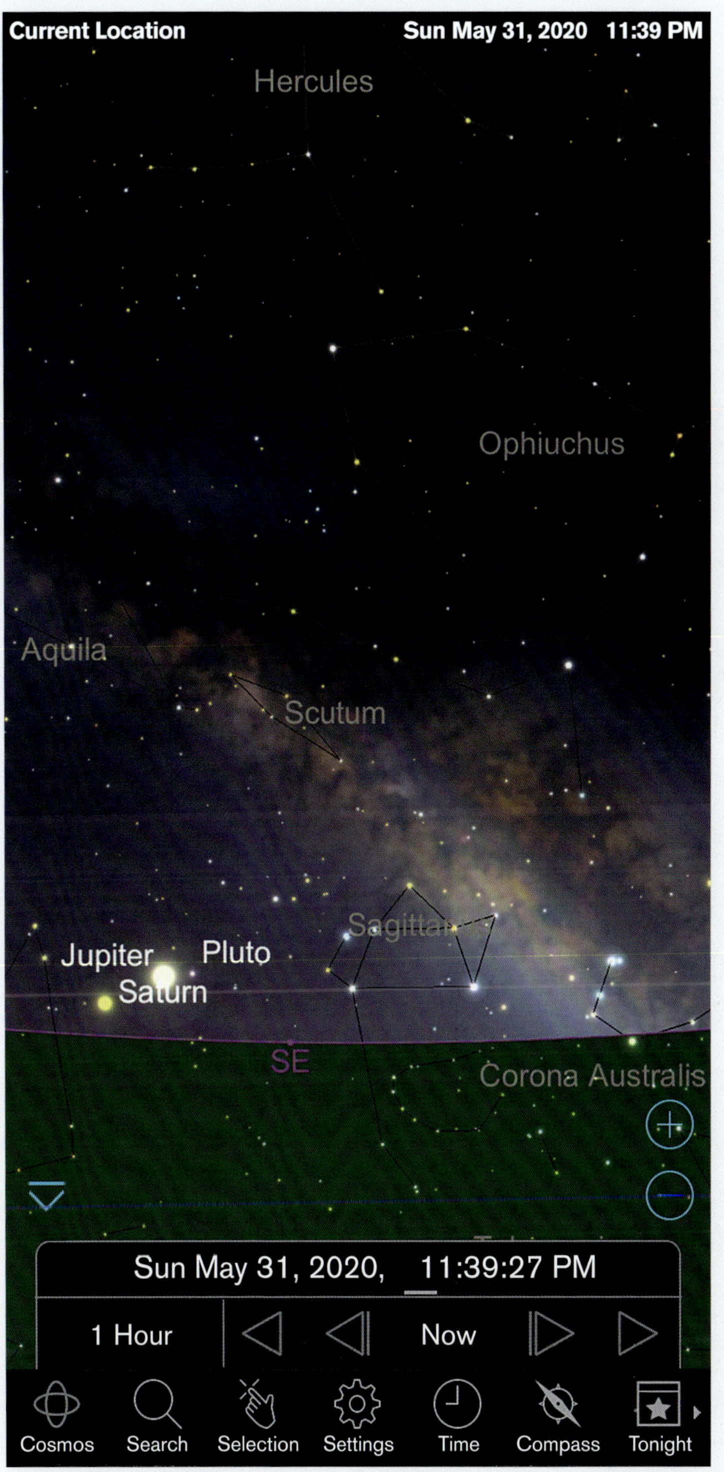

▲ The SkySafari app on an iPhone.

11.3 USING PHOTOPILLS FOR MILKY WAY PLANNING

There are a number of iOS and Android apps available for planning photos of the Milky Way. In fact, these apps will help you plan any sunrise, sunset, moonrise or moonset photo.

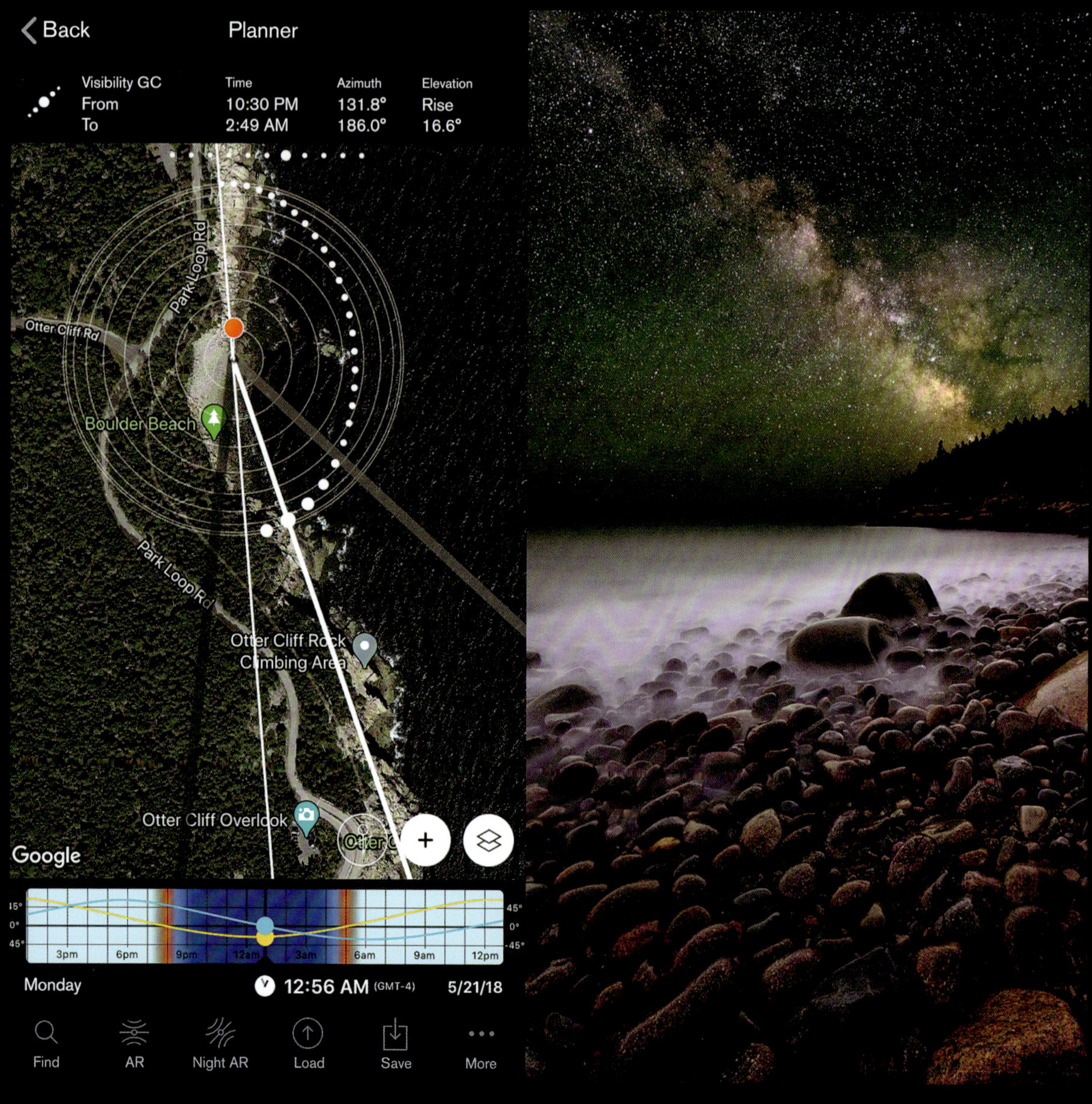

◀ An example of a plan with PhotoPills and the shot that resulted.

The major apps available are PhotoPills, The Photographer's Ephemeris, and Planit Pro. I use PhotoPills the most and we'll look at that here.

THE PLANNER

PhotoPills has tons of tools — we've already looked at the Spot Stars tool (see page 106). A full explanation of PhotoPills is beyond the scope of this book, but check out the many free tutorials available within the app and on the **photopills.com** website. I also offer a webinar that covers PhotoPills on my website, **adamwoodworth.com**. However, its real standout feature is the "Planner." This is basically a 2D map that lets you plan sun, moon and Milky Way shots for any location on the planet, for any date.

The Planner uses a red pin to indicate the position of your camera. This must be placed exactly where you intend to be with your camera. All the other details (sunrise, moonrise, Milky Way visibility times and so on) are based on the location of this pin, as well as the date and time you input at the bottom of the planner. You can move the pin by tapping and holding on it, then dragging it around, or just tap and hold somewhere on the map for a couple seconds. If you want to find your current location, then use the compass and pin button. To reveal this button, tap the "plus sign" (+) button to open the toolbox.

Lines that indicate the angle of the sun, moon or Milky Way will all extend from this red pin, showing you the angle to the Milky Way's center, for example, from that point on Earth. You can turn layers off or on that show the angle of the sun, moon or Milky Way by clicking the "Layers" button in the bottom right of the screen, just above the timeline.

The PhotoPills planner indicates the angle and elevation of the Milky Way with white dots and concentric circles. The white dots indicate the arc of the Milky Way, with the largest dots representing the Galactic Core. The thin white line indicates where the Galactic Center is, and the thick white lines indicate where the Milky Way arc hits the horizon. The concentric circles indicate its elevation; the closer the arc is to the center circle, the higher in the sky the Milky Way will appear, and vice versa. You can change the time by swiping on the timeline at the bottom of the planner. Double-click on the clock or date icon to set the date and time.

The top of the planner contains details relevant to the location and date, such as times of sunrise/set or moonrise/set, and the visibility of the Milky Way. Swipe left or right on the top part of the screen to see other panels of information. This information is very important! It will tell you when the Galactic Core will be visible during the night based on the set location and date. Combine this information with the moonrise and set times to determine when you will have dark skies.

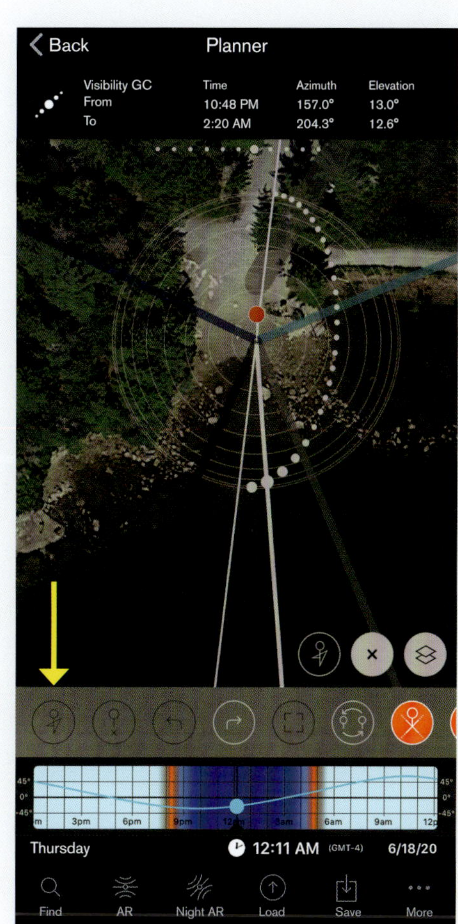

▲ Find your location with GPS.

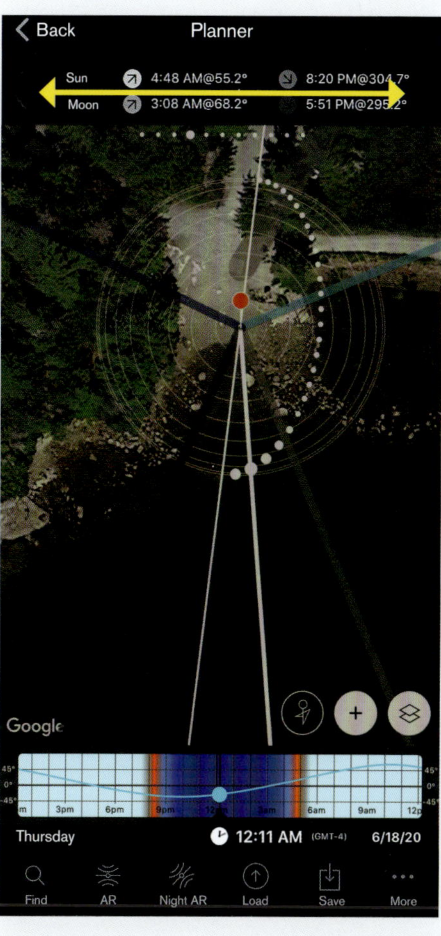

▲ Swipe the top panel left or right for more information.

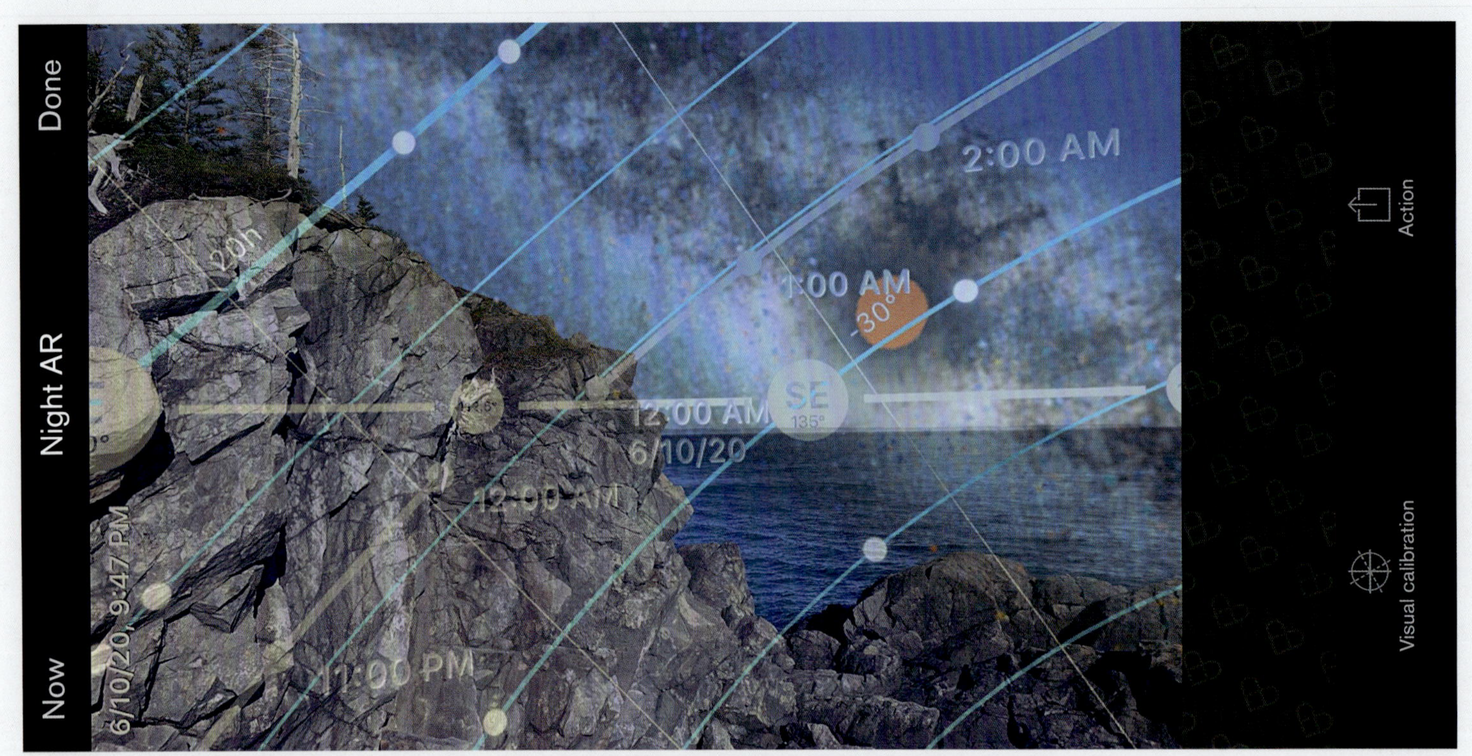

▲ The Milky Way is displayed over your phone's live camera view in PhotoPill's augmented reality mode. I held the phone horizontally to get a landscape view of the scene.

AUGMENTED REALITY

Augmented reality is a great tool for scouting locations. It allows you to view the scene in front of you live through your phone's camera with an image of the Milky Way overlaid on top of it. You can change the time to see how the Milky Way moves through the sky and see if it lines up with your desired foreground. Make sure you have the location (red pin) set to your current location.

Within the PhotoPills planner, click the "Night AR" button at the bottom of the screen to be taken to augmented reality view of the night sky that will show the Milky Way.

Once in Augmented Reality mode, you will see a "Visual Calibration" button at the bottom of the screen. This allows you to adjust the virtual view so that it matches reality to ensure that the Milky Way (or sun or moon) will show up in the correct position. Clicking this will temporarily set the date and time to the current date and time and will add a sun or moon to the AR view. Point your phone at the sun or moon to see if it lines up with the sun or moon icon in the AR view. If it does not, put your finger on the icon and drag it around until it lines up with the actual sun or moon. Then click "Confirm Calibration" at the bottom of the screen to set the view back to the date and time you had selected.

You will want to do this every time you use Augmented Reality for the first time at a new spot. Even putting your phone in your pocket and moving slightly to another spot in the same immediate area can throw off the accuracy, so always use Visual Calibration to ensure that PhotoPills is showing you the correct position of the Milky Way.

If you can't see the sun or moon because your view is blocked (by trees or clouds, for example) then you won't be able to complete the calibration. Instead take the readings with a

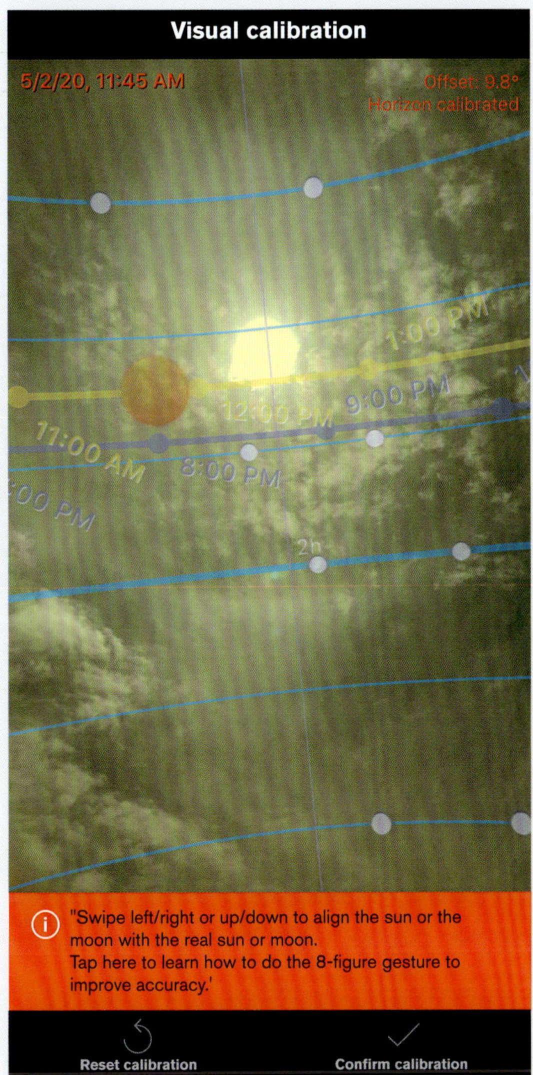

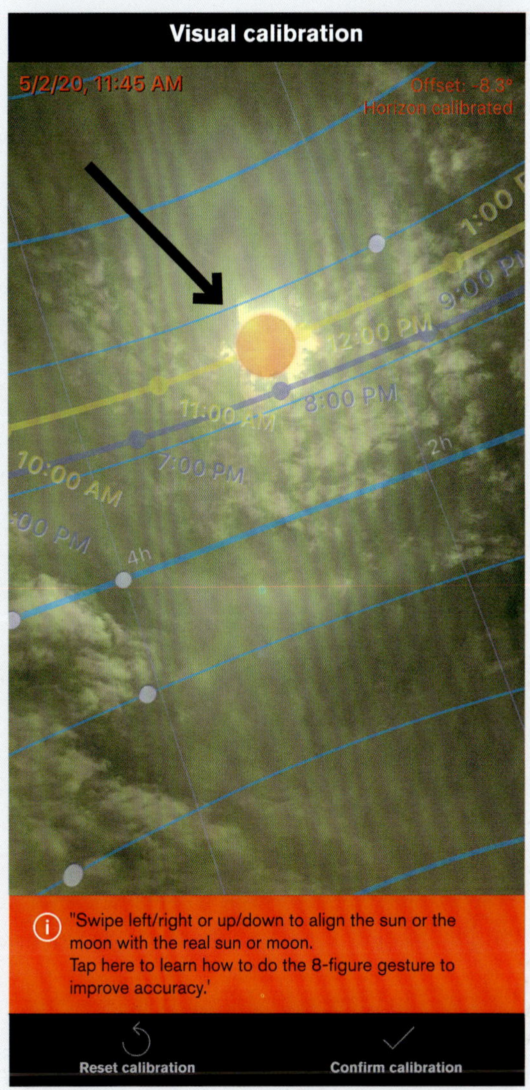

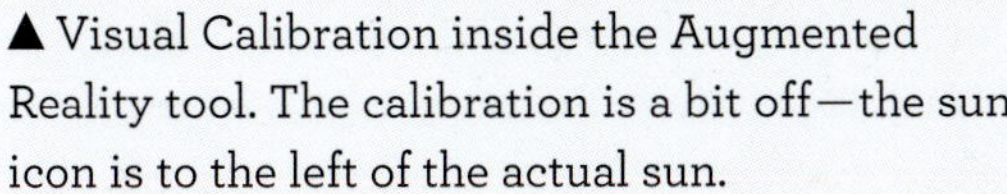

▲ Visual Calibration inside the Augmented Reality tool. The calibration is a bit off—the sun icon is to the left of the actual sun.

▲ Visual Calibration is carried out by placing your finger on the screen and dragging the image around until the sun icon is on top of the real sun.

hefty pinch of salt, since they could be off by a little or a lot depending on your mobile device.

You can also use the other "AR" button at the bottom of the planner for planning sun and moon shots. Again, use Visual Calibration to check it matches with reality.

When using the AR modes, make sure you consider when it will be dark outside. The app gives you a visual indication of this by changing the background color, but it's easy to miss. You don't want to head out at 9pm to catch the Milky Way, forgetting it is the middle of summer and the sky is still light outside.

11.4 MILKY WAY CALENDAR IN PLANIT PRO

Planit Pro is very similar to PhotoPills, but it has an additional tool that I absolutely love: the Milky Way Calendar. Based on the camera location you set in Planit Pro, the Milky Way Calendar shows you which days of a month will have visibility of the Milky Way's Galactic Core under dark skies.

This means that the Milky Way Core is not only above the horizon, but that the moon is also not up for at least part of the night. The calendar indicates how many hours of dark Milky Way Core time there is per night with green dots on each date. One dot is less than two hours, two dots is more than two hours, and three dots is more than four hours. No green dots means that either the moon is up all night or the Milky Way Core is never above the horizon.

This calendar is incredibly useful for planning when you might want to take a trip to a certain location to capture the Milky Way. You can pick any month of any year. I also use it to plan dates for my workshops.

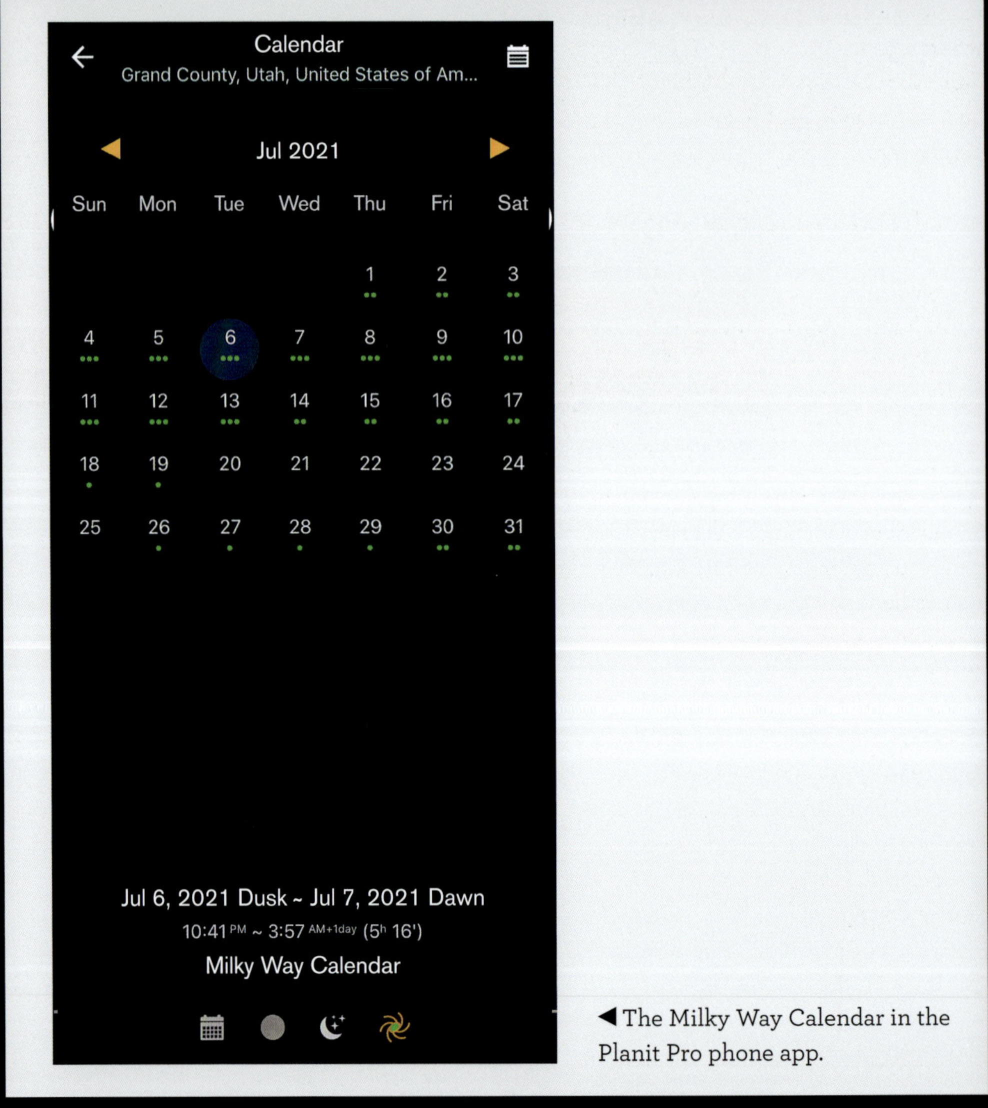

◀ The Milky Way Calendar in the Planit Pro phone app.

11.5 WEATHER FORECASTING

Cloudy skies are the bane of the landscape astrophotographer's existence, so a reliable weather forecast is very helpful for planning. However, don't give up hope if the forecast isn't for completely clear skies, a few clouds can add some really interesting texture to photos taken with long exposures.

There are myriad weather forecasting apps and websites available, but most of them do not provide enough detail to be particularly useful. You really want to know when and where the clouds will be. "Dumbed down" daily/nightly forecasts with smiling suns and moons will not tell you much about the cloud cover.

In the US, my favorite general weather source is NOAA. Their website is **weather.gov**. If you carefully inspect the hourly forecast graph it will give you a much better idea of the forecasted cloud cover. The NOAA website works on a phone as well. Look for the "sky cover" line on the graph. Lower numbers for sky cover indicate less cloud cover and more open sky.

As for phone apps, I have found that the best cloud cover app for the US and Canada is Astrospheric. It will show a detailed hour-by-hour forecast of the cloud cover percentage for a particular location, as well as a cloud forecast map. The forecast map is very useful in determining where you might want to go for clear skies.

Another handy app is Clear Outside. It also features hour-by-hour cloud cover percentages, however it does not have a map of cloud cover like Astrospheric.

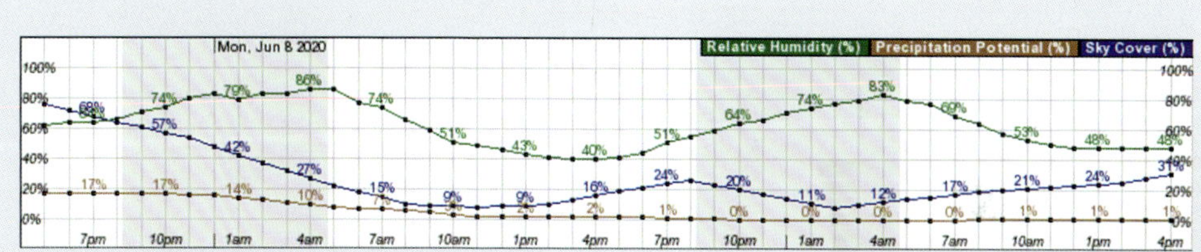

▲ An example of the Sky Cover graph from NOAA's weather.gov website. The blue line is sky cover. Lower values indicate fewer clouds.

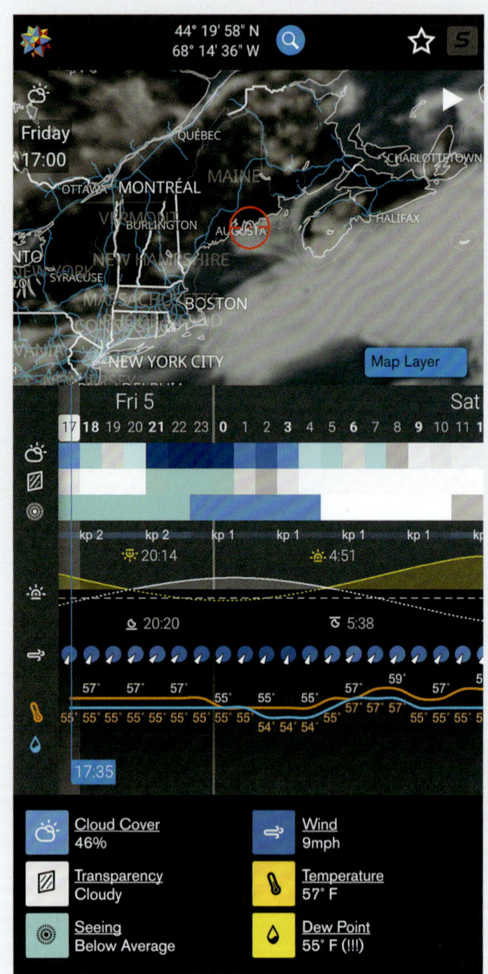

▲ Hourly cloud cover graph in Astrospheric.

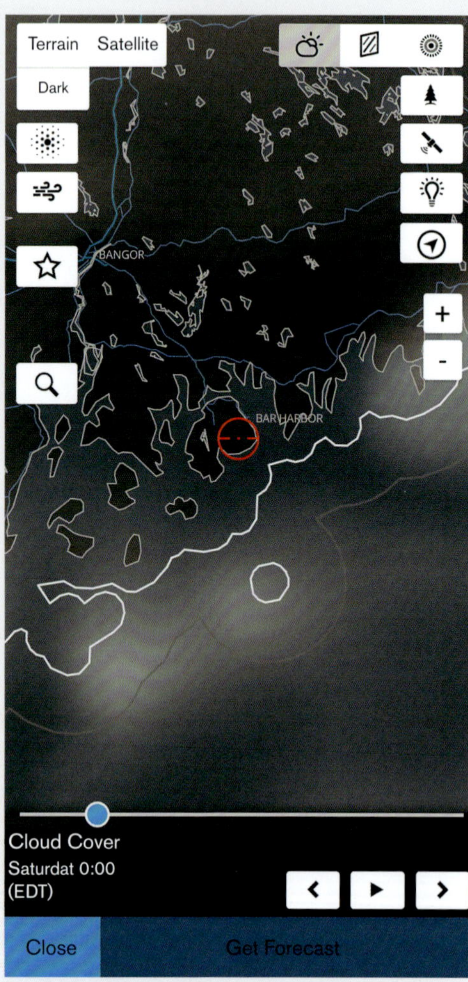

▲ Cloud cover forecast map in Astrospheric.

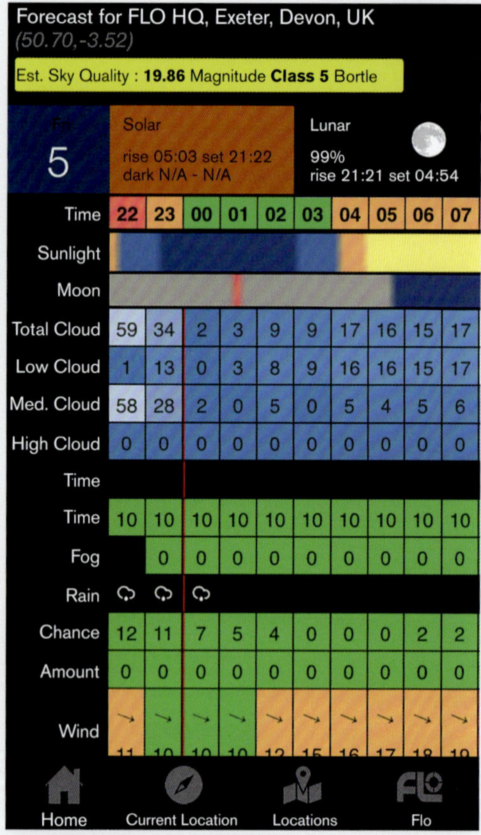

▲ The hourly forecast in the Clear Outside app.

11.6 FINDING A DARK SKY

Light pollution really limits the visibility of the night sky, and the further you can get from big sources of light pollution, the better. Using your planner, such as PhotoPills, you can determine which direction you want to face for the Milky Way, and then use that information to see what cities might be in that direction as well. If there's a big city within 50 miles (80km) you'll have some glow on the horizon, but it might be tolerable. The further you can get from big cities, the better.

You can use a dark sky map to find locations with less light pollution. Such a map is available in the previously mentioned apps Astrospheric and Planit Pro, and freely available at the website **darksitefinder.com**. These maps use the Bortle scale, which is a standard way to measure light pollution overhead. The higher the number on the scale, the worse the light pollution overhead at that location. Keep in mind that you'll likely be shooting with the horizon in view, so you'll want to take that into consideration when looking at a Bortle map—the Bortle number might be low overhead where you want to be, but it could be much higher in the direction you want to face.

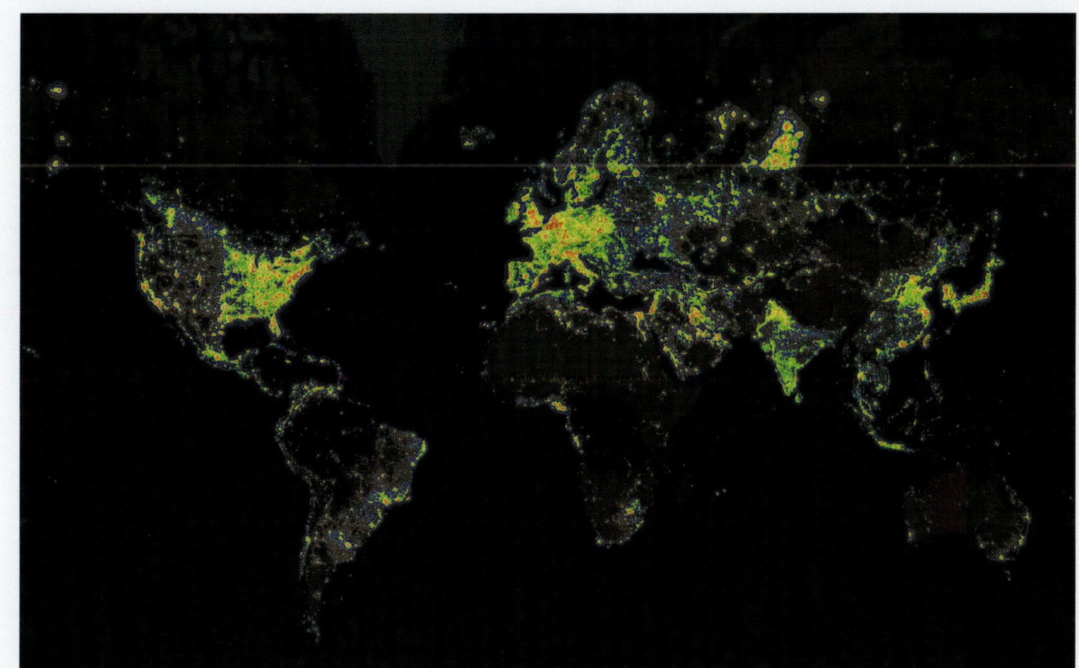

▲ Bortle scale map at **darksitefinder.com.**

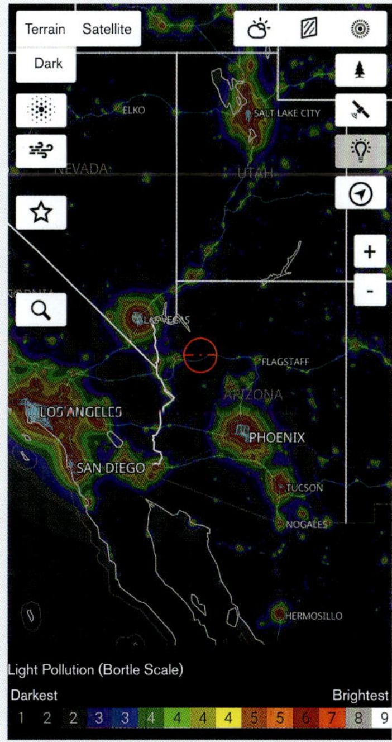

▲ Bortle scale map in the Astrospheric app.

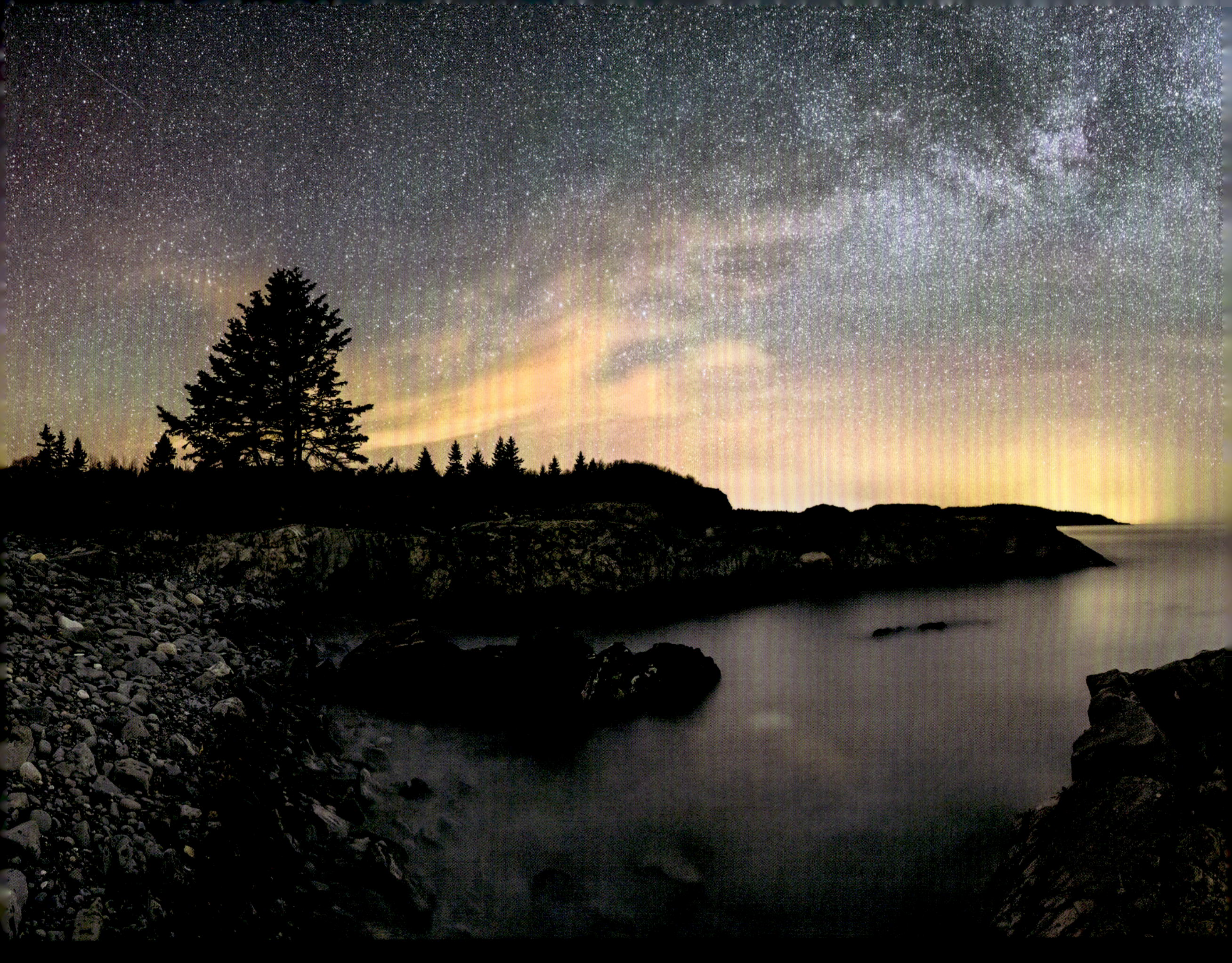

12 MILKY WAY PANORAMAS

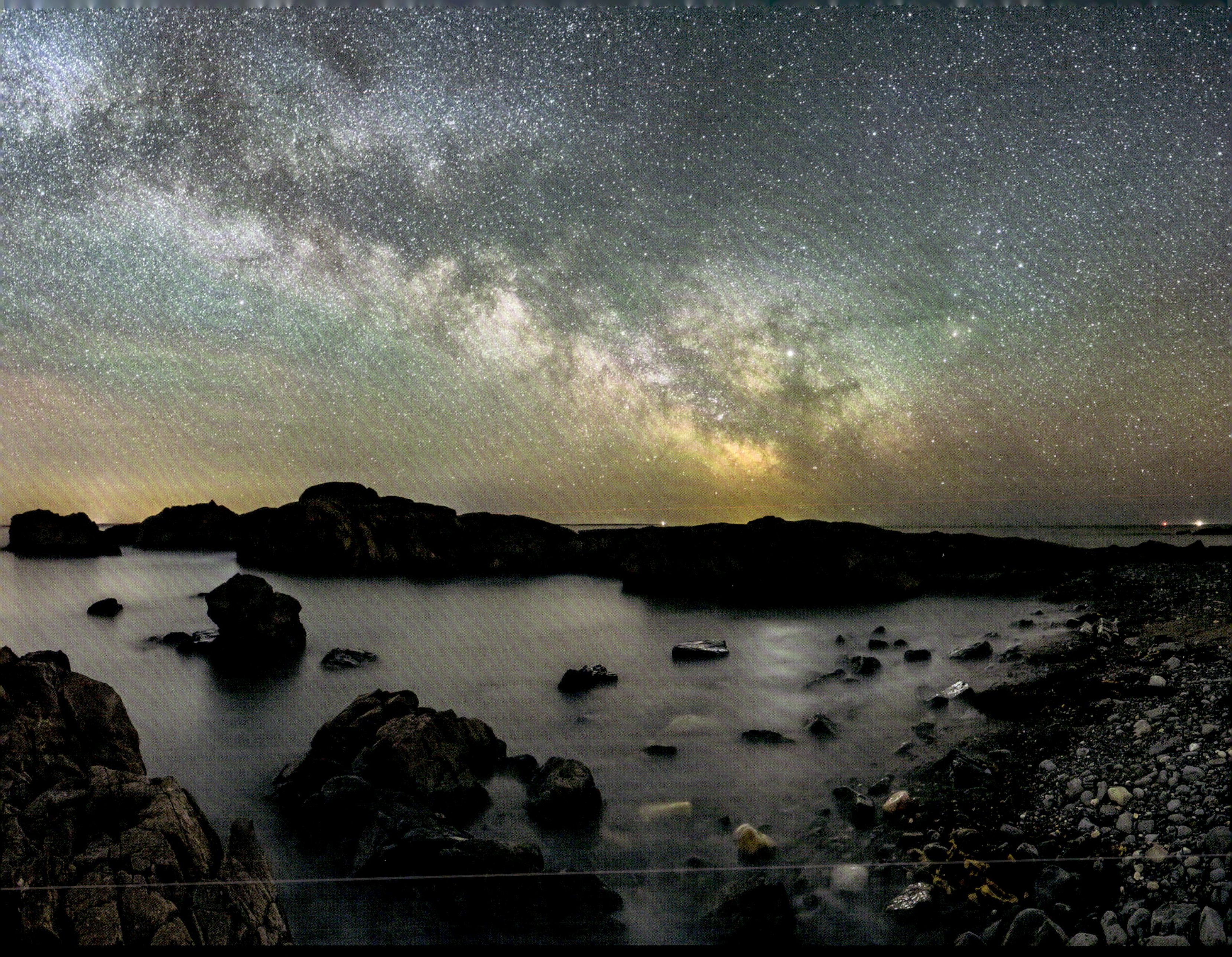

▲ This is a panorama created from two separate panoramas—one panorama exposed for the sky and another with longer shutter speeds for the foreground. I used the Nodal Ninja RD16-II rotator to make this easy in the dark. You can set "click stop" settings on the rotator, so I set it to 30 degrees and then I could just pan the head until it clicked into place at the next stop without having to turn on my headlamp and find the next 30-degree increment manually. This makes shooting panoramas much faster.

Nikon Z 6 with FTZ lens adapter and Nikon 14-24mm f/2.8 lens at 14mm, f/2.8 for all shots.

Sky: Eight shots at 20 seconds, ISO 6400. Foreground: Eight shots at ISO 6400 for 2 minutes.

The sky and foreground panoramas were stitched in Photoshop and then manually blended into one single panorama to have short stars trails and more detail in the foreground.

12.1 SHOOTING PANORAMAS

There's something particularly fun about creating panoramic photographs of the Milky Way arcing across the sky. With the arc positioned over a striking foreground, panoramas can really make for impactful photographs that show a huge amount of the night sky and landscape.

Panoramas are created by taking lots of exposures at different angles and then stitching them together in software to create the single panoramic image. Horizontal panoramas like the one on the previous page are usually created with many individual vertical shots, and vertical panoramas like the one opposite are usually created with horizontal shots. Capturing the photographs in the opposite orientation of your intended panorama gives you the most flexibility and the best results when stitching and cropping. For panoramas of the Milky Way, you'll need a tall field of view to capture the top of the Milky Way arc, as it can be quite high in the sky.

Once the Milky Way is in the position that you want it to be in for the panorama, start taking your shots from either the left or right side of the Milky Way (or top/bottom for vertical panoramas) and then pan your camera so that half of the next frame will overlap with the previous frame. You need this overlap so that the stitching software can properly align all the images and create the panorama. You might be able to get away with less overlap depending on your focal length and the stitching software you are using.

If you have a ballhead with a panning base that has degree marks on it, you can note the number of degrees that you need to pan the camera at the focal length you're using until the next frame overlaps half with the previous frame. You can then keep using that same measurement between each shot for that focal length. For example, with a 14mm lens on a full-frame camera, I can pan the camera 30 degrees between each frame of the panorama to get a 50 percent overlap.

You will need to shoot at least one extra frame on either side of the panorama, beyond what you think you will need for your desired composition. You will lose some of the image on the left and right (or top and bottom) sides of your panorama during the stitching process due to the warping needed to stitch the single frames together, so make sure you have space on both sides of the panorama that can be cropped off later.

▶ West Quoddy Head Lighthouse.

A vertical panorama created from five horizontal frames stitched together.

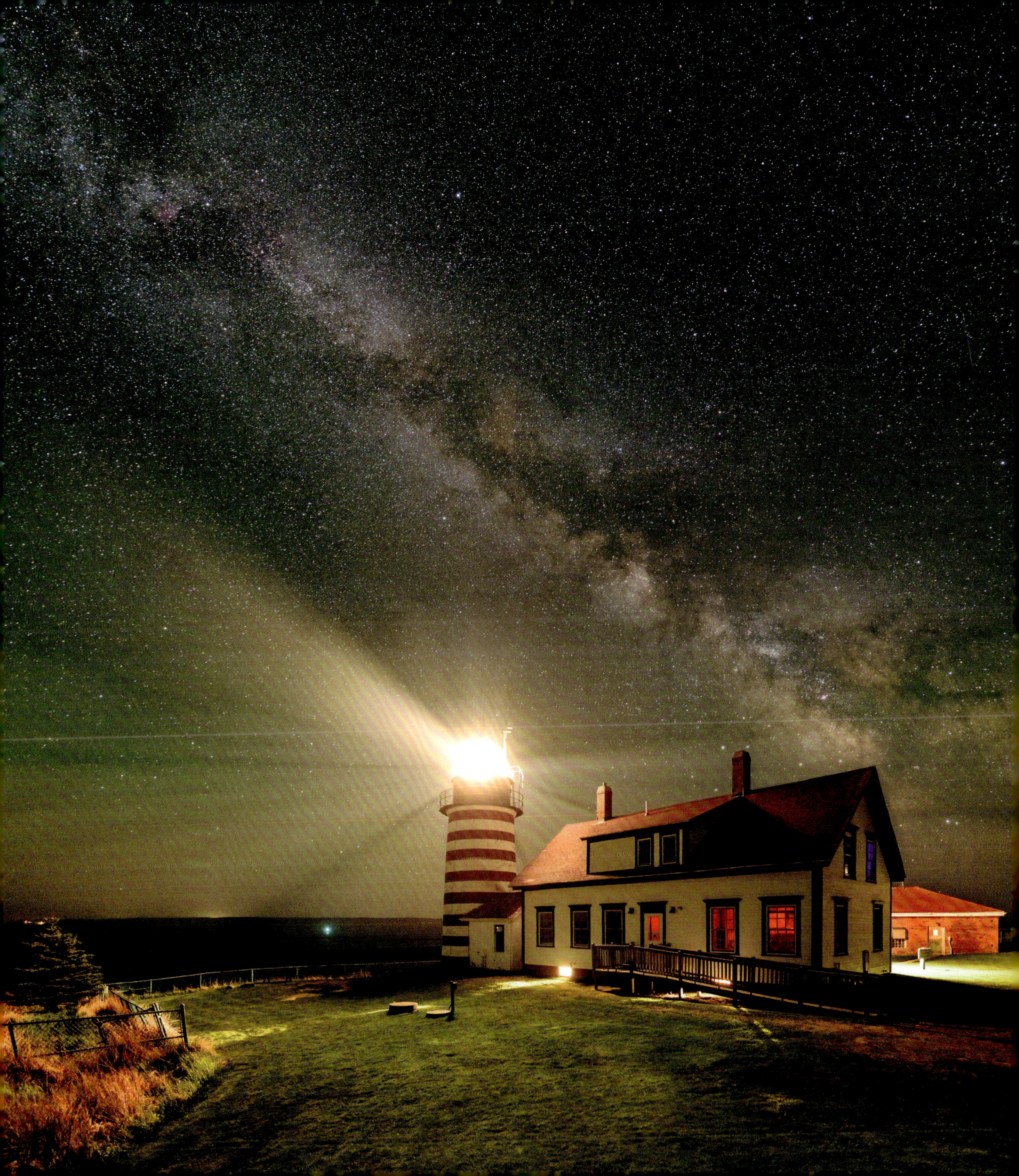

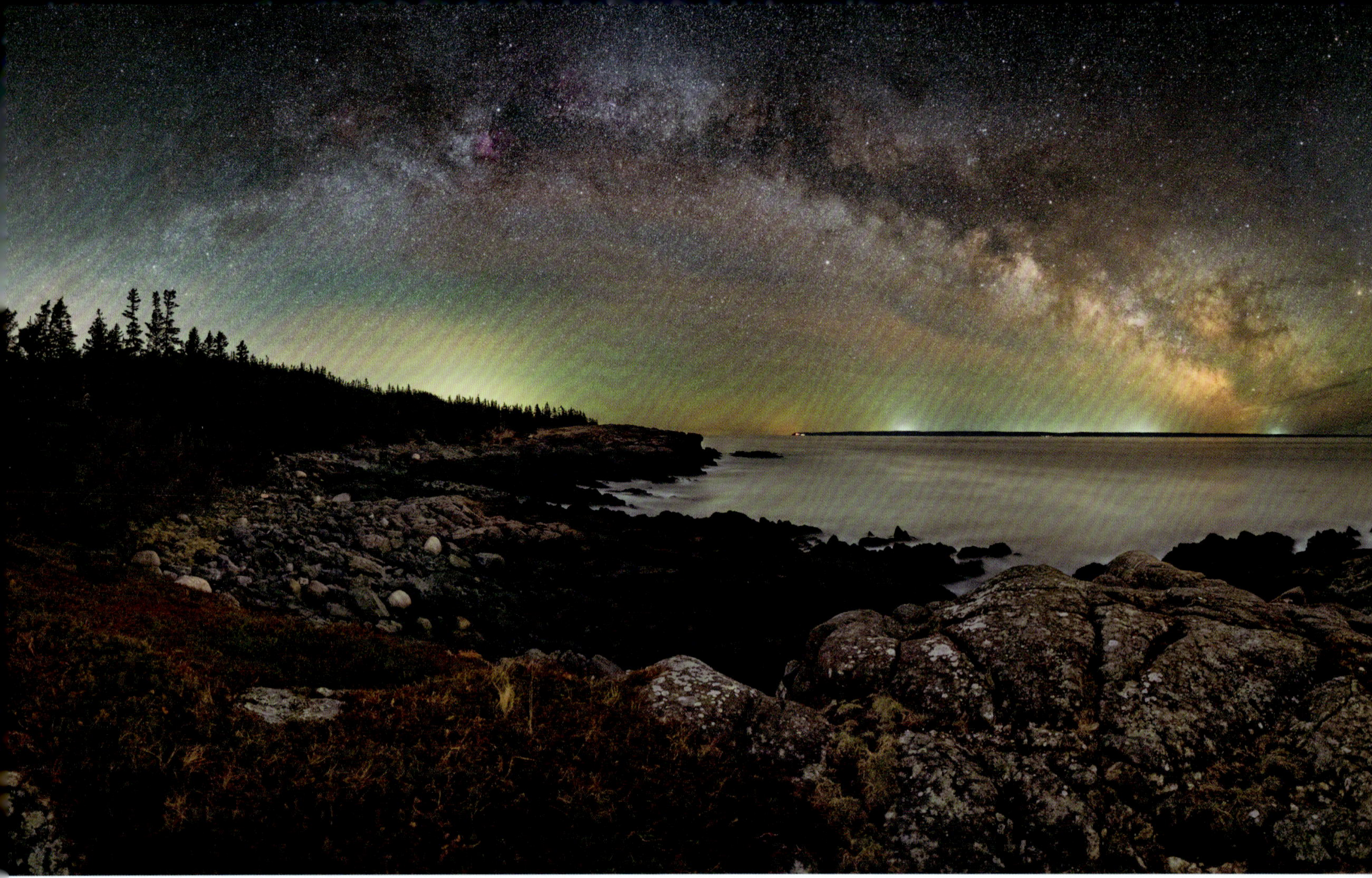

▲ This panorama is a blend of two separate panoramas, one created for the sky and one for the foreground. Each panorama consists of six separate frames.

For panoramas, I'll take single images for each sky frame, as opposed to multiple images for star stacking. If you're stitching 10, 20 or more frames, then shooting and processing all these shots adds up to a lot of extra work. I will still take separate foreground photographs, but normally I will use a shorter shutter speed than I would for a non-panoramic image, again to save time.

This results in an increase in noise, but requires substantially less time to capture and edit. This means I will have two panoramas, one exposed for the sky and the other exposed for the foreground. Just like with a non-panorama, I will blend these together to create the final image.

MULTI-ROW PANORAMAS

If the highest point in the Milky Way arc is too high to fit in the frame with your camera oriented vertically, then you will not be able to capture the entire arc in a single-row panorama with your camera leveled. You could tilt the camera up enough to capture the highest point of the arc in the frame and take a single row that way, but then you're cutting out a lot of your foreground. It's better to capture multiple rows for the panorama, one with the camera tilted up, one with the camera level, and optionally another row for the foreground with the camera tilted down. This will give you massive coverage of the scene, capturing the entire Milky Way arc and lots of foreground with room for cropping later.

PANORAMA GEAR

You can take panorama exposures with your regular ballhead, but there are panorama-specific pieces of gear that can help make the capture and stitching process much easier.

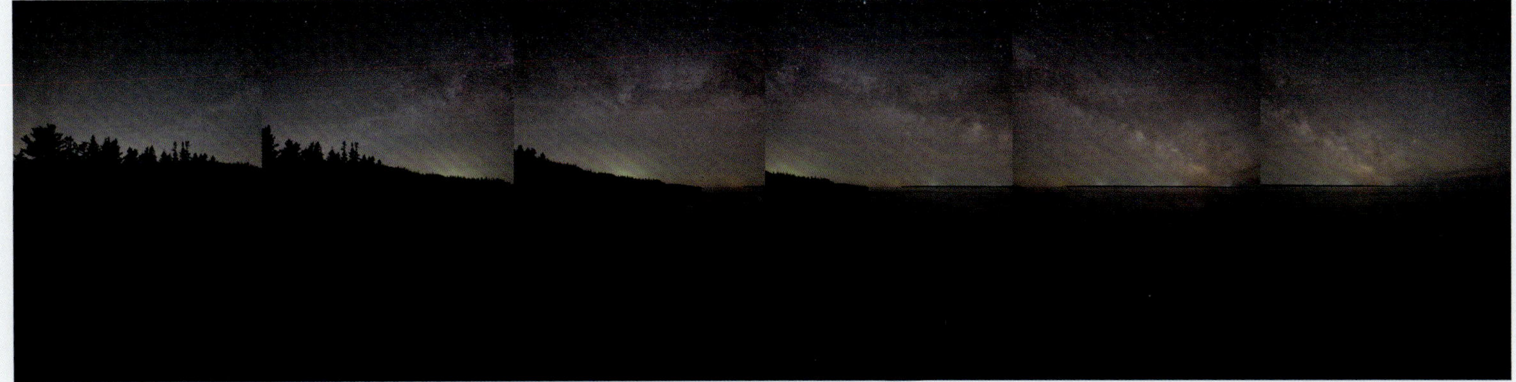

▲ The sky frames.

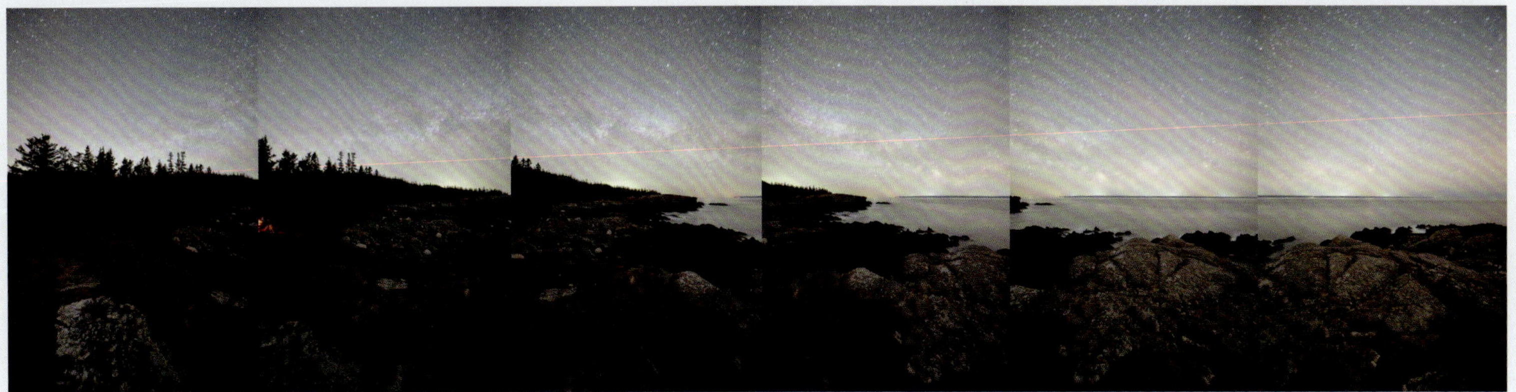

▲ The foreground frames.

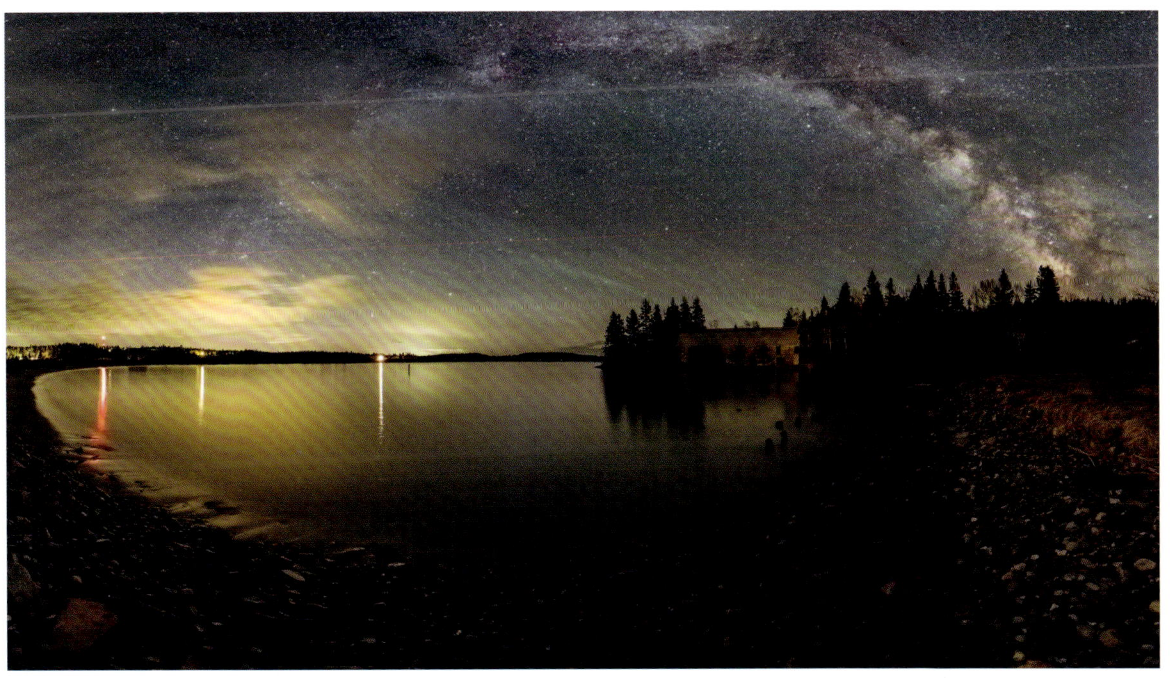

◀ This is a three-row panorama to get the high arc of the Milky Way and the beach in frame. I used the same exposure settings for all the frames in this panorama, which meant I could stitch them together without a separate panorama of longer foreground exposures. This was possible because the lights from the nearby houses lit up the foreground, enabling me to capture enough detail in 20 seconds. Nikon D810A, Nikon 14-24mm f/2.8 lens at 14mm, f/2.8, ISO 12800, 20 seconds for each image, 24 total images.

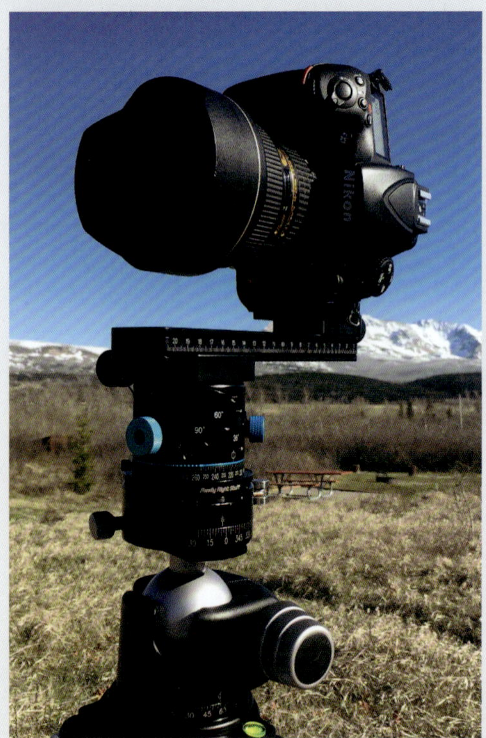

▲ A nodal rail mounted onto a rotator, both by Nodal Ninja (Fanotec).

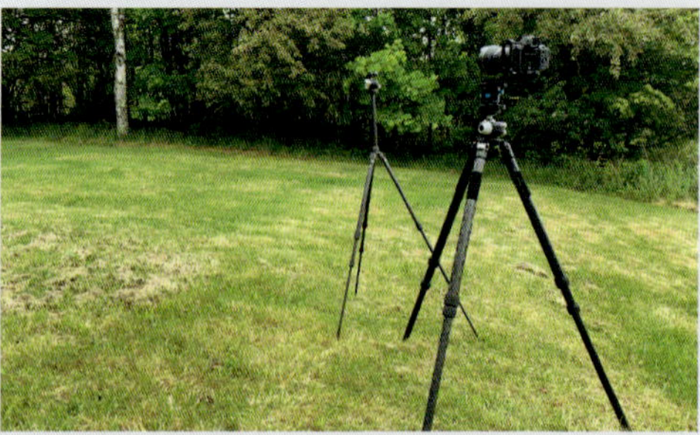

▲ Here I am using a spare tripod close to my camera lens to compare against the birch tree in the background.

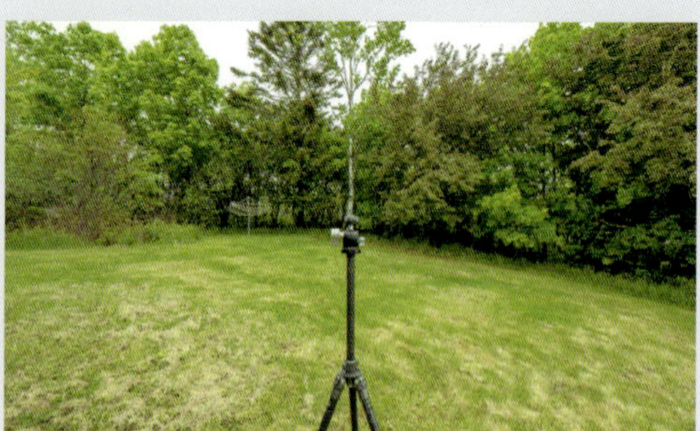

▲ Line the camera up so that the spare tripod and tree are in alignment when the camera is level and centered.

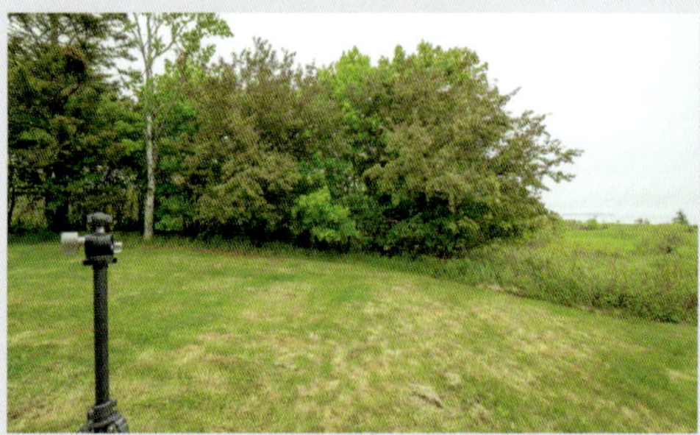

▲ Without correcting for parallax the tripod and tree will not line up when panning the camera.

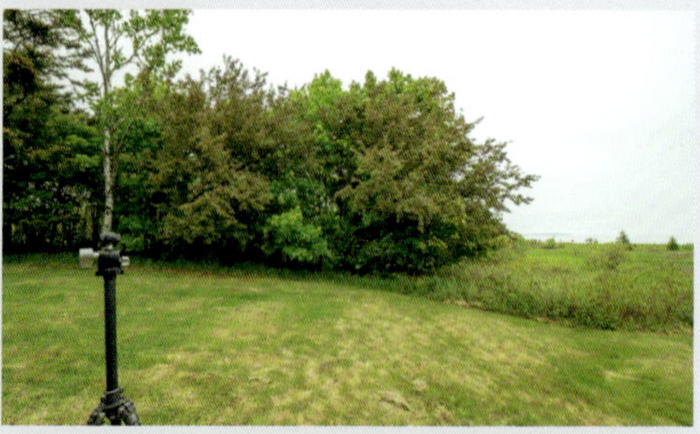

▲ I moved the nodal rail back and forth in the tripod head until the spare tripod and tree lined up with the camera panned to the right.

NODAL RAIL

A key piece of equipment you'll need for panoramas is a nodal rail (also called a nodal slide). A nodal rail allows you to position the camera lens over the center of your ballhead at the lens' "no-parallax point" to eliminate parallax. This is also often called the nodal point in panoramas, hence the name of the rail, but the no-parallax point is not the same as an actual nodal point in the lens. Parallax is what you see when you close one eye, then switch eyes—objects in the foreground appear to move left or right in relation to objects in the background. This is caused by your two eyes having a view of the world from sightly different points, so the view isn't exactly the same. Your brain takes care of this and blends the perspectives of both of your eyes together into one view.

When you take frames for your panorama, the view, of course, changes between each frame, and without using a nodal rail you will have parallax issues. Objects in the foreground of one frame will seem to be in a different spot in relation to background objects when you compare it with another frame containing the same objects. Using a nodal rail, you can move the lens to its no-parallax point, which means objects in the foreground and background will line up the same regardless of the camera panning angle. This makes it much easier for stitching software to line up the images and create a successful panorama. Without a nodal rail, you may have a very difficult time getting some panoramas to stitch, particularly those with complex foregrounds.

When buying a nodal rail, you'll need to get one that is long enough for your lens but not so long that it shows up in the frame. Nodal Ninja (Fanotec), Really Right Stuff, Acratech and many others all produce nodal rails—consult the manufacturer's recommendations for the length of rail you will need.

You can find the no-parallax point for your lens fairly easily by placing your camera (mounted on the nodal rail, ballhead and tripod) somewhere where you have a distinct foreground object and a distinct background object. Pan the camera side to side while looking through the viewfinder or using live view, and move the camera back and forth on the rail until it looks like the foreground and background objects line up no matter how much you pan the camera. Make sure to zoom in on live view to clearly see the alignment. For example, you can place a spare tripod close to your lens and compare it with a telephone pole, tree or similar object in the distance. If you're using a zoom lens you will have to check the no-parallax point for the specific focal lengths you want to use for your panoramas.

The nodal rail should have markings on it so you can make a note of how far you need to slide it for the next time you use it for that same lens and focal length. Keep this number handy so you don't have to find the no-parallax point each time you use the same lens with the same focal length.

ROTATOR

Once you know how far you need to pan your camera between each shot for the panorama, it's easy to do so with the markings on a panning base, if you have one. However, that means having to turn on your headlamp or other light at night to see the markings. While not a big deal if you are able to do so without disrupting the photos of those around you, a rotator with "click stops" enables you to pan your camera without having to turn on a light. You choose an increment of rotation in degrees that you want, and then when you're shooting a panorama, all you need to do between shots is to pan the rotator until it clicks into the next set increment, then take your picture. Easy, fast and no light needed.

I use the Nodal Ninja RD16-II Advanced Rotator. It features configurable click stops for easy panning.

MULTI-AXIS PANO HEAD

A specialist panorama head, like the Nodal Ninja line of gear produced by Fanotec, makes it easy to capture panoramas with multiple rows, and allows you to keep the camera lens centered on the no-parallax point when tilting the camera up or down. A single nodal rail will let you eliminate parallax when panning horizontally, but panning vertically requires another axis to keep the lens centered.

I currently use a Nodal Ninja M1-L with the RD16-II rotator mentioned previously when I want to take multiple-row panoramas. This setup makes the stitching process much more likely to work smoothly.

PANORAMA STITCHING

Many image-editing programs are capable of panorama stitching, including Adobe Lightroom Classic, Adobe Photoshop, ON1 Photo Raw, Affinity Photo and so on. So if you're using one of these as your Raw editor, you can try it for stitching your panorama exposures. But if you're having difficulty, you might need to use a dedicated panorama-stitching program, such as PTGui. PTGui achieves better alignment than most other panorama software, and makes it easy to work with very complicated panoramas.

It's worth noting that, as of writing, Lightroom often has a hard time blending night sky images, resulting in bad seams and color issues in the sky. Give it a try; sometimes it works great, but if not, try using Photoshop, or even better, PTGui.

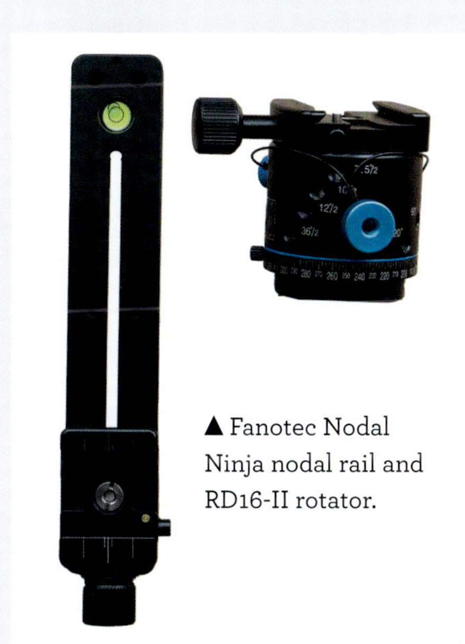

▲ Fanotec Nodal Ninja nodal rail and RD16-II rotator.

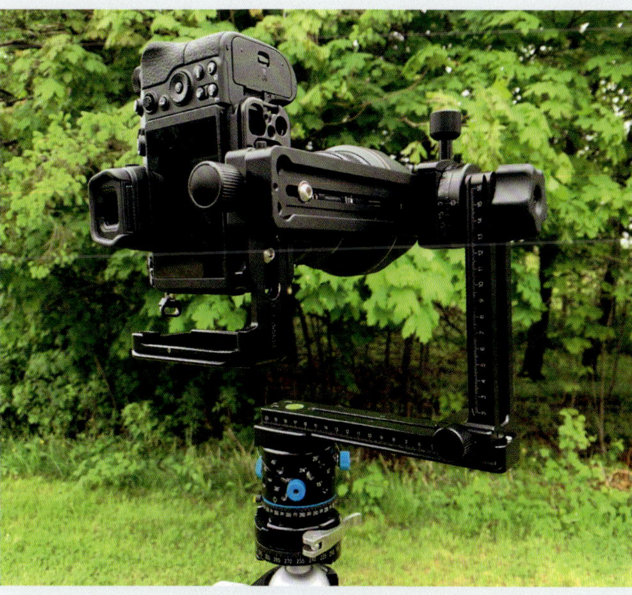

◀ M1-L multi-axis panorama head and RD16-II rotator, both by Nodal Ninja.

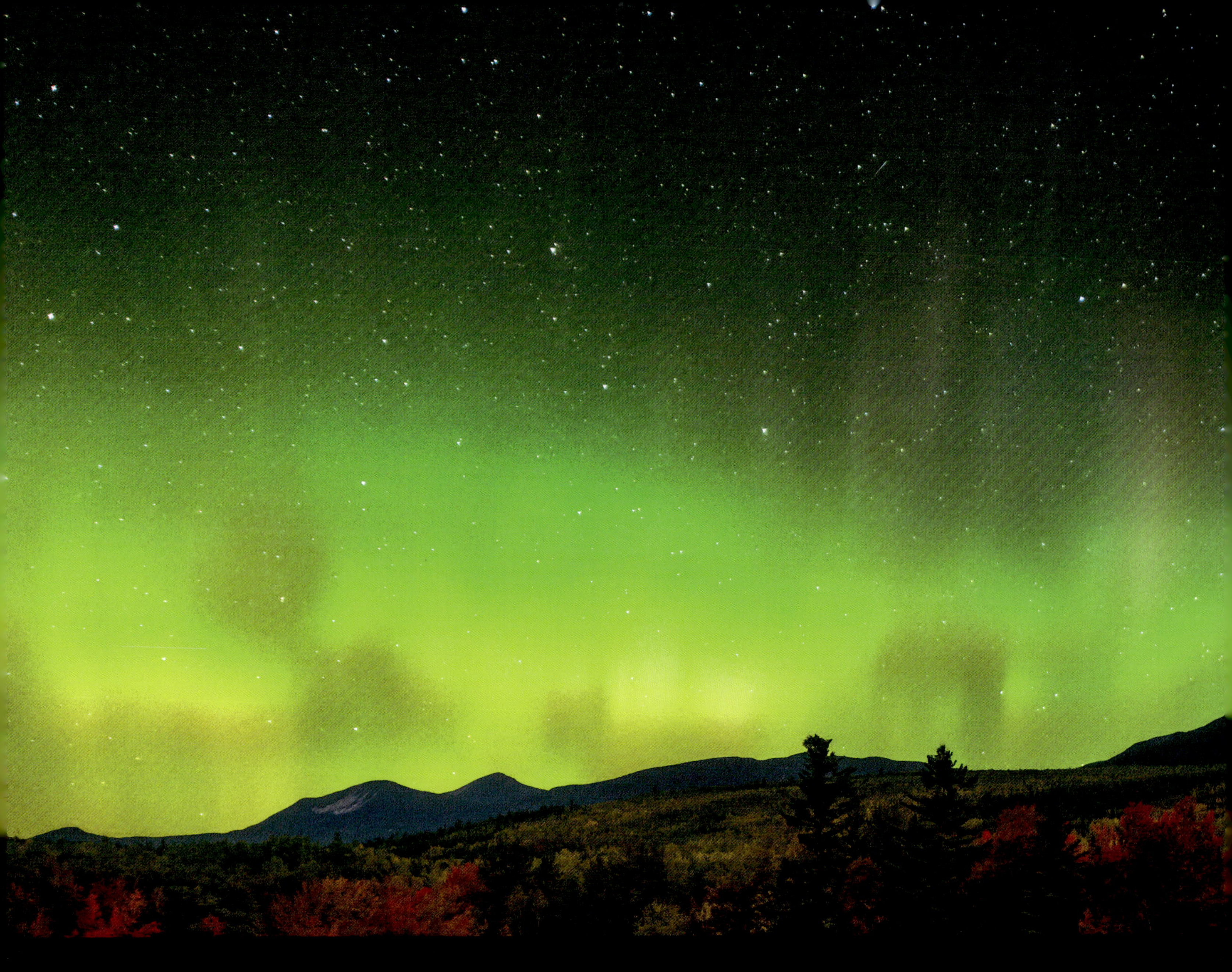

13 AURORA PHOTOGRAPHY

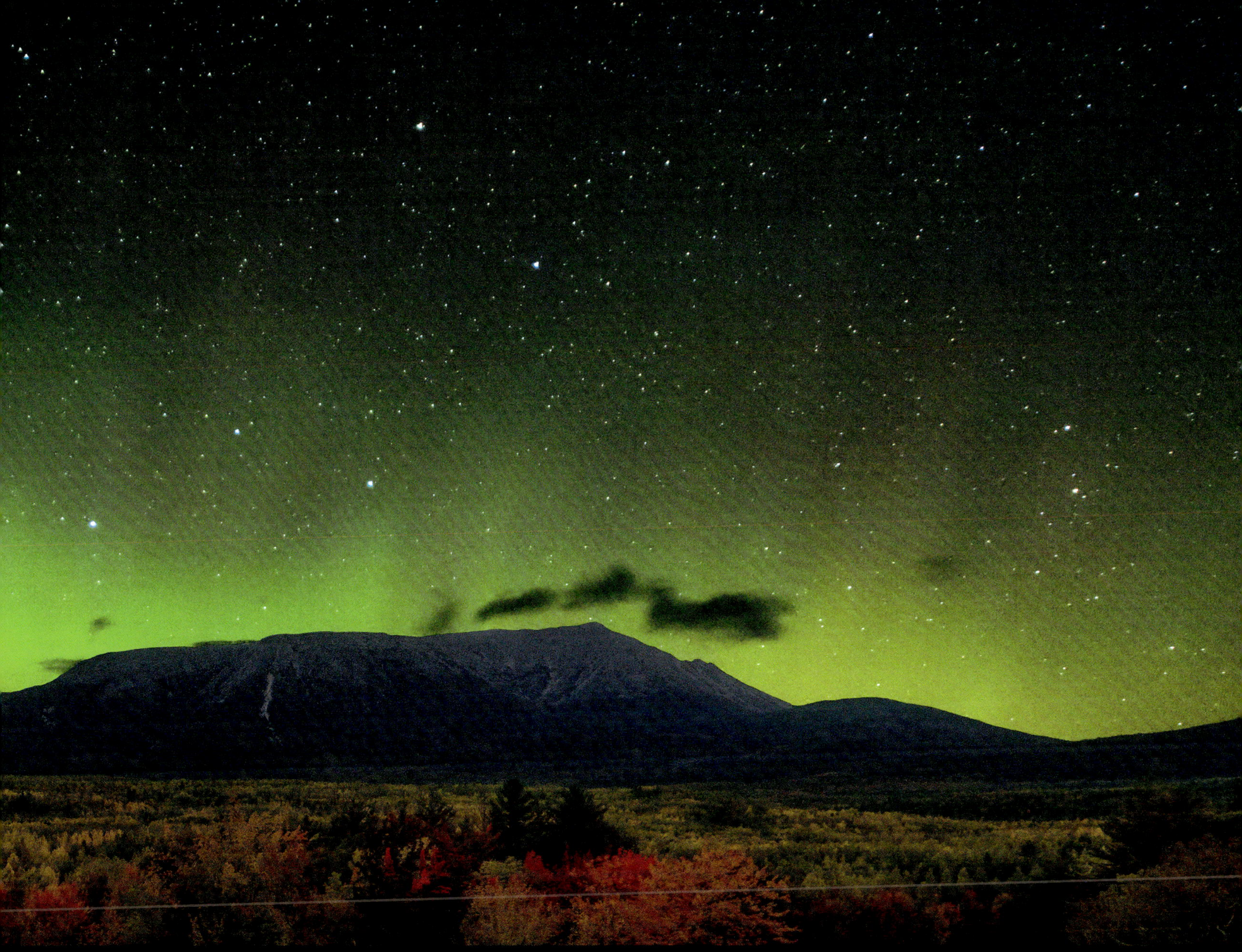

Nikon D810A with Nikon 14-24mm f/2.8 lens. This is a blend of three images, one for the sky at f/2.8, ISO 12800, 6 seconds. One of the foreground images was at f/2.8, ISO 1600, for 15 minutes, and another was at f/4, ISO 1600, for 20 minutes. These foreground shots were used to get detail in the trees and mountain. The aurora was moving so fast that I had to use a relatively quick shutter speed for the sky—6 seconds was about as long as I could stretch to without blurring the aurora too much and losing detail in the spikes and curtains.

13.1 EXPOSURE SETTINGS

More commonly known as the northern lights (aurora borealis) or southern lights (aurora australis), the aurora is easily the most amazing thing you'll ever see in the sky, should you be so lucky to witness it.

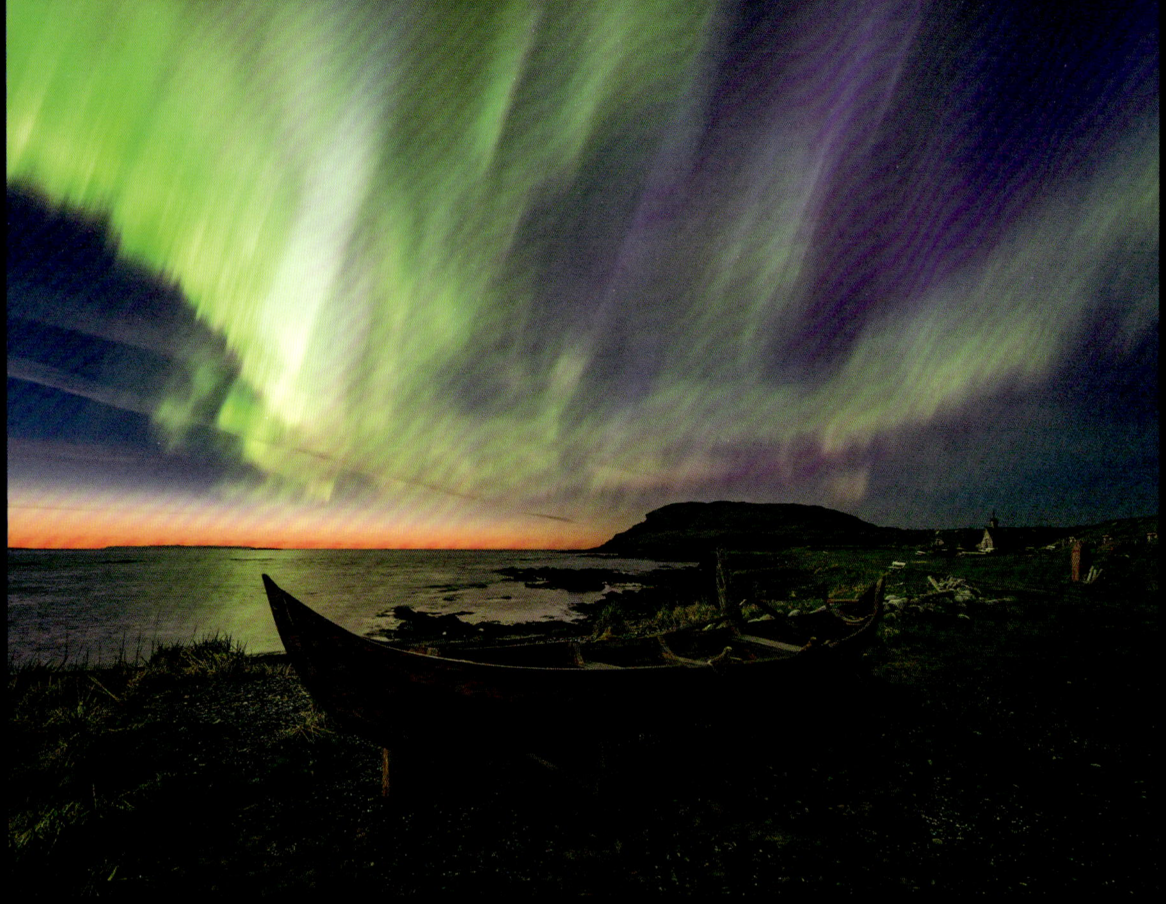

◀ Newfoundland.

Nikon D810A, Nikon 14-24mm f/2.8 lens.

Sky: Single shot at 14mm, f/2.8, ISO 3200, 1 second.

Foreground: Single shot at 14mm, f/5.6, ISO 1600, 2 minutes.

When photographing the aurora, the same exposure and camera settings apply as those for sky exposures of the stars and the Milky Way (see Exposure Settings, from page 94). However, you likely won't want to take multiple exposures for stacking, and you should adjust your shutter speed based on the activity of the aurora.

If the aurora is moving very fast, then a short shutter speed will capture the ribbons and pillars with more detail, while a long shutter speed could blur them so much that you see nothing but a solid color in the sky. For example, in the photo above, the aurora was moving very fast, so I used a shutter speed of 1 second for the sky, and a separate 2-minute exposure for the foreground.

You can take a separate foreground photograph (see page 58) to capture a more detailed, lower noise foreground to be blended with the sky image later in Adobe Photoshop or similar software.

13.2 PLANNING & FORECASTING

The aurora is the result of charged particles ejected from the sun hitting the Earth's magnetic field and reacting in a way that emits the marvelous colors and ribbons that we see in the sky.

These charged particles come from a coronal mass ejection (CME) from the sun during a solar storm. The intensity of the aurora is measured by the Kp index, from 0 to 9. The higher the Kp number, the stronger the storm and the brighter the aurora. A stronger storm also means that the aurora will be visible further south or north of the poles.

A Kp 3 storm might be a good storm to photograph if you're way up in Alaska, but it won't look like much further south. But a Kp 7 storm will be clearly visible in Maine, and the glow might be visible low on the horizon much farther south. I've captured the aurora as far south as Utah during a Kp 7 storm!

There is a common misconception that the aurora is only visible in the winter. In fact, solar storms don't care what season it is. But the aurora is more visible in the winter due to the longer nights that come with winter. Also, as you have a better view of the aurora far to the north or south of the globe, it is more common to see the aurora in the winter because at very high or very low latitudes the summer nights are incredibly short or non-existent.

There are a number of aurora forecast websites and apps available. Some of these can even send you text or phone notifications to alert you of upcoming solar storms. Here are a few that I use: Soft Serve News, **softservenews.com**, provides a simple, easy-to-understand, immediate forecast on its home page. You can create a paid account to get custom text alerts when the aurora is active or forecast to be active. The websites **spaceweather.com** and **solarham.net** are both great places to geek out on the nitty gritty details of current and upcoming solar storms.

All three websites have links to the OVATION model maps provided by NOAA that give a visual representation of where you can see the aurora (if at all) over the next 30–40 minutes. The best viewpoints are within yellow or red areas of the map, if they are present for the forecast. Note it must be dark, of course, for you to see the aurora.

On iOS and Android devices you can get the My Aurora Forecast app. You can pay to receive notifications when the aurora is active.

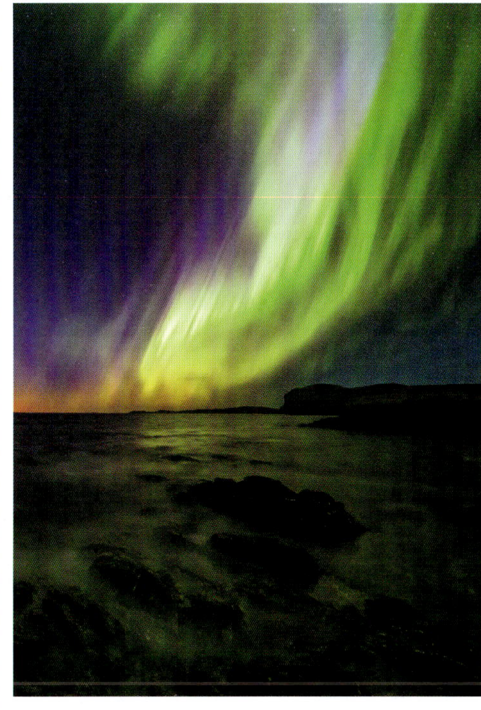

▲ Newfoundland.

Nikon D810A with Nikon 14-24mm f/2.8 lens, 14mm, f/2.8 for all exposures.

Sky: Single shot at ISO 10000, 2.5 seconds.

Foreground: Focus stack of three shots at various shutter speeds and ISOs.

14

▶ The Milky Way rises over a sunflower field during twilight.

Young sunflowers follow the sun through the sky each day, turning back east during the night to greet the sun again the next day, but when they mature they stop that and only face east – as was the case with this mature field of sunflowers. With the Milky Way core in the south/southwest, it was a little tricky to find a composition with sunflowers at least somewhat facing the camera, but I liked this angle with the road leading toward the Galactic Core. I really love shooting during twilight because of the blue tones. Of course it also makes getting foreground exposures quite a bit easier, especially with flowers that could move with any hint of wind. And with enough ambient light, you can stop down the lens for greater depth of field without the exposure taking an eternity.

The biggest challenge was getting the sunflower that sticks up into the sky to focus stack cleanly. In the sky image, the focus is on the stars of course, so the prominent sunflower was way out of focus and blurred quite a bit beyond the sharp edges of the in-focus version in the foreground image. This is where manual editing techniques come into play: I ended up using a combination of warping and clone-stamping to manually do that part of the focus stacking.

Nikon Z 7 with FTZ lens adapter and Nikon 14-24mm f/2.8 lens @ 14mm and f/2.8 for all shots.

Sky: Star stack of 20 exposures, each at 10 seconds and ISO 3200.

Foreground: Focus stack of two exposures, one at 2 minutes and one at 1 minute, both at f/5.6 and ISO 1600.

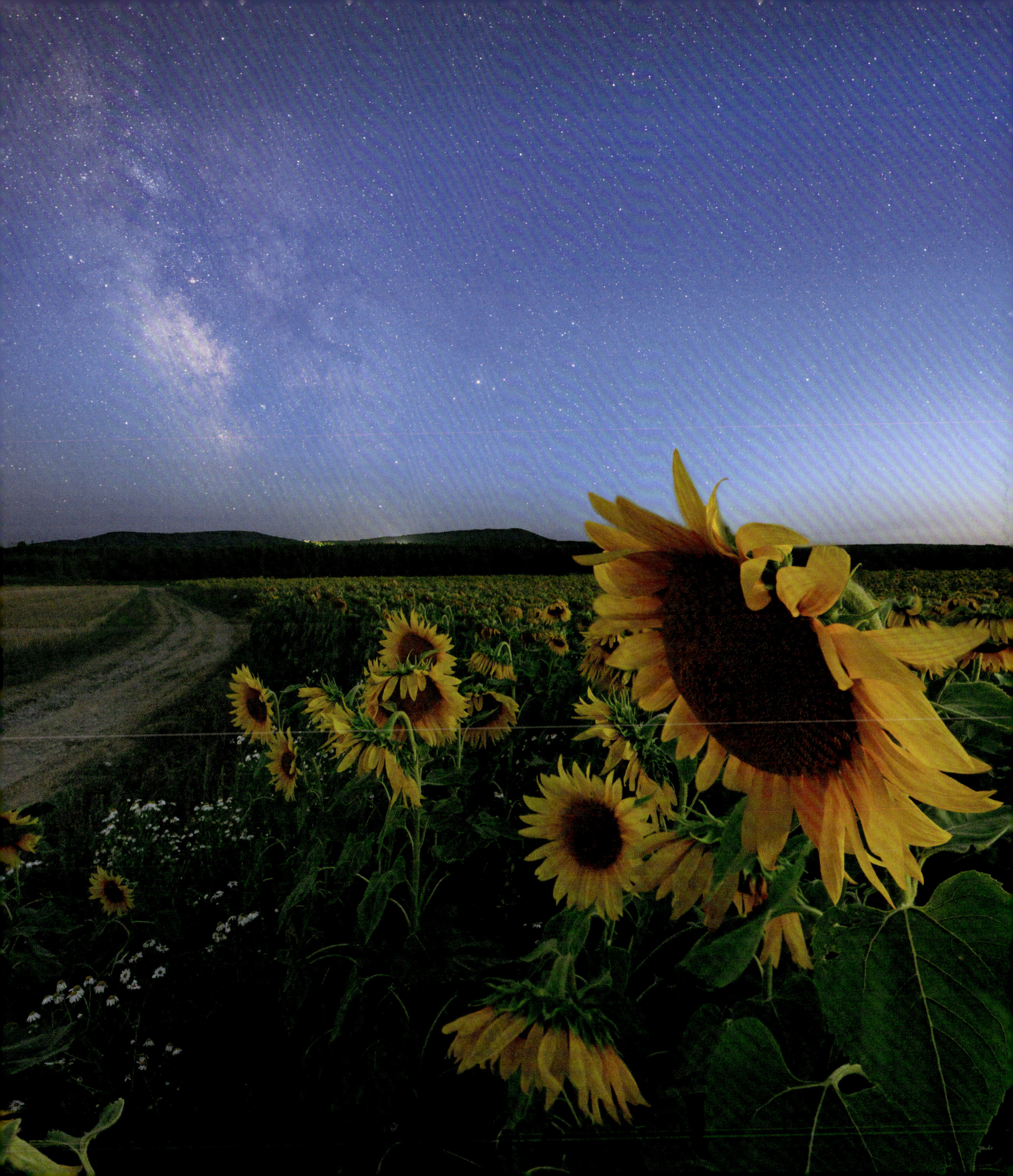

14.1 WORKFLOW

If you're following the methodology laid out in this book, you will have a set of various images that need to be stacked and blended to create a final image where the entire scene is in focus, well exposed, and has low noise. To achieve this, I have a four-step workflow that I follow and have been teaching for years.

In my workflow, I split the editing process into four major stages that I execute in order: Raw preparation, star stacking, blending, and creative adjustments. If you are using a single photograph then you only need to follow the Raw preparation and creative adjustments steps, and possibly apply some noise reduction.

1 Raw Preparation The goal here is to apply basic adjustments to the Raw files to get them ready for star stacking and/or blending. No creative adjustments are done at this point.

2 Star Stacking This is where you take the multiple sky shots and stack them in a dedicated star-stacking program to create a single image with low noise. As of writing, I do this with TIFF files exported from Adobe Lightroom Classic, but you may be able to load your Raw files directly into your stacking program depending on which one you use.

3 Exposure Blending and Focus Stacking Here you blend the sky and foreground images together to create a seamless image that has detail in both the sky and foreground. You can also use the technique of focus stacking to blend multiple foreground shots together for better depth of field. This is done using an image-editing program like Photoshop that supports layers and masking.

4 Creative Adjustments After all the prep work and blending is out of the way, now you can apply your own personal touch to your photo.

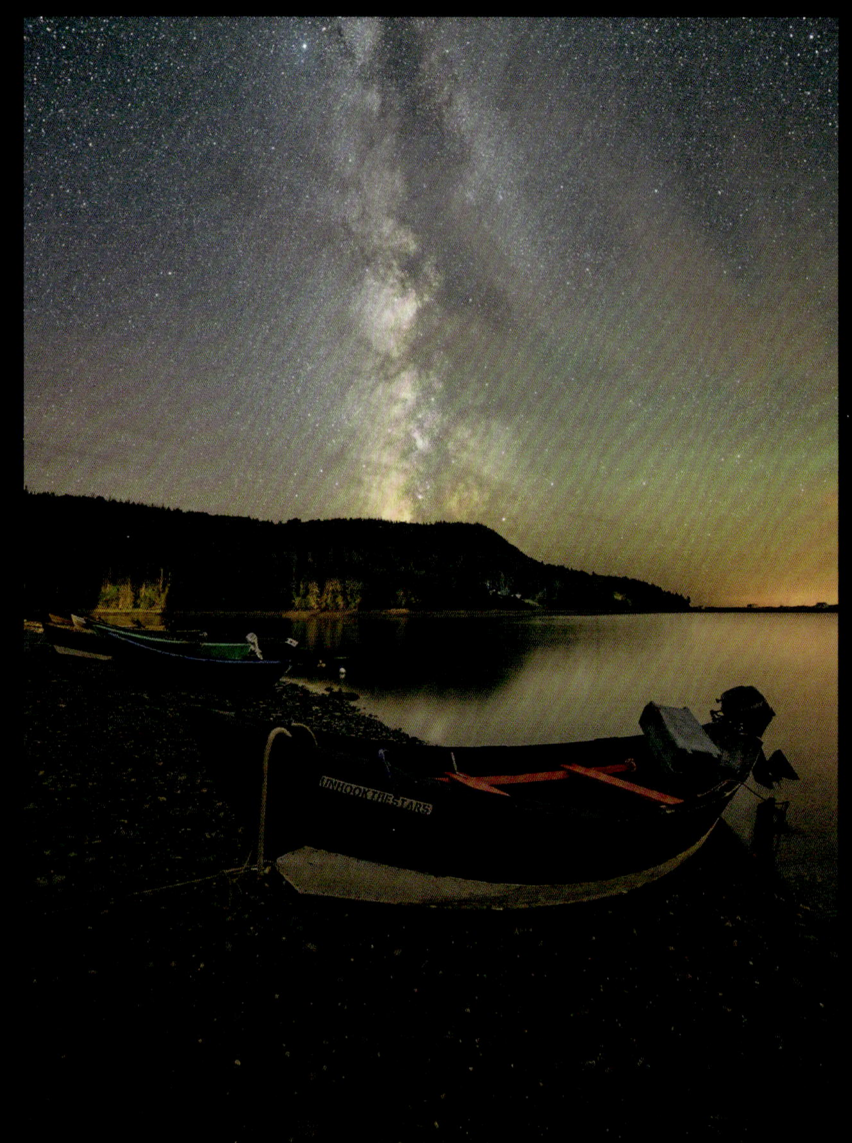

▲ Dories on the coast of the Bay of Fundy.

To demonstrate the different stages and processes that make up the workflow I will be using this photo of dories (fishing boats) on the coast of the Bay of Fundy. It consists of a star-stacked sky and two separate foreground photographs, taken with a Nikon D850 and the Nikon 14-24mm f/2.8 lens set at 14mm and f/2.8 for all exposures.

Note: This book teaches techniques for Adobe Lightroom Classic and Photoshop, but the same techniques can generally be applied to other Raw editors and image-editing programs.

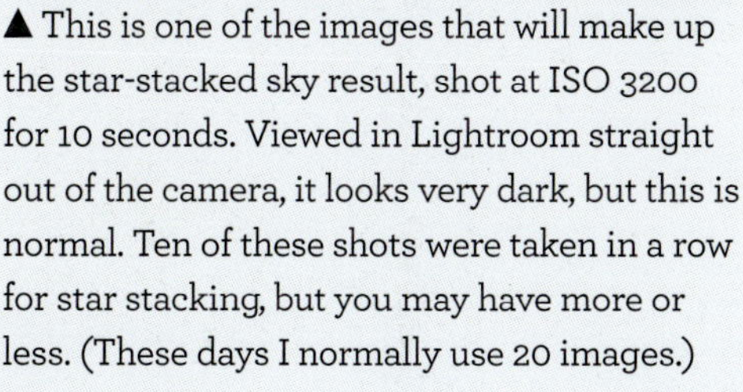

▲ This is one of the images that will make up the star-stacked sky result, shot at ISO 3200 for 10 seconds. Viewed in Lightroom straight out of the camera, it looks very dark, but this is normal. Ten of these shots were taken in a row for star stacking, but you may have more or less. (These days I normally use 20 images.)

▲ This and the next image are the two foreground exposures, each shot at ISO 1600 for 8 minutes. Again, they look very dark straight out of the camera, except for the sky. The one on the left is in focus from the horizon to the boat, and the one on the right has the focus on the very close foreground rocks. These images will be focus stacked and blended with the sky.

PREPARATION

The first part of the workflow is to get all your Raw images of the sky edited so that they are ready for stacking in Starry Landscape Stacker or Sequator. Even if you aren't stacking your images, the same Raw prep still applies to exposure blending. You want to adjust the white balance, exposure, highlights, shadows, whites, blacks, sharpening, noise, and correct lens issues in order to get the sky and foreground images to a sort of "flat" point where they are not punched with lots of added contrast and saturation and will blend together more easily.

At the time of writing, Starry Landscape Stacker doesn't read Raw files, but it will do by the time you're reading this. Sequator already does. You may prefer to load your Raw files into your stacking program directly instead of processing them as described here, however these are useful adjustments to make to your files before or after stacking.

For the foreground images, I find it is often helpful to bring the Highlights and possibly White Point sliders way down to darken the sky so that blending them with the star-stacked sky result is easier.

You don't want to make any creative edits at this point, as doing so will usually introduce noise and make blending your images more difficult. Wait until after stacking and blending to make any creative edits.

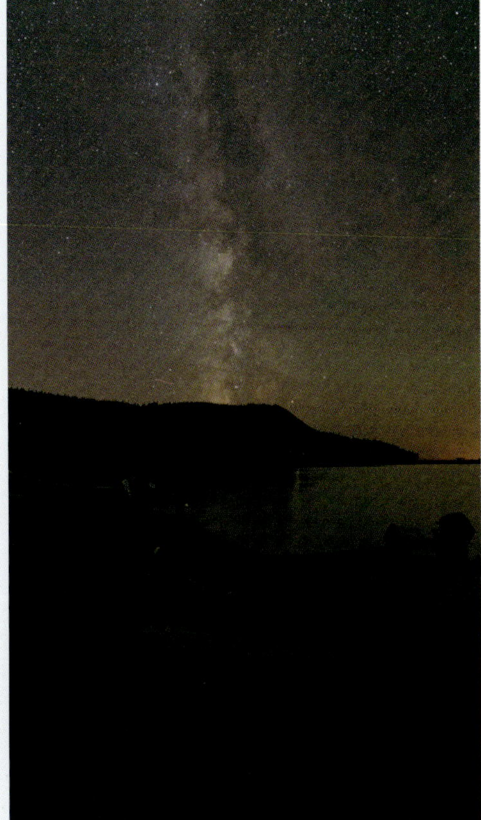

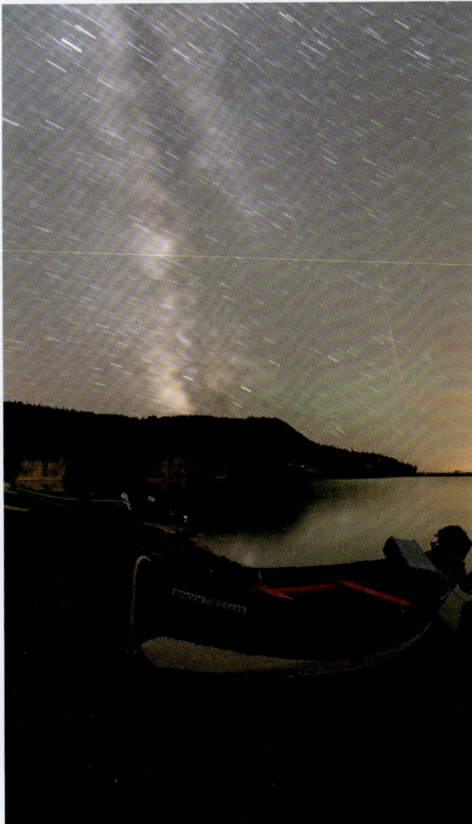

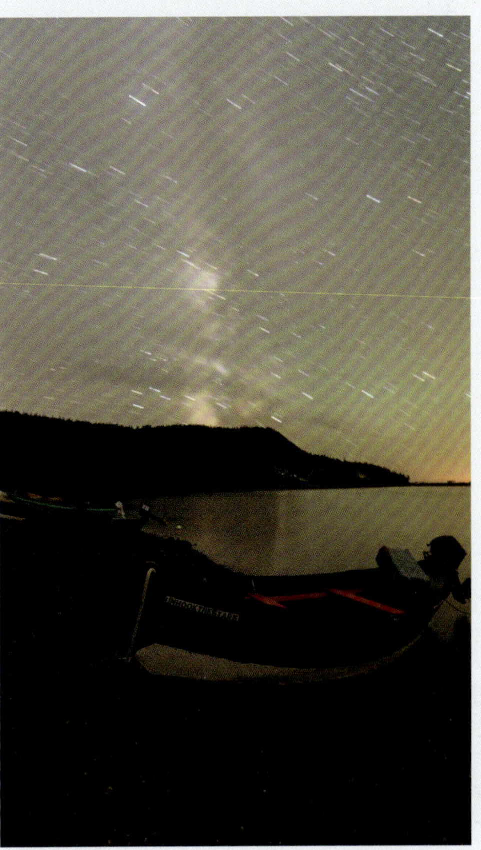

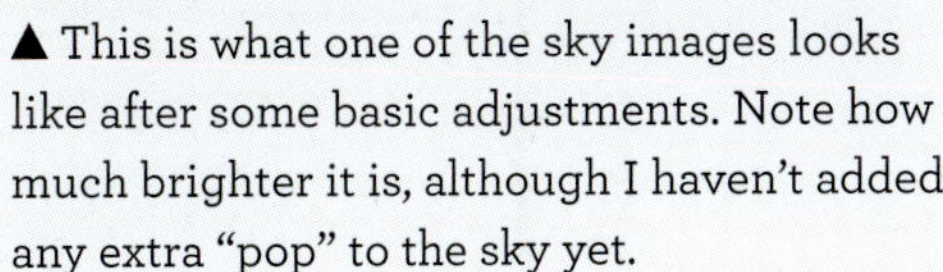

▲ This is what one of the sky images looks like after some basic adjustments. Note how much brighter it is, although I haven't added any extra "pop" to the sky yet.

▲ Here are the two foreground shots after some basic adjustments. I brought the highlights down so the sky is darker, which will usually make it easier to blend with the star-stacked sky image.

WHITE BALANCE

White balance is not absolutely critical here, as you can work more on color later, but you should try to get the white balance in the ballpark of your desired endpoint. You can try using the White Balance color picker in your Raw editor to pick out a blank area of the sky (away from light pollution and airglow) that you think should be neutral (if you can even find such a spot), but this method can be tricky with noisy images, resulting in all kinds of wild white balance results. You may need to just manually drag the Temperature and Tint sliders to something reasonable, and then you can focus on balancing the color more carefully after you've star-stacked your images, when you can work on a less noisy image.

SHARPENING

Sharpening should be disabled for the sky images. In Adobe Lightroom Classic or Adobe Camera Raw, sharpening is enabled by default and applied to the entire image, sharpening every little detail, including the noise. By setting the Sharpening slider to "0" you disable it entirely and reduce the crunch of the noise a bit. You can always increase the sharpening later in the creative process.

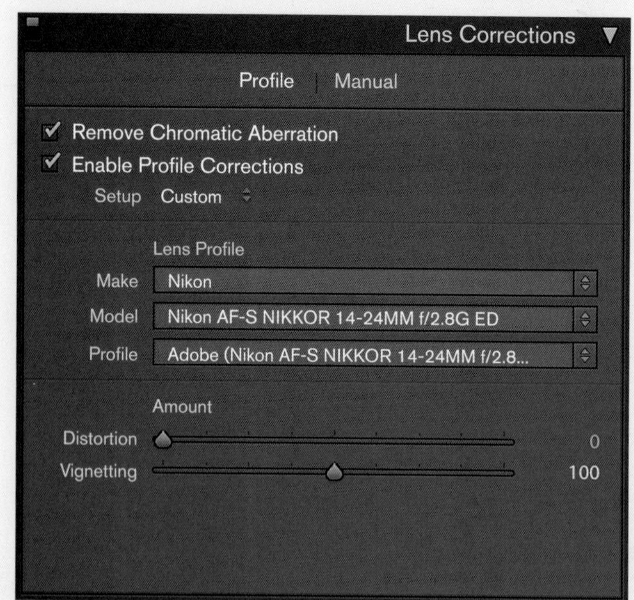

▲ In Lightroom Classic (or Camera Raw) make sure you set Distortion Correction to "0."

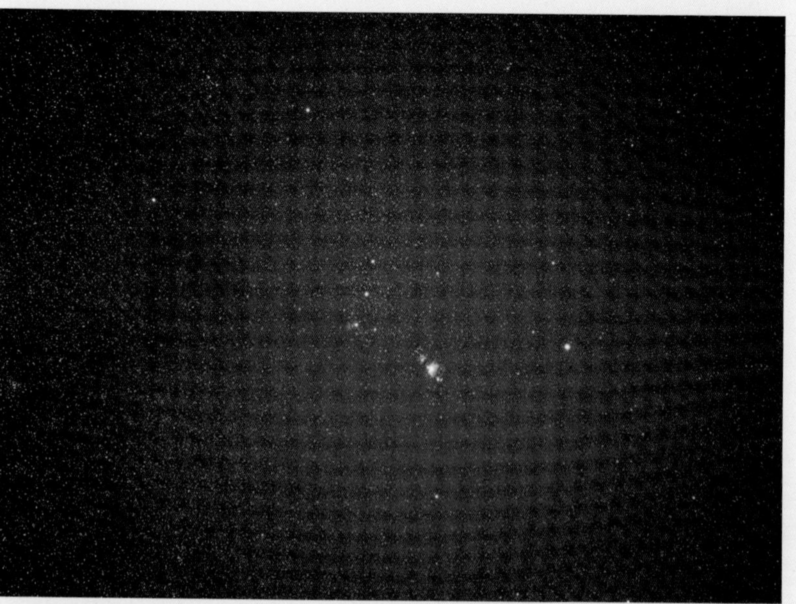

▲ An example of the waffle pattern caused by Lightroom Classic and Camera Raw's problematic Distortion Correction on dark photos. The image has been enhanced with contrast to really show the issue.

For the foreground shots I recommend disabling Sharpening as well, unless you have a foreground image with very low noise.

LENS CORRECTIONS

Make use of the Chromatic and Vignetting Corrections in your Raw editor, but avoid the Distortion Correction. It may cause dark areas of the image to have warping artifacts that will look like lines running through the image, sort of like a warped waffle pattern. This is certainly the case with Lightroom (and Camera Raw), and may occur with other Raw editors as well. As far as I can tell, this is due to a limitation in the Raw editor's Distortion Correction algorithm and essentially ruins any images that are dark enough for it to occur. You may not even notice these "stretch marks," but they may become more visible once you've stacked your images or when you start making creative edits to alter the tone and color of the image.

Even worse, if you are using a camera that has lens corrections built into the Raw files, as many modern mirrorless cameras do, you will have no way at all to disable those lens corrections from being applied inside of Lightroom Classic or Adobe Camera Raw. Even if you disable all lens corrections, they will still apply the profiles built into the Raw file. Again, you may or may not see the issue depending on your workflow and how dark your images are, and it may not even be an issue for many of your night images, but it will probably pop up at some point and cause you grief.

There are two ways to deal with this:

1 You can convert the Raw files to DNG files using Adobe's DNG Converter (or by exporting them to DNG from Lightroom), strip the built-in lens profile data from the DNG files using a program such as ExifTool, and then import the DNG files into Lightroom (or Camera Raw). Since the lens profiles have been removed from those DNG files, they will not be forced upon you, and you can turn them off in the Lens Corrections panel.

2 Most other Raw editors will allow you to disable all lens distortions, even the ones embedded in Raw files. Try using a different one even if only for preparing your images for star stacking and blending, and then storing the results in Lightroom. .

LUMINANCE NOISE REDUCTION

Set Luminance Noise Reduction to "0" for the sky exposures. I recommend doing it this way and letting the star-stacking process reduce the noise before using any other noise-reduction technique on the sky. You may find that star stacking alone cleans the sky up enough to not need any further noise reduction.

For the foreground images you can increase the Noise Reduction a bit. Try somewhere between "10" and "20" when using Lightroom. Don't go overboard here, as excessive noise reduction will always look worse than having a bit of noise.

COLOR NOISE REDUCTION

This should almost always be enabled. Set it to somewhere between "10" and "50." If you zoom in on your photos and adjust this slider you can inspect how it may be affecting the color of stars. Too much and you will lose all color in the stars, but too little and there will be way too much color noise in the image. When working on foreground shots you can generally crank this up to "50" or beyond to help reduce ugly color splotches.

SYNCHRONIZE SETTINGS

Once you have completed the Raw prep on one of your sky exposures, synchronize the settings to all other sky exposures in the stack (if you are star stacking your images). To sync settings, select the Library module, highlight the images you want to sync (by selecting the one to sync from first, then selecting the rest of the images) and click Sync Settings. Similarly, you can edit one foreground photo and then synchronize the settings to your other foreground photos, but it is not uncommon to have to adjust White Balance or other exposure settings separately to make the foreground shots all look similar.

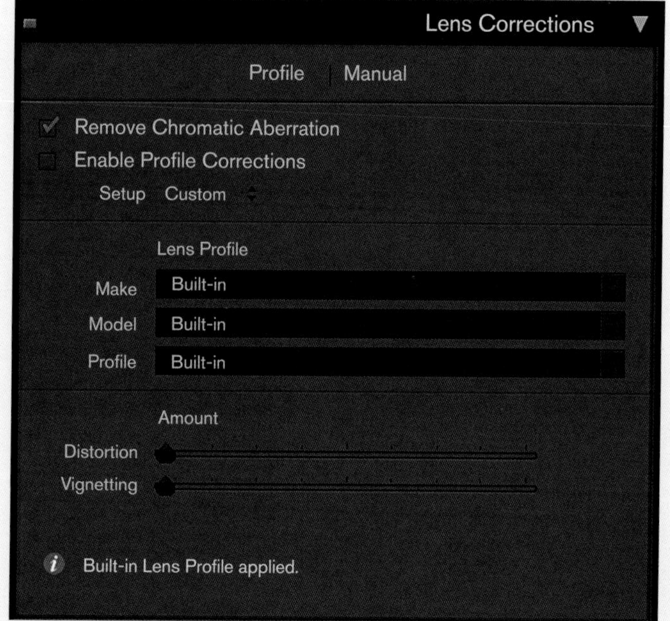

◀ For any cameras with built-in lens profiles, even though the Lens Corrections panel has been completely disabled, the little "i" icon is indicating that lens correction profiles embedded in the Raw file are still being applied. There is no way to disable them!

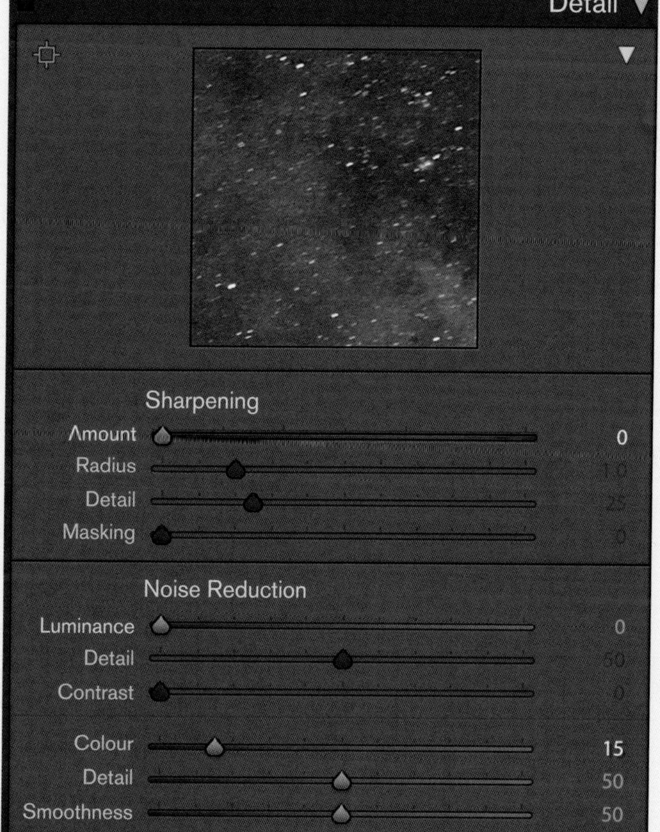

◀ Suggested Sharpening and Noise Reduction settings for sky images. Adjust the Color Noise Reduction slider to avoid excess color noise in the sky without destroying the color of stars and nebulae.

14.3 PART 2: STAR STACKING

Starry Landscape Stacker (Mac) and Sequator (Windows) are star-stacking programs that take the foreground into consideration. Most stacking programs are designed for stacking images of the stars only and will either get confused with a foreground in the frame or will cause the foreground to blur, since all the images are aligned based on the stars. But Starry Landscape Stacker and Sequator separate the sky and foreground during stacking, so you end up with low noise across the entire image without blurring the foreground.

As of this writing, I am using TIFF files exported from Lightroom Classic for star stacking, but you may wish to bring your Raw files straight into your stacking program, if it supports Raw files. My workflow is often in flux – in the past I've usually preferred to prep my Raw files before stacking, but I'm looking forward to working with Raw files when they are supported in Starry Landscape Stacker, for example. Feel free to experiment and find what works best for you.

When exporting TIFF files, make sure you are using the ProPhoto RGB color space for Starry Landscape Stacker, or the Adobe RGB color space for Sequator. ProPhoto RGB is a bigger color space so ideally you want to work in that space as much as possible. Unfortunately, as of writing, Sequator can't handle ProPhoto RGB's non-linear gamma well. The workaround is fairly complicated and makes it very difficult to see what you're doing because the image will look very dark, so it's probably not worth the extra hassle.

Be sure to disable Resizing or Output Sharpening when exporting the TIFF files, as you want to export them at full resolution.

We will now look at how to use both Starry Landscape Stacker and Sequator.

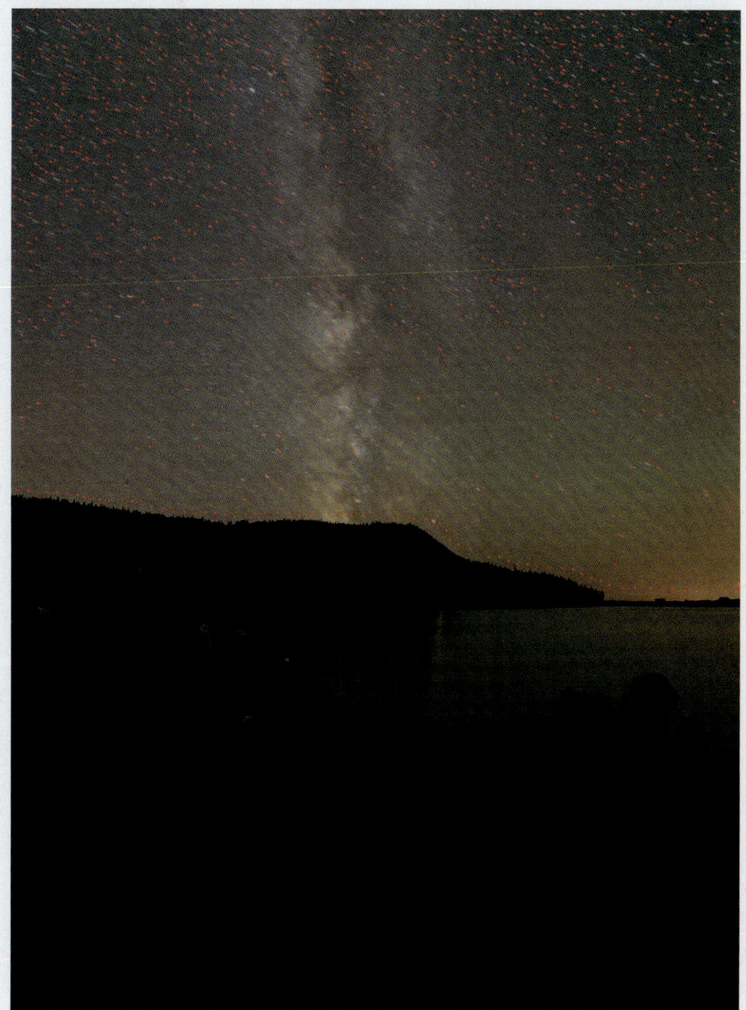

▲ The red dots indicate the stars.

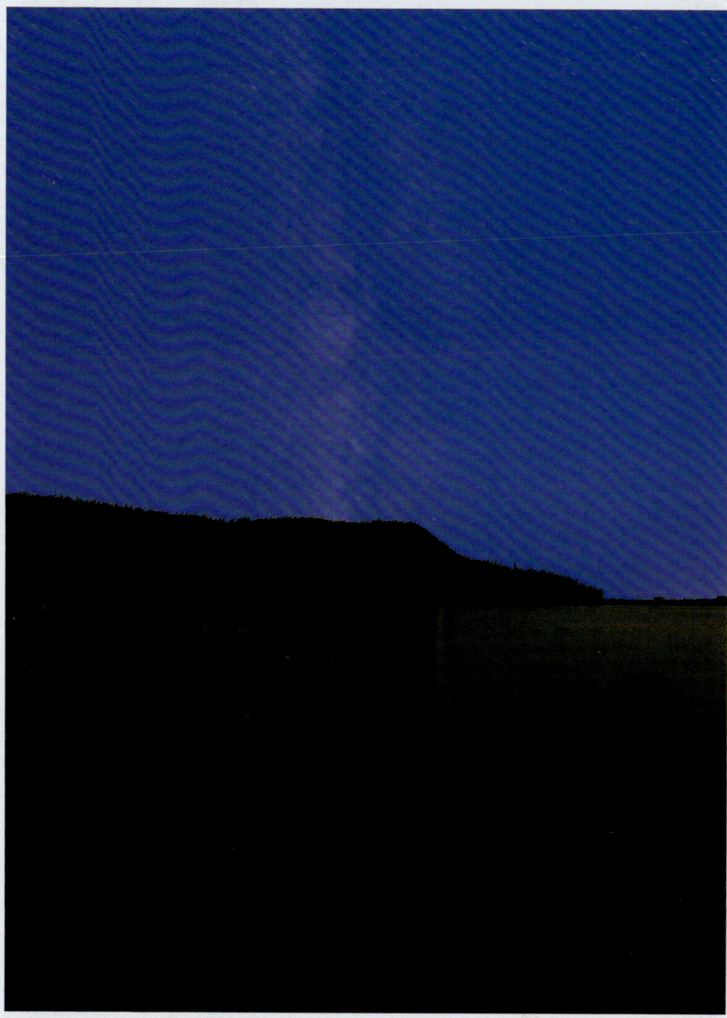

▲ The blue mask indicates the sky.

STARRY LANDSCAPE STACKER (MAC COMPUTERS)

This program is available for Mac computers only, if you are using Windows you can use Sequator.

1 When you open Starry Landscape Stacker, you will be prompted to load your images. Locate the TIFF files you exported from your Raw editor as previously described.

Once a TIFF file has been loaded into Starry Landscape Stacker, the program will analyze the image and try to find stars, placing red dots on many of them. You can add or remove red dots as needed. The red dots are an aid to tell the algorithm where the sky is located. You don't need red dots on every star by any means, but do make sure that there are red dots along the horizon and in tricky spots, for example, between tree branches—any areas where the stars are visible.

2 Next click the **Find Sky** button. This causes Starry Landscape Stacker to use the red dots as hints to determine where the sky is located in the image. It will generate a blue mask to indicate the sky area. If it is not perfect you can use the **Brush tool** to add bits to the blue mask or erase parts of it that overlap the foreground. You just need to make sure that the blue mask covers as much of the sky as possible in areas where the stars appear.

3 Then click **Align and Composite** and Starry Landscape Stacker will align and take an average of all the images. Save the file with a useful name.

▲ With an irregular mask applied.

SEQUATOR (WINDOWS COMPUTERS)

This program is available for Windows computers only, if you are using a Mac you can use Starry Landscape Stacker.

1 Load the TIFF files you exported earlier into Sequator by using the **File > Star images** menu item. (Use the **File > Output** menu item to specify the name and location of your output file.)

2 Click on **Sky region** then click **Irregular mask**. This puts you in mask-drawing mode. Draw the mask around the sky as much as you can with the mouse. If you have complex horizon areas, such as areas with trees, just get close to them, don't worry about being exact. The mask helps the algorithm work out where the sky is located.

3 Find the **Color space** option in the lower left panel, right-click it and select **Adobe RGB**.

4 Click the **Start** button to begin the alignment and averaging process. The file will be saved using the location you specified earlier.

Sequator has a lot of other image-processing options that you may wish to experiment with.

CATALOG

When you have generated your stacked image, import the file back into Lightroom Classic or your cataloguing program.

When I finish working in my stacking program and have the final TIFF file saved to my computer, I import that file into my Lightroom catalog, alongside the other files for that particular image. This keeps everything organized and makes it easier to find the file. Later, it will be blended with the foreground images in Photoshop.

14.4 PART 3: EXPOSURE BLENDING & FOCUS STACKING

Blending is where you combine the star-stacked sky result with your foreground exposures in Photoshop to create an image that has everything in good focus, and should look as "natural" as possible in terms of hiding blend lines and balancing brightness and color across the image. For a more realistic image, keep in mind that the sky should always be brighter than the foreground unless there is additional light in the foreground. Similarly, reflections should always be darker than the objects (e.g., sky) being reflected. But you can certainly break these rules when it comes to artistic choices.

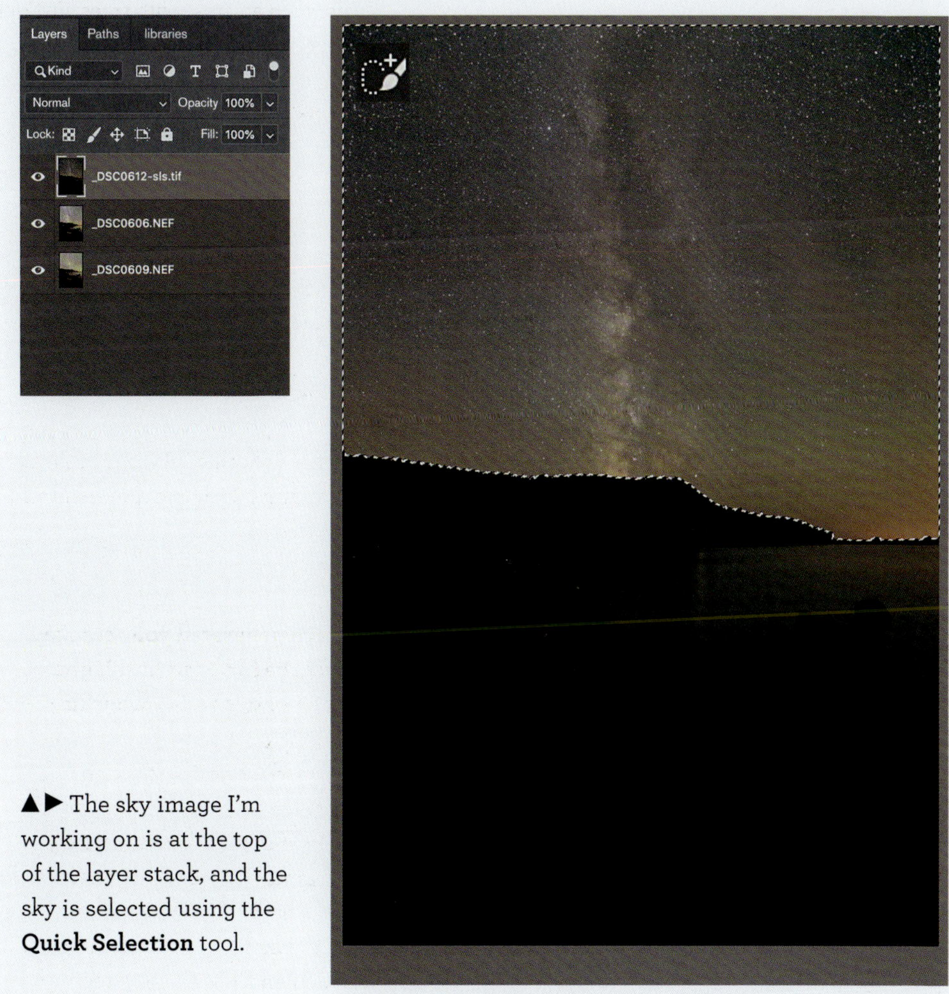

▲▶ The sky image I'm working on is at the top of the layer stack, and the sky is selected using the **Quick Selection** tool.

You can use layer masks in Photoshop to manually blend your images.

1 Begin by placing the sky on the top of your layer stack, with the foreground images below and in order of closest focus distance to farthest focus distance.

2 You may need to align the images so that the horizon and other foreground features all line up. If the images are out of alignment it will be difficult to blend. You can try selecting all the layers and using Photoshop's **Edit > Auto-Align Layers** menu item. If this doesn't work, try adding a mask to each layer that masks out the sky (use black paint) and try again—the mask will force the alignment to work on just the foreground areas. Crop the image after alignment to get rid of the rough edges.

3 With the sky layer highlighted, use the **Quick Selection** tool and drag it through the sky to create a rough selection. You can change the size of the Quick Selection brush to get into smaller areas of the sky, such as in between tree branches, or the railings on a building, and so on. This selection doesn't have to be perfect, but try to include as much of the sky as you can.

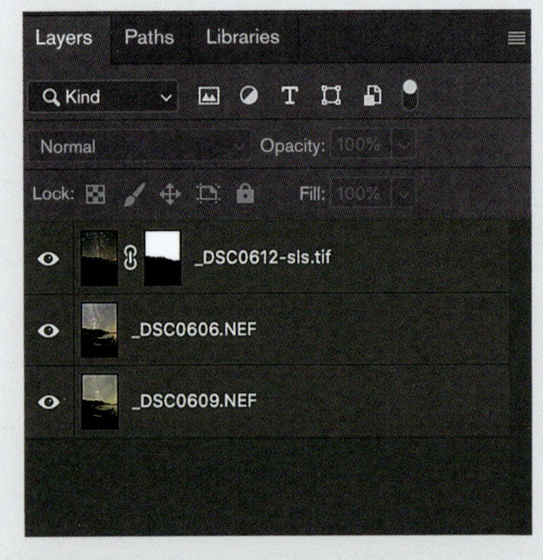

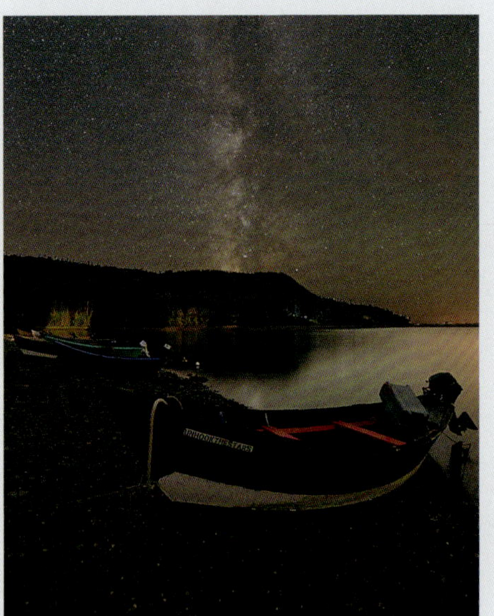

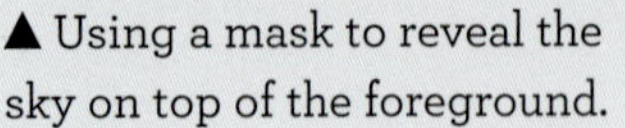
▲ Using a mask to reveal the sky on top of the foreground.

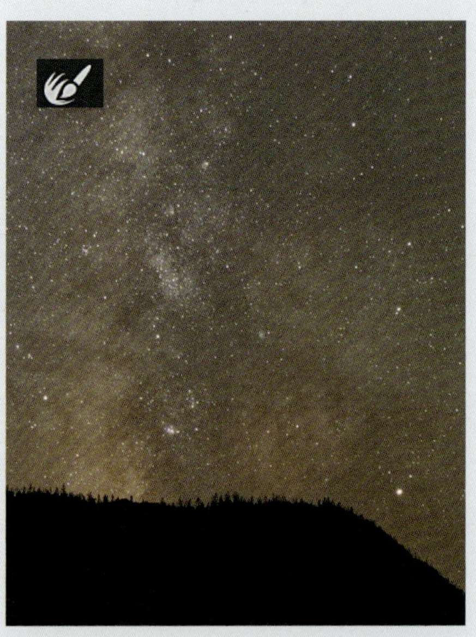

▲ Using the **Select & Mask** tool to refine the selection.

4 Once you have made your selection around the sky you can use that selection to create a mask on the sky layer. The selected areas will become the white part of the mask, and the non-selected areas will be black. This will reveal the sky on top of the foreground layers. Already we have a pretty good blend and the foreground is now clearly visible.

5 If the mask has rough edges around trees, buildings or any part of the horizon, then use the **Select & Mask** tool to refine the selection. Use the **Refine Edge** brush tool and drag it along all the edges in the mask to (hopefully) make those edges blend together better. Use the sliders in the right half of the screen to adjust the mask edge. The Shift Edge slider will be the most effective here. Try the Decontaminate Colors option in the bottom right section of the screen (it can be a huge help when blending), drag the slider back and forth until it has the effect you want.

6 When your mask edge looks good, you can leave the **Select & Mask** tool. Double-check that the blend looks clean and there are no halos around hard edges. Be sure to save your file at this point if you haven't done so already. You should always save often to avoid losing your work. Photoshop has a built-in auto-save feature that runs periodically, but you should save whenever you get to a point where you definitely don't want to lose your work.

7 Once the sky is blended with the top foreground layer, you can move onto blending the rest of the foreground layers to give you a wide depth of field — this is called focus stacking. Add an empty mask to each foreground layer, except for the bottom layer. Then, starting with the layer that has the same focus as the sky, use a black paint brush to mask out the parts of the image that are out of focus. This should reveal the more in-focus areas from the layer below. Move onto the next layer and do the same thing. The last layer at the bottom of the stack will not need a mask.

You could also try Photoshop's Auto-Blend Layers option for just the foreground layers, or you can use a dedicated focus-stacking program like Helicon Focus or Zerene Stacker. The best method will often vary from image to image, so experiment and see what works for you.

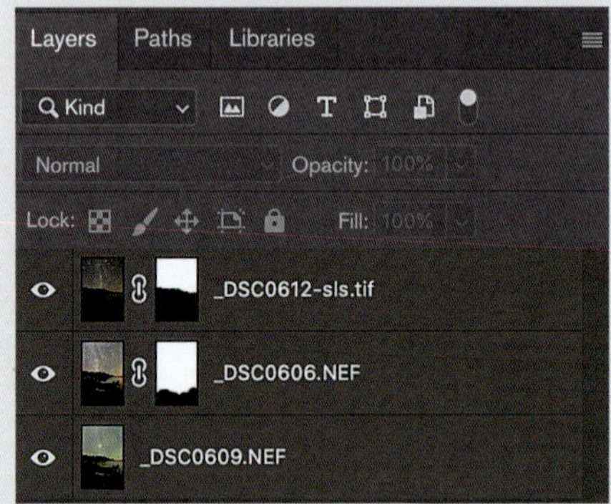

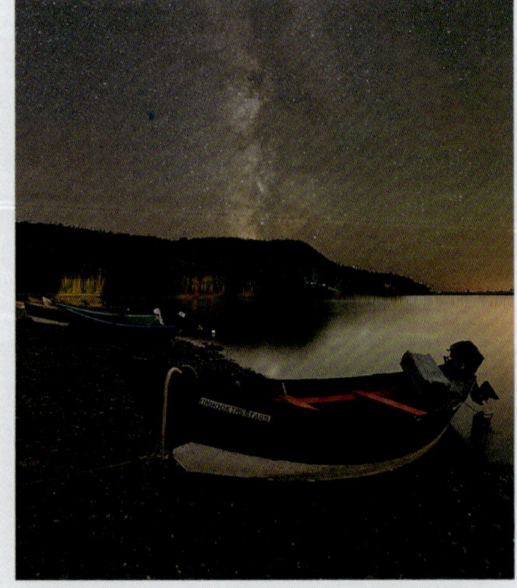

▲ Blending the foreground layers.

14.5 PART 4: CREATIVE ADJUSTMENTS

This is where you can let your inner artist really go wild or stay completely tame, depending on your style. I generally prefer a more "realistic" approach here, but the term "realistic" is hard to qualify when you're talking about something you can't see very well with the naked eye, certainly with nowhere near as much detail as your camera.

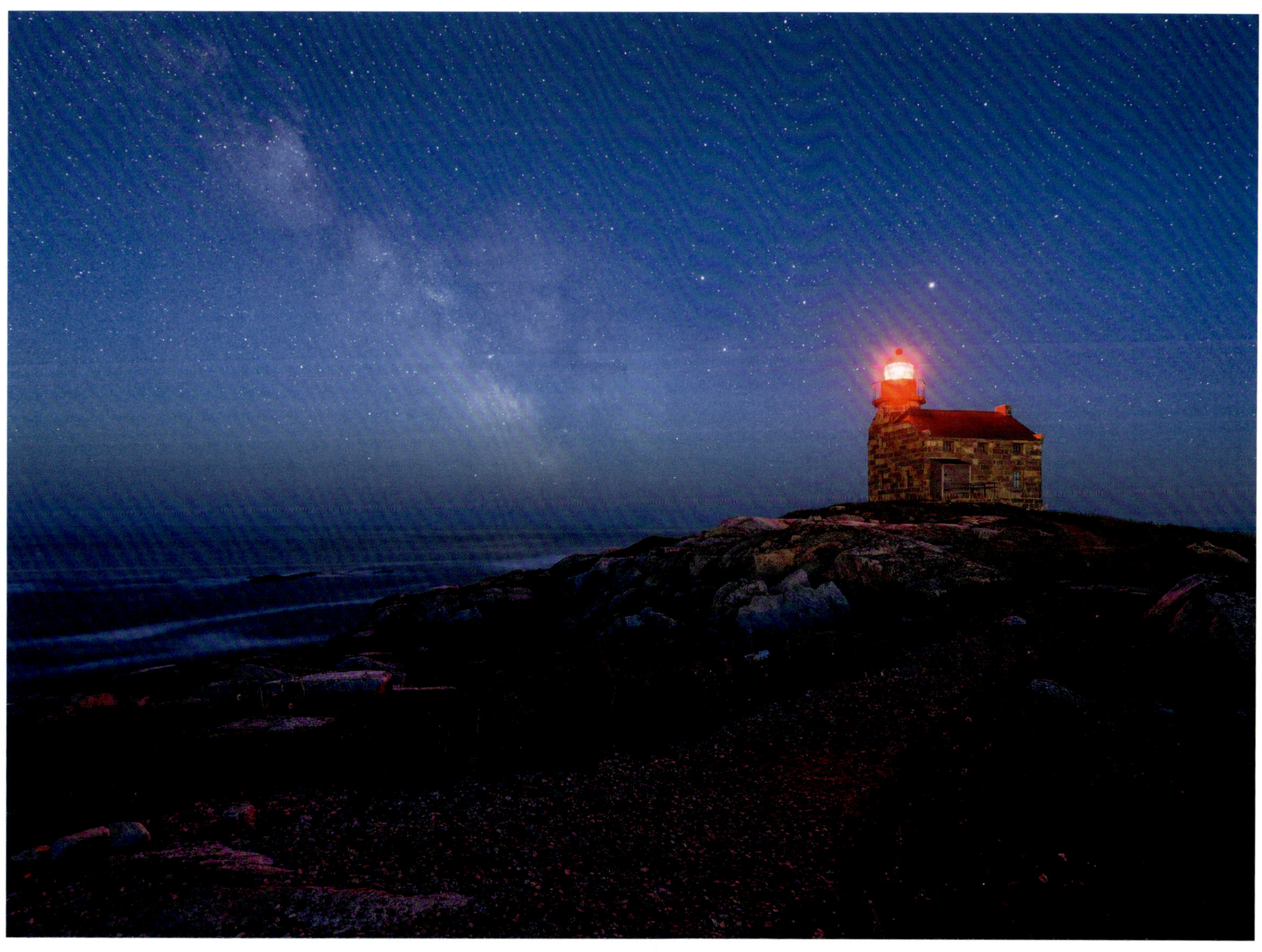

▲ Rose Blanche Lighthouse, Newfoundland. Deep blue dominates the sky during twilight.

14.5.1 COLOR BALANCE

When standing out under the stars, our perception of the night sky consists of various shades of gray. Human vision is essentially color blind at night, so it's hard to see any color with the unaided eye in the dark. You can see the red color of Mars if it is visible that night, and maybe the color of some of the very brightest stars, but even the aurora can look gray-white if it is not strong enough to overcome our color blindness in the dark.

However, your camera captures a world of color, which is easy to see once you open your photos in your Raw editor. The Milky Way's Galactic Core, any airglow (however faint), and stars will have colors you would never have seen with the naked eye.

This makes dealing with the color of night sky photos an interesting experience. What is the "right" color? Should I process the image to look more like I perceived it, without much color? Or should I take advantage of all that color and process it in a scientifically accurate way? Or should I balance the colors to my own personal liking? This gets even trickier with mixed lighting situations, such as when there's a lighthouse, light pollution, strong airglow, a light painting source, and so on. Balancing color for just one light source can make the others appear wildly off, but balancing them all can be a challenge (although it is relatively easy to color balance the sky separately from the foreground using layer masking).

I personally like to strike a balance between accurate color for the night sky, accurate color for the foreground and pleasing color overall. As much as I want the night sky to look accurate, I don't want to do so at the expense of the entire scene looking like it got hit with a can of orange paint. If that means adjusting the sky to have more blue in it than it technically should, then I will just do that.

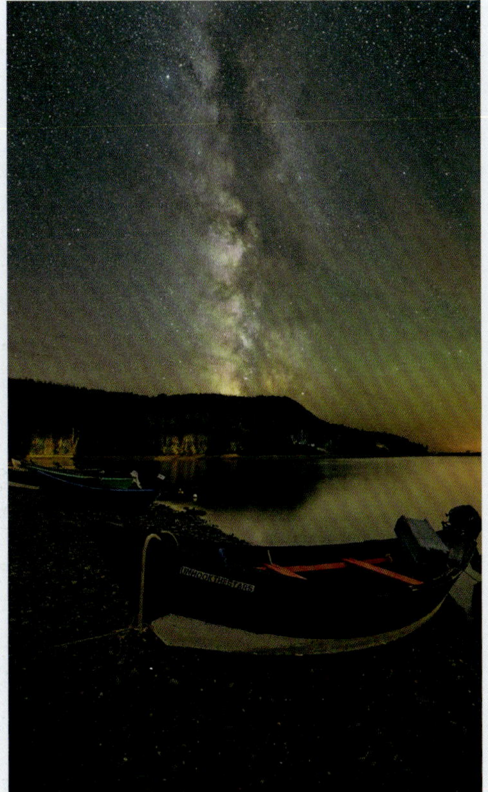
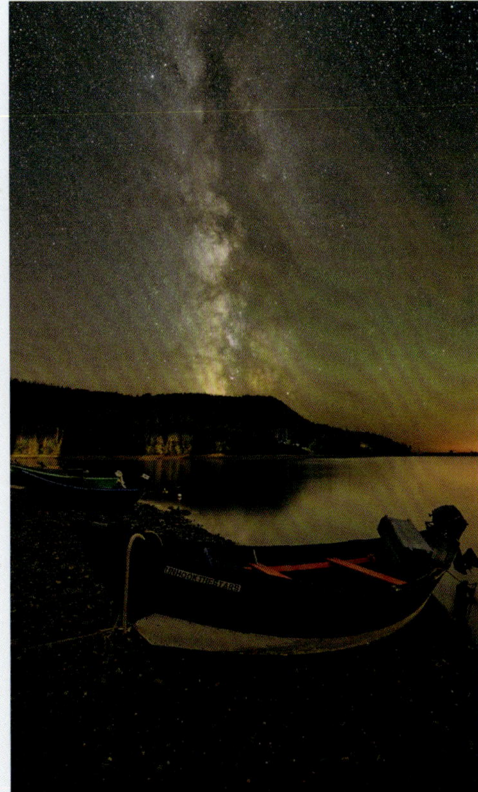
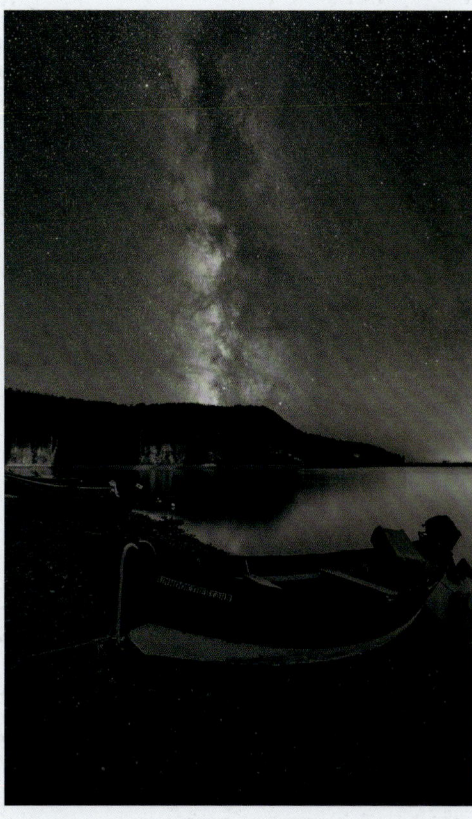

▲ Three different treatments of the same image.

Ultimately the choice is yours, and color balance is one of the many ways you can impart your own artistic style to your images, but it's helpful to know some basics on what the actual colors of things should be.

The true color of the bright Milky Way core is a rust-brown color. But it can dramatically shift in color due to airglow or the aurora, appearing green-yellow or something similar. And when it is low in the sky, as it often is in the Northern Hemisphere, the core can appear reddish-orange due to Rayleigh scattering—the light from the Milky Way shines through more of the atmosphere when it is low in the sky, and the atmosphere will filter the light and cause it to look more red-orange. This is the same reason the sun and moon (or Venus or any celestial object) appear red-orange when they are low in the sky. And, of course, light pollution will effect the color of the sky, making it appear more orange-yellow.

Sometimes when the moon is up or you're shooting around twilight the sky can actually be blue due to the Rayleigh scattering of the sunlight in the atmosphere (remember that moonlight is actually reflected sunlight). This is down to the same reason that the sky is blue during the day. In these cases there will be less visible detail in the Milky Way. If the sky is bright enough, all color detail in the Milky Way will be lost and everything will look blue.

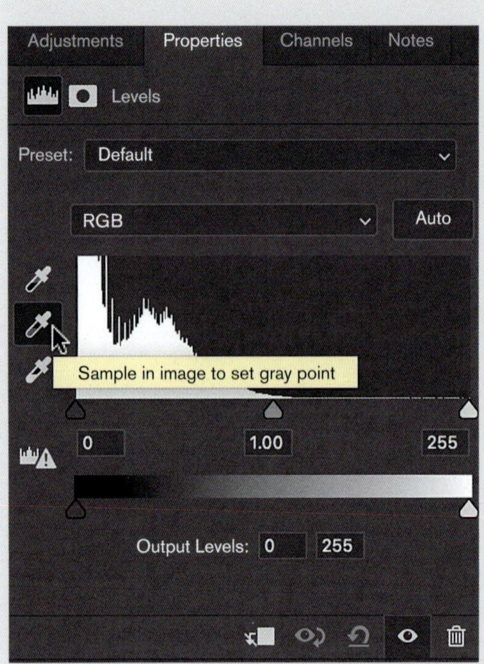

▲ The location of the Gray Point Sample tool in the Levels Adjustment Properties.

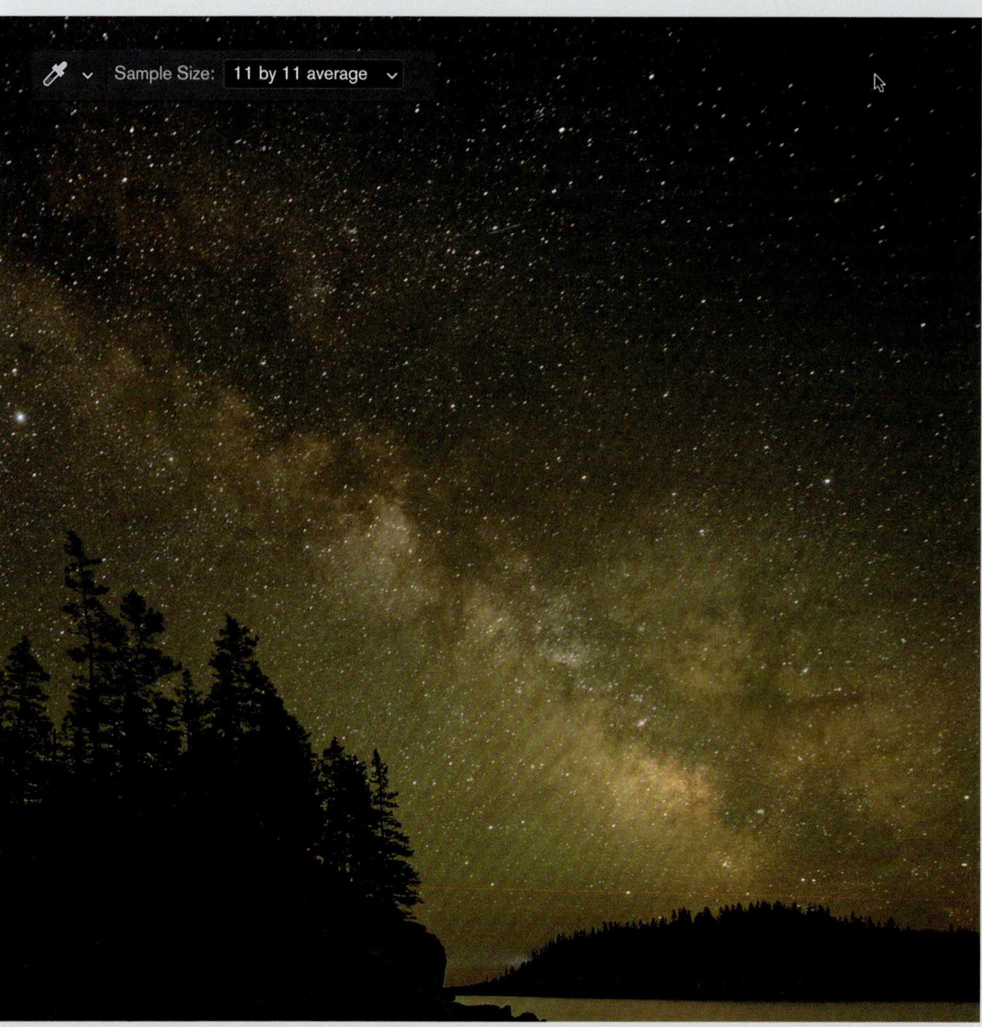

▲ I clicked an area in the upper right of the image away from light pollution and the Milky Way, and where the effect of airglow is less visible.

Make sure to set the sample size for the eye-dropper to 5 x 5 pixels or larger, and zoom in on the image when selecting a sample point—avoid including any stars in the sample. Whether you find a good sample point or not, you can always adjust color to taste.

USING LEVELS OR CURVES TO SET GRAY POINT

1 In Photoshop, the Levels and Curves Adjustments panels have color sampling tools (eye-droppers) that can be used to set the black point, gray point and white point. I tend to ignore the black and white point with landscape astrophotography, but the gray point can be quite useful for setting the overall color balance. Look for an area devoid of any strong light sources, such as stars, intense airglow, light pollution, the Milky Way, nebulae and so on. Sample that area with the Gray Sample tool in the Levels or Curves Adjustments options. A cloud can also be used for setting the gray point if it is not reflecting light pollution.

Setting the gray point will cause Photoshop to balance the colors so that the area you sampled will be considered neutral (a shade of gray), bringing all the other colors in the image “in line” based on that gray point.

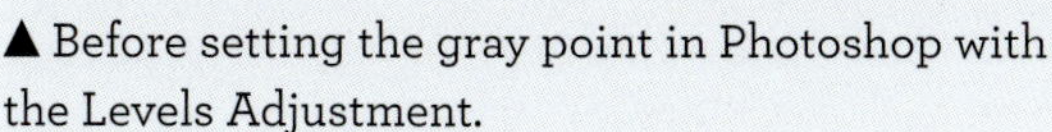

▲ Before setting the gray point in Photoshop with the Levels Adjustment.

▲ After setting the gray point to a sample in the upper right of the photo.

2 If a suitable area of blank sky (or cloud) can't be found, you can try sampling something in the foreground that should be gray (or white) that is not lit up by any artificial light, such as a white or gray building (with no nearby lights), a vehicle, a boat, a very neutral-colored rock and so on. It will take some experimentation. You may need to color balance the sky separately from the foreground. Alternatively, this method might not work for your image at all, in which case you can just judge the color by eye instead.

14.5.2 LEVELS & CURVES

Two of the most useful creative adjustment tools are the Levels and Curves tools, available in many image-editing programs, including Photoshop. These simple but very powerful tools allow you to adjust the tones in your images, which can result in dramatic changes, especially when combined with layer masking to affect only part of the image.

Using the fishing boat image again as an example, we can see just how dramatic an impact the Curves tool alone can have.

1 After blending, the image, particularly the sky, looks a little dull.

2 A few quick adjustments using the Curves tool in Photoshop adds punch to the sky.

It's often best to use multiple adjustment layers, making small changes and masking them in where needed.

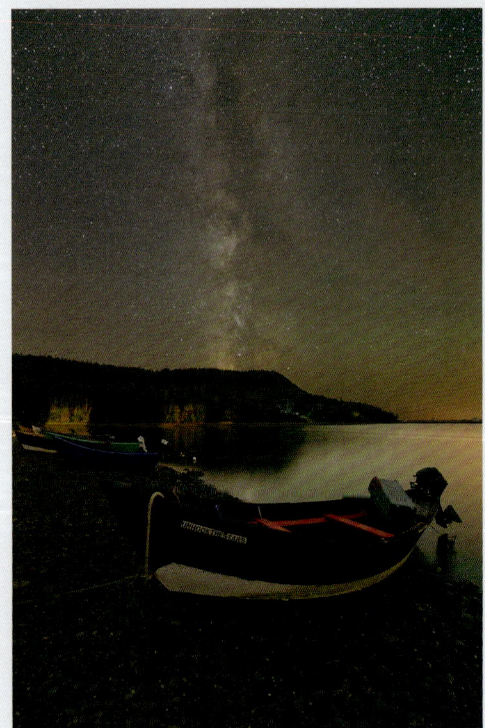

▲ The original blended image.

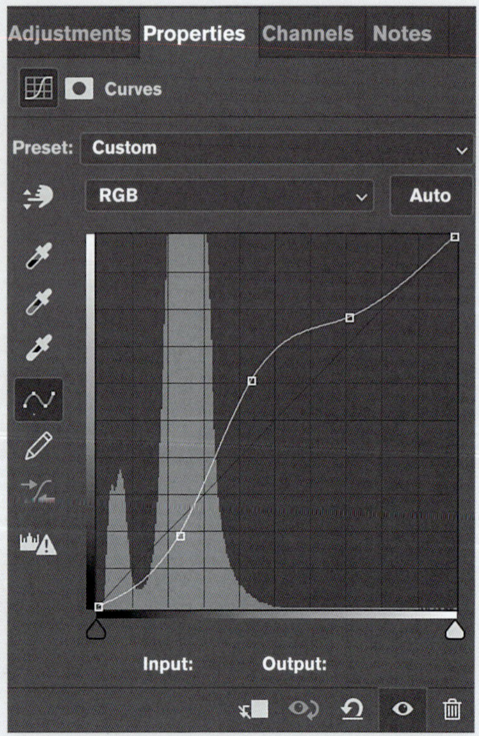

▲ Making adjustments with the Curves tool.

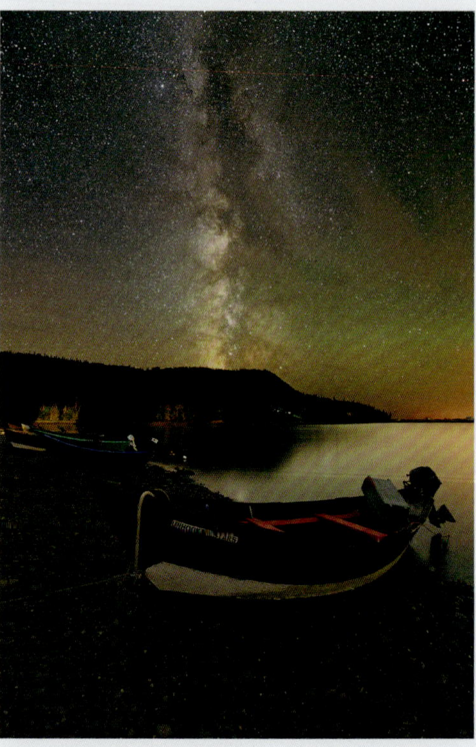

▲ The adjusted image.

14.6 MORE CREATIVE ADJUSTMENTS

There is an enormous number of effects packages and plugins available for Adobe Lightroom Classic and Photoshop from companies such as Nik, Topaz and Skylum, as well as a zillion creative tools within Photoshop, including the built-in Layer Adjustment tools and Blending Modes.

If you have used Photoshop for the blending process, continue editing within Photoshop rather than going back to Lightroom. Photoshop is better suited to the fine-tuning that you may need to apply to certain parts of an image. Lightroom has a Brush tool for applying edits in this way, but the types of edits you can make in Lightroom are limited. The creative possibilities are endless once you are comfortable using Photoshop or a similarly advanced image-editing program.

ADOBE CAMERA RAW FILTER

Adobe Camera Raw is a tool on its own and a filter in Photoshop. It features all the same tools as Lightroom for editing Raw files, and you can use them to great creative effect. Try adjusting the Dehaze or Clarity slider, but be careful, a little goes a long way. I also use the regular Tone Adjustments (exposure, contrast, highlights, whites, shadows, blacks) to make the image "punchier." Just increasing the Whites slider a bit can make a huge difference in contrast, really bringing out the Galactic Core.

Whatever edit I'm applying, I'll often only add it to a certain part of the image by using a mask. For example, I may add some punch and saturation to the sky by using a layer mask that only applies those adjustments to the sky.

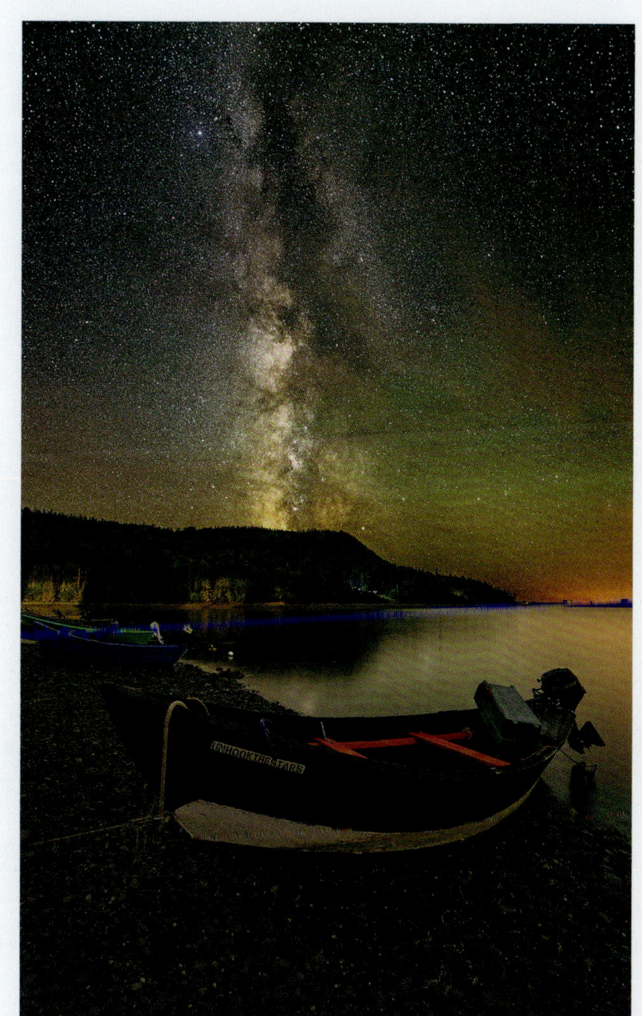

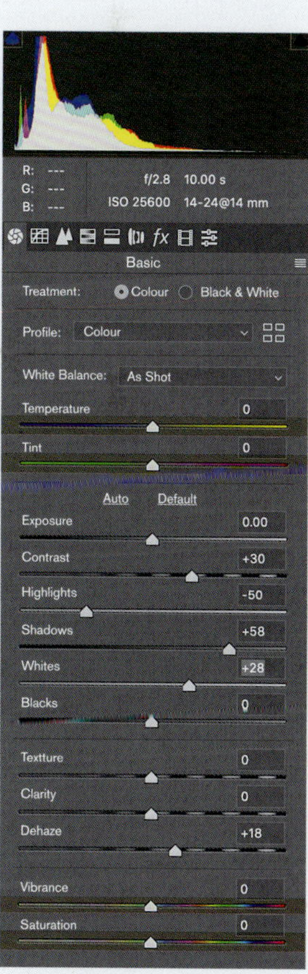

▲ Using the Adobe Camera Raw filter in Photoshop, you can use all the sliders and tools normally available in Adobe Camera Raw, such as adding a vignette.

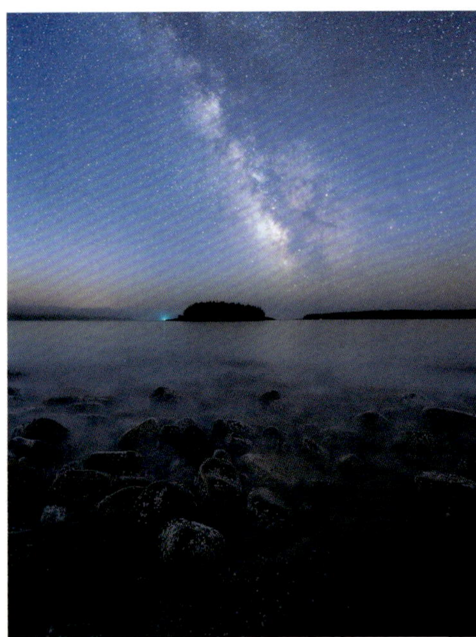

▲ Here is an image without any creative adjustments.

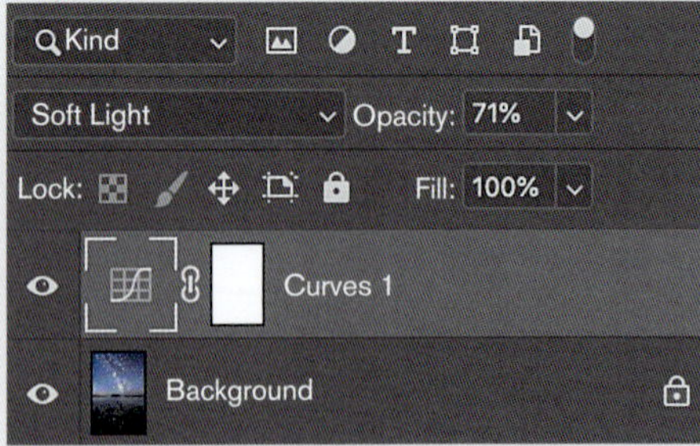

◀ I have added a Levels adjustment layer with no changes to the Levels, but I have changed the blending mode to Soft Light and reduced the Opacity of the layer. The contrast and saturation have increased.

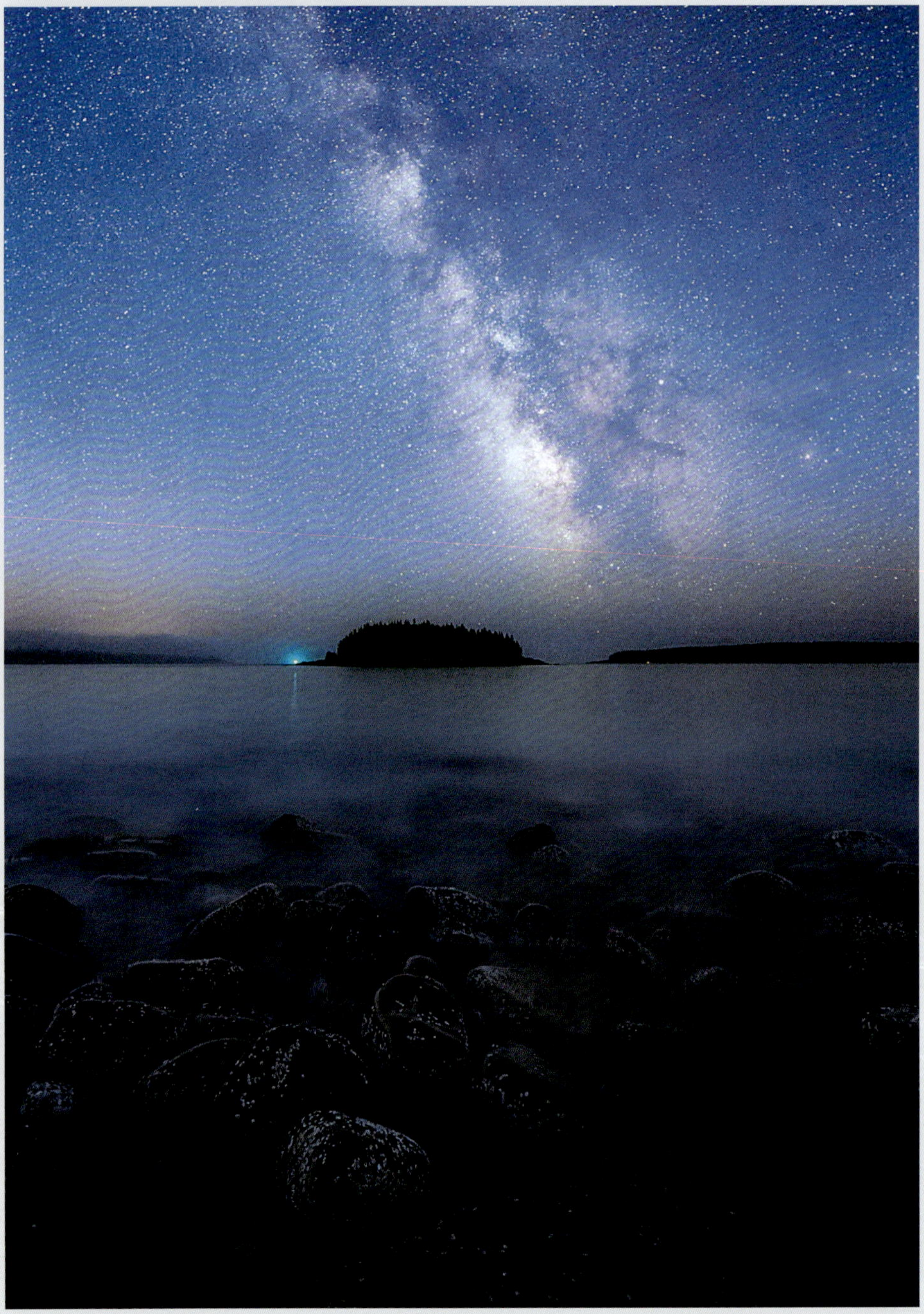

BLENDING MODES

A good way to add punch to an image is to add an adjustment layer (such as Levels or Curves) on top of the image layers in Photoshop, and change the blending mode of that new layer to Soft Light (my favorite), Overlay or Hard Light. You can then adjust the Opacity of the layer to taste. At 100% (the default opacity), the image will probably look way too dark, so bring the Opacity down until you get something you're happy with.

You could duplicate the image to have another pixel layer that you apply the blend mode to, but you will save file space by just using an adjustment layer instead. You don't have to make any changes to the sliders or buttons of the adjustment layer, it is just acting as a way to blend the image with itself.

14.6.1 PROTECTING THE STARS

When making any creative adjustments that affect the sky it is important to protect the stars from being blown out to pure white and losing all color and detail. There are a few ways to do this.

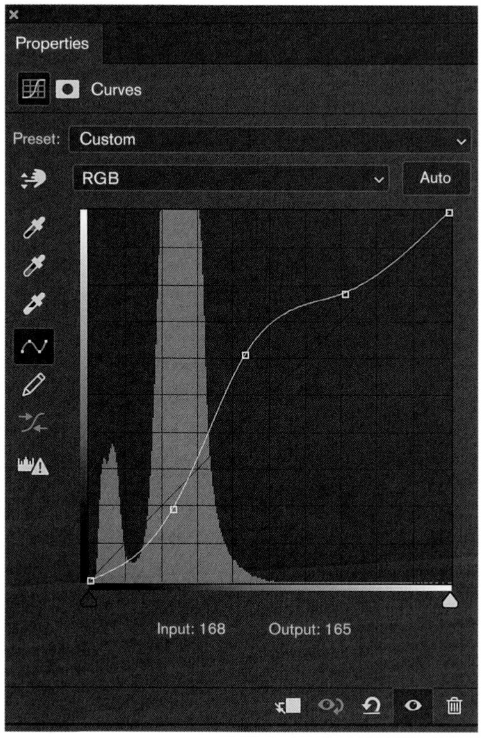

▲ An example of a curve with the line keeping close to the diagonal center.

1 With the **Curves** tool this can be accomplished by keeping the top right section of the curve (the highlights) close to the diagonal middle line of the curve window. Be careful here, a steep curve can create weird effects.

2 Alternatively, you can use **Blend If** in the Layer Style options. Click on the appropriate sky layer in the layers panel, then select **Layer > Layer Style > Blending Options** from the menus. Set **Blend If** to **Gray**. Hold down the Alt or Option key and click on the white triangle beneath the This Layer gradient bar on the right-hand side. This will split the triangle in two and allow you to pull the left half toward the middle of the gradient bar and bring the right half of the triangle inward as well. Zoom in on the image to see what effect this is having—you want it to protect the stars without causing other issues.

3 You can also protect the stars by using a layer mask to select everything but the stars. You can generate a mask using the **Select > Color Range** tool in Photoshop. Change the **Select** drop-down menu to **Highlights**, and choose **Grayscale** from the **Selection Preview** drop-down. Since we want to protect the stars, we want them to be black in the mask, so check the **Invert** box. Zoom in on the image to see the stars. Drag the **Fuzziness** and **Range** sliders around until you get a mask where most of the stars are black. Click **OK** and you will now have a selection of everything but the stars (and anything else that is really bright). You can add this selection as a layer mask to adjustment layers, or group your layers and apply the mask to the entire group. Examine the mask for accuracy and use white or black paint to fix it if needed. For example, if some bright foreground objects have been selected that you want to be affected by an adjustment, then you can paint them white to remove them from the mask.

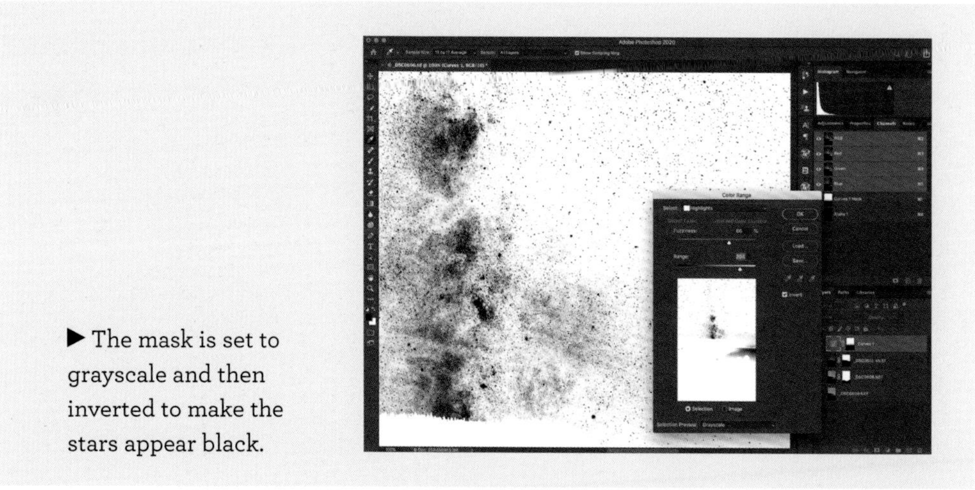

▶ The mask is set to grayscale and then inverted to make the stars appear black.

14.6.2 STAR REDUCTION

Star reduction is a technique that makes the stars a little smaller so that the color and detail of another celestial object (such as the Milky Way) is more visible in the image. This is a technique taken from deep space astrophotography and it can make a huge difference in how your Milky Way photos look.

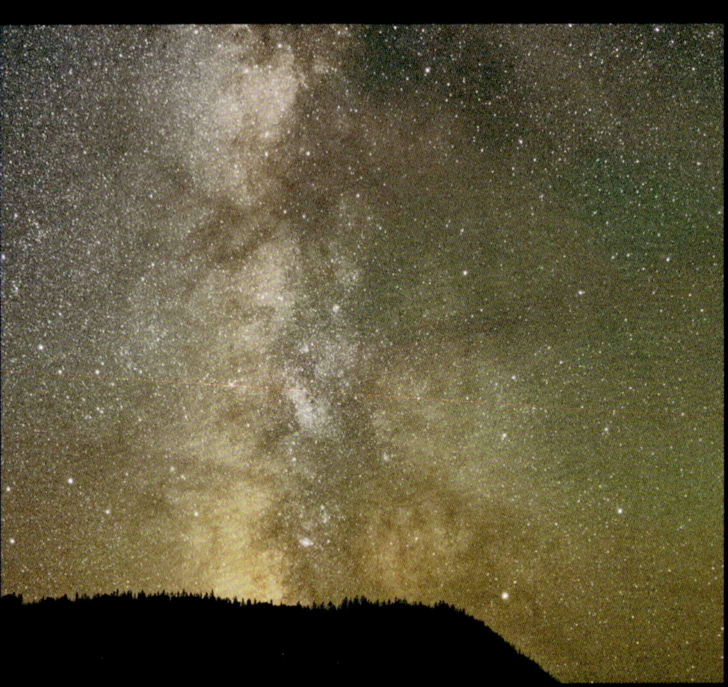

▲ No star reduction.

▲ With star reduction. The stars are not as prominent, allowing detail in the Milky Way to come through more.

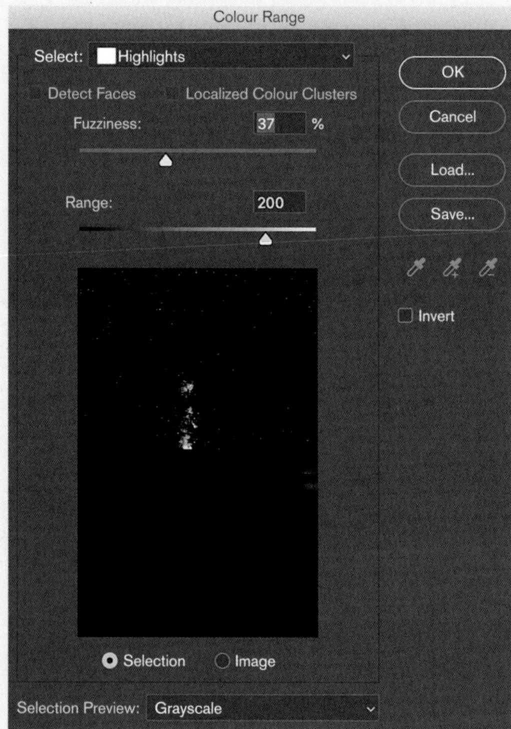

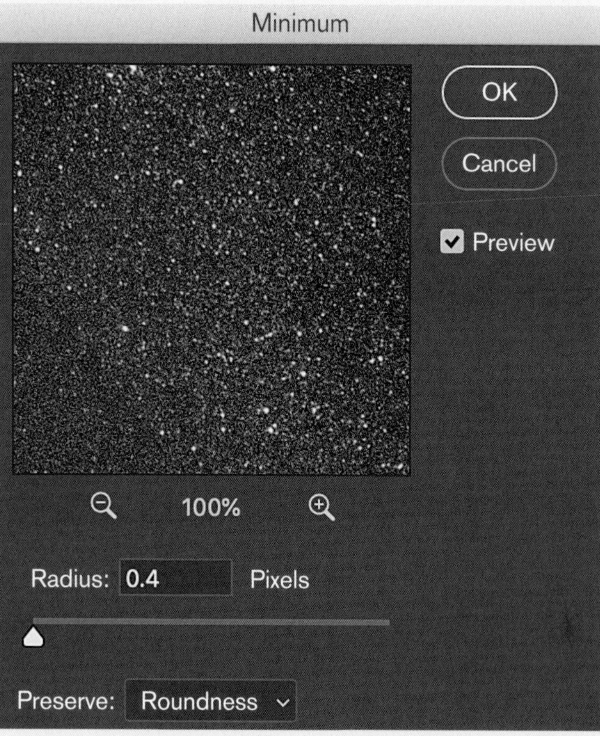

This technique is fairly simple:

1 Create a new **Merge Visible** layer on top of all the other layers. Select this layer in the layer stack.

2 Use the same method outlined in the previous section (Step 3; page 183) on using the **Color Range** tool, but instead don't check the **Invert** box. We want to select the stars this time, so they should appear white in the mask.

3 After clicking **OK** in the **Color Range** tool, use the **Select › Modify › Expand** menu option to increase the selection so that it includes a small, immediate area around the stars. Try a value of 2 pixels. This will expand the selection border by an additional 2 pixels around each star already selected.

4 Use this selection to create a mask on the layer you created in Step 1. (Or leave the section loaded and continue onward, just remember to de-select the selection after applying the Minimum Filter in Step 6.)

5 Click on the pixel layer (not the mask) to make it active.

6 Launch the Minimum Filter from the **Filter › Other › Minimum** menu item. Set the **Preserve** drop-down menu to **Roundness**. Set the **Radius** as low as it will go (0.2 pixels) and examine the preview. Zoom in on the image to an area with lots of stars. Look at how the image now looks with the Radius at 0.2. Toggle the preview on and off. Increase the Radius by 0.1 pixels at a time and examine the preview. You should see the stars getting smaller and less pronounced the higher you go with the Radius. A low Radius is probably all you'll need. Don't go too high or you'll have very strange looking stars.

7 Click the **OK** button to apply the result. It should be applied just to the new **Merge Visible** layer you created in Step 1.

8 Adjust the Opacity of this layer as needed if the effect is too strong.

9 Check the mask and paint out areas where the effect should not apply with black paint, such as anything in the foreground, and maybe any areas of the sky where it is too strong.

14.6.3 NOISE REDUCTION

If you've been following the techniques I laid out earlier in the book for creating low-noise images using star stacking (or a tracker) and long-exposure foreground shots, then you will likely not need to apply an enormous amount of noise reduction during post-processing. In fact, you might not need any at all. However, if you're taking a single short exposure for the sky/and or the foreground, then you will likely have a lot more noise to deal with in post-processing.

LESS IS (SOMETIMES) MORE

While reading the next few sections on noise-reduction methods, keep in mind that going too far will often be much worse than having a bit of noise in your image. You can spot a heavily noise-reduced image from a mile away due to the splotchy, plasticky look of the image. Having a little bit of noise is perfectly fine. It actually adds a bit of "bite" to the image, making the image appear sharper. So, there's a balance to be found, and when in doubt, less is more.

WORKFLOW TIPS

Noise reduction is often done in iterations, at various stages throughout the workflow. Some degree of noise reduction can be applied in the Raw editor. When in Photoshop, you can use noise-reduction tools on the sky and foreground separately before blending, after blending and after any subsequent creative edits that may have brought out more noise. Stretching the tones and colors of an image will almost always make noise more visible, so it's good practice to reduce noise before making any creative adjustments, and you may need to reduce it yet again after making the creative adjustments.

Note that you do not want to apply any noise reduction to sky shots before star stacking them into a single image.

NOISE REDUCTION TOOLS

Your Raw editor willl have some noise-reduction tools. Photoshop has built-in noise reduction tools, and there are a number of third-party noise-reduction plugins available for both Adobe Lightroom Classic and Photoshop (or in some cases standalone programs) that do amazing work at getting rid of noise. One of my longstanding favorites has been Nik Dfine, although Topaz has been making some great strides in the AI (artificial intelligence) area of noise reduction with their DeNoise AI standalone program.

NOISE MATCHING

Sometimes you'll notice that your image has very different levels of noise from one area to another. This is often true after blending your star-stacked (or star-tracked) sky with your long-exposure foreground—the noise pattern in the sky is likely to be different to the noise pattern in the foreground, and it might be vastly different compared to smooth surfaces that will show noise much more easily, like a body of water or the side of a building or vehicle. These differences can sometimes be distracting, interrupting the viewer from what should feel like a seamless, immersive image.

This is where what I call "noise matching" comes into play. Areas of the image that really stand out because they are lower or higher in noise than the surrounding areas can be helped by either adding or removing noise selectively within the image.

Take a close look at the example image. There is more noise in the sky than in the water. To help make this a more seamless-looking blend we can match the noise between the sky and water, either by reducing noise in the sky or adding noise to the water.

Using Nik Dfine, I sampled the noise in the sky and reduced it significantly to more closely match the noise in the water of the previous image. Ignore how the water looks in this image from Nik Dfine, as noise reduction

▲ Zooming in shows how noise is clearly visible in the sky compared to the water.

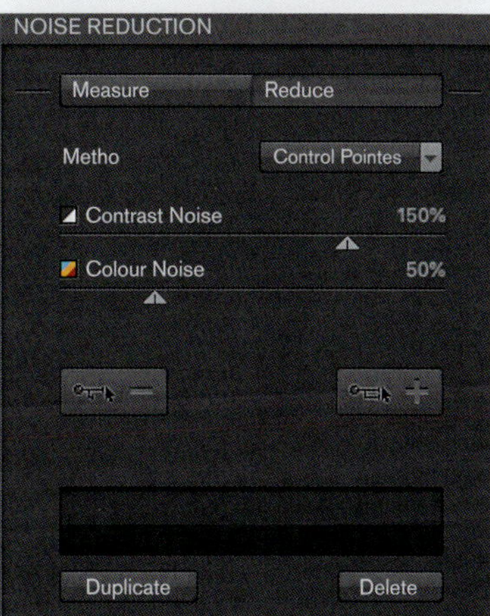

◀ Using Nik Dfine to better match the sky to the water.

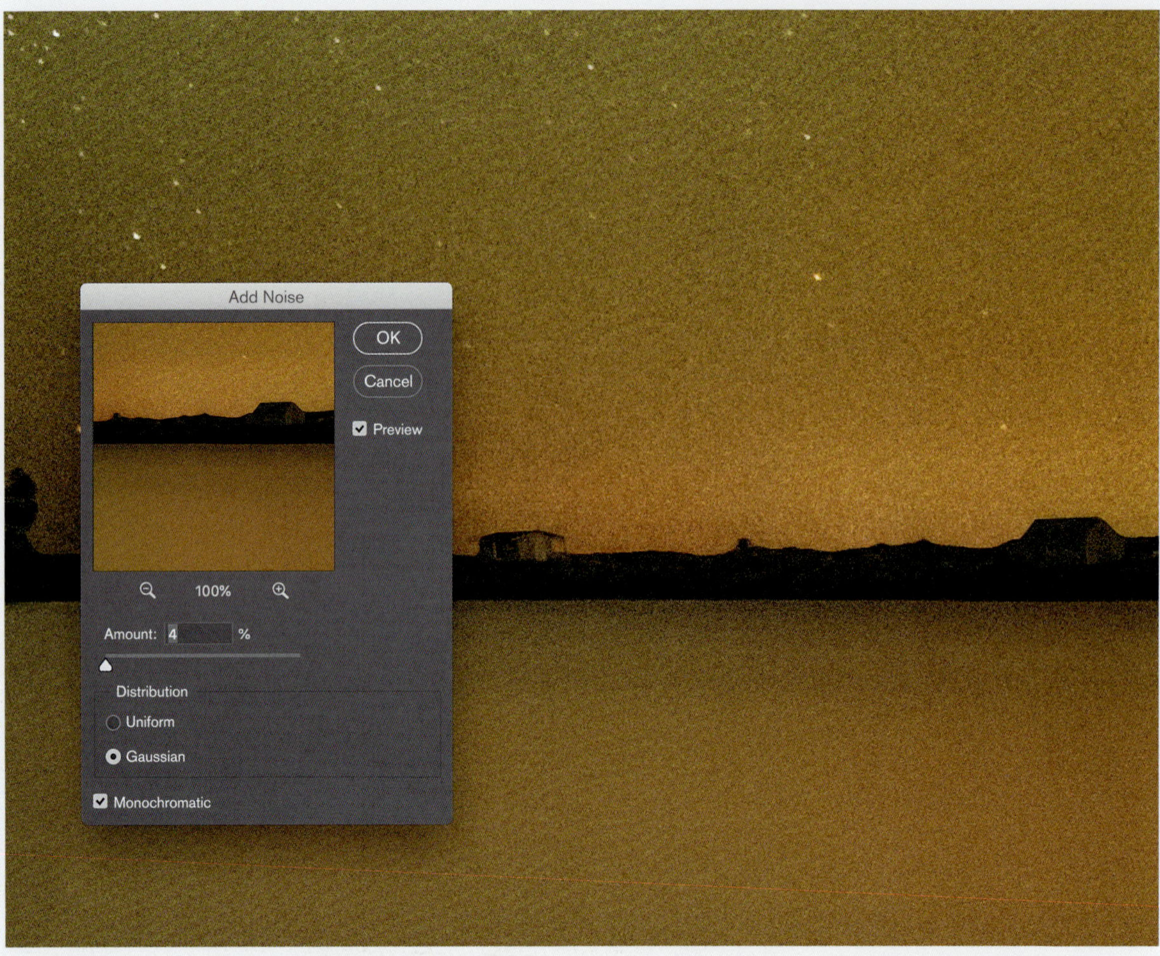

is being applied to the entire image and we are just worrying about reducing it in the sky.

However, the noise reduction is too much. Even though it now more closely matches the water, the noise reduction is causing the sky to look splotchy and pixelated. In situations like this, where reducing noise is causing ugly artifacts, you can try adding noise to the less-noisy areas. This may sound counterintuitive — why would you want to *add* noise to your image? In this case, noise reduction is making the image worse, so adding a little noise will make the blend look better.

You can use Photoshop's **Add Noise** filter to add noise to the water. Create a new layer that is a copy of the entire image (or just the relevant layer) to use with the filter. Check the **Monochrome** option in the **Add Noise** filter window. For **Distribution** try both **Uniform** and **Gaussian** and see what works best. I usually prefer **Gaussian**. Adjust the **Amount** slider until the additional noise looks like the noise you're trying to match. It helps to add a mask to the layer that only selects the area that needs more noise before launching the filter, otherwise the filter will affect the entire image and it will be hard to determine how much noise to add. After applying the filter you can adjust the Opacity of the layer to fine-tune how much noise is added.

Whichever method you use (and it will vary based on the image), make sure you mask in the noise reduction or noise addition only where needed in the image.

▲ Adding noise to the water to match the sky, where noise reduction reduces the image quality.

REMOVING HOT PIXELS

If your image only has a few hot pixels it is easy to remove them with the **Clone Stamp** or **Spot Removal** tool in Photoshop (or your Raw editor), but if you have a lot of hot pixels to deal with it's best to get rid of them in Photoshop using the **Dust & Scratches** filter. (Many thanks to Jon Secord for telling me about this method years ago, it is a lifesaver!)

Here's a step-by-step process for using Dust & Scratches to remove hot pixels:

1 Create a new layer that is a copy of the entire image (or just the relevant layer) to use with the filter.

2 Zoom in on your photo to get a good view of the hot pixels.

3 Open the filter from the **Filter > Noise > Dust & Scratches** menu item. Drag the **Radius** and **Threshold** sliders as low as they will go. Enable the **Preview** checkbox so that you can see the effect take place on your zoomed-in image.

4 Slowly increase the **Radius** value until all the hot pixels disappear. This will cause the entire image to look a bit soft, which we will fix with the **Threshold** slider.

5 Increase the **Threshold** slider until the hot pixels start to come back, then decrease until they are gone again. Find the best point where most of the hot pixels are gone without removing detail from the image.

6 Click **OK** to apply the filter.

7 Examine the image close up and mask the effect out of any areas where it is causing trouble. This filter will destroy your stars so make sure to mask it out of the sky.

▲ An extreme example of hot pixels.

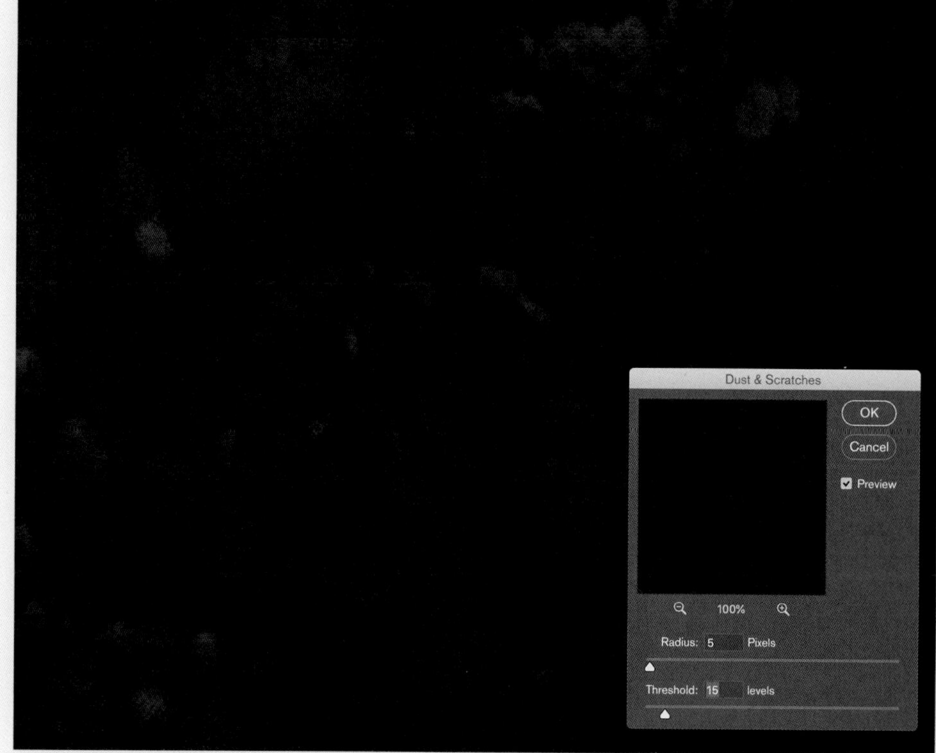

▲ Using the Dust & Scratches filter to remove hot pixels.

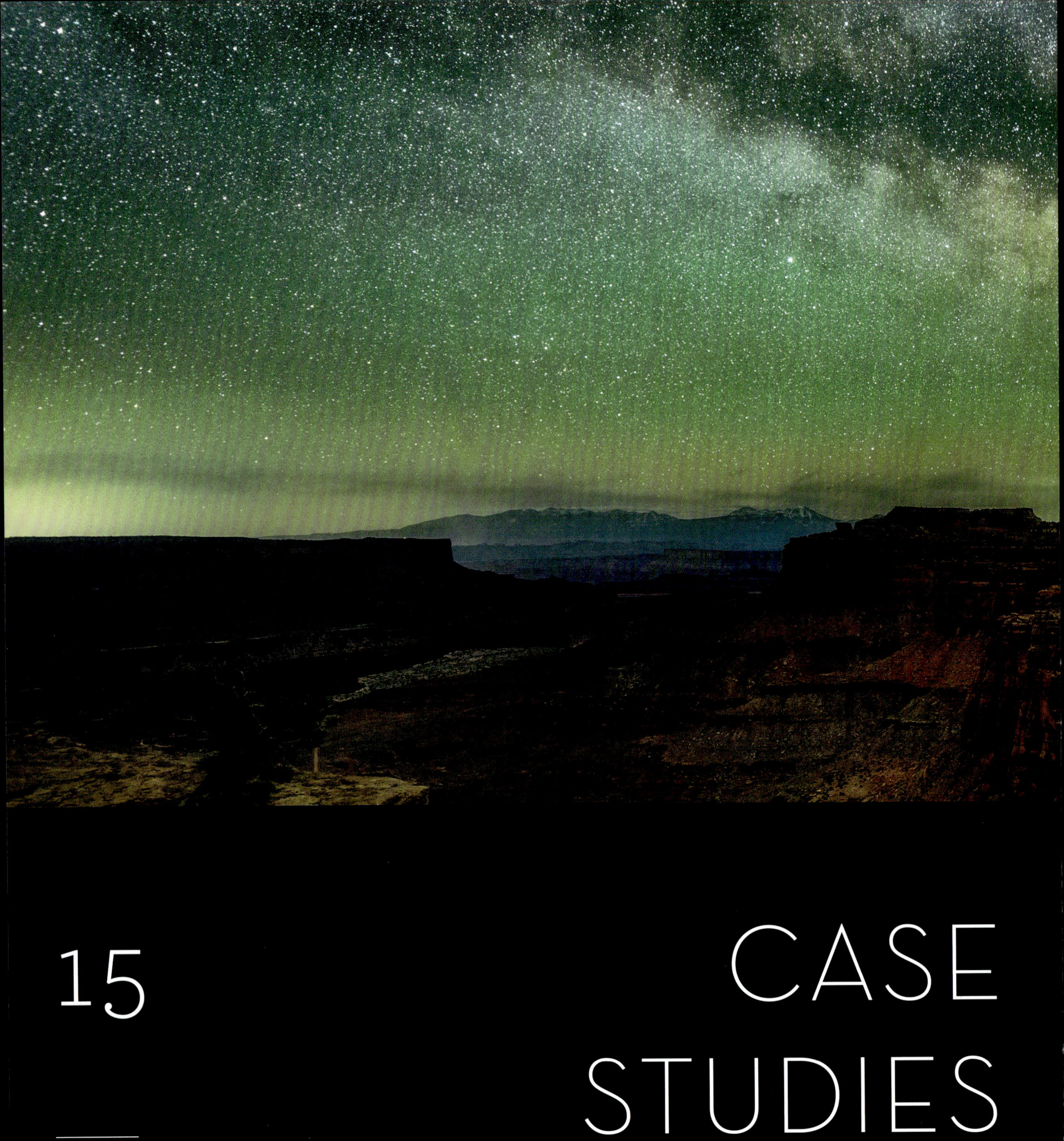

15

CASE STUDIES

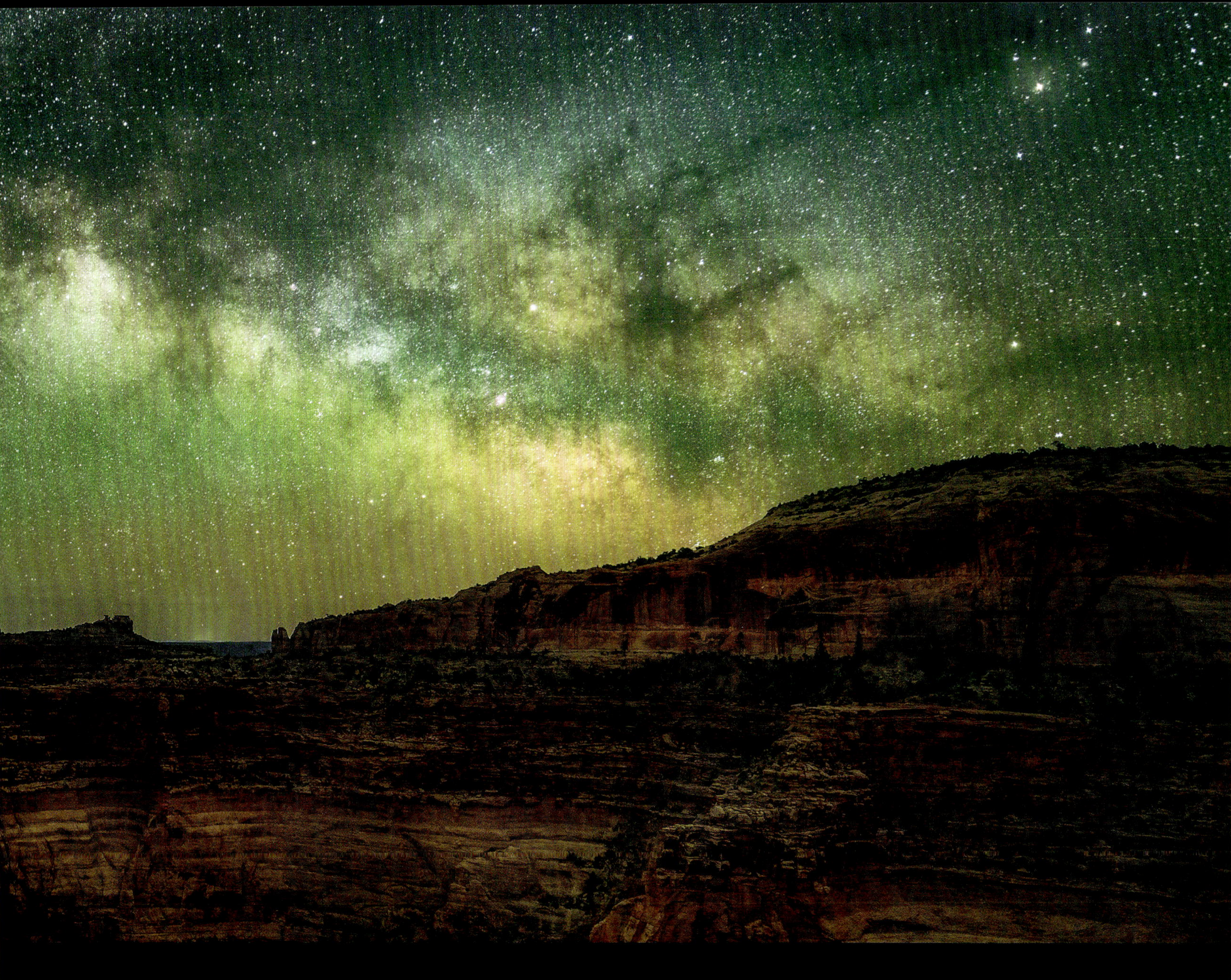

Here we will look at a few case studies that will help put the techniques described in this book into context and demonstrate how they can be used to capture a variety of different landscape astrophotography images.

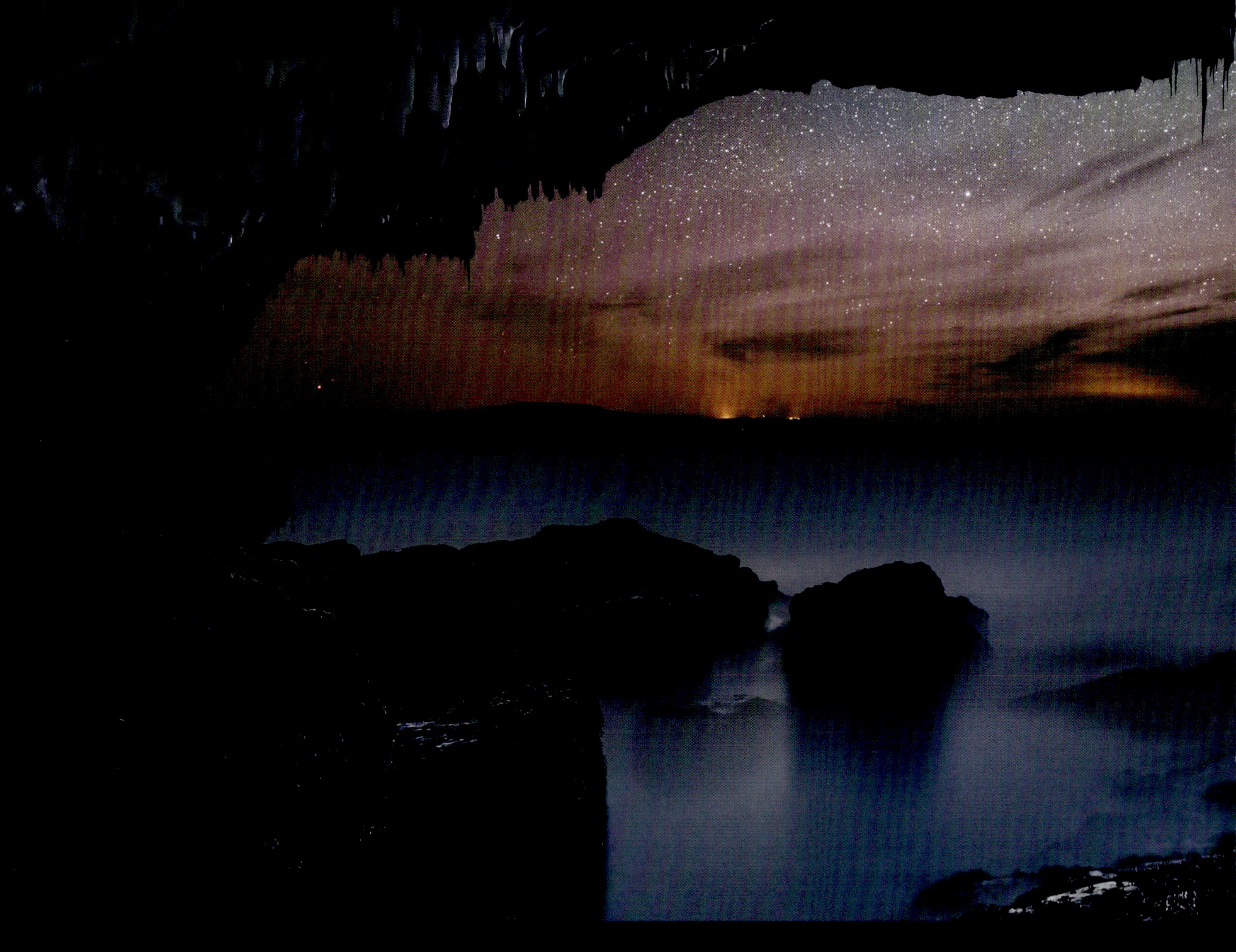

15.1 GALACTIC CAVE

Case Study:
A Well-Timed Shot

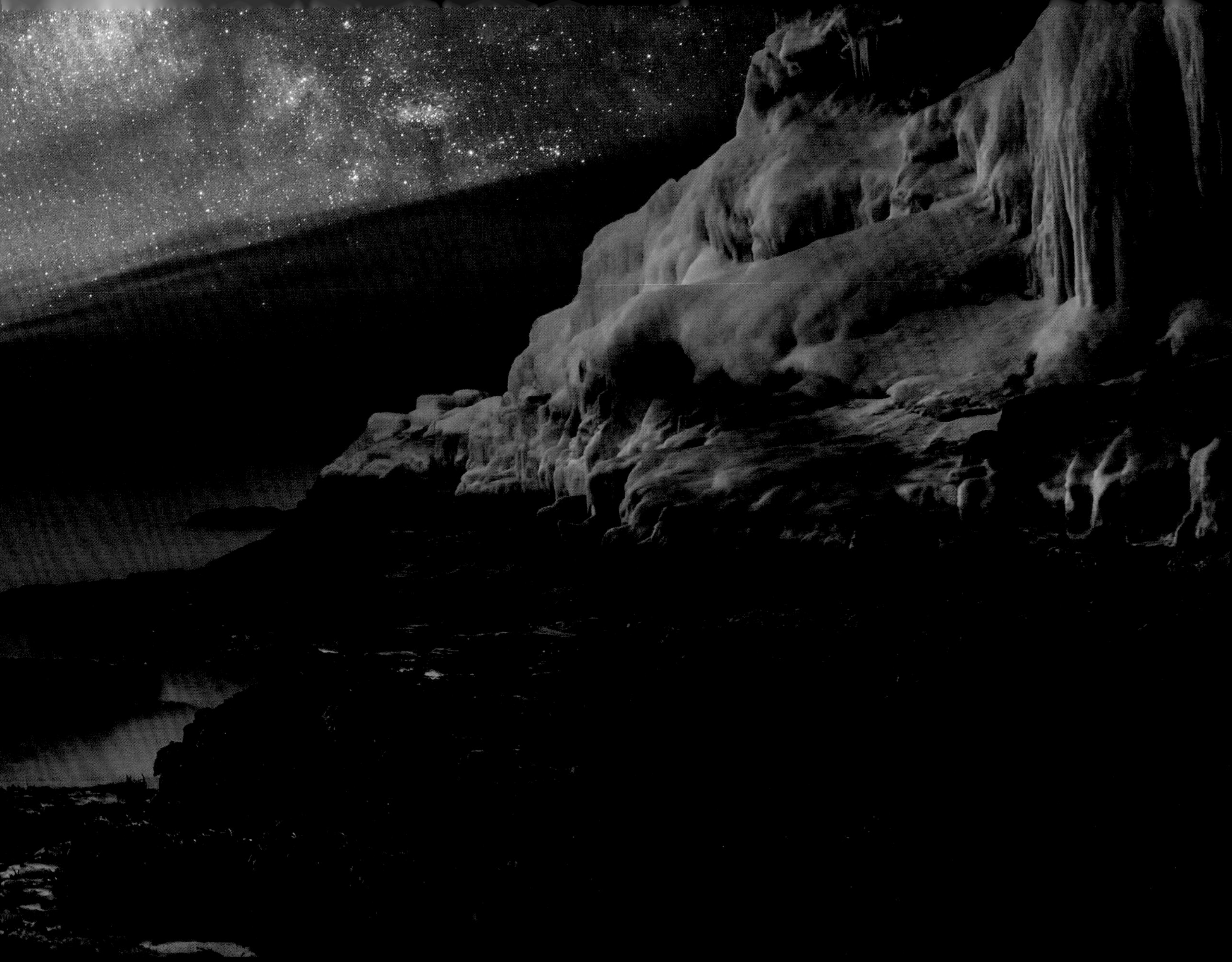

When I took this photo in February 2015, I had already been planning it for about two years. A lot of things needed to come together for it to work. It had to be early in the year (at the start of "Milky Way season") in order to see the Milky Way from inside the cave. I needed clear skies during the new moon when the tide was low enough for me to get in and out of the cave safely and still have enough time to try out various angles and take all the shots I would need.

When the time came around, it was bitterly cold and very windy, although it was calm inside the cave. The ambient temperature was somewhere between 0 and 5 degrees Fahrenheit. Wearing snowshoes, I had to trek knee and waist-deep in snow down the hillside through the woods to the shore. Then I had to slide down what was essentially a frozen waterfall from a drainage from the woods down to the rocks next to the ocean, before putting on crampons to cross the ice-covered rocks and carefully make my way over to and inside the cave. All alone and in the dark, but for a headlamp, of course.

This was taken with a Nikon D800E and a Nikon 14-24mm f/2.8 lens at 17mm. Like most of my night photos, this is a blend of multiple shots to get the scene in focus and well exposed from the foreground to the stars. Technically, 13 shots were used to create this final image. Ten frames of the sky of 10 seconds each at ISO 6400 were star stacked to get pinpoint stars with low noise. Then three other frames were used for the foreground at ISO 1600 and at different focus distances, f-stops and exposures lengths to capture an in-focus, low-noise foreground. The single image that resulted from the star stacking was then blended with all the foreground images. Creative edits were then applied to enhance contrast and bring out details in the sky.

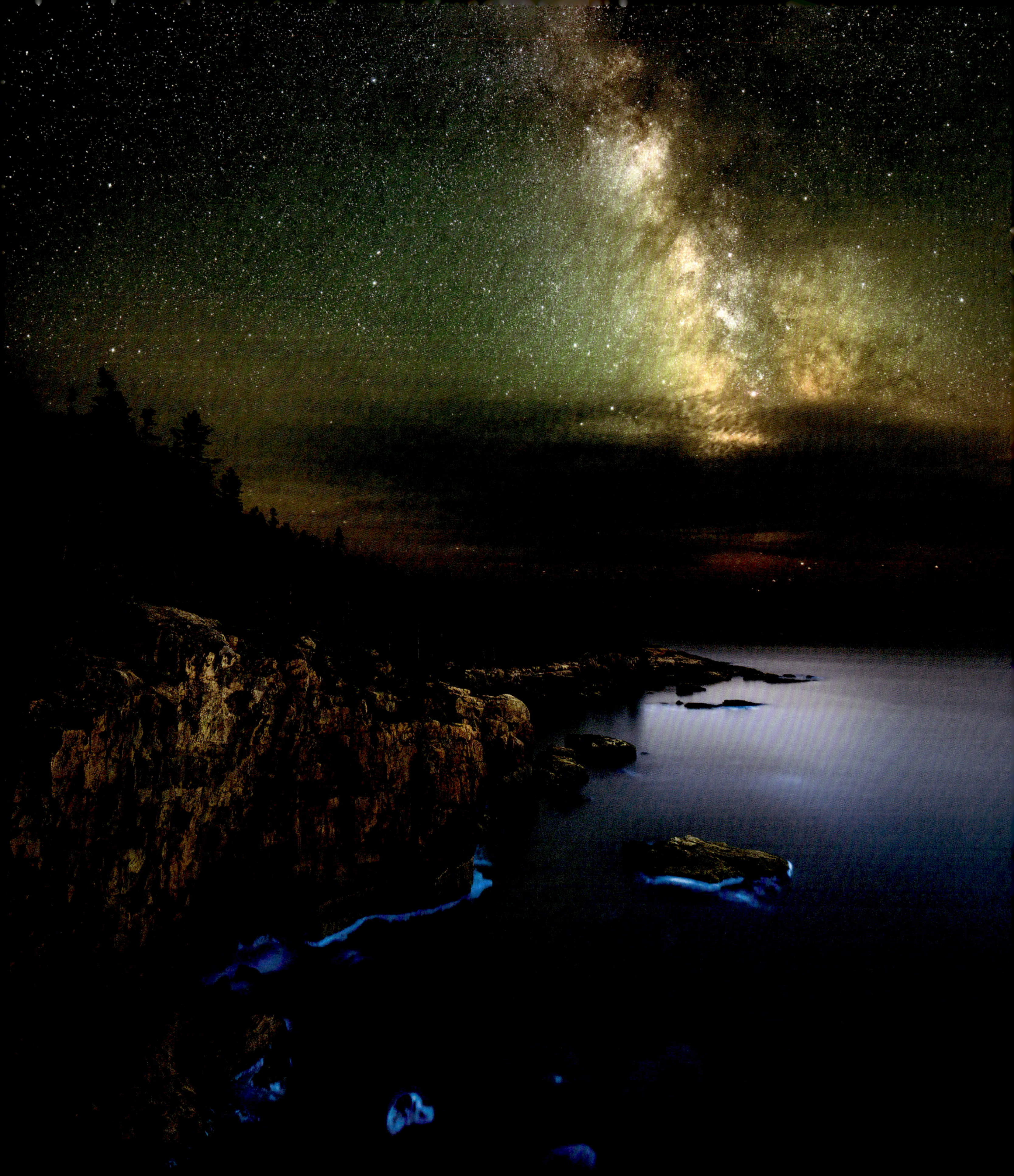

15.2 GLOWING COAST

Case Study: **Seizing the Opportunity**

This was one of those amazing summer nights on the coast of Maine — and an experience that I will never forget.

I had just finished teaching a small landscape astrophotography workshop in Lubec, Maine, when I heard from my friend and fellow photographer Benjamin Williamson that there was bioluminescence along some dramatic coves a couple of hours away in Acadia National Park. One of the workshop participants was able to stay longer, so we both bolted down the coast to check out this scene with our own eyes.

Due to the limitations of human vision in low light, we didn't see the blue color with our naked eyes—what we saw were white pulses of light in the water. But just as with the starry night sky, the camera is able to capture much more light and all the color that was there. Even so, it was an amazing sight to behold with such a dramatic foreground.

The blue light is real, and is just how my camera captured it, I didn't do anything to boost the blue. The blue light comes from microorganisms called "dinoflagellates" that emit light (bioluminescence) when they get "excited" by being tossed around in the water by the waves. This phenomenon is visible in many places in the world, although it is more common in warmer waters.

This is a blend of 10 photographs for the sky and two for the foreground. Ten shots for the sky were each taken at ISO 10000 (although nowadays I would recommend using a lower ISO to prevent heavily blown-out stars), f/2.8, 10 seconds, and then stacked with Starry Landscape Stacker for pinpoint stars and low noise. The two foreground shots were taken at lower ISOs and longer shutter speeds for a cleaner foreground; one at ISO 1600 for 20 minutes and the other at ISO 6400 for 2 minutes, both at f/2.8. These shots were then blended in Photoshop to create a single image with low noise and sharp focus. All shots were taken with the Nikon D810A and Nikon 14-24mm f/2.8 lens at 14mm.

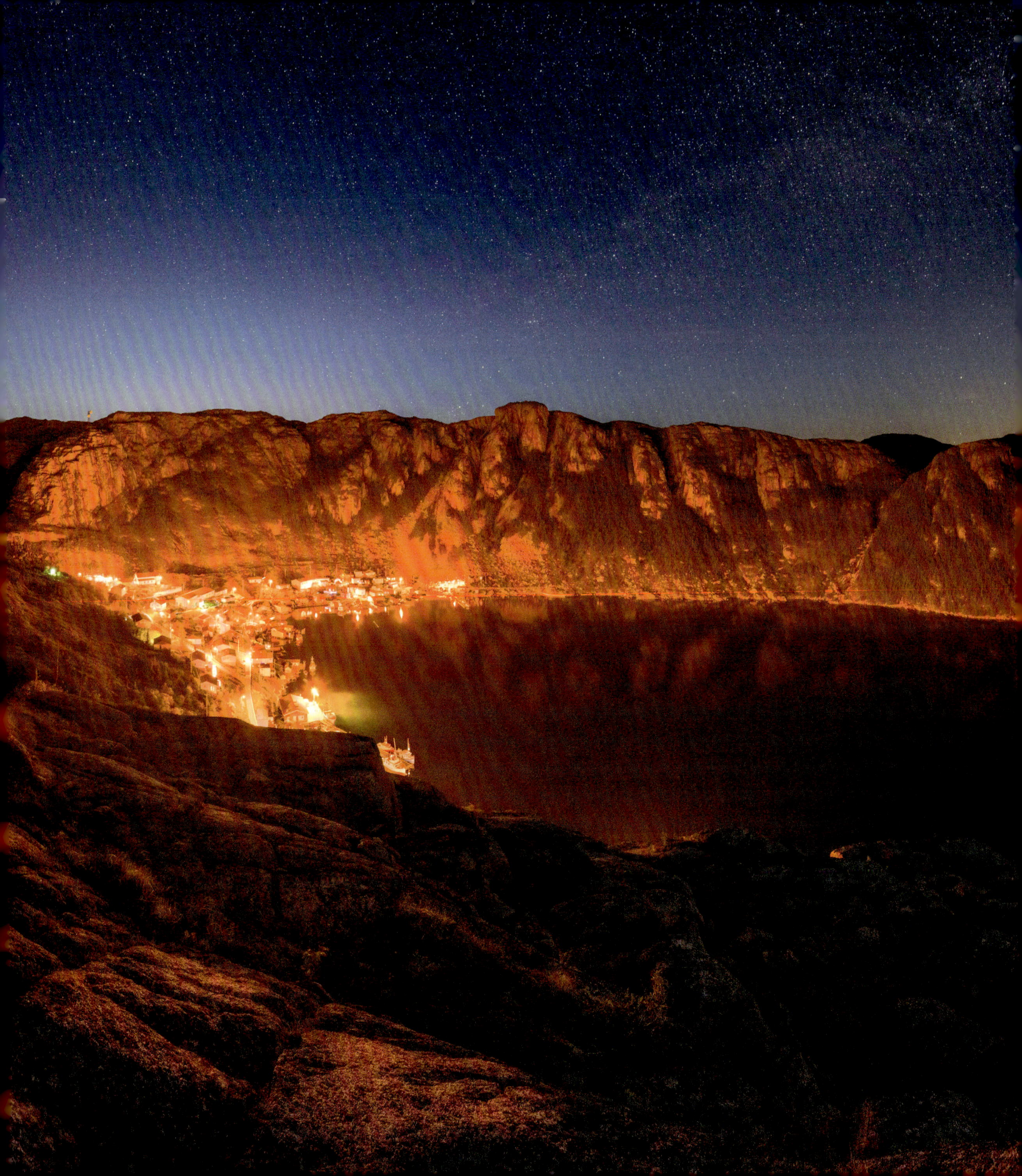

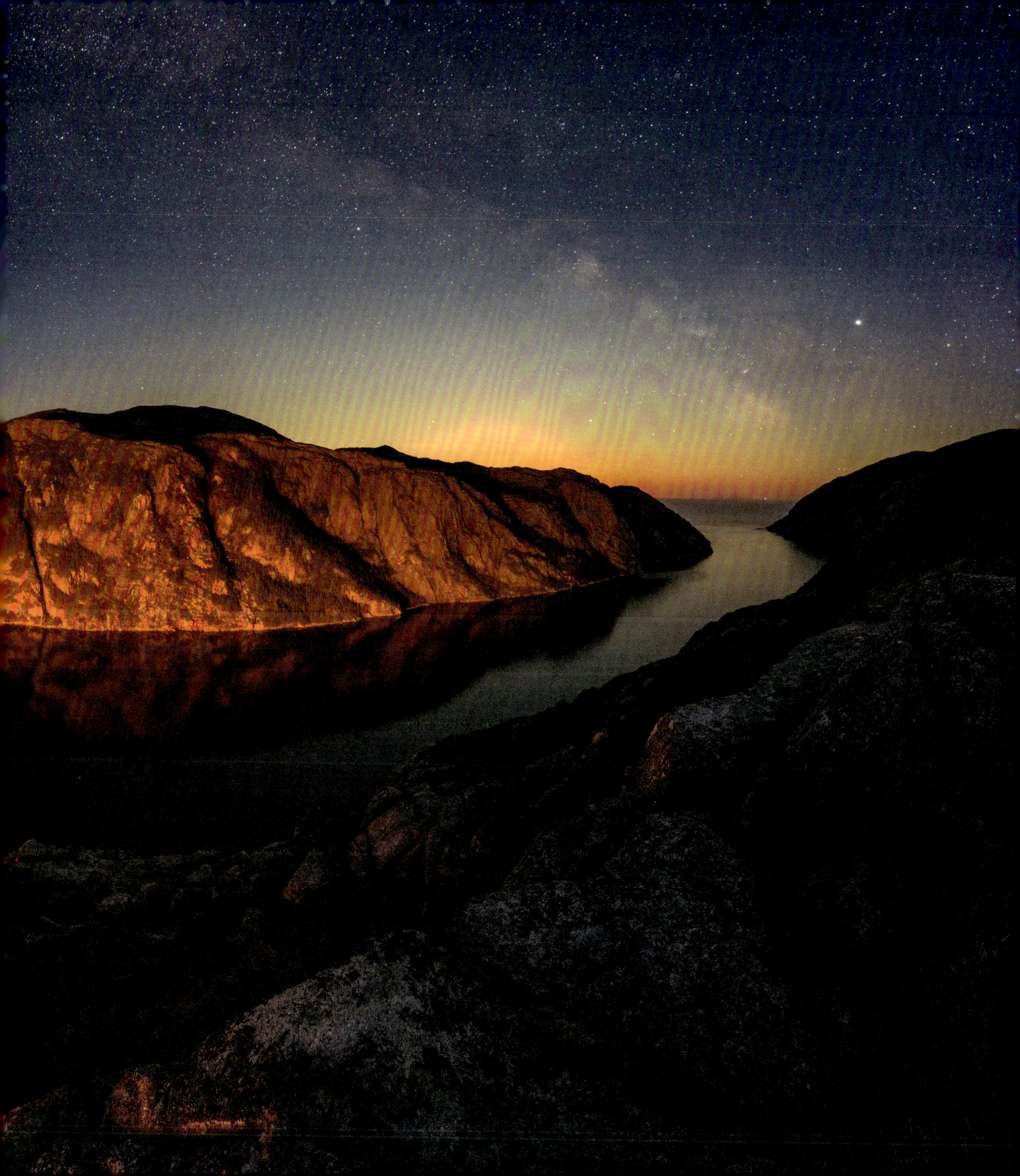

Case Study:
A Perfectly Planned Pano

There's a lot going on in this panaroma (previous page), taken above the remote village of François, Newfoundland. The Milky Way is arcing over the fjord; the moon has just risen to the east (left) of the Milky Way, which is why the horizon in that area is very orange (from the glow of the rising moon); it is still astronomical twilight, so the entire sky is still blue-ish all over; and the town lights are illuminating the fjord walls in a yellow-orange color.

None of this was an accident. I had planned it all out using PhotoPills. Using the app, I could determine where the Milky Way would be, whether it would be during twilight or darkness when it was in the position I wanted, and when and where the moon would rise. Learning to use planning tools like PhotoPills is an essential skill to have for night photography. If the app had shown the Milky Way in a very different position, then I would have known that this particular shot wouldn't be possible (although it would still be pretty without the Milky Way).

I hiked up to this view with the intention of using my NIKKOR 14-24mm f/2.8 lens for this shot, but when I was lightening my pack before the hike I forgot to include the FTZ lens adapter, so I ended up having to use the Z 14-30mm f/4 S lens, which is a great lens but at f/4 I was only getting half as much light, and less light means more noise. Luckily, it still worked out. I could have taken multiple shots for star stacking for each vertical image of this panorama to get less noise, but I opted to save time and take single shots.

I used a Nikon Z 7 with a NIKKOR Z 14-30mm f/4 S lens at 14mm, f/4, ISO 3200, 20 seconds, for all 10 vertical shots in this panorama. I used the Nodal Ninja RD16-II rotator with 30-degree click stops to make panning the camera easy, meaning no headlamp was required to look at the panning base to manually find the next 30-degree increment.

15.4 WEST QUODDY HEAD LIGHTHOUSE

Case Study: Adapting to Challenges

I'd had this photo (overleaf) in mind for about a year before I was finally able to make it happen, but not without quite a few challenges. First there are the porcupines, which for anyone who visits this lighthouse at night knows all too well. They don't run at you, but you have to be careful not to walk into them, especially in the bushes that I had to go through to get to the cliff where I wanted to stand. But the biggest problem was the dew in the air; my lens would fog up very quickly. It wasn't an issue for the sky shots, but the foreground shots were a challenge. I couldn't capture a long exposure without the lens fogging over pretty badly, despite wrapping chemical handwarmers on the lens. Nowadays I use (and recommend) an electronic lens heater such as the Protage brand lens heater. Electric lens heaters are much more reliable.

So, in order to get some shots of the foreground that weren't washed out with fog, I used shorter exposures at high ISOs, wiped off the lens, and then took another shot. These shorter (60-second and 120-second) exposures didn't have as much fog, and using the stacking method in Photoshop I was able to get a median of the exposures, resulting in less noise. Turn the layers into a Smart Object, set the Smart Object blend mode to Median, and you'll have less noise due to the averaging of the layers. Unfortunately, I didn't take enough of these high-ISO foreground shots; I could have used a few more to bring the levels of noise way down. But I was able to use the Nik Dfine noise-reduction plugin for Photoshop to reduce the noise further in the foreground.

The "light beams" from the lighthouse are real, they are caused by the intense and hard directional light being broken up by the window posts in the lighthouse, and show up like this in a long exposure. The reason they don't overexpose the entire scene is due to the fact that the light is a blinking light, and it only goes off for 2 seconds every 9 seconds. This means that most of the time the scene is dark. So there's enough darkness to capture the night sky and enough light to easily illuminate the foreground.

I used a focal length of 24mm on a full-frame camera for this shot. I often shoot at 14mm to get a big sky, but I liked the composition from this angle better at 24mm, and it has the added effect of making the Galactic Core of the Milky Way look quite prominent in the frame. Normally, if you're shooting a single shot for the sky at 24mm, you'd probably end up with more star trails than you'd like, or more noise than you'd like, since the farther you're zoomed in the faster the stars appear to move across the frame. So you need to either take a shorter exposure at a higher ISO, or deal with some trails with a lower ISO and longer exposure. However, with the star-stacking technique, you can get pinpoint stars and low noise even at 24mm. In hindsight, I should have shot even shorter sky exposures to get sharper pinpoint stars, as there's a little streaking.

This image is made up of 15 exposures. Ten for the sky at 24mm, f/2.8, ISO 4000 for 10 seconds each (I should have been using 5 seconds to get pinpoint stars at 24mm according to the Spot Stars tool in the PhotoPills app). The sky shots were then stacked with Starry Landscape Stacker (available in the Mac App Store) to get lower noise. The foreground is made up of five shots at 24mm. Some of the foreground exposures are f/5.6, some are f/4, some are 60 seconds, some are 120 seconds, all are ISO 3200. The foreground shots were stacked in Photoshop to reduce noise.

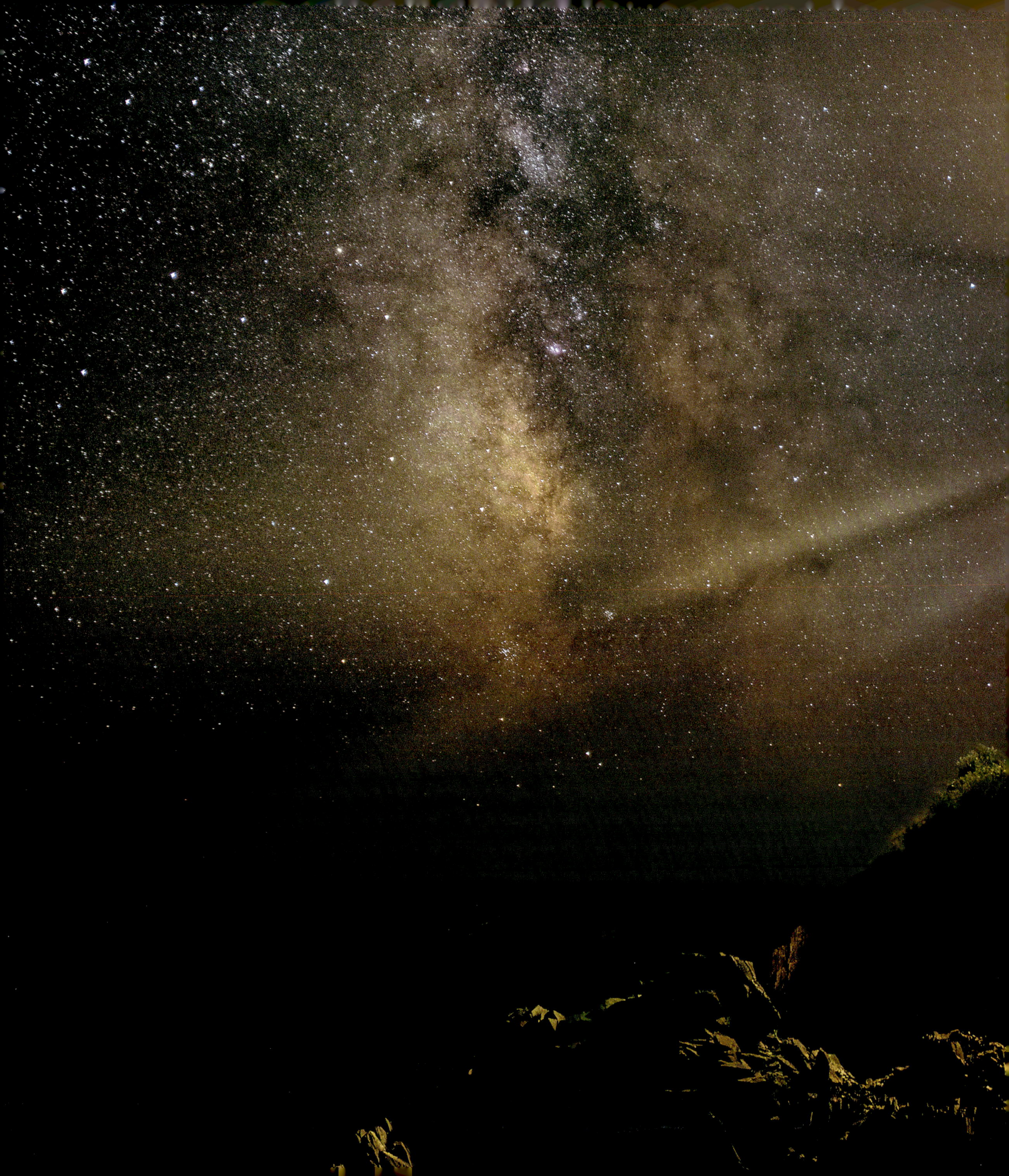

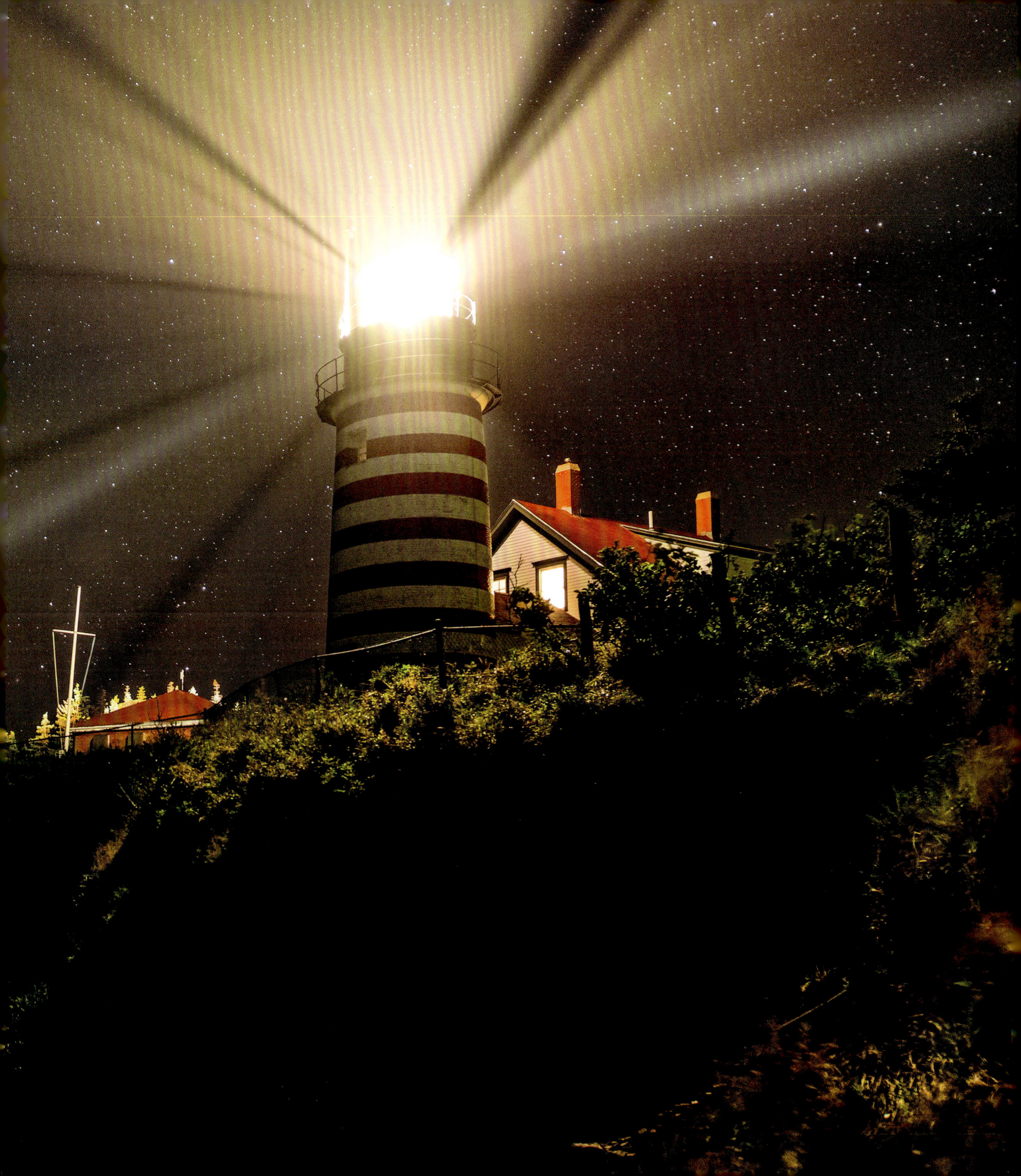

HAPPY SHOOTING!

I get asked a lot about how long my photos take to create. This one took a few hours out on the coast of Maine waiting for the skies to clear and for the Milky Way to move into position. It was an amazing experience by itself, especially since I had some great company for this hike. Then back home, it took hours to edit, at least 5 or so in total, which included star stacking, blending the sky and foreground shots, and the final edits.

Nikon Z 7 with FTZ lens adapter and NIKKOR 14-24mm f/2.8 lens at 14mm, f/2.8.

The sky is a star-stacked blend of 20 shots taken at ISO 6400 for 10 seconds to capture pinpoint stars. The foreground is from two exposures, both at ISO 1600 for 10 minutes, with one focused on the foreground grass.

16

I hope you enjoyed this journey through the ins and outs of photographing the night sky. Now you can figure out what gear you may need, plan shots, capture great images and process your final edits. Have fun out there and enjoy your time under the stars!

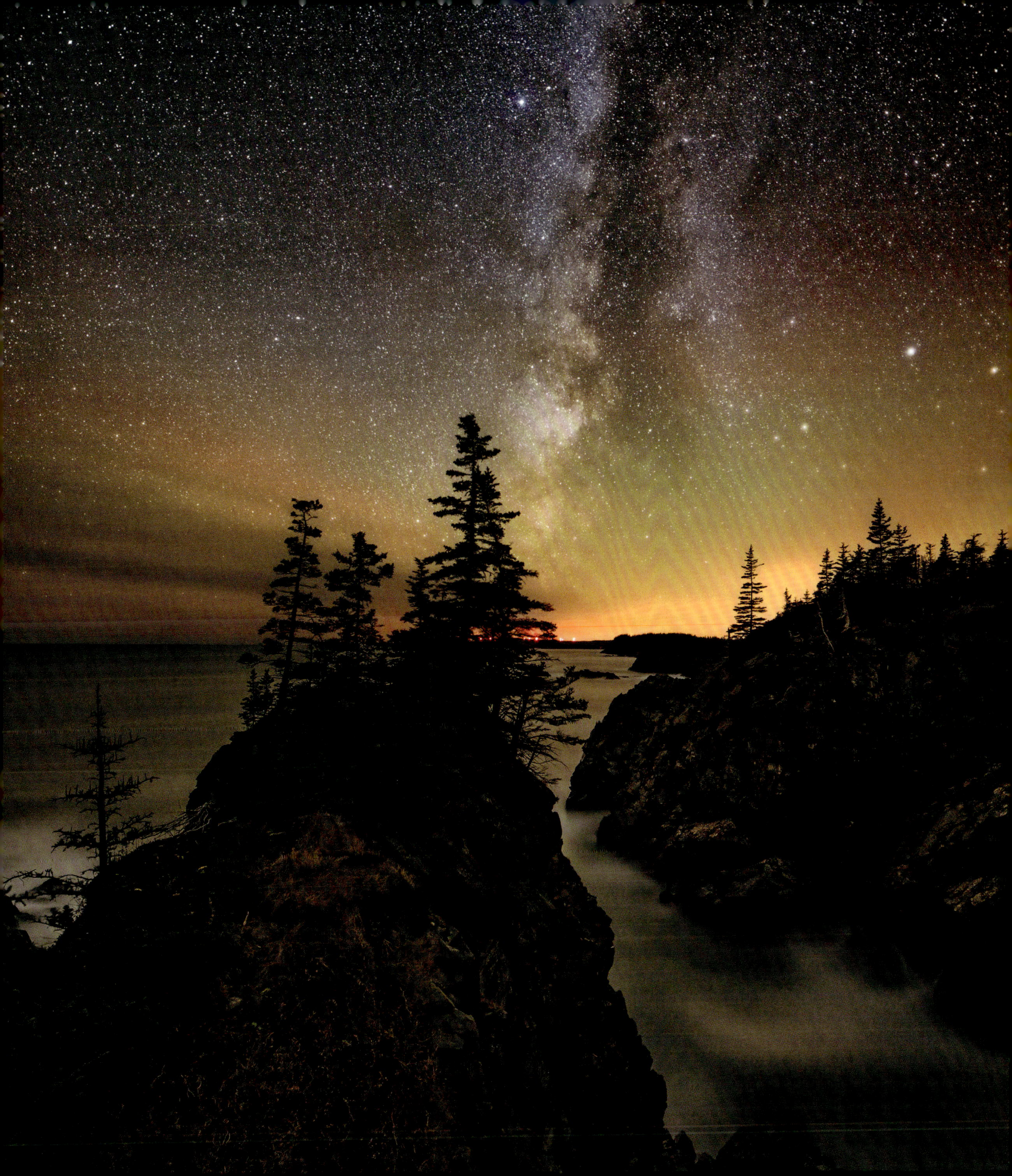

INDEX

ACKNOWLEDGMENTS

THANK YOU:

To everyone who helped me review this book, provide feedback, and answer questions.

To the publisher for approaching me about this book and encouraging me to write it.

To all the photographers that have inspired me over the years.

And to my partner, Linda, for her support during all the long days of writing that went into this book.

ADDITIONAL IMAGES:

© Yuri Beletsky, 22, 139
© Eric Tirrell, 84–5, 110–11